The Field Archaeology of Dartmoor

Dedicated to:

Norman Victor Quinnell FSA 1925–2008

Field Archaeologist

The Field Archaeology of Dartmoor

Phil Newman

 Historic England

Published by Historic England, The Engine House, Fire Fly Avenue, Swindon SN2 2EH
www.HistoricEngland.org.uk

Historic England is a Government service championing England's heritage and giving expert, constructive advice, and the English Heritage Trust is a charity caring for the National Heritage Collection of more than 400 historic properties and their collections.

First published by English Heritage 2011
Reprinted with corrections by Historic England 2016

ISBN 978-1-84802-033-7

British Library Cataloguing in Publication data
A CIP catalogue record for this book is available from the British Library.

Historic England holds an unparalleled archive of 12 million photographs, drawings, reports and publications on England's places. It is one of the largest archives in the UK, the biggest dedicated to the historic environment, and a priceless resource for anyone interested in England's buildings, archaeology, landscape and social history. Viewed collectively, its photographic collections document the changing face of England from the 1850s to the present day. It is a treasure trove that helps us understand and interpret the past, informs the present and assists with future management and appreciation of the historic environment.

For more information about images from the Archive, contact Archives Services Team, Historic England, The Engine House, Fire Fly Avenue, Swindon SN2 2EH; telephone (01793) 414600.

Brought to publication by David M Jones and Victoria Trainor, Publishing, Historic England

Typeset in 9.5pt Charter

Edited by David M Jones
Indexed by Alan Rutter
Page layout by Mark Simmons, revisions by Pauline Hull

Printed in the Belgium by Deckers Snoeck

Cover
The Grey Wethers Stone Circles

CONTENTS

ACKNOWLEDGEMENTS

The archaeological fieldwork that makes up the content of this monograph, and the publication of the book itself has only been possible through the cooperation of a number of organisations with whom English Heritage (EH) has worked in partnership and to all of whom we owe a huge debt of gratitude. Of these the Dartmoor National Park Authority, in the form of the Cultural Heritage team, led by Debbie Griffiths, have supported, encouraged and, at times, funded our work, over the 20 years that this research represents. Defence Estates, led by John Lock, Martin Brown and the training areas commandant Lt Col Anthony Clark, commissioned and funded surveys of all five of the Dartmoor training areas. The National Trust, under the archaeological leadership of Shirley Blaylock, funded research in the Plym Valley and various smaller sites within their estate.

Numerous individual landowners and tenants have cooperated fully over the years, some being particularly supportive and encouraging. Special thanks must go in particular to Min Cullom of Challacombe and to the Hurrell family. Many landowning estates have been helpful, some allowing vehicular access including Maristow, Duchy of Cornwall, Forest Enterprise, SW Lakes, Defence Estates, and the National Trust.

Most of the fieldwork presented in this monograph was undertaken by Simon Probert, Phil Newman and Martin Fletcher, with some individual surveys executed by Hazel Riley, Robert Wilson-North, Ian Sainsbury, Paul Pattison, Elaine Jamieson and Henry Chapman. Catherine Grindey, Ben Moore and Kate Page-Smith all contributed to the work while on one-year English Heritage (EPPIC) professional placements. A number of students also assisted while on shorter placements from Exeter, Bristol and Oxford universities: Jonathen Dempsey, Wesley Keir, Rod Lane, Phil Marter, Pena Monageng, Colin Wakeham and Duncan Wright.

Colour aerial photography is the work of Damian Grady. Specialist ground and finds photography is by James Davies. Other photographs are by Phil Newman and Simon Probert. Hachured earthwork illustrations are by Deborah Cunliffe. All other computer-generated illustrations are by Phil Newman, with assistance from Eddie Lyons. Other members of EH and former-RCHME staff who have eased the production of this work include the NMRC library, the archive teams and Ian Savage of photographic services. Thanks are due to Dr Robin Taylor of English Heritage Publications section for seeing the potential in a publication on Dartmoor's archaeology and for advising the author through the proposal process. The work has been edited and brought to press by Dr David Jones, with assistance from other members of the production team.

Fiona Pitt of Plymouth City Museums Service assisted greatly with the photography of pottery and finds from the museum collection. Throughout the duration of our work on Dartmoor, cooperation and assistance by staff at the Westcountry Studies Library, Devon Record Office, Cornwall Record Office and Devon HER was willingly given and much appreciated. Exeter Archaeology, The Dartmoor Trust, the Dartmoor Tinworking Research Group, West Country Studies Library, Plymouth City Museum and Art Gallery, The Devonshire Association and The Duchy of Cornwall have all kindly allowed publication of photographic and illustrative material.

The book benefited greatly from comments and advice from Mark Bowden, Graham Brown, Lt Col Anthony Clark, Wayne Cockroft, Jane Marchand, Henrietta Quinnell and others, each of whom read various drafts of the text and offered a number of major improvements. Dr Ralph Fyfe of Plymouth University and John Valentin of AC Archaeology also freely gave information and advice.

These contributions have all been much appreciated, though all errors, factual or interpretive, remain the responsibility of the author.

SUMMARY

Dartmoor, which lies wholly within the county of Devonshire, is southern England's largest tract of upland. The natural landform is an exposed pluton of the granite massif rising through and surrounded by earlier Devonian shales, and forms a high plateau of moorland that provides the source for many of Devon's larger rivers. The moorland areas of Dartmoor, which make up approximately 50% of the National Park, occupy the upper and middle ground. The character of this moorland varies between areas of peat bogs, granite outcrops and heathland, but on the slightly lower ground, as the rivers descend from the upland, it changes to one dominated by grassland and heathland. As the rivers progress towards the hinterland, they have incised steep-sided valleys where lush woodland has evolved. These diverse natural qualities assured Dartmoor its designation as one of England's first National Parks in 1951.

Despite the acknowledged natural appeal of Dartmoor as sometimes wild and rugged and sometimes beautiful, this landscape is not a place comprised only of natural spectacle, for the human dimension, or historic environment, has pervaded that of the natural environment for thousands of years. People have adapted and exploited Dartmoor for its natural resources, since at least the Mesolithic period, while settlement and farming has occurred here since the early 2nd millennium BC. There is no part of Dartmoor where human intervention has not played a role in shaping the character of the landscape, led by the environmental possibilities that the place may offer, although nature has itself adapted to the human induced changes that resulted. The landscape of Dartmoor today therefore represents a synergy between man and the environment, not a wilderness as often portrayed.

This book explores the role of humans on Dartmoor and attempts to reconstruct aspects of the past, particularly but not exclusively on the uplands, through a study of the archaeological evidence that is present in the landscape and representing aspects of the human past. It is the result of fieldwork undertaken by members of the English Heritage Archaeological Survey and Investigation team (since 1999 but formerly the Royal Commission on the Historical Monuments of England), over a period of approximately 20 years from 1989–2009. The archaeology of Dartmoor has been explored over the past two centuries by a variety of researchers, acting as individuals or as groups, undertaking fieldwork, excavation and, in some cases, restorations. Their activities and findings are also discussed.

The first certain indications of a human activity on Dartmoor are of the Mesolithic period from c 6500 years ago. These people left indications of their presence only in the form of scattered stone tools and environmental evidence captured in the pollen record, which hint at their activities. By the time of the Neolithic period (c 4000–2000 BC) permanent stone monuments, including a dolmen, and earthwork long barrows for burial of the dead were being constructed, and represent the first durable evidence from the material past. The enigmatic tor enclosures probably date from this period too, though evidence of where or if Neolithic people resided on Dartmoor has not been forthcoming. By the late 3rd millennium BC and the start of the Bronze Age, additional forms of monuments began to be built. Stone circles and stone alignments may have fulfilled ritual or perhaps religious roles, about which we can only conjecture on the basis of the evidence we possess, but the presence of round barrows early in this period and afterwards is indicative of human burial. The round barrows and cairns represent our first encounter with individuals from the past, who were often buried in them with their possessions, including pottery, metalwork and other artefacts. The first evidence of permanent occupation on Dartmoor is available from the early 2nd millennium BC, when round houses were build and lived in on the upland, of which their remains in the form of stone hut circles are perhaps Dartmoor's most superlative archaeological resource. More than 4,000 examples survive. Some were grouped into settlements, many of which were enclosed, while others were associated with a series of land divisions known as reaves. These systems of parallel banks dominate the landscape on parts of the moor and were established in about 1600 BC.

By the later Bronze Age and the start of the 1st millennium BC, evidence for permanent human activity is more scarce than at any other period since before the Neolithic and afterwards, and we have to assume the landscape was less intensively occupied until the later prehistoric period. Accumulating evidence from archaeological excavations is slowly painting a picture of partial occupation of the uplands in the Iron Age, when round houses were still the preferred option for domestic occupation. However, Dartmoor's Iron Age archaeology is dominated by the presence of lightly defended settlements that encircle the upland, including hillforts and hillslope enclosures.

The Roman and post-Roman periods and the so-called Dark Ages that followed are periods for which material evidence for human presence is lacking on upland Dartmoor. It is likely, however, that settlement was increasing within the lower-lying valleys and places such as Widecombe-in-the-Moor, perhaps two centuries before the Norman Conquest of 1066.

It was during the medieval period that the character of Dartmoor – which survives today as a place of farming, small villages, hamlets and farmsteads – came into being. The patchwork of fields that gradually spread up the sheltered valleys towards the upland, served as the framework onto which all later expansion became attached. The high moors, however, always favoured as common land for grazing, remained untouched. While many settlements and their associated farmland from this period remain occupied today, others, usually those on the higher ground, became abandoned, and now provide archaeological snapshots of medieval life, including field systems designed both for arable crop growing and for livestock pasturage, as well as ruined domestic structures such as longhouses and barns.

From the 17th century, some areas of Dartmoor were adapted for the farming of rabbits. The evidence of these rabbit warrens is spread across places such as the Plym Valley and comprises the earthen mounds or buries in which the animals were encouraged to breed and the vermin traps needed to catch predators. A further interesting dimension of the agricultural landscape was the arrival of the 'improvers' of the 18th and 19th centuries, when large portions of the remaining open moors were enclosed using stone walls, in the pursuit of more 'modern' farming methods.

Of industrial activity on Dartmoor, the exploitation of tin must take precedence, with origins at least in the 12th century if not before. The evidence of alluvial tin stream works and opencast lode workings bring a contrasting and somewhat destructive dimension, resulting from an activity that radically and permanently altered many hundreds of hectares of the landscape in its wake. Associated archaeological features include the network of abandoned artificial water courses needed to supply the workings, and the places where ore was processed and smelted – known as stamping and blowing mills. Other industries with medieval origins were certainly peat cutting, which in part supplied the demands of the tin smelters, and granite working, harvesting the abundant supply of moorstone for buildings on and away from the moors.

All of these industries developed further in the 18th and 19th centuries as the spirit of capitalism brought investors to finance them. Metal mining expanded to include copper and silver-lead, which along with a revitalised tin industry utilised underground mining techniques for which extensive evidence of shafts, wheel pits, dressing floors, large spoil heaps, some engine houses and traces of infrastructure survive. The granite industry developed on a dramatic scale with the advent of quarrying techniques c 1800, leaving huge quarries scaring the landscape, while commercial peat cutting has stripped away the surface of large swathes of upland. China clay was a late comer to Dartmoor; nevertheless its impact on the southern peripheries of the National Park has been dramatic and it still survives as a viable industry. Aspects of this industry's early archaeology, such as clay processing works have survived despite the massive and destructive spread of the more recent activity.

The training of military personnel has been taking place on Dartmoor since the early 19th century. The most notable evidence is found within the training areas, the first of which was established in the 1870s, though others followed. In Okehampton and Willsworthy ranges are the remnants of earthworks and structures associated with early forms of training. Dartmoor's role in the Second World War and later defensive efforts have also survived in places, mainly associated with aerial defence including radar.

Thus the story of Dartmoor concludes for the time being, although of course the narrative for the historic environment is ongoing. In the future there will be more to tell, particularly regarding Dartmoor's role in the late 20th and early 21st centuries as a National Park, and how the conservation ethos in which national parks have their roots influenced the development of the landscape. Hopefully, the evidence of past human activity will continue to survive through the ongoing efforts of the National Park and other governmental and voluntary bodies, but also the often unsung efforts of some landowners. Crucial to this survival is support by the public, whose enthusiasm for the historic landscape can be greatly stimulated by an understanding of it. It is hoped that this book will play a part in stimulating the interest and debates necessary to help with this aim.

RÉSUMÉ

Le Dartmoor, situé entièrement à l'intérieur du comté de Devonshire, constitue la région de hautes terres la plus étendue du sud de l'Angleterre. Son relief est constitué d'un pluton du massif granitique affleurant dans des schistes dévoniens antérieurs ; il forme un haut plateau de landes où naissent plusieurs des grandes rivières du Devon. Les landes du Dartmoor, qui couvrent à peu près la moitié du parc national, occupent les sommets et zones intermédiaires. Elles se composent de tourbières, d'affleurements granitiques et de bruyères, tandis qu'un peu plus bas, là où les rivières descendent des sommets, ce sont les prairies et les bruyères qui prédominent. En descendant, ces rivières ont creusé dans l'arrière-pays des vallées encaissées revêtues de forêts verdoyantes. Ces qualités naturelles diverses ont garanti au Dartmoor une place parmi les premiers parcs nationaux anglais établis en 1951.

Bien que l'attrait naturel de cette région parfois sauvage et rude, parfois d'une grande beauté, soit reconnu, ce paysage n'offre pas un spectacle uniquement naturel car la dimension humaine – l'environnement historique – a commencé à marquer de son empreinte l'environnement naturel il y a des milliers d'années. L'homme s'est adapté au milieu du Dartmoor dont il exploite les ressources depuis au moins le mésolithique, les premiers peuplements et l'agriculture y étant arrivés dès le début du deuxième millénaire av. J.-C. Aucune partie du Dartmoor n'a échappé à l'intervention de l'homme qui, incité par les possibilités que présentait l'environnement, a partout influencé le caractère du paysage, bien que la nature se soit elle-même aussi adaptée aux changements qui ont résulté de son action. Le paysage du Dartmoor est donc aujourd'hui l'aboutissement d'une synergie entre l'homme et l'environnement, plutôt que l'étendue sauvage souvent dépeinte.

Le présent ouvrage examine l'influence de l'être humain sur le Dartmoor et tente de reconstituer certains éléments de ce passé, en particulier, mais pas uniquement, sur les hautes terres, au moyen d'une étude des vestiges archéologiques qui sont disséminés dans le paysage et qui représentent des aspects du passé anthropique. Il est l'aboutissement du travail mené sur le terrain par les membres de l'English Heritage Archaeological Survey and Investigation Team (Royal Commission on the Historical Monuments of England jusqu'en 1999) au cours d'une vingtaine d'années (1989-2009). L'archéologie du Dartmoor a été étudiée au cours des deux siècles écoulés par divers chercheurs qui, travaillant seuls ou collectivement, ont exécuté des travaux de terrain, des fouilles et, dans certains cas, des restaurations. Leurs activités et découvertes sont aussi examinées.

Les premières indications incontestables d'une activité de l'homme dans le Dartmoor datent du mésolithique, il y a 6 500 ans. Les seules traces de cette présence prennent la forme d'outils en pierre éparpillés et de vestiges environnementaux détectés au moyen d'études polliniques, qui donnent une idée de ses activités. À partir du néolithique (vers 4000-2000 av. J.-C.), on s'est mis à construire des monuments en pierre permanents, dont un dolmen, et des tumulus de terre allongés destinés à ensevelir les morts ; ce sont les premiers vestiges durables du passé matériel. Les « enceintes de *tors* » dont l'origine reste inexpliquée, datent sans doute aussi de cette période, bien qu'aucun vestige permettant de savoir si des peuples du néolithique vivaient dans cette région, ni à quelle période, n'ait été découvert. À partir de la fin du troisième millénaire av. J.-C., au début de l'Âge du bronze, on commença à construire d'autres types de monuments. Les cercles et alignements de pierre jouaient un rôle peut-être rituel ou religieux, sur lequel les vestiges qui nous sont parvenus ne nous permettent que des conjectures, mais la présence de tumulus circulaires au début de cette période et par la suite indique que des êtres humains y étaient ensevelis. Les tumulus circulaires et les cairns représentent notre première rencontre avec les hommes de cette époque, qui étaient souvent ensevelis avec leurs possessions, dont des poteries, des objets en métal et d'autres objets. Les premières preuves de l'occupation permanente du Dartmoor remontent au début du deuxième millénaire av. J.-C., époque de la construction d'habitations circulaires sur les hautes terres, dont les vestiges, qui prennent la forme de cercle de pierres, constituent peut-être le matériel archéologique le meilleur du Dartmoor. Plus de 4 000 exemples subsistent. Certaines forment des villages, dont la plupart étaient entourés d'une enceinte, tandis que d'autres sont associées à des séries de limites appelées *reaves*. Ces systèmes de talus parallèles dominent le paysage dans certaines parties de la lande et remontent à vers 1600 av. J.-C.

Dès la fin de l'Âge du bronze et au début du premier millénaire av. J.-C., les traces d'activités humaines permanentes se font plus rares qu'à tout autre période précédant ou suivant le néolithique : il nous faut donc conclure que ce paysage fut occupé de manière moins intensive jusqu'à la fin de la période préhistorique. Les vestiges croissants accumulés dans le cadre de fouilles archéologiques permettent de dégager lentement un tableau partiel des hautes terres à l'Âge du fer, époque où les habitations circulaires continuaient d'être la forme d'occupation domestique préférée. Cependant, dans le Dartmoor, les vestiges archéologiques de cette époque sont dominés par la présence de villages légèrement fortifiés qui encerclent les hautes terres, y compris des « forts de colline » (hill-forts) et des « enceintes de pentes » (hillslope enclosures).

Les périodes romaines et post-romaines et le Haut Moyen-Âge qui ont fait suite n'ont laissé que peu de vestiges de la présence de l'homme dans les hautes terres du Dartmoor. Il est probable cependant que les vallées de basse altitude et des villages comme Widecombe-in-the-Moor se soient peuplés de manière croissante, peut-être deux siècles avant la conquête de l'Angleterre par les Normands en 1066. C'est durant la période médiévale que s'est dessiné le caractère du Dartmoor – qui reste aujourd'hui une région agricole ponctuée de petits villages, de hameaux et de fermes isolées. La mosaïque de champs qui s'est étendue progressivement des vallées abritées vers les hautes terres a formé le cadre à partir duquel a eu lieu toute l'expansion ultérieure. Les landes de haute altitude, cependant, toujours réservées aux pâturages communaux, n'ont pas changé. Bien que de nombreux villages de cette époque, ainsi que les terres qui leur étaient associées, demeurent occupés aujourd'hui, d'autres, situés en général à plus haute altitude, ont été abandonnés et offrent un aperçu archéologique de la vie médiévale, y compris les systèmes agraires conçus à la fois pour les cultures et le pacage ainsi que les structures en ruine telles que les « longères » et les granges.

À partir du XVIIe siècle, certaines parties du Dartmoor ont été aménagées pour l'élevage des lapins. Des vestiges de garennes subsistent dans des endroits comme la vallée de la Plym et comportent des tumulus ou buries, dans lesquels les animaux étaient encouragés à se reproduire, ainsi que des pièges, qui servaient à attraper leurs prédateurs. Parmi les autres influences intéressantes qui s'exercèrent sur le paysage agricole, figurent les « modernisateurs » (improvers) des XVIIIe et XIXe siècles, qui clôturèrent de vastes étendues des landes ouvertes restantes au moyen de murets de pierre pour « moderniser » les méthodes d'agriculture.

En ce qui concerne l'activité industrielle, l'exploitation de l'étain, qui remonte au moins au XIIe siècle est incontestablement la plus importante. Les vestiges des installations d'extraction de l'étain alluvial dans les ruisseaux et d'exploitation à ciel ouvert des filons offrent une dimension contrastée et pour le moins destructrice, résultant d'une activité qui modifia radicalement et à jamais plusieurs centaines d'hectares de paysage. Parmi les vestiges archéologiques associés figurent le réseau de cours d'eau artificiels abandonnés qui alimentaient les chantiers de mine et les lieux où le minerai était transformé et fondu, les bocards et « fonderies à soufflets » (blowing mills). Parmi les autres industries d'origine médiévale figuraient certainement l'exploitation de la tourbe, qui servait en partie à alimenter les fonderies d'étain, ainsi que le travail du granit, présent en abondance, qui était utilisé dans la construction sur place et dans d'autres régions.

Toutes ces industries continuèrent à se développer aux XVIIIe et XIXe siècles sous l'effet des capitaux apportés par les investisseurs mûs par l'esprit de capitalisme. L'extraction des métaux se développa pour englober désormais l'extraction du cuivre et du plomb argentifère qui faisait appel à des techniques d'extraction souterraine. Ces techniques, qui redonnèrent une impulsion à l'industrie de l'étain, laissèrent d'importants vestiges: puits, fosses de roue, laveries, terrils ainsi que quelques bâtiments de machines et des traces d'infrastructures. L'industrie du granit se développa à une vitesse spectaculaire avec l'arrivée des techniques d'extraction vers 1800, marquant le paysage de grandes cicatrices, tandis qu'avec l'exploitation commerciale de la tourbe, de vastes étendues des hautes terres furent dénudées. L'exploitation du kaolin arriva tardivement, mais son impact sur les abords méridionaux du parc national est spectaculaire, et cette industrie demeure rentable. Des vestiges de ses débuts survivent, tels que des usines de kaolin, malgré le développement massif et destructeur des activités plus récentes.

Le Dartmoor sert pour l'entraînement du personnel militaire depuis le début du XIXe siècle. Les vestiges les plus importants se trouvent dans les zones d'entraînement, dont la première fut créée dans les années 1870, bien que d'autres aient fait suite. Dans les champs de tir d'Okehampton et de Willsworthy se trouvent les traces des levées de terres et structures associées aux anciennes formes d'entraînement. Le rôle joué par le Dartmoor durant la Seconde Guerre mondiale et dans les efforts défensifs postérieurs, principalement lié à la défense aérienne, radars compris, a également laissé des traces à différents endroits.

Ainsi, l'histoire du Dartmoor se conclut pour le moment, même si la transformation de cet environnement historique se poursuit. Il y aura d'autre choses à dire à l'avenir en particulier sur le rôle du Dartmoor à la fin du XXe siècle et au début du XXIe en tant que parc national, et sur celui que joueront les principes de conservation qui sont à la base des parcs nationaux dans le développement du paysage. Les vestiges de l'activité humaine ancienne continueront d'être préservés, on l'espère, grâce aux efforts déployés actuellement par le parc national et d'autres organismes publics et bénévoles, mais aussi grâce à ceux, moins connus, de certains propriétaires. Cette préservation dépend de manière cruciale du soutien que lui apportera le public, dont l'enthousiasme à l'égard des paysages historiques peut être favorisé considérablement s'il y est sensibilisé. Nous espérons que le présent ouvrage contribuera à stimuler l'intérêt et les débats nécessaires à la réalisation de cet objectif.

Traduction: Muriel de Grey
in association with First Edition Translations Ltd,
Cambridge, UK

ZUSAMENFASSUNG

Dartmoor liegt ganz in der Grafschaft Devonshire und ist Südenglands größtes Hochlandgebiet. Die natürliche geographische Form der Landschaft ist ein freiliegendes Plutonit des Granitmassivs, das den älteren devonischen Schiefer durchbricht und davon umgeben ist. Sie formt ein Hochplateau aus Moorland, in dem viele der größeren Flüsse Devons entspringen. Die Moorlandgebiete von Dartmoor, die rund 50 % des Nationalparks ausmachen, bedecken die mittleren und hohen Ebenen. Der Charakter des Moorlands variiert von Torfmoorlandschaften, Felsnasen aus Granit bis hin zu Heideland. In den etwas tiefer gelegenen Gebieten, durch die sich die Flüsse aus dem Hochland ihren Weg bahnen, besteht die Landschaft hauptsächlich aus Gras- und Heideland. Auf ihrem Weg durch das Hinterland haben die Flüsse tiefe Täler ins Gestein geschnitten, in denen dichte Wälder gewachsen sind. Diesen vielfältigen natürlichen Facetten verdankt Dartmoor die Tatsache, dass es 1951 einer der ersten Nationalparks Englands wurde.

Trotz der anerkannt attraktiven, wilden, zerklüfteten und schönen Natur Dartmoors findet sich hier keine reine Naturlandschaft, stattdessen ist sie von einer Jahrtausende währenden menschlichen Dimension oder Geschichte geprägt. Menschen haben Dartmoor verändert und die natürlichen Ressourcen spätestens seit der mittleren Steinzeit, dem Mesolithikum, ausgebeutet. Seit dem frühen 2. Jahrtausend v. Chr. haben sich Menschen hier angesiedelt und Ackerbau betrieben. Es gibt keinen Teil Dartmoors, in dem keine menschliche Aktivitäten die Landschaft im Rahmen der Umweltbedingungen, die das jeweilige Gebiet bot, geformt haben, wobei sich die Natur selbst den vom Menschen verursachten Veränderungen angepasst hat. Demzufolge zeigt die Landschaft von Dartmoor heute eine Synergie von Mensch und Umwelt und nicht die Wildnis, die oft portraitiert wurde.

Dieses Buch untersucht die Rolle, die Menschen für Dartmoor gespielt haben und versucht, Aspekte der Geschichte zu rekonstruieren, und zwar insbesondere, aber nicht ausschließlich, des Hochlands. Dies geschieht anhand einer Studie von archäologischen Nachweisen in der Landschaft, die Aspekte menschlichen Lebens in der Vergangenheit zeigen. Die Nachweise sind das Ergebnis von Feldforschung, die von Mitgliedern des English Heritage Archaeological Survey and Investigation Teams (seit 1999, zuvor die Royal Commission of the Historical Monuments of England) in einem Zeitraum von rund 20 Jahren zwischen 1989 und 2009 betrieben wurde. Die Archäologie von Dartmoor wurde in den letzten zwei Jahrhunderten von einer Vielzahl von Forschern allein oder in Gruppen erforscht. Dabei wurde Feldforschung betrieben, Ausgrabungen und in einigen Fällen Restauratione vorgenommen. Die Forschungsaktivitäten und -ergebnisse werden ebenfalls besprochen.

Die ersten sicheren Anzeichen menschlicher Aktivitäten in Dartmoor stammen aus dem mesolithischen Zeitalter vor etwa 6500 Jahren. Als einzige Spuren haben diese Menschen zerbrochene Steinwerkzeuge hinterlassen und Umweltspuren in der Pollenanalyse, die Aufschluss über ihre Aktivitäten geben. Seit dem Neolithikum (etwa 4000-2000 v. Chr.) wurden dauerhafte steinerne Monumente wie Dolmen und Erdarbeiten für Grabhügel zur Bestattung der Toten errichtet. Dies sind die ersten dauerhaften Nachweise aus der materiellen Geschichte. Die rätselhaften „Tors" stammen vermutlich auch aus dieser Zeit, wobei es keine Nachweise dafür gibt, ob und wo jungsteinzeitliche Menschen in Dartmoor wohnten. Gegen Ende des 3. Jahrtausends v. Chr. und zu Beginn der Bronzezeit wurden zusätzliche Monumente errichtet. Steinkreise und Anordnungen von Steinen spielten eine rituelle oder vielleicht religiöse Rolle, über die wir anhand der Nachweise, die wir haben, nur Vermutungen anstellen können. Die runden Hügel, die zu Anfang dieses Zeitalters und später errichtet wurden, weisen auf Begräbnisse hin. Die runden Erdhügel und Steinhaufen sind unsere erste Begegnung mit Menschen aus der Vergangenheit, die häufig mit ihren Habseligkeiten wie Töpferwaren, Metallarbeiten und anderen Artefakten darin bestattet wurden. Der erste Nachweis einer permanenten Besiedlung in Dartmoor stammt aus dem frühen 2. Jahrhundert v. Chr., als runde Hütten im Hochland gebaut und bewohnt wurden. Die steinernen Hüttenkreise sind wahrscheinlich die bemerkenswerteste archäologische Ressource Dartmoors. Davon haben über 4.000 Exemplare überdauert. Einige waren in Siedlungen gruppiert, viele eingefriedet, andere standen in Zusammenhang mit einer Reihe von Landaufteilungen, die als „Reaves" bezeichnet werden. Diese Systeme paralleler Aufschichtungen dominieren die Landschaft in Teilen des Moors und wurden um 1600 v. Chr. angelegt.

In der jüngeren Bronzezeit und zu Beginn des 1. Jahrhundert v. Chr. Sind die Nachweise dauerhafter menschlicher Aktivität seltener als in irgendeiner anderen Periode vor der Jungsteinzeit und danach, was uns zu der

Vermutung veranlasst, dass die Landschaft bis zur späteren prähistorischen Periode weniger intensiv besiedelt wurde. Gesammelte Nachweise aus archäologischen Ausgrabungen setzen allmählich das Bild einer teilweisen Besiedelung des Hochlands in der Eisenzeit zusammen. Zu dieser Zeit waren runde Hütten noch immer die bevorzugten Behausungen. Allerdings ist Dartmoors Archäologie der Eisenzeit vom Vorhandensein leicht befestigter Siedlungen geprägt wie Bergfesten und eingefriedeten Hängen.

In der römischen und nachrömischen Ära und dem sogenannten finsteren Mittelalter fehlen materielle Nachweise für menschliche Besiedlung im Hochland von Dartmoor. Es ist jedoch wahrscheinlich, dass Siedlungen in den tiefer gelegenen Tälern und an Orten wie Widecombe-in-the-Moor wuchsen. Wahrscheinlich fand dies zwei Jahrhunderte vor der normannischen Eroberung im Jahr 1066 statt.

Während des Mittelalters wurde der Charakter von Dartmoor geprägt, für den auch heute noch eine von Ackerbau, Kleinstädten, Dörfern und Gehöften geprägte Landschaft typisch ist. Der Flickenteppich von Feldern, der sich nach und nach über die geschützten Täler zum Hochland hin ausbreitete, bildete den Rahmen, auf dem sich später alle Expansionen abspielten. Die Hochmoore hingegen, die immer als Weideland bevorzugt wurden, blieben unberührt. Viele Siedlungen und das dazugehörige Ackerland aus dieser Zeit sind noch immer bewohnt während andere, meist höher gelegene, verlassen wurden und jetzt archäologische Momentaufnahmen des mittelalterlichen Lebens bieten. Dazu gehören Feldsysteme für Ackerbau oder Viehhaltung sowie verfallene Gebäudestrukturen wie Bauernhäuser und Scheunen.

Ab dem 17. Jahrhundert wurden einige Gebiete von Dartmoor angepasst, um Kaninchen zu halten. Die Nachweise dieser Kaninchenzucht erstrecken sich über Orte wie Plym Valley und beinhalten die Erdhügel, in denen die Tiere gezüchtet wurden und Köderfallen, die dazu benötigt wurden, Raubtiere zu fangen. Ein weiterer interessanter Aspekt der landwirtschaftlich genutzten Landschaft war die Ankunft der „Verbesserer" des 18. und 19. Jahrhunderts, als große Bereiche der restlichen offenen Moore mit Steinmauern eingefasst wurden, um „modernere" landwirtschaftliche Methoden zu praktizieren.

Bezüglich industrieller Aktivitäten in Dartmoor muss vornehmlich der Abbau von Zinn genannt werden, der spätestens im 12. Jahrhundert begann, wenn nicht früher. Die Nachweise für Seifenzinnwerke und Schmelzöfen bieten eine kontrastierende und recht zerstörerische Dimension, die durch Aktivitäten verursacht wurde, in deren Zuge viele hundert Hektar der Landschaft dauerhaft und radikal verändert wurden. Zu den dazugehörigen archäologischen Eigenschaften gehört das Netzwerk aufgegebener künstlicher Wasserläufe für die Werke und die Orte, wo das Metall bearbeitet und geschmolzen wurde, die Stampf- und Blaswerke. Andere Industriebereiche mittelalterlichen Ursprungs waren sicherlich das Torfstechen, das zum Teil den Schmelzöfen diente, und die Granitverarbeitung. Die reichen Vorkommen der Moorsteine dienten für Gebäude im und außerhalb des Moors.

All diese Industrien wurden im 18. und 19. Jahrhundert weiterentwickelt, als der Kapitalismus Investoren hervorbrachte, von denen sie finanziert wurden. Der Metallabbau wurde ausgeweitet, um Kupfer und Silber-Blei zu gewinnen. Dabei erlebte auch die Zinnindustrie eine Renaissance, und Bergbaumethoden kamen zum Einsatz, wie die Überreste von Schächten, Gruben, Waschwerken, großen Halden, Maschinenhäusern und Spuren einer Infrastruktur bezeugen. Die Granitindustrie erlebte um 1800 mit Einführung der Steinabbautechniken ein dramatisches Ausmaß, als riesige Steinbrüche Narben in die Landschaft schlugen, während durch die Torfstecherei große Teile der Oberflächen des Hochlands abgetragen wurden. Porzellanerde kam spät nach Dartmoor, hatte jedoch dramatische Auswirkungen auf die südliche Peripherie des Nationalparks und ist immer noch ein rentabler Industriebereich. Aspekten der frühen Archäologie dieser Industrie wie Töpfereiwerke haben trotz der massiven und zerstörerischen Ausbreitung der jüngeren Aktivitäten überdauert.

Seit dem frühen 19. Jahrhundert wurden Soldaten in Dartmoor ausgebildet. Die wichtigsten Nachweise finden sich in den Ausbildungsbereichen. Der erste wurde in den 1870er Jahren gegründet, andere folgten. In Okehampton und Willsworthy finden sich Reste von Erdarbeiten und Strukturen, die für frühe Formen der militärischen Ausbildung dienten. Dartmoors Rolle im Zweiten Weltkrieg und spätere defensive Bemühungen haben auch mancherorts überdauert, viele in Zusammenhang mit der Luftabwehr wie Radar.

Bis dahin geht die Geschichte von Dartmoor bisher, wobei das Auslesen der historischen Umgebung weiter fortgeführt wird. Künftig wird es mehr zu sagen geben, insbesondere bezüglich Dartmoors Rolle im späten 20. und frühen 21. Jahrhundert als Nationalpark und wie die Umweltschutzbewegung, in der die Nationalparks wurzeln, die Entwicklung der Landschaft beeinflusst hat. Hoffentlich wird es weiterhin Nachweise für Aktivitäten nach den Menschen durch die Bemühungen des Nationalparks und andere staatliche und gemeinnützige Organisationen geben. Auch Landbesitzer leisten einen Beitrag, auch wenn er weniger spektakulär erscheinen mag. Ausschlaggebend ist die Unterstützung der Öffentlichkeit, deren Enthusiasmus für diese historische Landschaft dadurch stimuliert werden kann, dass sie sie besser versteht. Wir tragen die Hoffnung, dass dieses Buch einen Beitrag dazu leistet, Interesse zu wecken und Diskussionen zu fördern, die dieses Ziel unterstützen.

Übersetzung: Tamara Benscheidt
in association with First Edition Translations Ltd, Cambridge, UK

Introduction

The modern visitor to Devon, travelling west on the main roads into the region, is greeted by a panorama of high ground and rocky outcrops that make up the southern and eastern flanks of Dartmoor, providing a tantalising sample of what lies beyond. In a county renowned for its 'rolling hills', Dartmoor surpasses expectation; the large rounded summits of the high moors, topped by granite tors, preside over the massive folds of its peripheral valleys, incised by the fast-moving moorland rivers and streams as they flow towards the hinterland. It is often this natural beauty, the tranquil, rural character of its landscape and the outdoor experience of an apparently sparsely inhabited upland that initially attracts people to Dartmoor, but an appreciation of this landscape should not be confined to the aesthetic beauty of its natural assets, for the human or cultural dimension is equally compelling.

Dartmoor is southern England's largest tract of upland and is frequently misrepresented as 'wilderness', incorrectly implying that the presence of humans has had little impact on the way the landscape has developed. Despite its appearance of – in places, an apparently wild and occasionally harsh environment – its character has as much to do with past human intervention as any piece of land in England; and even today, though often promoted as 'England's last wilderness', it is a managed landscape, maintained to function in a certain way. The human activity, in particular the traditional forms of hill farming and woodland management carried on for many centuries, has resulted in a diversity of habitats, providing a unique combination of vegetation, and resulting in a landscape of varied character, where the diverse elements of the natural environment have been adapted through the human response to it and vice versa.

People only half familiar with Dartmoor, and many who visit the moor from afar, may associate the region culturally with some of its more internationally renowned attributes, including Dartmoor Prison, Widecombe Fair (notable for being the haunt of Uncle Tom Cobley and associates), Dartmoor Pixies (or Piskies) and Conan Doyle's *Hound of the Baskerville's*. A visit to any of the tourist 'hotspots' will only serve to reinforce these preconceptions, indeed all of these are important components of Dartmoor's modern cultural identity.

However, those who care to investigate further will find that Dartmoor, far from having only legend and literature, has a landscape that is rich in cultural meaning, manifest through the phenomenal profuseness of its historic environment. Dartmoor, arguably, has the most dense concentration of upstanding prehistoric archaeological remains in England; human activity is evident for a period extending from the Neolithic (4000–2000 BC) until very recent times, with field evidence representing a wide spectrum of human behaviour and all leaving their mark in the landscape, including domestic, sepulchral, ritual, spiritual, agricultural, industrial and military features. Whether consciously or not, the estimated 4.3 million people who make day-visits to Dartmoor every year (DNPA 2007, 64), are witnessing a landscape moulded by people.

This book offers an exploration of the elements that comprise the historic landscape of Dartmoor, particularly the archaeology of the open and freely accessible areas of moorland, but includes some of the outlying areas, and attempts to explain some of the human activities that have contributed to the shaping and character of the modern landscape through the results of archaeological investigation.

618m

Key
to
Relief
Range

>150m

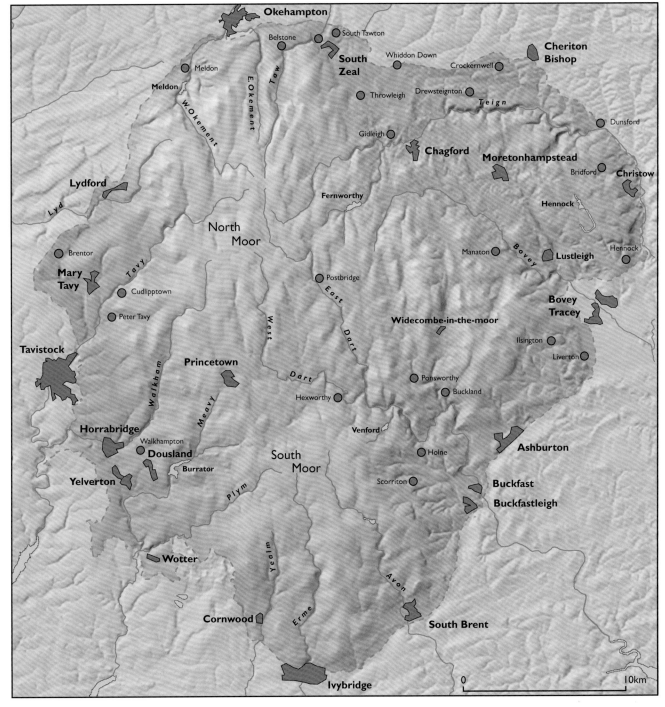

Okehampton

Belstone

South Tawton

Meldon

Meldon

South
Zeal

Whiddon Down

Cheriton
Bishop

Crockernwell

E. Okement

Taw

Throwleigh

Drewsteignton

Teign

W. Okement

Gidleigh

Chagford

Moretonhampstead

Dunsford

Lydford

Lyd

Fernworthy

Bridford

Christow

Hennock

North
Moor

Brentor

Manaton

Bovey

Lustleigh

Hennock

Mary
Tavy

Tavy

Postbridge

Bovey
Tracey

Cudlipptown

East Dart

Widecombe-in-the-moor

Ilsington

Peter Tavy

West

Liverton

Tavistock

Walkham

Princetown

Dart

Ponsworthy

Meavy

Hexworthy

Buckland

Horrabridge

Walkhampton

Venford

Ashburton

Dousland

South
Moor

Holne

Burrator

Yelverton

Buckfast

Scorriton

Buckfastleigh

Plym

Wotter

Yealm

Cornwood

Erme

Avon

South Brent

0   10km

Ivybridge

The Dartmoor landscape

Location and description

Dartmoor lies wholly within the county of Devonshire, between Exeter and Plymouth in the southern part of the county (Fig 0.1). The area, 954 sq km in total, became a National Park in 1951, the fourth region in Britain to be so designated. The natural landform is a granite massif rising through and surrounded by earlier Devonian shales, and forms a high plateau of moorland that provides the source for the majority of Devon's larger rivers, including the Dart, Erme, Plym, Tavy, Taw and Teign. There is only one major settlement on the high moors, at Princetown, although on the peripheries of the moor are several small country towns, including Okehampton, Moretonhampstead, Bovey Tracey, Ashburton, Buckfastleigh, Ivybridge, Yelverton, Horrabridge and Tavistock; and an a number of smaller settlements are found around and on Dartmoor itself. The highest point on Dartmoor, and indeed in the south-west peninsula, is High Willhays at 621m OD, with land over 300m occupying more than 50% of the national park territory.

Dartmoor is a national park, but it is not owned by the state, and although the open moors and many areas of the peripheries offer mostly free access to the modern visitor, the majority of the land is in the private ownership of individuals, public bodies and charitable trusts.

From barren wasteland to National Park

Like most upland regions in Britain, Devon's early topographic and historical writers had a very negative perception of Dartmoor, many advising their readers to avoid the place if possible. Thomas Westcote for example, writing in the early 17th century, warned of:

The peril of deep tinworks, steep tors, high mountains, low valleys, bogs, plains, being neither in any hazard or fear of danger, without wetting you're your foot in the many meers, or fouling your shoes in the many mires (Oliver and Jones 1845, 89)

Such attitudes may have been due in part to the remote and inaccessible nature of the upland, which before the 19th century had no roads, other than what were essentially well-used footpaths, and the central areas of the moor were visited by few people besides those whose presence was necessitated by the nature of their labours, either graziers, tinners or peat cutters. The arrival of those driven by a sense of investigation – such as antiquaries, naturalist and topographers, or seekers of Dartmoor's inspirational qualities – including artists, poets and writers, did not come until the roads and general accessibility of the place were improved in the 19th century. But come they did, followed eventually by others wishing to share in the many qualities that the landscape of Dartmoor provides. The changing attitudes of those writers and artists, who altered the perception of Dartmoor through their works, have been eloquently set out by Patricia Milton (2006), who tells how the barren, unwelcoming 'wilderness', described in the work of 17th- and 18th-century writers, was transformed into a land of rugged beauty and a source of inspiration to those of the 19th and 20th centuries. The inspirational qualities coupled with the tranquillity and rural peace are of course among the main attractions of Dartmoor today for the many people who enjoy visiting the National Park. Although now it is more fashionable and more appropriate to perceive Dartmoor not only through its natural assets but also through understanding it as a place where past human activity is as much to be credited for its present aesthetic beauty as that of nature; as the Dartmoor National Park Authority (DNPA) management plan expresses it, Dartmoor is:

… a cultural landscape created through the interaction of distinctive land management practices with the physical environment (DNPA 2007, 16)

Although in the past, the concept behind protected landscapes in Britain was weighted in favour of 'natural beauty', today the importance of the cultural or human landscape is fully acknowledged by the national parks movement and enshrined in the legislation regarding the purposes of the parks, with equal stature given to that of the natural landscape (DNPA 2007, 9).

The natural environment

Topography and vegetation

The moorland areas of Dartmoor, of which there are 46,000ha in total, approximately 50% of the National Park (DNPA 2007, 30), offer the

Fig 0.1 (opposite)
Map of Dartmoor, showing topography, major water courses, towns, villages and hamlets, and the National Park boundary (height data licensed to English Heritage for PGA through Next Perspectives™).

Fig 0.2
Geological map of South Devon showing the granite mass of Dartmoor as a clear intrusion into the older sedimentary rocks (© British Geological Survey, with permission).

greatest contrast to the landscape of the hinterland of Devon, occupying the upper and middle ground. The uplands represent the highest ground, of which there are two separate highland zones, the south moor and the north moor, separated by a central belt of slightly lower ground. The higher peaks of these uplands, topped by granite tors, fall away to form shallow basins within their folds, where large peat bogs retain the water that provides the source for many of Devon's infant rivers, which, as they escape their cradles, cut valleys through the undulating terrain. Where these water courses leave the plateaux, and smaller streams merge with the larger rivers, the ground becomes firmer and the land is bound together by the granite, which makes its presence known at frequent intervals in the form of tors, outcrops and clitter fields. Here, the heathlands begin to dominate, comprising heather, gorse and whortleberry, but also swards of open grassland that have been highly valued for summer grazing since humans first settled here in the early 2nd millennium BC. In recent decades these middle and lower altitude areas have increasingly been encroached by bracken, owing in no small part, to the reduction in the numbers of grazing animals. The outer edge of the moorland zone is marked by enclosure walls demarcating the upper limits of farmland, a majority of which was established in the medieval period, though with earlier elements also much in evidence. Today, the character of this farmed landscape is a patchwork of irregular pasture fields and hay meadows, separated by stone walls and hedge banks. The fields have expanded in an organic, piecemeal fashion, encroaching into areas of former moorland along the gentler slopes of the river valleys and hillsides, and in many cases still function much as they have for more than a thousand years. The rivers gain momentum and the valleys widen and become deeper as they approach the peripheries of the moors, possessing steep flanks where woodlands and forests thrive as the sheltered valleys descend towards the hinterland. The wooded river valleys include those of the Teign, Dart, Erme, Walkham and Plym; they have in the past been a highly valued resource, providing timber for building and charcoal managed through coppicing. Deciduous woodland is rare on the moorlands, with three notable exceptions: Wistman's Wood, Blackator Beare and Piles Copse. These are relict ancient oak woodlands, survivors from an earlier regime of landscape management. Despite the diminutive proportions and withered appearance of the trees, a result of poor soils and harsh weather conditions, some are believed to be hundreds of years old (Simmons 1965, 232).

Despite Dartmoor's many attractive qualities, it undeniably possesses a wet and often cold climate by comparison with other areas of

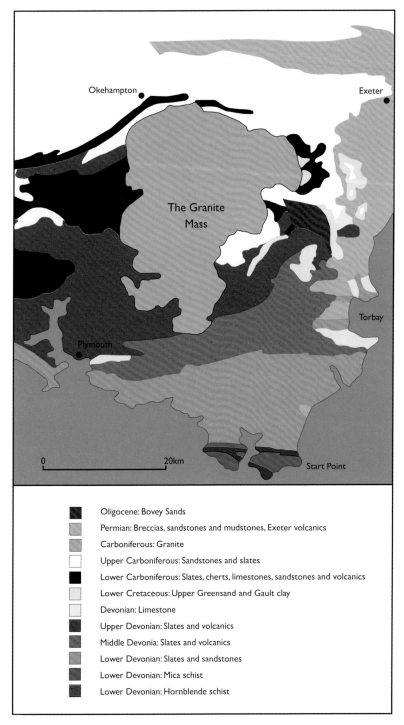

Okehampton

Exeter

The Granite
Mass

Torbay

Plymouth

0   20km

Start Point

■ Oligocene: Bovey Sands

▨ Permian: Breccias, sandstones and mudstones, Exeter volcanics

▨ Carboniferous: Granite

□ Upper Carboniferous: Sandstones and slates

■ Lower Carboniferous: Slates, cherts, limestones, sandstones and volcanics

▨ Lower Cretaceous: Upper Greensand and Gault clay

▨ Devonian: Limestone

▨ Upper Devonian: Slates and volcanics

▨ Middle Devonia: Slates and volcanics

▨ Lower Devonian: Slates and sandstones

▨ Lower Devonian: Mica schist

▨ Lower Devonian: Hornblende schist

southern England, dominated by south-westerly winds, with short summers and harsh winters; the current average annual rainfall for Princetown is 2,150mm (DNPA 2004). These conditions are most acute on the higher exposed ground of the uplands and it is for this reason that, in farming terms, parts of Dartmoor have to be seen as marginal, whereby their viability as places to eke out a living through farming will always be dependent on minor changes to the climate. This is evident for several periods in Dartmoor's past (*see* chapters 4 and 7), when phases of favourable and unfavourable climate may have influenced the extent of human activity.

Geology

(The following is a synthesis which summarises the works of Dines 1994, Durrance and Laming 1982 and Perkins 1984.)

In a landscape such as Dartmoor, the underlying geology to a great extent dictates certain aspects of human behaviour, particularly the economic activities essential to the survival and prosperity of groups and societies. The fertility and richness of soils, together with mineral wealth are unique to an area; the behaviour of those who have made that area their home, although subject to many other agencies, has usually developed to work with it in an advantageous manner.

Dartmoor is well known for its granite tors, but this igneous granite massif is a later intrusion, set amid and surrounded by much earlier sedimentary rocks. The earliest dateable rocks in Devon were formed in the Lower Devonian Period, 395 million (Ma) years ago, and comprise sands, muds and intermittent deposits of calcareous material, which settled and accumulated as silts beneath the sea, later to become compressed by their own weight to form sandstones, shales and limestones (Fig 0.2).

During the later Carboniferous Period there occurred a series of tectonic events, collectively known as the Variscan Orogeny. During this time folding, faulting and contraction of the various sedimentary layers generated great frictional heating between plates, melting the lower structures and forcing an intrusion of magma from below. The magma then cooled and solidified to form the granite batholith of the south-west peninsula. Only a small portion of the upper sections of the batholith is visible at surface, forming separate bodies or plutons, including the massifs of Bodmin Moor and

Dartmoor; the spectacular granite tors that characterise these moorlands are the visible outcome of this event. Granite was derived from the melting of sedimentary rocks and is composed of four major minerals: quartz, feldspar, biotite and mica. Accessory minerals include tourmaline, which is very common on Dartmoor, where a course- to medium-grained granite rich in magacrysts (ie crystal grains set within the rock that are larger than the surrounding matrix) is most usual. The heat generated by the rising magma during the intrusion also transformed the composition of the older rocks in the contact zone around the granite plutons, creating a concentric ring of baked sedimentary rocks known as the Metamorphic Aureole (Fig 0.3). This band of metamorphic rocks is between *c.* 0.75 and 3.25km wide at the surface.

During the period of cooling, the magma, along with the altered rocks of the Metamorphic Aureole, contracted fractured and underwent some movement. This process produced fissures within and between the rocks. Some of these were filled by porphyry to form the Elvan Dykes of hard quartz, while others were filled by hydrothermal or metalliferous veins, formed by hot gases and mineral rich solutions, which emanated from the magma in areas believed to be still molten after most of the batholith had cooled.

The elements contained within the mineralised solutions, which flowed into the fissures, solidified at varying temperatures to form metallic rocks, including Cassiterite

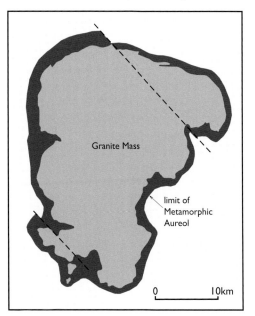

Fig 0.3
The granite mass and the Metamorphic Aureol (© British Geological Survey, with permission).

(tin oxide), Chalcopyrite (copper sulphide), Galena (lead sulphide) and Blende (zinc sulphide). The metalliferous veins are found within both the granite batholith and the Metamorphic Aureole, but the combinations of metallic minerals within each differs.

One of the outcomes of the Variscan Orogeny, was an uplifting process that resulted in the formation of mountains rising from the sea to form the land mass, later to become the south-west peninsula. This land was from the very start subject to weathering and erosion of the upper layers, but particularly during the Permian and Triassic periods, causing massive deposits of alluvium eroded from the upland to be washed down and built up in all the river valleys of Devon. Any metamorphic rocks that remained covering the granite boss, together with the upper sections of the granite itself, eroded away over millions of years, taking with it the upper levels of any exposed mineral veins. As part of this process, within the granite zone, the weathered veins or 'lodes' of tin became redeposited in the form of alluvial or 'stream' tin in low-lying valleys, basins and river plains and were successfully exploited by the medieval and post-medieval tin streamers (*see* chapter 8). Off the granite, in the areas still covered by the baked sedimentary rocks of the Metamorphic Aureole, a wider range of mineral veins survived, including tin, copper, lead, wolfram and iron. Silver and manganese occur in isolated areas together with minor minerals such as blende (zinc), magnetite, micaceous hematite and arsenopyrite or mispickle (arsenic).

The fractured granite that broke away from the outcrops to settle on the slopes, known as 'clitter', served as a useful source of building stone from the late 3rd millennium BC. As masonry skills developed in the medieval period, 'moorstone' as it became known, was used in the construction of many fine buildings on and around the moors, and continued to be used until the development of quarrying techniques in the 19th century (*see* chapter 10).

Other economic benefits derived from the geology of Dartmoor and exploited by its inhabitants over several millennium include tin, copper and silver-lead. Although it is probable that the latter two metals were only mined economically from the 18th century onwards (*see* chapter 11), tin was certainly being exploited by the 12th century (*see* chapter 8), although possibly much earlier, with origins perhaps even in the prehistoric period. Finally, china clay, which as an industry still enjoys economic prosperity on and around Dartmoor, is extracted from a deposit called kaolin. This is granite that has been subject to rotting to become a crumbly white substance, which when separated from all its associate minerals is a highly versatile material with a wide spectrum of commercial uses (*see* chapter 12).

Modern human activity

The modern landscape of Dartmoor, so valued for its aesthetic beauty and rural charm, is largely the result of land management practices by hill farmers, which were being put into place before Domesday in 1086, and have developed over the thousand years that followed in a mostly unaltered form. It is a regrettable truth therefore that this very way of life, which contributed so much to the appearance of this landscape, is itself so threatened, as the modern economics of agriculture and the changed priorities of farming policy have gradually driven hill farming towards diminishing sustainability, which in turn must mean change to the landscape in the future. Nevertheless, although on a much reduced scale, thankfully many farmers continue to raise livestock on Dartmoor, though with a notable decline in stocking levels on the open moors and commons.

For the landscape archaeologist, whose field of study may extend over thousands of years, the decline and even the collapse of farming communities are familiar global occurrences, as past climates, demographic movements, plagues and changing economics would often lead to the partial or complete abandonment of entire landscapes in times of difficulty. Dartmoor is no stranger to major change caused by varying degrees of human presence, as is evident in the chapters that follow. But on 20th- and 21st-century Dartmoor there is a difference, because, although the traditional stewards of the land are declining in number, the public at large rather likes what it is their predecessors have created and want it to be maintained and enjoyed as a recreational resource. Here, ironically, is where Dartmoor's economic present and future lie. Management of the land today, including planning policy and the encouragement of economic activity, is a balance between the interests of farming and conservation, and is aimed at maintaining the

Fig 0.4
Aerial view of Fernworthy
Forest and reservoir
(NMR 24673/030;
© English Heritage. NMR).

appearance of the landscape through fostering the traditional land management practices that make that aim possible. Although this may be perceived by some as a way of stopping Dartmoor's traditional history in its tracks, by micro-managing and even preventing change, in the longer view of history it is quite the opposite, for the system of management that prevails in any landscape at any period can only be a reflection of the social order of its time; in the late-20th and 21st centuries AD this is manifest on Dartmoor through the existence of a national park, managed for all the reasons described above and more. By contrast, in the 11th and 12th centuries AD a similar 'managed' approach maintained Dartmoor Forest solely as a hunting ground where 'beasts of the chase' could flourish, but where people could not farm or build houses (*see* chapter 7). Recreational landscapes are no less relevant, and in future their significance as a product of 20th- and 21st-century British society will be recognised.

It will become clear as various chapters of this book are explored, that Dartmoor has always been perceived by some as a place for economic opportunity; whether it was the early graziers who utilised its summer pastures, the tinners, miners, peat cutters and stoneworkers exploiting the mineral resources or the 18th- and 19th-century improvers wishing to accrue wealth through agriculture, the land has been a base for diverse forms of economic activity. In the 20th and 21st

centuries, tourism is a somewhat unusual industry in that it places very different pressures on the land without the land itself producing anything. Other economic benefits come from the wet climate and water-retentive nature of the ground, providing an ideal location for reservoirs to supply water to the lowland inhabitants of Devon. There are five large reservoirs on and around the uplands of Dartmoor: Avon, Burrator, Fernworthy (Fig 0.4), Venford (Fig 0.5) and Meldon, and a further three in the hinterland of the National Park at Hennock. Burrator, the earliest reservoir was built in 1898 and the most recent was Meldon in 1972.

Conifer plantations cover a total of 3,290ha within the National Park, planted between the 1920s and the 1950s. The Dartmoor climate provides an ideal environment for conifers, encouraging rapid growth rates and good-quality timber. The plantations have provided an economic benefit for the region, and as they have matured they have also become valued as a recreational resource. Their presence on the uplands of a National Park, however, remains controversial and one stated

Fig 0.5
Aerial view of Venford reservoir and the south-east Dartmoor hinterland beyond (NMR 24675/077; © English Heritage. NMR).

long-term aim of the DNPA is the removal of conifer plantation from the high moorland areas (DNPA 2007, 32).

Of all the extractive industries that have occurred on and around Dartmoor, china clay is the only one that survives in any substantive form, occupying large areas around south-west Dartmoor, both within and outside the National Park. Historically, it is one of the regions youngest extractive industries (*see* chapter 12) and although its past economic benefits to the area are undeniable, its continued presence and the incredibly destructive nature of its operations, which irreversibly alter the landscape, remain hugely controversial.

The work of previous writers

Dartmoor is one of the most written about topics of any in Devon, reflecting the fact that it has, for a long time, been a favourite place to visit and explore, possessing the rare qualities of remoteness and tranquillity, which provide spirituality and inspiration to those who visit or reside in the area, as well as a fascination for those with an instinct for inquiry into the past.

Among the literary output has been a strong tradition of archaeological writing, commencing with Samuel Rowe's *Perambulation of Dartmoor* in 1848, and followed by Sabine Baring-Gould (1900), John Lloyd-Warden Page (1892) and Robert Burnard (1890–4). Many of these writers included the information that was available to them on the antiquities – and indeed several were actively engaged in archaeological investigations – through their association with the Devon Committee on Barrows and the Dartmoor Exploration Committee (DEC), whose activities are described in chapter 1; both of these groups published the results of archaeological research in various learned journals. Curiously, no dedicated book on archaeology resulted from early antiquarian investigations or from the work of the DEC, and the first writer to make a really substantive contribution to the publication of Dartmoor's archaeology, making his work more widely available, was R Hansford Worth. His collected papers, covering prehistoric archaeology, aspects of the medieval period and the early tin industry, were published in a single volume entitled *Worth's Dartmoor* in 1953 following his death

(Spooner and Russell 1953); it has been reprinted many times since and the work remains in print.

In 1974 Paul Pettit published the first book dedicated to the prehistoric archaeology of Dartmoor. *Prehistoric Dartmoor* was a brave attempt by the author to place the work of the early antiquarians within a more up-to-date framework of understanding relevant to the 1970s, in an accessible, non-specialist format. However, apart from new material that had become available from excavations in the 1950s by Aileen Fox, discussed below, he was unable to add a great deal to the interpretation, due to a lack of fresh data.

Other works worth drawing attention to are *Dartmoor: a New Study*, first published in 1970, edited by Crispin Gill, a collection of essays written by leading researchers of the period, discussing a broad range of topics covering history, archaeology and landscape from 'Early Men' to the 20th century. This fine volume, also the subject of several reprints, remains one of the core texts for the student of Dartmoor's past, bringing out of learned journals and into the public domain topics previously neglected, such as medieval settlement, tinworking and the influence of the improvers.

The list of essential core texts must also include Helen Harris's *Industrial Archaeology of Dartmoor* (1968). The significance of this work is discussed in chapter 10, but its seminal importance as the first book to highlight the surviving material evidence of Dartmoor's more recent industries cannot be overstated.

A series of prehistoric land divisions, known on Dartmoor as the 'reaves', formed the focus for a major research project in the late 1970s and 1980s (discussed in chapter 3), which culminated in Andrew Fleming's landmark publication *The Dartmoor Reaves* in 1988. This book changed archaeologists' perceptions towards prehistoric Dartmoor from a limited approach, based on the collective analysis of a number of individual 'sites', to one whereby past human interventions were viewed more holistically as components of a prehistoric 'landscape'. The scale of analysis shifted from localised issues surrounding settlement, domesticity and burial practice, to questions about how society developed and utilised the landscape in a practical, economic, social and political sense. Since that time others have contributed to discussions on the reaves at an academic level, but in 2008, a revised edition of Fleming's work brings this subject up to date regarding current thinking on this topic.

The prehistoric period also constituted the major focus of a series of important volumes by Jeremy Butler, during the 1990s (1991a, 1991b, 1993, 1994 and 1997). Butler combined the technique of aerial photographic transcription with selective ground recording, to amass a highly detailed set of data, presented as maps, drawings and photographs, covering all aspects of the field archaeology, from the Neolithic to the 19th century AD, focussing in particular on the 2nd millennium BC. Excellent though Butler's work is, it is descriptive rather than analytical, and its importance lies in providing an essential guide and starting point for anyone wishing to embark on an exploration of Dartmoor's archaeological landscape, whether professionally or for his or her own interest.

The most recent contribution to Dartmoor's general archaeological writing is Sandy Gerrard's *Dartmoor* (1997). This was the first modern volume to offer an updated introduction to the topic aimed at the general reader; Gerrard provided basic explanations of the usual Dartmoor themes but included medieval tinworking, which had not been previously considered in any archaeological sense. The topic was expanded further with Gerrard's *Early British Tin Industry* (2000) and by Newman (1998) in the *Dartmoor Tin Industry: a Field Guide*.

Background to this volume

The book forms one of a series of regional monographs published by English Heritage (EH), which present the results of fieldwork by EH (formerly the RCHME) Archaeological Survey and Investigation teams (AS&I). Other regions described in the series include Bodmin Moor (Johnson and Rose 1994; Herring *et al* 2008, Exmoor (Riley and Wilson-North 2001), the Salisbury Plain Training Area (McOmish *et al* 2002), the Malverns (Bowden 2005), the Quantock Hills (Riley 2006) and), and Northamptonshire (Deegan 2007). Although conforming with the general style and format, it differs slightly from others in the series in that it does not represent the culmination of a single project, but celebrates 20 years of smaller projects and focussed surveys, each undertaken as a response to changing research priorities and conservation requirements over

that period. Together this work, adds up to a substantive body of data, covering most aspects and all periods of Dartmoor's archaeological landscape, and the aim is to present the collective results of surveys undertaken, offering an interpretation of some aspects of Dartmoor's historic landscape informed by the new survey material and presented within a contemporary archaeological context.

Interest in the past has developed from a hobby practised by 19th-century clergymen with spare time on their hands, to become the modern discipline of archaeology, encompassing a broad range of techniques, period specialisms and interpretive theories. The accounts of early researchers provide a rich social history, which is intriguing enough in itself, but it is also fundamental to how current understanding of the material past, through interpretation and dating of the many facets of the archaeological landscape, is achieved. A summary narrative of past investigation, excavations and discovery, where of interest, is therefore offered for each of the themes presented.

Although the material presented here represents as broad a sample as is possible, both in terms of the periods of the past covered and the topics discussed, there are limitations within this brief; for example, the main subject material of the book has to be the open moorland and uplands that are freely accessible to the public. Although the peripheries of the moor are frequently referred to in the text, this is necessary to provide context, but it has not been deemed appropriate in a publication of this type, to discuss a great number of sites that are on private land and may not be visited, although there are one or two exceptions.

The topics and themes discussed are constrained to some extent by the investigation methods used and by the ground covered as a result. This book is about landscape archaeology and although ideally this term should include all facets of past human intervention within a landscape, it has not been possible to include most aspects of the built environment. Parish churches, towns, villages, farms and vernacular buildings generally are therefore not included. Indeed, although piecemeal work to examine the historic buildings and major settlement of Dartmoor has taken place in the past, this is often due only to threats to the structures; with the exception perhaps of Gawn's study of early farmhouses (Gawne and Sanders 1998), no structured programme of architectural research with broad academic aims has yet been undertaken, although this is surely a priority for the future. The topic of movement through the landscape – including trackways, guidestones, stone crosses and droveways – has also been omitted, while the discussion of later tramways and railways is limited. Also, in a themed monograph of this type, it has not been possible to engage too deeply with the social history of Dartmoor, though this is well covered by authors such as Hemery (1983), Stanbrook (1994a) and numerous magazine articles of recent years.

The survival of Dartmoor's archaeology

In any region of the world, evidence from the past is under constant threat from change and artefacts surviving from earlier use of the landscape are destroyed or subsumed by human progress. However, the archaeology of Dartmoor has suffered far less from these forces of attrition than many of the more intensively farmed lowland areas of Britain, resulting in high survival rate for archaeological sites, particularly upstanding stone and earthwork features. This not only reflects the lack of intensity of modern farming but demonstrates that radical disruption to the upland in particular, has been rare over its entire history, where the material evidence for the activities of one generation has rarely been entirely effaced by those of the next. This survival of many layers of evidence, from more than four thousand years of human interaction with the land, has provided a landscape in which material remains have accumulated, enabling a view of change in both the recent and the remote pasts. For most areas of Britain, such as towns, cities and intensively farmed rural areas, accumulative landscapes will be dominated by evidence of the recent past, and the archaeologist needs to look much harder to find earlier material. On Dartmoor not only are those living in the present able to explore all periods of the past, because it is so visible to those who investigate this landscape, but it is also possible to reflect on how the existence of earlier features may have influenced the imposition of those from later times by investigating the relationships of remains from different periods.

The survival of monuments depends mostly on the activities of later occupants in an area.

For example, prehistoric archaeological remains, especially the enclosures, settlements and reave systems for which high Dartmoor is so renowned, once extended off the open moors into the present-day enclosed lands and beyond. Unfortunately, the medieval wall builders who created later enclosures, utilised the ruined prehistoric walls either to serve as foundations for a refurbished walls or, along with hut circles, cairns and stone monuments in the vicinity, to make convenient quarries for stone. The enclosed fields were often improved for ploughing, so any stony monuments that remained would also be removed as a result. For this reason the best of the highly visible prehistoric archaeology survives on areas of the open moors where the wall builders were not active, and ploughing never took place. Even so, there were further threats to these sites in the modern period as road builders, stone cutters and 'newtake' wall builders were all responsible for the despoiling of sites as a source of stone.

Burial sites, barrows and cairns, were also the victims of disturbance when dug into by treasure seekers and barrow diggers. The accounts of 18th- and 19th-century writers on Dartmoor's antiquities record that many were being actively destroyed at that time. The extent of the destruction may only be estimated, but if the thousands of sites that do survive on this single area of upland are considered, it is sobering to reflect on what must have once existed in Britain as a whole, before a thousand years of intensive farming effaced the evidence in the lowland areas. It is therefore important not to perceive Dartmoor as in some way 'other' or different, particularly in the prehistoric period, and its relevance needs to be understood in terms of the archaeology found elsewhere in Devon (compare Griffith 1994) and Britain as a whole. In this context its importance is as a place where the archaeological evidence has survived rather better than most.

As later uses of the moors came and went they each left their mark on the evidence of previous ages. Tinners', quarrymen's, miners' and farmers' activities may all be seen to have destroyed, disturbed, altered or utilised earlier features in the landscape. Where the destruction of earlier evidence was only partial, and evidence for many activities may be found in a single location, the accumulative landscape is at its best, providing a number of timed snapshots as the human landscape developed.

Part One
Prehistoric Dartmoor

1

From antiquaries to landscape archaeologists: the discovery of prehistoric archaeology on Dartmoor

Early investigations: the 'ancient British' and the Druids

Interest in British archaeology has origins in the 16th century with nationally renowned antiquarian figures such as William Camden, author of *Britannia* in 1586, who it was that first described Stonehenge, and a little later, John Aubrey, whose *Monumenta Britannica* (1665–93) contained his published investigations at some of Britain's most notable prehistoric monuments, including Avebury and Stonehenge. However, although William Camden mentioned Dartmoor briefly in *Britannia* it is unlikely that he ever visited and no scholar of that period paid any regard to Dartmoor's antiquities. In a manuscript copy of Aubrey's volume, there is a scribbled note in the margin 'stones of Dartmoor, ask Mr Bovey' (J Marchand DNPA, pers com) but it seems improbable that Aubrey ever visited the region either. This is hardly surprising: Dartmoor, unlike the developed agricultural landscape of Aubrey's Wiltshire, was an inaccessible and inhospitable place. There were no good roads across the moors and the landscape was hostile to the unfamiliar traveller crossing many miles of open moorland on the few narrow trackways and at the mercy of the weather, which was, and still is, notoriously wet, cold, windy and frequently enshrouded by mist. The 16th-century Devon historian, John Hooker, claimed that '… this one thing is to be observed that all the yere through it rayneth or is fowle wether in that more or desert' (Blake 1915, 345*)*.

But there were other reasons not to explore Dartmoor and one 18th-century visitor wrote of the place that it '… has long been considered as an inhospitable desert, where strangers were anxiously warned to avoid passing over it, and a thousand stories told of people being pillaged and murdered, and of others perishing in the floods and the snow' (Fraser 1794, 56).

It is little wonder therefore that Dartmoor's antiquities escaped the notice of early antiquarian investigators. Perhaps one exception was Tristram Risdon, the 17th-century historian who mentioned Dartmoor briefly in his *Chorographical Description of the County of Devon* in about 1630, and although he probably did not consider antiquities to be part of his brief, he noted that: 'In this forest are three remarkable things: the first is a high rock called Crocken-Tor, where the parliament for the stannary causes is kept; … the second is Child's of Plimstock's tomb; … The third is some acres of wood and trees … called Wistman's Wood' (Risdon 1810, 222–3).

It is significant that one of these 'remarkable things', Childe's Tomb, a prehistoric burial chamber near Foxtor, was an antiquity but the close proximity of these three places, suggests that when exploring central Dartmoor, if indeed he ever went there himself, Risdon did not venture very far from the trackways of the time.

It was not until 1779 that the first account of what we would today consider an archaeological site was reported by Chapple with a description and interpretation of Spinsters' Rock, a Neolithic portal dolmen on the eastern border country near Drewsteignton (Timms 1993, 4). Chapple firmly believed, based on his notes and observations, that this monument was a Druidic astronomical observatory. However, the next writer to describe this and several other Dartmoor

Fig 1.1
Extract from Benjamin
Donn's map of 1765,
showing the area around
Chagford and including
'A Druid Cromlech'
(Spinster's Rock) and
'Wooston Castle', an Iron
Age Hillfort.

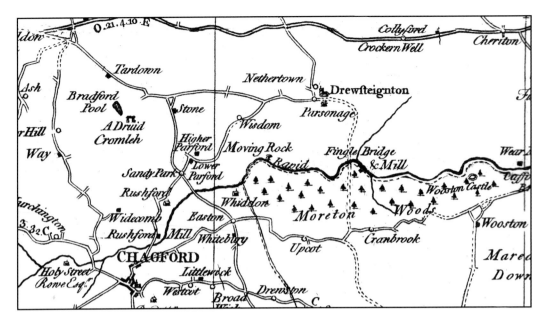

Fig 1.2
An untitled etching of
Spinster's Rock in which
the scale has been
exaggerated, with a
Druid-like figure in the
foreground; T H Williams
1804 (© Westcountry
Studies Library, with
permission).

artefacts had even stronger opinions as to its Druidic origins and purpose. Richard Polwhele, the vicar of Kenton near Exeter, in his *History of Devonshire* (1793–1806 [1799]), dismissed Chapple's theories, claiming that Spinsters' Rock was actually the burial place of an Archdruid, and he went on to attribute Druidic origins to several other features of the Dartmoor landscape. Although Polwhele's work is concerned with the whole of the county, his explorations of Dartmoor had clearly penetrated the upland a little deeper than those before him such as Risdon, as he also describes Grimspound, near Manaton (a prehistoric enclosed settlement), as well as

Crockerntor near the centre of the moor, which he believed had been 'the seats of judicature for Druidic cantreds' (administrative districts) long before the tinners' parliament met there. Polwhele also had a fascination for rock basins, a geological phenomenon found on some of the granite tors, which he considered to be associated with Druid ritual.

It is perhaps likely that both Polwhele and Chapple were familiar with the first reasonably accurate map of Devon, published by Benjamin Donn in 1765 (Fig 1.1); although as a navigational aid for the Dartmoor upland the map leaves much to be desired, it does depict some antiquities, including Crockern Tor (*see* Fig 8.1) and 'A Druid Cromlech' near Drewsteignton (Spinster's Rock). The druidic interpretation of Spinsters' Rock therefore clearly had origins earlier in the mid-18th century.

Druidism had been a universal explanation in Britain for certain classes of 'ancient' monuments, since the time of John Aubrey, who, in the 17th century, had believed Stonehenge to be a Druid temple. It was in some ways quite logical for 17th- and 18th-century antiquaries to interpret aspects of the past in this way, given the lack of accumulated knowledge within their infant discipline. The Druid idea evolved from a reinterpretation of some classical texts, such as Julius Caesar's *Gaelic Wars,* recording his encounters with the 'British' inhabitants of these islands at the time of the first Roman invasion in 55 BC, and Diodorus Siculus a

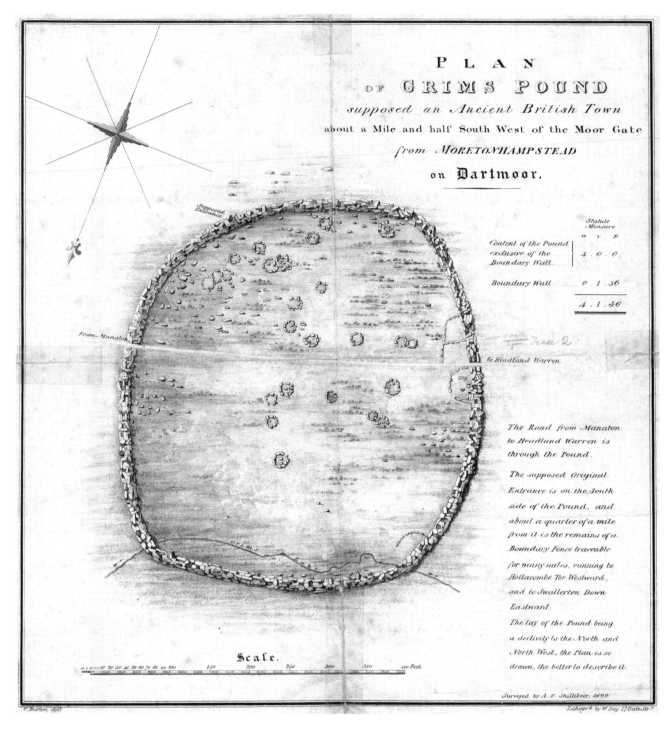

Greek writer who described Britain and its people in the 1st century BC. To the 18th-century mind the Classical period defined early civilisation and culture and it was Roman antiquities and architecture that had first come to the attention of the early investigators. The so-called 'rude stone' monuments such as Stonehenge and Avebury were a clear contrast in style to the precise and skilfully executed ruined buildings of Roman Britain and Europe, and could therefore be attributed to the 'British' inhabitants who occupied the land beforehand (Fig 1.2).

It must have seemed too irresistible a coincidence for these early scholars, that a group known as the Druids were recorded, by these seemingly 'reliable' sources, inhabiting Britain before the coming of the Romans,

Fig 1.3
Shillabeer's 1829 plan of Grimspound, 'arguably the first adequate plan of a prehistoric settlement site to be drawn in Britain' (Fleming 2008, 19) (© Westcountry Studies Library, with permission).

15

and who must surely have been responsible for these earlier remains. Caesar had described the Druids as a religious elite who were 'Concerned with divine worship, the due performance of sacrifice, public and private, and the interpretation of ritual questions.' It was then just a matter of interpreting what purpose the monuments served within this framework of inference and this served the antiquaries very well for another three centuries.

Once the genie was out of the bottle, Druidism continued to pervade the interpretations by Dartmoor's antiquaries well into the 19th century. After Polwhele's time even worse was to come, as described below in the discussion of stone rows, and as late as 1862 Sir Gardner Wilkinson, known foremost as an Egyptologist, continued to argue in favour of Druidic origins for many of Dartmoor's monuments in an otherwise very comprehensive and useful account of the region's prehistoric landscape (Wilkinson 1862, 22–53; 111–33).

The influence of Druidism also emerged in the popular literature of the period, such as the work of Anna Eliza Bray (1879), for whom in

Druids could be found an explanation for every curiously shaped rock formation or stony antiquity – and this served to further embed these myths in the culture of Dartmoor.

Druidism aside, the enthusiasm for investigating Dartmoor's 'antiquities' was gaining momentum in the first decades of the 19th century. This was an exciting time for archaeological investigation, particularly in Devon. Successive excavations at Kent's cavern, a cave in Torbay, by Revd John Northmore in 1824 and MacEnery in 1825 had recovered bones of species such as the cave bear and hyena, known to have been long extinct in Britain, but found in association with human remains. This discovery would, some decades later, have profound implications for the dating of British prehistory. Northmore later turned his attention to Dartmoor and Andrew Fleming has related the events that brought Northmore together with two other clergymen, James Holman Mason and John Pike Jones. Their explorations ultimately lead to the recognition of the Dartmoor reaves, the land divisions that are now known to date from the 2nd millennium BC (Fleming 1988, 12–17) and discussed below in chapter 3. It was Mason who in 1829

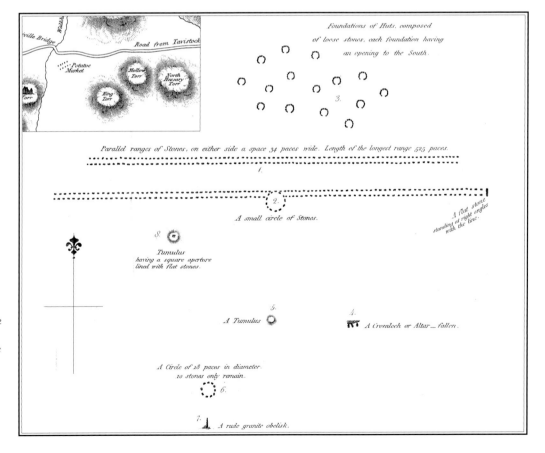

Fig 1.4
Alfred Kemp's plan of Merrivale c.1828. Clearly based on a sketch and entitled 'Vestiges supposed Druidical, on Dartmoor near Tavistock, Devon'. This may be contrasted with a modern survey of the complex (see Fig 2.43). Note the 'Tumulus' (8), described as 'having a square aperture lined with flat stones'. Although today vestiges of this ring cairn survive, the stone feature described, which is a cist, has since been robbed (see Fig 2.26).

commissioned A C Shillabeer to survey Grimspound (Fig 1.3), Dartmoor's most well-known prehistoric settlement, which is certainly the first accurate scale plan to be drawn of a Dartmoor archaeological feature and, according to Fleming, 'arguably the first adequate plan of a prehistoric settlement to be drawn in Britain' (Fleming 1988, 12).

Other antiquaries were active at this time too, and it is obvious from their choice of media for publication, that Dartmoor's archaeology was coming to the attention of a much wider group of investigators. In 1829 Alfred J Kemp published a letter in *Archaeologia*, the prestigious journal of the Society of Antiquaries of London. He began his letter: 'On the mountainous, wild, and barren tract of Dartmoor … are some curious vestiges of a druidical character, hitherto, I believe, but little noticed by topographical writers in the County …' (Kemp 1829, 429–35).

Dartmoor, according to this writer, was still considered a place only for the adventurous, but Kemp goes on to describe the remains at Merrivale, providing a stylised sketch plan of the site, which nevertheless includes most of the features surviving today, including the two double stone rows, the settlement, cist, stone circle and standing stone (Fig 1.4); and, interestingly, he alludes to 'numerous similar remains, scattered over the whole surface of the moor', which indicates that investigations were extending to elsewhere on Dartmoor other than the 'usual' sites close to the few roads at the time. The spectre of Druidism remains over this piece, however, as Kemp describes one of the cists as a 'Druidical alter' and observed that the stone rows are aligned with Vixen Tor (which they are not) because it contains a rock basin 'considered by some as intended to retain water to be used in the lustrations of the Druid Priests'.

Early excavations and the first signs of scholarship

The investigation of Dartmoor's archaeology continued to gain momentum in this period, as the subject came to the attention of a wider public. Although the Society of Antiquaries of London (SoAL) had been founded in 1717, it was more than a century later that learned societies with more parochial aims came into existence in Devon, such as the Plymouth Institution, which was founded in 1812 and which published its first journal in 1830, followed by the Torquay Natural History Society founded in 1844. Both provided forums and outlets for the gathering number of Devon's antiquaries to present, discuss and publish their findings; indeed a specialist antiquarian group was formed within the Plymouth Institution (J Marchand DNPA pers com). One of its members was Samuel Rowe, another clergyman, who was perhaps the man to whom the title of first 'Dartmoor antiquary' may be applied, publishing a seminal paper on the subject in 1830. Within Rowe's work, an element of scholarship had been introduced into the study of Dartmoor's archaeology, for he was the first to offer a classification for a majority of the elements of what today would be referred to as the prehistoric archaeology, describing the field evidence in terms to which we in the 21st century can still relate. Eventually Rowe's observations on antiquities were published alongside much of his other Dartmoor work in his *A Perambulation of Dartmoor*, 1848. However, although authors like Rowe were increasing the quantity of data by broadening the field of study beyond stone monuments to include many settlements and barrows, the interpretations continued to be hampered by the lack of understanding of prehistory, and the continuing tradition of Druidism as one of its cornerstones.

Rowe was not alone in offering classifications and descriptions of archaeological sites and only 14 years later, in 1862, Gardner Wilkinson provided a very detailed description of most aspects of prehistoric Dartmoor (Wilkinson 1862), followed in 1871 by C Spence Bate, who also discussed the physical evidence exhaustively (Bate 1871). As an aside, Bate mentioned that he had cut a trench through a stone circle at Merrivale, and his report marks a new departure for Dartmoor archaeology – that of the archaeological excavation. The excavation of archaeological sites had occurred ever since an interest in the subject first developed but, until the late 19th century, the results often went unrecorded, so the contribution of artefacts towards understanding and dating the field archaeology had been nil. The great majority of Dartmoor's round barrows, for example, have been dug into at some point in the past, although for most, no information about what was found has been passed down to us. Some may have been dug many centuries ago in search of 'treasure', while others were probably investigated by early antiquaries, before the days when recording ones actions and finds became standard practice, especially if no objects considered worthy of note were found. On rare occasions anecdotal evidence or a passing reference survives, such as Polwhele's recollection of a barrow being 'opened' where 'ashes, burnt wood and pieces of earthen vessels' were found (Polwhele 1793–1806 [1797]), or in another case 'an old jar or two' (Butler 1997, 205), and Mrs Bray's aside that her husband, Rev A E Bray had dug into the central cairn at Merrivale south row on October 7th 1802 (Bray 1879, 155).

In 1872 Spence Bate published a more detailed account of one of his Dartmoor excavations. The work was published in volume 5 of the *Transactions of the Devonshire Association for the Advancement of Science, Literature and the Arts*, a relatively new learned society founded in 1868, which, in the decades that followed, would have profound influence on the way Dartmoor archaeology developed.

Bate's explorations focussed on round barrows or cairns, a class of monument not greatly discussed by his predecessors. His descriptions of the cairns seem fairly routine, outlining how they were constructed and mentioning that several had evidently been interfered with prior to his own interventions. However, at Two Barrows on Hameldown, he found a previously undisturbed cairn, where he unearthed one of Dartmoor's most spectacular prehistoric metal finds to date; a corroded bronze dagger with a broken off amber pommel, decorated with gold pins. Unfortunately, these finds were destroyed when the Plymouth Athenaeum, which housed the finds, was bombed in the Second World War, but the modern interpretation of the pieces would place them in the Early Bronze Age, or mid-2nd millennium BC, about 1650 BC to 1450 BC (Pearce 1983, 90).

Prehistory gets older

Bate's own understanding of the date of the Hameldown Barrow was rather confused, for he claimed: 'I think that the evidence tends

to the direction, that the barrow was erected by some old Viking, who, in the early bronze age, crept up the Dart in search of tin' (Bate 1872, 557).

Although Bate mentions the 'bronze age', curiously he associated the period with Vikings.

The so-called 'Three-Age System' of stone, bronze and iron had been around since 1819, and developed into a useful method of categorizing finds held in museum collections. It was based on the assumption that, in terms of human technological accomplishment, stone tools and weapons were the least advanced and iron the most advanced (Bahn 1996). At that time, however, there was little idea as to the true ages of any prehistoric artefacts in terms of even approximate calendar years.

For scholars of this period, interpretation of the very remote past was hampered to a great extent by the doctrines of the Church. The Old Testament was still taken literally and the Creation, as calculated by Archbishop James Ussher in 1650, was believed to have occurred on October 23rd 4004 BC. The great majority of Devon's antiquaries at the end of the 18th century, and into the second half of the 19th, were clergymen – including Polwhele, MacEnery, Northmore, Mason, Rowe and others – and their allegiance to the Church must have prevented them from thinking too far 'outside the box'.

The Three-Age System was introduced to Britain in the 1850s but it was not until the 1860s that geologist William Pengelly, who was the founder of the Torbay Natural History Society and of the Devonshire Association, was able to shed more light on the prehistoric period in Devon and indeed globally. While excavating a cave at Windmill Hill, Brixham, Pengelly discovered flint tools in association with the bones of animal species long extinct; this was a major breakthrough (Pengelly 1877). During his later work at Kents Cavern, Pengelly's experience as a geologist and his knowledge of stratigraphy, enabled him to establish without doubt that human beings had been occupying the caves tens of thousands of years ago, pushing the origins of mankind into a more remote past than previously believed, and helping to support theories about human origins put forward by Charles Darwin, among others. Such discoveries made it possible to discard for good chronologies based on biblical and classical writings.

Enter the archaeologist

Archaeological research in Devon, in the period so far discussed, had been pursued by individuals or by small groups of like-minded individuals, but with no common agenda. One exception was a detailed investigation commissioned by the Society of Antiquaries of London (SoAL) in the 1870s to investigate stone rows and circles. The work was carried out by the Rev W C Lukis, but was, regrettably, never published, although the plans were archived in the SoAL archive. Nevertheless, Lukis was clearly enamoured of Dartmoor and inspired to declare to his fellow antiquaries that '... no portion of the British dominions is more deserving of the closest attention of antiquaries. For the student of prehistoric archaeology, it is a veritable paradise' (Lukis 1881, 471).

In the late 19th century two important events brought a wider base of researchers together with intent to follow a more focussed and shared research agenda for Dartmoor. The first of these was the formation of the Devon Barrow Committee, of the Devonshire Association, in 1878, which consisted of several prominent researchers of the day, including C S Bate, J Brooking Rowe (Samuel Rowe's nephew), P O Hutchinson and R N Worth, and later included S Baring-Gould, R Burnard and R H Worth. This committee's brief, as its title suggests, was to investigate the literature and physical remains of Devon's barrows and, 'where possible take steps for their scientific investigation' (Barr Comm 1879). Although originally the committee excluded Dartmoor from this brief, by 1882 this had changed and the Dartmoor barrows soon became the main focus of their investigations; it was not long before they began undertaking excavations and recording their findings in the society's *Transactions* (Fig 1.5).

The second important event was the formation of the Dartmoor Exploration Committee (DEC), which was responsible for the most intensive period of archaeological activity Dartmoor has ever seen, between 1893 and 1906. Also under the auspices of the Devonshire Association, this committee included many of the same members as the Barrow Committee. The circumstance that lay behind the formation of the DEC is retold in the committee's first report in 1894 (DEC 1894, 101–21). In 1893 Robert Burnard, assisted by

Rev Sabine Baring-Gould, directed the first recorded archaeological excavation of a Dartmoor settlement at Broadun and Broadun Ring, where they excavated 20 hut circles, or prehistoric houses, in a space of three weeks.

Burnard's excavation technique was essentially to remove all the soil from the interior of each hut until the natural undisturbed subsoil was reached, then pass all the removed material through a sieve in search of small artefacts. Trenches were also extended outside the entrances in search of middens (rubbish heaps). Of the many small items unearthed, including flint, bone and cooking stones, Burnard was puzzled not to find any metal or pottery and concluded that the occupants were of a 'neolithic age' from before the use of metals (Burnard 1890–4, 185–96). In the same year, the Rev Sabine Baring Gould excavated four huts of an unenclosed settlement at Ger Tor, Tavy Cleave, though with unspectacular results. Following these two excavations Burnard and Gould, together with R N & R H Worth (father and son) and W A Gray formed the DEC, although others would join later. The first joint project was the excavation of Grimspound, where 20 hut circles were excavated using the same techniques that

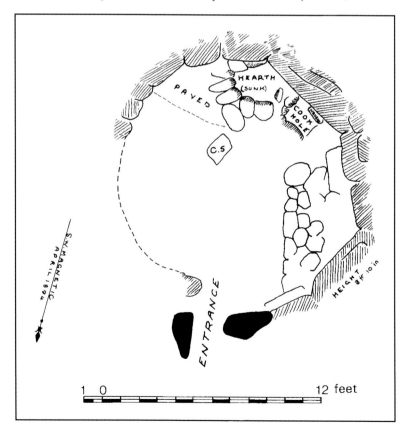

Fig 1.5
Plan of an excavated hut circle at Grimspound (redrawn) from the 1894 DEC report (© The Devonshire Association, with permission).

Fig 1.6
The reconstruction of one of the Grimspound huts, following the excavations of 1894. The figure apparently overseeing the labourers is likely to be the Rev Sabine Baring-Gould (photo: Robert Burnard; © Manaton Community History Group).

Burnard had used at Broadun. A new plan of the site was surveyed and the huts were individually planned (Fig 1.5) and sectioned at large scale and a detailed report appeared in the Devonshire Association's *Transactions* for 1894.

Over the next 12 years the DEC prosecuted an extraordinary programme of archaeological research, including excavations, field recording, survey and restoration (Fig 1.6), summarised in their annual reports in the *Transactions*. Unfortunately their research agenda was not as focussed as we would expect today, as they moved their attention rapidly between different sites before giving due consideration to the implications of work already completed. In the second year they resorted to 'spade investigation' at Langstone Moor, Merrivale, Crapps Ring and Shapley Common (DEC 1895, 81–92). In year three they excavated four settlements, totalling 43 huts, together with the Lakehead cists and other sites. And so it continued, inhibited only by the weather, and their unregulated enthusiasm over the following years led to excavations occurring almost on an yearly basis, culminating in 1906 with the excavation of a staggering 94 huts in a period of just seven weeks at Watern Oke by Rev I K Anderson (DEC 1906, 101–13).

Despite their shortcomings, the DEC episode may be seen in a mostly positive light. On the whole, although working within the limitations of available techniques at the time, the excavations were approached methodically.

There was a serious attempt to be scientific and bags of bone, charcoal and cremated ash from these excavations, all neatly labelled, survive in Plymouth City Museum today. Also, both the DEC and the Barrow Committee did make some important discoveries, such as Burnard's excavation of a barrow on Raddick Hill (Barr Comm 1899, 98) containing a complete Trevisker style urn that was successfully retrieved (*see* Fig 3.6), and the unearthing of a various ceramic vessels from barrows on Hurston Ridge, Watern Down and Fernworthy (Fig 1.7; *see* Figs 2.39–2.41). Indeed much current knowledge of prehistoric ceramics on Dartmoor is derived from the DEC's excavations. In a broader context, their work linked into the early days of the work of the Dartmoor Preservation Association (DPA), which had been formed in 1883 (Somers Cocks 1983, 7). Robert Burnard was a founder member of the DPA and through his and the work of others in the DEC, attention could be brought to bear on the increasing destruction of Dartmoor's stone monuments as a source of wall-building material, highlighted in his publication *Plundered Dartmoor* in 1896.

However, with hindsight, certain aspects of the DEC's activities had a negative effect on the archaeology. Some of the later work was motivated seemingly only by unbridled curiosity, rather than by the more restrained research questions with which they had set out. There may also have been a certain amount of rivalry and the servicing of egos among a group of men who each considered themselves to be experts in the field; and the quality of the work seems also to have varied between the members. The excavations at Watern Oke, which stands out as a particularly unfortunate example of over-exuberance, were very poorly recorded (DEC 1906, 101–13). The 94 excavated huts, when published, were condensed into a short tabulated summary with no individual plans, and thus fell far short of the standard of the DEC's earlier work, and indeed the standard of archaeological recording that had evolved elsewhere in the country, exemplified by the work of Pitt-Rivers who had been developing more sophisticated and effective recording methodologies since the 1870s (Bowden 1991).

It would be wrong to judge these early archaeologists too harshly, however; given the freedom they had to dig wherever they pleased in a landscape filled with fascinating archaeology, which on Dartmoor was still not subject to any form of statutory protection (although the first Ancient Monuments Act had been passed in 1882, none of Dartmoor's monuments were affected by it), it is little wonder their enthusiasm ran away with them.

The DEC's activities were not, however, only confined to excavation archaeology. Together with the Barrow Committee, they made a major contribution towards the recording and survey of Dartmoor's archaeology, forming the foundations for the database from which we work to this day.

Some of the DEC's finest surveys were undertaken by R Hansford Worth, the youngest and perhaps the most accomplished and cautious archaeologist of the group, who later earned a reputation for his work as an individual rather than as part of the DEC. There followed a gap of 29 years after the 1906 report when in 1935, Worth, the sole survivor of the original committee, reported excavations he had undertaken at Ryder's Rings and Metheral. By comparison with the extravagant projects of earlier days, these are restrained excavations: at Ryder's Rings small trenches were opened to answer specific questions and at Metheral, huts were excavated only because they were soon to be submerged by the flooding of Fernworthy Reservoir (DEC 1935, 115–30). This more thorough approach paid off and within the Metheral huts Worth was able to postulate later phases of occupation after the prehistoric period.

The extraordinary zeal and energy of the DEC was in decline by the end of the 20th century's first decade, and it was 50 years before excavation on any sort of scale occurred again on Dartmoor, with the exception of those undertaken by R H Worth. Aspects of the DEC's earlier work were summarised in the *Victoria County History of Devon* in 1906 (Page 1906), and in 1952 Raleigh Radford, the last survivor of the DEC, evaluated the knowledge that had been gained through the DEC's work (Radford 1952, 55–84). Although his interpretations may not necessarily be those of modern prehistorians, his paper provided a statement of their collective achievements and the knowledge gained, to form a basis onto which others could build.

The 1950s witnessed what may be termed the inception of 'modern' excavation techniques to Dartmoor archaeology, when Lady Aileen Fox, an experienced excavator, who had learned her craft at excavations in the bombed-out city centre of post-war Exeter, turned her attention to a number of prehistoric hut settlements on Dartmoor. By this time the concept of the restrained research project had developed. The realisation that excavation is an essentially destructive process, and that archaeological remains are a finite resource, can only be excavated once and should not be squandered in the way, on reflection, some activities of the DEC had done, lead to Fox's more focussed work at Kestor in 1951–2 (A Fox 1954, 21–62), where only a portion of the huts were excavated. However, research ethics aside, opportunities to dig archaeological sites were still available, when they were threatened by various other developments on Dartmoor,

Fig 1.7
Prehistoric pottery from Dartmoor. All these items, with the exception of the small vessel in the foreground, were recovered from Dartmoor excavations by the Dartmoor Exploration and Devon Barrow Committees. The small vessel was a later chance find retrieved from a fissure in the rock face of the Dewerstone (NMR DP099396; © English Heritage. NMR. Photographed with permission of Plymouth City Museum and Art Gallery).

including the construction of the reservoir at Dean Moor on the River Avon, where in 1954 Fox excavated an enclosed settlement containing nine hut circles and a medieval farmstead (A Fox 1957, 18–77).

Excavation on Dartmoor continues and the contribution of 20th century projects by Wainwright, Fleming, Gibson, Eogan, Minter and Austin, are discussed in the chapters that follow. Hopefully, research into Dartmoor's past through focussed excavations, and with precise research aims, will continue; it is extremely unlikely, however, that the scale of this activity will ever again equal that of the DEC during its zenith.

Landscape investigation

Although the results of excavations have contributed greatly to the understanding and dating of Dartmoor's archaeological sites, establishing their function and in some cases their chronology, it needs to be said that answers to many of the questions that archaeologists tend to ask have come with more difficulty here than in many other parts of the British Isles – and in most cases remain inconclusive, in particular the sequential relationship of the prehistoric ritual and burial monuments, and the settlements. Dartmoor is a difficult place to dig: the soil is very shallow and peaty, lacking the deep stratigraphy that archaeologists need for dating sequences. The acidity of the soil has destroyed much of the organic evidence that might be expected elsewhere, such as bone, wood and leather. Although this problem has probably been exaggerated in the past, as an excuse for inexperience by early practitioners who overlooked much important data, it has meant that few samples have been available for radiocarbon dating, a scientific technique that relies on stratified samples of organic material. Unfortunately, because the great majority of excavated prehistoric sites were dug in the pre-radiocarbon era, the dating of Dartmoor's prehistoric landscape features are still piecemeal and uncertain by comparison with other regions. Modern excavation techniques and the application of science are beginning to redress the problem, but building up the necessary data will take time. There is also a problem with the emphasis of research excavations, which in the 20th and early 21st

centuries have focussed mainly on hut circles and reaves, while burial and ritual monuments have taken second place, restricted to one small cairn group on Shaugh Moor (Wainwright *et al* 1979, 10–33) and a stone row at Cholwichtown (Eogan 1964, 25–38). Both were under imminent threat of destruction but neither perhaps would have been a first choice for a research excavation, while other sites might have revealed more information.

People are often surprised therefore to realise how poorly many aspects of Dartmoor's past are understood from excavated evidence, and that much of the knowledge we possess has been established through survey and field investigation, a tradition that extends back to Milles, Chappel and Polwhele in the 18th century and to Rowe in the 19th century. It requires the investigator firstly to explore the landscape, searching for anomalies within it that have been caused by human intervention, and to make considered observations about the sites they encounter, taking measurements, notes and, if possible, to carry out measured surveys. These practices will not only help to understand the sites, but will also assist in passing on knowledge to others and provide a permanent record; Shilabeer's plan of Grimspound, surveyed in 1829 (*see* Fig 1.3) serves as a particularly fine example. Some notable practitioners emerged in the 19th century, and many of the antiquaries mentioned above, including Wilkinson, Bate, Gould and other members of the DEC, carried out field investigation before they went on to excavate, often providing small plans of archaeological sites. The work of Lukis described above was a particularly well-resourced research project to examine prehistoric stone monuments, and resulted in some of the finest survey drawings of the period, though sadly the drawings remain unpublished (Lukis 1881, 470–81).

Of all the 19th–early 20th-century investigators, R H Worth stands out as having made an exceptional contribution, discovering, recording and publishing a large number of new sites while re-evaluating and re-surveying many established examples. Worth was a polymath, whose publication list, covering Dartmoor topics ranging from ecology, geology, etymology, history and archaeology, was so vast that an entire volume of his papers was published together in 1953 as *Worth's Dartmoor* (Spooner and Russell 1967); this important publication remains one of the core sources of reference on most aspects of Dartmoor field archaeology.

Most independent researchers, like Worth, concentrated on surveying individual, mostly quite small sites, at large scale; but since the 1880s the Ordnance Survey had been including prehistoric features on their county series maps at scales of 25 inches to the mile (1:2500) and 6 inches to the mile (1:10560). Many of the hut settlements, cairns, stone rows and stone circles marked on modern OS maps were first recorded by them in the late 19th century. This was carried out somewhat sporadically to start with; Baring-Gould, who was dissatisfied with the level of depiction, recalled leading an OS surveyor to see some sites he felt needed including in 1891 (Baring-Gould 1900, 9). In 1920, the Ordnance Survey appointed its first archaeological officer, O G S Crawford, whose task it was to investigate and map Britain's archaeological landscape features, which could be reproduced on the OS maps at various scales. By 1939, Crawford had an assistant, but after the Second World War the archaeological team became more developed, to become a Division (OSAD) within the OS by the 1960s (Bowden *et al* 1989). Not every site investigated by the team was marked on the published maps, but the database that the OSAD established through survey and field recording was later to form the basis of both the county Historic Environment Records (HERs) and the National Monument Record Inventory for England (NMR). The latter responsibility was transferred from the OS to the Royal Commission on the Historical Monuments of England (RCHME) in 1983, and is now curated and kept up to date by English Heritage.

Therein lies in part the origin of this book, which follows the tradition and spirit of archaeological landscape investigation as practised by these bodies past and present, and has continued through the work of the English Heritage Archaeological Survey and Investigation Team. Technology and survey technique may have changed completely since the early investigators started to record Dartmoor, but the basic skills of searching for, identifying, recording and interpreting the evidence of past human intervention within the landscape remains the same. In the 21st century, however, we may be more confident that the chronologies we use to date the field remains, be they still far from perfect, are at least based on empirical evidence and scientific reasoning. Also, it is not just the remote periods of prehistory that are of interest but, thanks to the modern concept of artefacts from the past as 'heritage', as a society we are more inclined to see the value of recording and understanding landscape elements of more recent times past. As a result our understanding of Dartmoor has extended far beyond the prehistoric archaeology that so fascinated the antiquaries, to embrace the medieval and modern periods, including military and industrial landscapes.

2

Mesolithic to Early Bronze Age

Note on dating: It is normal practice to express dates within the Palaeolithic period in terms of years BP (before present) ie 20,000 BP = 20,000 years ago. In the case of the Mesolithic period onwards, for which radiocarbon (RC) dates are available, the raw results from the laboratories are also in years BP, but when calibrated to calendar years they are expressed as BC. For the purpose of this volume all dates from the Mesolithic onwards are therefore in years BC. Uncalibrated RC dates are not included.

There can be no certainty as to the date of the first human presence in the upland area today known as Dartmoor. The earliest human artefact so far retrieved is a hand-axe found on Brent Moor (Worth 1931, 359–60), of a type associated with the Lower and Middle Palaeolithic periods, between 60,000 and 500,000 years BP; but the circumstance of its discovery, as an out-of-context chance find, constrains the conclusions that may be drawn from it. It may have been a secondary deposit, found elsewhere and carried to Brent Moor at any time since its date of manufacture. However, if deposited or lost by its original owner at this place, it certainly implies that very early humans visited Dartmoor, although the extent or nature of their business there is as yet unknown. Although finds of this period are not uncommon in the south-west, most examples so far have come from the river valleys of south-east Devon (Straw 1999, 44), and they are far less numerous in the upland areas. Exmoor, like Dartmoor, has so far produced only one example (Riley and Wilson North 2001, 16) and none are known from Bodmin Moor. This may reflect the statistical problems associated with the distribution of chance finds, in which case no conclusions should be drawn, or may imply a genuine absence of humans on the higher ground.

Modern humans (*Homo sapiens*) may have migrated into much of northern Europe around 30–40,000 years ago, at the start of the Upper Palaeolithic, when Britain was still part of the European landmass, and before the onset of the last major ice age. Upper Palaeolithic cave dwellers are known to have occupied Kent's Cavern in Torquay (Straw 1999, 46), but our knowledge of their activities elsewhere in the Devon landscape at that time is limited. In the latter part of the Upper Palaeolithic age, during the coldest part of the ice age, which was at its most severe in *c* 18,000 BP, the British Isles were again uninhabited, although it is believed that humans had returned by *c* 12, 600 BP, during a subsequent warmer period. A final cold phase, known as the Loch Lomond Stadial, may have led to a further exodus, but it had an abrupt end *c* 10,000 BP, after which migration from northern Europe resumed (Roberts 2000, 480). This is the point at which more enduring human activity becomes evident on Dartmoor, in the period known as the Mesolithic.

The Mesolithic period (*c* 9000 BC–*c* 4000 BC)

Today, the concept of moorland, as applied to regions like Dartmoor, is one of large open areas, covered by grassland, with some heathland species, such as gorse, heather, and wortleberry. Economically, moorland is used for grazing rather than for intensive farming, and woodland is confined to the river valleys around the peripheries of the moor. In the remote past, the vegetation was very different, a fact that prompted the prehistorian, Andrew Fleming, to claim that: 'around four or five thousand years before the birth of Christ, there was really no such thing as Dartmoor' (Fleming 1988, 94). His statement was inspired by what is currently understood of the natural environment and vegetation of the upland in the prehistoric period, derived from the analysis of ancient pollen and plant remains – material that was deposited in the peat before humans began to settle on this highland region that later would become Dartmoor. This evidence is somewhat limited and open to various interpretations, but it can provide an outline sketch of what the environmental conditions may have been (Fig 2.1).

Following the Loch Lomond Stadial, which ended c 10,000 years ago, woodland evolved over a large portion of Dartmoor, leaving only the highest peaks and rocky outcrops exposed. The pattern of expansion of the trees varied between species but by c 6,500 years ago, all the native tree varieties are represented in the pollen record. There is some evidence that human intervention began to play a role in shaping the environment from that point onwards, as an increase in charcoal found within the peat samples is matched by a reduction in tree pollen, suggesting that clearance and burning accompanied the arrival of humans. This activity may eventually have caused the tree

line to recede and have helped to facilitate the formation of peat and the expansion of blanket bog in these higher exposed areas (Casseldine and Hatton 1994, 39).

Beyond the environmental evidence, material evidence for Mesolithic occupation of Dartmoor exists in the form of stone tools. Mesolithic toolkits are highly distinctive and composed of much smaller pieces of flint than those of Palaeolithic origin. Many of these sharpened pieces served as projectile tips, specifically in some cases for arrows, as archery became fully developed as a hunting technique during the Mesolithic. Others may have served as craft tools for fashioning bone, wood and leather. Several Mesolithic flint assemblages have been recorded on and around Dartmoor (Roberts 2000, 48), including at East Week in an area of enclosed ground in the north-west corner of the National Park (Greig and Rankin 1953, 8–26) and Batworthy near the eastern edge of the upland, where a scatter of material recently unearthed is, at the time of writing, undergoing analysis (Webster 2008, 76). Few have been found on the higher moors, particularly where the peat is at its deepest, but the existence of those that are known confirms

Fig 2.1
Aerial view of north Dartmoor (NMR 24965/035; © English Heritage. NMR).

the presence of these hunter-gatherers in the region. Lack of any evidence for domestic sites on Dartmoor leads to the conclusion either that these were seasonal visitors to the moors, which was just one place in an itinerary that included varied hunting grounds, following herds of deer or wild cattle, and gathering seasonal plant foods; or alternatively, the evidence for Mesolithic domestic sites is yet to be discovered on Dartmoor, as in much of Britain.

The Neolithic period (*c* 4000 BC–2000 BC)

The earliest human activity on Dartmoor to provide lasting, physical, landscape evidence was the building of barrows and chambered tombs. This occurred in the early Neolithic period, when people of the British Isles generally, were beginning to adopt a less transitory lifestyle compared with that of their Mesolithic predecessors. The 'Neolithic', which simply translates as 'New Stone Age', is a term developed in the 19th century as a way of distinguishing it from the later part of what had previously been simply described as the Stone Age. Originally this distinction was based solely on the type of stone technology used, which was notably more advanced than the larger stone hand-axes and spearheads of the Palaeolithic or Old Stone Age (Mesolithic or Middle Stone Age was coined even later as a means to cover the transitional nature of the technology in that period as further distinctions became recognised). The term Neolithic, however, has come to embrace many other factors besides simply stone tool technology, within what is often now termed a 'neolithic package', used to define the period. These are:

- a comparatively settled lifestyle;
- an economic strategy that included domestication of certain crops and livestock;
- the use of pottery and certain other artefacts;
- distinctive stone tools, such as the leaf-shaped arrowhead;
- burial of the dead in chambered tombs and long barrows;
- and the building of stone or earthwork monuments. These include the above mentioned burial monuments, but also causeway enclosures and henges.

For all of these factors the Neolithic marks the period in which they become visible in the archaeological record. From the archaeologist's point of view, particularly those interested in landscape, it was also an important period of human development because it was the first to provide a legacy of permanent monuments. Implicit in the existence of such monuments, each representing major building projects, is the first indication for the existence of organised human communities capable of such schemes. Taken a stage further, the concepts of territory, ownership, sense of place and other societal attitudes towards, and perceptions of, the land, may have begun to evolve from this time.

But the definition, if applied to a fixed period of time, is misleading, because evidence of some of these practices varied in their occurrence, intensity and chronology depending on which region of Britain, or indeed of Europe, one examines. At the beginning and end of the Neolithic period a certain amount of temporal overlap has to be included as these cultural, technological, domestic and ceremonial practices underwent slow transition. With these shortcomings of the term highlighted, for the purposes of this discussion, the Neolithic covers the period from *c* 4000 BC to 2000 BC, based on radiocarbon dates from Neolithic sites throughout Britain.

The regional and chronological variation creates certain problems for the south-west of Britain because very few radiocarbon dates have been retrieved from the limited number of potentially Neolithic archaeological sites that survive in the region. However, some important research in recent years has added considerably to what is known of Neolithic Devon and Cornwall at sites off the moors, and although archaeological knowledge of Dartmoor in particular has been slow to advance on this topic, we are at least in a position to understand more of the Devonshire environs of which the upland was a part.

Long barrows and chambered tombs

The earliest surviving man-made structures on Dartmoor and its immediate environs are the Neolithic long barrows and chambered tombs. Within this group also are the portal dolmens of which Spinsters' Rock, Drewsteignton is

Devon's only surviving example (Fig 2.2), although it is not truly on the moors but in the hinterland to the east of Dartmoor.

Portal dolmens, often referred to in antiquarian literature as 'cromlechs', are a well-known feature of upland regions, mostly in the west of Britain, several surviving in Cornwall, Wales and Ireland. Typically, they comprise three or more upright stones closely arranged to support a large horizontal slab, sometimes described as a 'quoit'.

Spinsters' Rock now sits in the edge of a pasture field within enclosed farmland. Upright, earth-fast stones of granite form a three-legged pedestal on which the capstone is supported. Examples elsewhere in Britain have more closely spaced uprights forming a chamber with a distinct entrance or portal. It is probable therefore that at Spinsters' Rock some stone may have been removed, leaving a bare framework of the monument and the somewhat open appearance it has today. In Cornwall, where several portal dolmens survive, both Lanyon and Carwynnen Quoits have similar characteristics and have been similarly interpreted (Barnatt 1982, 45). There is a possibility that some dolmens were covered by earth or stone mounds, but this too is uncertain because at many of these places there is no surviving trace of a mound, Spinsters' Rock being a clear example. Early descriptions of Spinsters' rock and its immediate locality mention other stone monuments near by, including stone circles and avenues (Ormerod 1872, 73–4; Tyler 1930, 249–60), but unfortunately these were exploited as a source of stone during the 19th century and very little now remains (Rowe 1896, 117–18). In 1862 the monument collapsed but was re-erected two years later.

Reliable dating evidence for portal dolmens is limited, but pottery retrieved from Dyffryn Ardudwy in Wales is similar in character to examples excavated from known Neolithic sites in Cornwall, such as Carn Brea, which would suggest this form of monument was in use by about 3700 BC (Barnatt 1982, 43). Closer to Dartmoor, Zennor Quoit in Cornwall has produced radiocarbon dates of 3342 BC–3024 BC (Kytmannow 2008, 106), also firmly within the earlier portion of the Neolithic period.

What such monuments were used for and what their meaning was to those who built them is difficult to establish for certain, but it is most likely that their primary function was as a

tomb. Although no human remains have yet been retrieved from any of these sites using modern archaeological techniques, there is anecdotal evidence from Richard Polwhele, who mentioned that 'relics of the interred have been frequently discovered in the area of the Cromlech' (Polwhele 1793–1806 [1977], 154).

In the Neolithic period, remains of the dead were not simply disposed of by burial or cremation, but often preserved, as is evident from excavations in other types of Neolithic monument known as long barrows and chambered tombs, that were contemporaries of the portal dolmens. Frequently, these monuments are found to contain multiple inhumations or group burial, the bones sometimes sorted, indicating they were the material of mortuary practices long after the death of the owner. It is probably not too rash to speculate that ancestor veneration may be one of the reasons behind such practices.

Long barrows

There are several earthworks on Dartmoor that could be interpreted as long barrows, though none have been subject to scientific excavations. But on the basis of their form and through comparison with examples elsewhere, they are good candidates. These sites are at Corringdon Ball, Butterdon (Fig 2.3), Cuckoo Ball and Gidleigh, though it should be noted that several less likely sites have also been recorded. Long barrows are one of the defining monuments of the early Neolithic

Fig 2.2
Ground photo of Spinster's Rock, a portal dolmen near Drewsteignton (NMR DP082167; © English Heritage. NMR).

Fig 2.3
*Earthwork plans of
longbarrows at Corringdon
Ball and Butterdon. Both
have been extensively
disturbed and at Butterdon
the stones from the chamber
have been robbed out. At
Corringdon three large
slabs from the collapsed
chamber remain at the
south end of the mound
(EH 1:100 scale survey).*

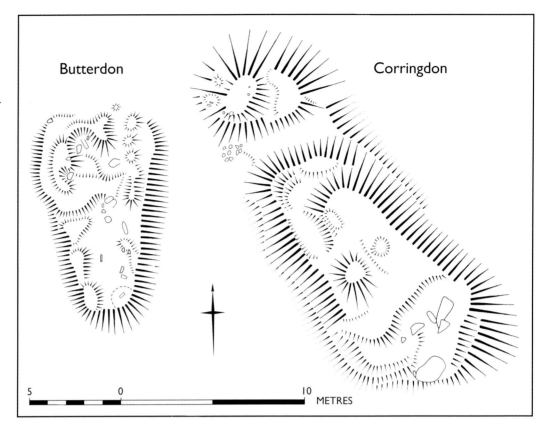

and are numerous in other parts of Britain, especially southern and eastern England and parts of Scotland. They comprise elongated earth mounds, which originally covered one or more chambers constructed from slabs of stone or timber, wherein the bones of the dead were deposited.

A study of long barrow earthworks on Salisbury Plain Training Area demonstrated that these mounds can be between 25m and 120m long, with substantial ditches on either side of the long axis (McOmish *et al* 2002, 21–31).

None of the Dartmoor long barrows are this large; neither are they as grand or well-defined as those found in Wiltshire. Corringdon Ball (Fig 2.3) is perhaps the best preserved example on Dartmoor; though the earthwork is somewhat broken up, three large boulders that formed a chamber at the south end lie collapsed within the fabric of the mound. At Butterdon (Fig 2.3), the earthwork survives as a single entity, but the stones from the chamber appear to have been robbed out, leaving a hollow, disturbed appearance to the central area; while at Cuckoo Ball, the chamber survives a little better, comprising two slabs on one side of the barrow, but with the earthwork badly disturbed.

As groups of people began to assimilate with localities, be it as hunter-gatherers or as farmers, they may have felt the need to impose some symbol of ownership, staking their claim over an area at a time when no other human imprint on the landscape existed. Constructing highly visible monuments such as the long barrows was a way of making such a statement. We cannot know the details of these peoples' beliefs when it came to the dead, but by placing the mortal remains of their ancestors within these monuments, they were reinforcing the message that their claim over a territory was based on an enduring presence by their group.

Although Dartmoor's surviving long barrows are few in number and small in size, their location, in all cases on the middle slopes of the upland, is of significance. Perhaps they were deliberately positioned to be on this slightly elevated terrain, beyond which lay the high ground. In such a location they remained visible and accessible to people occupying the lower slopes and hinterland, where social groups were beginning to experience the need to demonstrate claims over territory (*see* Fig 2.37). Their relatively small size, compared with long barrows elsewhere, may be due simply to the fact that smaller examples have survived less frequently in the lowland areas of Britain where intensive ploughing has taken place, and where only larger barrows remain upstanding. Studies have revealed that smaller long barrows often existed where larger examples are found, and may even have represented the norm either independently or as part of a group (Bradley 2007, 57).

It seems likely that the vegetation on Dartmoor, as experienced by the hunter-gatherers of the preceding millennium, was little changed by the activities of humans until the period leading up to the less transient lifestyle of the 4th millennium BC. This brought with it certain forms of landscape intervention, such as clearing wild vegetation, felling trees and burning as described above, but woodland still prevailed over the majority of the upland. By the time the long barrows were constructed they were sited within cleared areas, possibly cleared especially to contain them. Deliberate clearance of wild areas of woodland by humans was probably the result of changes to subsistence strategies by those who relied on the upland as a source of food, particularly the hunting of animals, which was much easier on open ground. Domestication of animals would also require some clearance for the grazing species such as cattle, thriving on pasture rather than on scrub.

Evidence to suggest where the people who frequented Neolithic Dartmoor were living has proved elusive. This is the case for much of Britain, where traces of domesticity prior to the Bronze Age are extremely rare. On the few occasions that Neolithic houses have been discovered, such as Lissmore Fields in Derbyshire (Barnatt and Smith 1997, 22), or Haldon in Devon (Willock 1936, 239) they usually prove to have been flimsy structures constructed from organic material, which have left extremely subtle remains. Whatever their houses and settlements were constructed of, they have not survived in a highly visible form within the archaeological record of Dartmoor. One explanation for this absence of evidence could be that the lifestyle of people in the Neolithic was not totally sedentary but was partly itinerant within an area of familiar territory; animals were becoming domesticated but were moved around the territory as seasonal grazing dictated, and permanent dwellings may not have been required. However, absence of evidence does not prove absence of human presence and future investigation may bring more data to this topic.

Tor enclosures

Two somewhat enigmatic sites that may offer evidence of a Neolithic presence, apart from the burial monuments, are the stone tor enclosures at Dewerstone (Fig 2.4) and Whittor (Fig 2.5).

At Whittor the enclosure sits on the summit of the tor, which has the form of a plateau; it overlooks much of western Dartmoor, west Devon and east Cornwall, including Bodmin Moor. Closely spaced parallel rubble walls define the edge of the plateau, forming a circuit, and take advantage of several prominent rock outcrops, which have been incorporated. Two of the outcrops also have cairns built around them. The walls, constructed from the blackish metamorphic rock of the tor (Fig 2.6), are now widely spread by the erosion of time, but may once have been upstanding features, though probably never that high judging by the volume of material. The interior of the enclosure is its most unusual element, for although isolated areas have been cleared, perhaps to accommodate small structures, and a cairn has been constructed around a boulder in the centre of the space, the majority of the interior has its original natural covering of clitter, deposited there in geological times (*see* Introduction). This terrain is awkward, even to walk over in places, and it seems almost certain that any activity that took place here, domestic or otherwise, would have been inhibited by the lack of clearance and must have been on a limited scale.

Fig 2.4
Aerial view of the Dewerstone, showing the stony rampart of the possible Neolithic tor enclosure (NMR 2458/00; © English Heritage. NMR).

Fig 2.5
Plan of Whittor, a possible
Neolithic enclosure sited on
the summit of the tor. The
stony ramparts are now
spread and two large cairns
appear to sit on the ramparts
(after an OSAD survey by
N V Quinnell; height data
licensed to English Heritage
for PGA through Next
PerspectivesTM).

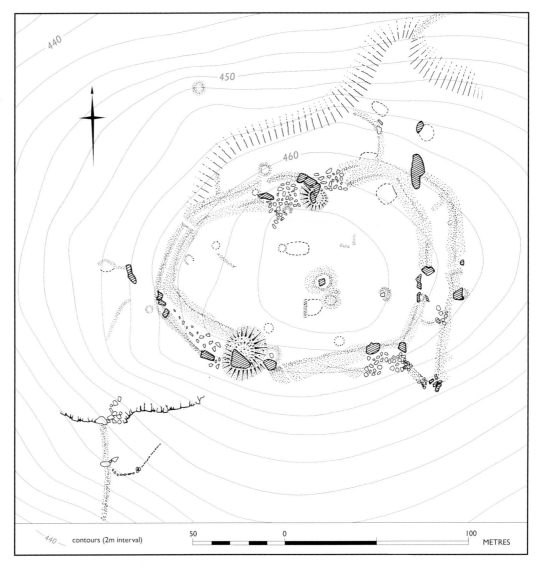

Fig 2.6
Aerial view of the possible
Neolithic tor enclosure at
Whittor (NMR 24959/036;
© English Heritage. NMR).

Dewerstone (Fig 2.4 and 2.7) occupies a steep-sided, south-west facing spur of land, overlooking south Devon, the Plym estuary and south-east Cornwall as far north as Kit Hill and Bodmin Moor. The south, west and eastern sides of the spur comprise precipitous slopes and granite cliffs, while to the north a broad ridge of land forms the surface of a peninsula, which merges into the gentler slopes of Wigford Down. A curving double stone wall encloses the neck of the spur providing a physical barrier between it and the land to the north. The walls, although mainly of rubble, have evidence of stone footings, suggesting a more built appearance, unlike Whittor, although they are now also very spread. There are two possible original entrances in the wall and one probable later breach. On the southern portion of the enclosed area, there is a second enclosure with a rectangular plan and remains of a round house built into one corner. These latter features can be more reliably associated with a 2nd-millennium BC date (*see below*), its familiar construction technique highlighting the less usual appearance of the outer enclosure.

No archaeological excavation is recorded at Dewerstone and the only excavation at Whittor, in 1898 (DEC 1899, 146–55), was inconclusive with regard the origin of the enclosure, providing no dating evidence, and this raises the question, why are these two sites considered of such potential importance in the context of Neolithic Devon?

Whittor and Dewerstone share few similarities with any later sites in Devon. Their commanding elevated positions are redolent of hillforts of the 1st millennium BC, although the slight proportions of the walls and high moorland location, in the case of Whittor, support an argument against this idea (*see* chapter 4). The method of construction of the walls also varies considerably from that used at 2nd-millennium BC (Bronze Age) enclosures, and during the 2nd millennium hilltop locations like Whittor appear to have been avoided as places of occupation. However, these two sites can be included in a growing body of evidence for enclosures with similar characteristics from uplands elsewhere in Britain, where stony walls enclose the rocky peaks of tors. In Cornwall, excavations at two such places, Helman Tor and Carn Brea, have provided evidence for a Neolithic occupation (Mercer 1981). It is therefore possible that Whittor and Dewerstone were constructed as part of a similar culture and at a similar date,

Fig 2.7
Earthwork plan of the possible Neolithic enclosure above Dewerstone, showing the double stony bank, which cuts off the south-western end of a steep-sided spur of land and overlooks the confluence of the Rivers Plym and Meavy. The hut circle and small rectangular enclosure are believed to be later and of probable 2nd millennium date. A breach (a) in the outer enclosure is the possible original entrance (RCHME 1:1000 survey; height data licensed to English Heritage for PGA through Next PerspectivesTM).

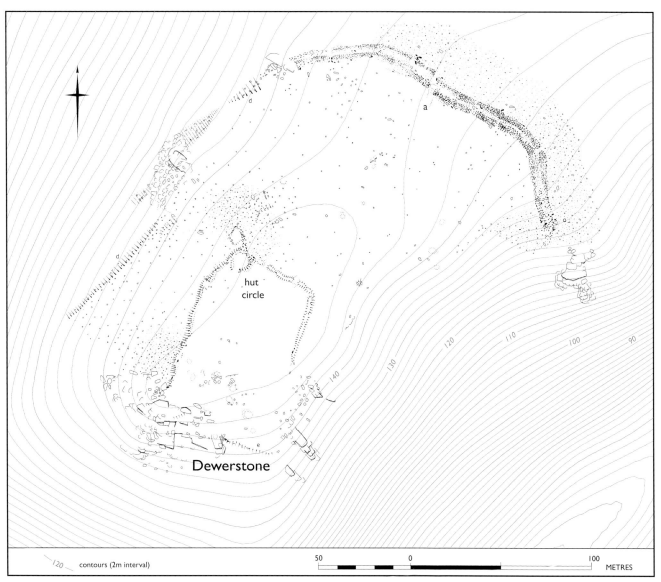

hut circle

Dewerstone

120 contours (2m interval)

50   0   100 METRES

but this will never be known for certain until these sites provide definitive radiocarbon dates of their own through excavation. This is a research priority for the future.

Archaeologists trying to make sense of this category of sites have recently begun to consider them as comparable in importance and date to another class of Neolithic monuments known as causewayed enclosures. The latter comprise ditched enclosures with multiple breaks or causeways across the ditch, and are common elsewhere in Britain where the underlying geology permits the digging of deep ditches. An example that was excavated within farmland at Raddon in east Devon has provided radiocarbon dates for Neolithic occupation of 3370 BC–3020 BC (Quinnell 1999, 21), and others are known in the east of the county. The tor enclosures may very plausibly be explained as offering an alternative in areas of granite where the digging of such ditches is not possible. As to function, this is less straightforward for both causewayed enclosures and tor enclosures and it cannot yet be assumed that both served precisely the same purpose anyway. For this we need to rely on theories informed by the evidence from excavations and landscape investigations elsewhere which, it has to be said, have not yet provided a definitive answer (Oswald *et al* 1999).

Settlement has been mostly ruled out as a function through a lack of domestic finds or house remains, but other theories mooted include communal activities such as feasting or seasonal festivals, gatherings for the purpose of exchange, and mortuary practices. It is indeed difficult in the 21st century to understand what lay behind the actions of people some 5–6,000 years ago from the meagre evidence we have, but, as is hinted with the long barrows, the lack of any physical human presence in the landscape before their construction, would make the first monuments of great significance to their builders. Similarly, the fact that the entire landscape was just 'space', unenclosed with no barriers built by humans, must surely hint that the very few deliberately enclosed spaces were immensely important, with cultural, political or spiritual significance that other places did not possess – so some of the theories regarding communal activities may not be that wide of the mark.

The siting of both Whittor and Dewerstone with vistas extending far into Cornwall would certainly suggest carefully chosen locations.

The late 3rd and early 2nd millennium BC

The idea of defining spaces for group activities could equally apply to stone circles, one of a series of monument types that may have origins towards the latter part of the Neolithic, but was also certainly an important component of the cultural landscape in the early part of the 2nd millennium BC. Together with other monuments of this period including stone rows and the early round cairns, they marked the transition from the Neolithic into the Early Bronze Age. However, as this millennium progressed, the domestic evidence of houses and settlements, as well as the land divisions known as reaves, come into the equation, providing evidence for a complex, developing society.

Evolutionary changes in prehistoric society on the scale we may witness through archaeology may have been less perceivable to those alive at the time, especially changes wrought through the availability and influence of technology, which are likely to have been gradual. Any account that discusses the end of the Neolithic and the beginning of a Bronze Age in terms of separate epochs would be misleading. However, to the archaeologist, these changes are perceivable, albeit over a period of several generations or even centuries rather than in precise terms of calendar years. Apart from changes in subsistence strategies and farming practices, there were also developments in domestic behaviour, material culture, mortuary practice and belief, all of which would eventually result in new forms of monuments and artefacts. Most notably among the material changes was the introduction of metals for the manufacture of prestige artefacts, including gold, but also copper, which later was alloyed with tin to produce bronze. Some of these changes may have been occurring by 2500 BC, but it is after 2000 BC that we can be more confident that life on Dartmoor was perceivably different.

Some of the emergent monument types in this period on Dartmoor have close associations, but each needs describing individually first.

Stone circles

Stone circles are a common feature in many parts of the British Isles, but tend to occur more frequently in western, south-western, and northern England, Wales and Scotland. An absence of stone circles in other areas, including

Fig 2.8
Ground photo of Scorhill
stone circle on Gidleigh
Common (NMR DP082151;
© English Heritage. NMR).

south-east, eastern England and the Midlands may be explained in a number of ways, but it is most likely that timber circles existed in areas where suitable stone was rare, or that earthwork equivalents to stone circles, such as henges, were serving a similar function. The archaeological evidence for timber circles in Britain, revealed through archaeological excavation, has been collated and published by Gibson (2005) and includes Durrington Walls and Boscombe Down in Wiltshire, and the remarkable Holme-next-the-Sea ('Seahenge') in Norfolk. At Machrie Moor in the Isle of Arran two stone circles were found to have had timber precursors dating to the late 3rd millennium BC (Heggarty 1991, 60).

In the south-west, both Devon and Cornwall are well endowed with stone circles, but the majority of Devon's examples are found on Dartmoor, where 12 have been recorded, together with some other doubtful examples. At this point it is important to highlight the difference between the open stone circles, currently the subject of discussion, and the cairn-circles found in association with burials and round barrows, which are discussed below. The open variety comprised only upright stones

with spaces between them, arranged into a circle. The area within the circle remained open and was probably intended to serve as a space where certain activities, as yet unknown to us, might take place; in other words the circle of stones was intended to define an accessible space that could be entered, rather than delimiting or containing a burial mound, which was the function served by cairn circles.

Stone circles, along with dolmens and stone rows, were among the first monuments to come to the attention of the early antiquaries such as Richard Polwhele in the 18th century. Samuel Rowe in his *Antiquarian Investigations* (1830) gave 'sacred circles' precedence among the descriptions of 'Druidical antiquities', citing the 'most striking' examples at Gidleigh Common (Scorhill) (Fig 2.8) and Grey Wethers (*see* Fig 2.11), and providing dimensions and statistics about the stones. In his descriptions Rowe mentions that although both these circles had stones upstanding and *in situ*, many were fallen and some were displaced or missing. That these monuments were still actively being destroyed in the 19th century is evident from Spence Bate's account, in which he describes the sockets of missing stones at Grey Wethers,

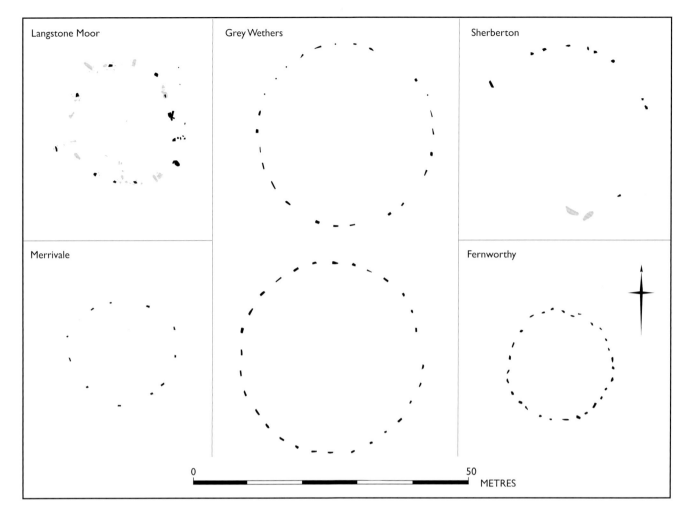

Langstone Moor

Grey Wethers

Sherberton

Merrivale

Fernworthy

0   50
METRES

Fig 2.9
Composite plan showing
stone circles at Grey
Wethers (near Sittaford
Tor), Fernworthy,
Merrivale, Langstone
Moor and the
incomplete example at
Sherberton (RCHME
1:100 scale surveys).

which had not grassed over, indicating that the stones had recently been robbed, probably to repair a nearby mine leat (Bate 1871, 514). In fact most of Dartmoor's stone circles, with a few exceptions, were in a fairly advanced state of decay at this time, and their appearance today is due largely to a programme of restoration carried out by the Dartmoor Exploration Committee (DEC) in the 1890s, which are described in their annual reports.

Fig 2.10
Ground photo of
Fernworthy stone circle
(NMR DP082123;
© English Heritage. NMR).

The first of these restorations was at Langstone Moor in 1894, where, after the circle was 'carefully examined' by the DEC, the stones were re-erected (DEC 1895). Although the restorers claim to have used the original sockets, it seems likely the restored circle does not reflect the original circular layout, now presenting a very irregular shape (Fig 2.9). In 1896 the stones of the Whitemoor circle were re-erected, the committee reporting that it had been badly despoiled as a source of stone (DEC 1897), and others followed, including Grey Wethers and Brisworthy. The DEC also carried out limited excavation at several of the circles, which in some cases resulted only in finds of wood charcoal, leading them to the conclusion that they were 'places of cremation or funerary feasts' (DEC 1899, 153).

The field evidence of stone circles

Twelve open stone circles survive on Dartmoor, but it is likely that others existed in areas now enclosed by farmland, and were robbed of stone leaving no trace. The survivors are located on the edges of the upper highland zone, in areas usually just beyond those occupied by prehistoric settlement, although chronological associations between the circles and any settlements in their locale have not yet been established. They stand on land that remained unenclosed until the 19th century, and most remain on open ground to this day. Each stone circle is unique: their size varies between 38m diameter at Mardon Down to c 18.5m at Merrivale (Fig 2.9), and the number, height, shape and spacing of the stones varies considerably. Fernworthy (Fig 2.10) has unevenly-shaped upright slabs of only 1.1m high maximum and the Grey Wethers (Fig 2.11) have distinctly square-topped slabs of up to 1.3m. In contrast, nearby Scorhill (see Fig 2.8) includes several tall, narrow pointed stone posts of up to 2.4m high..

Stone circles continue to be difficult monuments to interpret because of the lack of data so far retrieved from them. The few excavations that have taken place in Britain have proved inconclusive as to their function, and where material has been retrieved through excavation it is difficult to be certain that the activity it represents was contemporary with the stones. This lack of information has meant that those who have studied stone circles using archaeological principles have had to approach them on the basis of what can be said about them as features within a landscape, rather than from associated artefacts. By examining their distribution, nationally and locally, their type, size, location and altitude, as well as their topographic situation with reference to river valleys and other landscape features, Barnatt (1989) was able to make cautious statements regarding their landscape context.

He established that there are two classes of open circle on Dartmoor: symmetrical and irregular. Of these the first category, which includes Whitemoor and the Grey Wethers, are dominantly on the higher ground, located on

Fig 2.11
The Grey Wethers, a pair of stone circles near Sittaford Tor (NMR DP082125; © English Heritage. NMR).

Fig 2.12
Beardown Man, a standing
stone in the Cowsic Valley
(photo: Phil Newman).

watersheds with views in both directions. The irregular circles, such as Scorhill, tend to be sited in central locations within major valleys, perhaps each representing a focal point for separate groups or communities. But even this comprehensive study, in which the author was able to offer many new insights, he admits that, owing to limitations of the data, details of any activities that took place must remain conjectural. More recently, Bradley (1998, 116), in a discussion of monuments of this period, has referred to stone circles as 'permeable', as a means of expressing the idea that visually they were designed to look outwards from within; the spaces between the stones intended to allow the surrounding landscape to be seen rather than obscured by a barrier.

The dates of stone circles on Dartmoor are not known from radiocarbon, but nationally a range of dates has been obtained that places several examples within the period 2000 BC to 1300 BC (Quinnell 1994a, 56), firmly within the Early Bronze Age. Stone circles could therefore have had origins in the late Neolithic from before 2000 BC, although on Dartmoor their relationship with other monuments as components of the broader prehistoric landscape, which is discussed below, suggests their importance endured well into the 2nd millennium BC and the Bronze Age.

Menhirs or standing stones

Large stones, set artificially upright occur in many parts of Britain, and are likely to have once been more common, many in the lowlands probably having been reused in the post-prehistoric period for other purposes, when large elongated stones were needed as parts of farm buildings or as gate posts. Although assumed to be prehistoric, there is often little evidence to confirm this for individual examples, and their function and meaning are mostly lost to us. While likely to have a ceremonial or monumental function, they could also have served more practical purposes, such as territorial markers, meeting or rallying points within a landscape that possessed few other man-made features. Excavations in Cornwall have revealed associations with burials of Bronze Age date (Barnatt 1982, 96) but the stone and burial need not have been contemporary.

Few menhirs on Dartmoor are isolated – most share their location with other sepulchral and ceremonial monuments such as stone

rows. Beardown Man (Fig 2.12) is an exception. This 3m tall granite column stands to one side of Devil's Tor in the valley of the River Cowsic. Although this is a remote location on north Dartmoor, there is evidence of much prehistoric activity in this area, including settlements, a cairn of Bronze Age date and a stone row on Conies Down Tor. Beardown Man can be seen from some distance away to the south, but on the north and particularly the east sides, visibility is very restricted. Other isolated menhirs include the now fallen example at Longstone Hill, which takes its name from the presence of the stone, Hanging Stone on Lee Moor and White Moor Stone, although this latter example is close to the stone circle of the same name.

The majority of menhirs are associated with stone rows, forming the terminals at one end of the row. These may have existed before the rows were added or were erected as a deliberate element of the row. The three stone rows at Drizzlecombe each have a menhir incorporated in this way, including the tallest example on Dartmoor, standing to more than 3m high (Fig 2.13).

Stone rows

Stone rows, alignments of upright stones arranged in single, double or multiple rows, offer one of the greatest puzzles in the prehistoric Dartmoor landscape. Whereas it is easy to hypothesise a number of functions that stone circles may have served by defining a space within the stones, the essential function of stone rows is less obvious, which makes understanding their purpose and meaning almost impossible. They appear not to have formed either a boundary or a physical barrier and they do not conform to any particular type, orientation, size or aspect. In fact the term stone row covers a wide variety of monuments of different styles and layout, their one common feature being their linearity, and for all types of row there are often various associations with other monuments, such as barrows, ring cairns and menhirs, acting as terminal features on one or both ends, or sometimes placed centrally within the row (Fig 2.14).

Stone rows have in the past been termed, avenues, parallelitha, alignments and pro-cessional ways, which gives some indication as to the confusion over their variety and purpose. Generally, there has been little consensus as to their function or date. Theories have been mooted with frequency as to the Dartmoor stone rows serving as astronomical observatories (Lockyer 1906), in the same way that part of the function of Stonehenge appears to have been to isolate the midsummer solstice. Emmett (1979) was able to argue against such ideas regarding the Dartmoor rows, on the basis of their varying orientations and the inconsistencies within the individual alignments, many having been 'restored' in the 19th century. Such theories have tended to rely on evidence from only one or two stone rows, which may coincidentally have solar or lunar alignments, without providing sufficient evidence to explain the purpose of all the Dartmoor rows as a collective group (eg Walker 2005); Lockyer for example dismissed all but the straightest rows in his discourse. Although offering intriguing possibilities, such ideas are often based on constructs by those who advance the theories rather than being a product of empirical evidence, and as a result many are unconvincing. As yet such ideas have not contributed greatly to our understanding of these monuments and unfortunately, in recent years, no programme of archaeo-astronomical research has focused on the Dartmoor rows, though future investigation, if scientifically conducted, could throw light on this topic.

The distribution of stone rows in the British Isles is similar to that of other megalithic structures, including circles and portal dolmens, predominantly in the west and north of the country. Stone rows are also common in Brittany, where many multiple rows containing extremely large stones survive (Burl 1993). Dartmoor, however, has the single largest assemblage of stone rows in Britain, with between 75 and 80 examples, depending whether some debatable sites are included, though this figure continues to increase as new examples are brought to attention.

Many of the stone rows are fairly remote, which in the 18th and early 19th centuries meant that the antiquaries were mostly unaware of the existence of quite so many. Not so the Merrivale complex (Fig 2.15), which is close by the main trans-Dartmoor route as it was at that time – now the B3357 – and became the focus for several early accounts. In the early 19th century, Rev E A Bray realised the significance of the rows and

Fig 2.13
The massive standing stone at Drizzlecombe in the Plym Valley, which forms the terminal of one of the stone rows (see Fig 2.16) (NMR DP099107; © English Heritage. NMR).

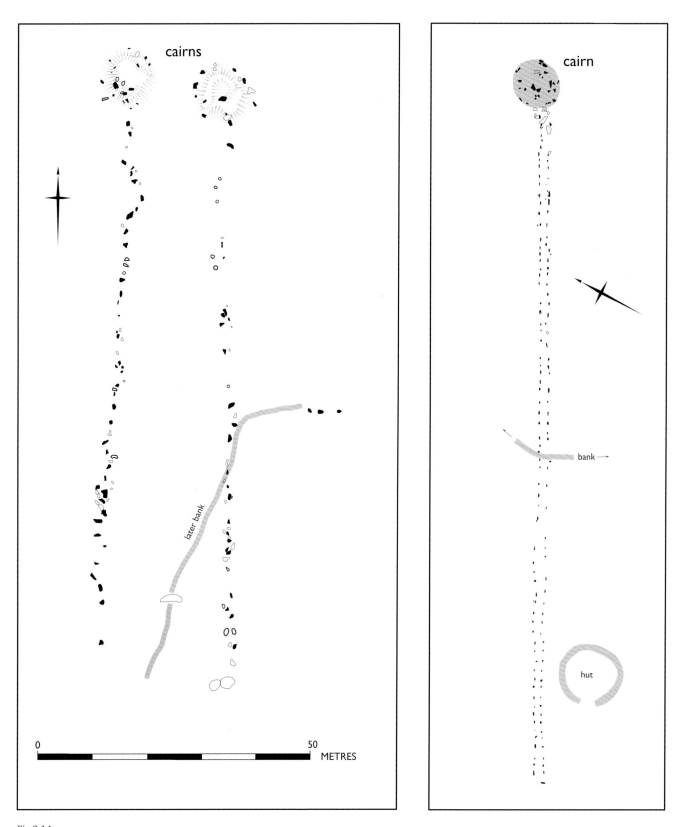

Fig 2.14
(left) Plan of two separate single stone rows with round cairn terminals at Wotter, both disturbed and ruinous;
(right) and the 'restored' Assacombe Stone Row in Fernworthy Forest (RCHME 1:100 scale survey).

Fig 2.15
Merrivale southern stone
row. View from the western
terminal looking east
(NMR DP055107;
© English Heritage. NMR).

much else at the site, for his wife Eliza recounts a visit in 1802, in her book *The Borders of Tamar and Tavy* (1879, 155). On this occasion, Bray excavated the central cairn but found nothing.

It was Samuel Rowe, with his usual thoroughness, who brought a far wider number of stone rows to public attention, laying the foundations for a corpus of data on these monuments. He noted their frequent association with other prehistoric remains but his usual obsession with Druids, unfortunately, guided his interpretations (Rowe 1830, 184).

Measured surveys of stone rows, as opposed to the sketch illustrations of earlier commentators, began with Gardner Wilkinson's plans (1862) of the rows near Hartor, Trowlesworthy and at Kestor. The discovery of stone rows continued towards the end of the 19th century and all new finds were reported by R N Worth and his son R Hansford Worth in a series of papers between 1892 and 1932, which though thorough was, due to a lack of interpretive data, little more than a cataloguing exercise.

In the early 1960s the first and only modern opportunity to archaeologically excavate a stone row arose when the row at Cholwichtown was threatened by the advance of china clay working. This was a single row, 216m long with a small circle on one end. The site was excavated totally, exposing all components, but, sadly, no finds or any datable evidence were retrieved, although environmental evidence suggested the site was built within a clearing of either grassland or heathland among woodland and scrub (Eogan 1964, 25). More recently, a newly recorded stone row on Cut Hill, which appears to have been exposed by post-medieval peat cutting, has provided radiocarbon dates from peat samples trapped beneath one of the fallen stones. Although interpretation of the results has proved far from straightforward in this case, the dates obtained at least suggest that the stones were in place by between 3700 BC and 3500 BC (Fyfe and Greeves in press). This is much earlier than previously believed for the origins of these monuments, and further work will be necessary to provide more certainty.

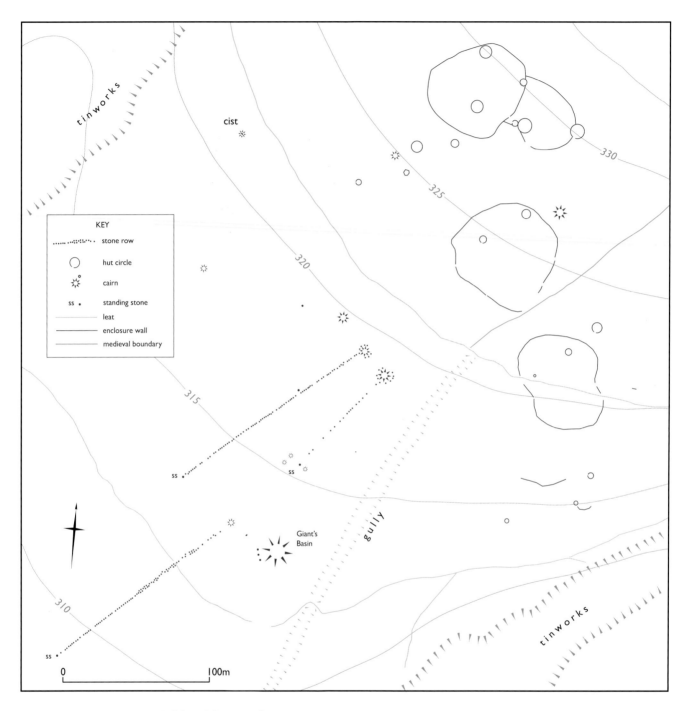

Fig 2.16
Plan of the Drizzlecombe
stone rows, ceremonial
complex and enclosed
settlements in the Plym
Valley (based on an RCHME
1:2500 scale survey).

Field evidence of stone rows

There are three main variants: firstly the single alignment – simply one line of individual stones. The rows at Wotter (*see* Fig 2.14) and Hingston Hill (*see* Fig 2.24) are of this type. Double rows, as the name suggests, comprise two parallel lines, the stones arranged in close pairs as at Merrivale (*see* Fig 2.43) and Assacombe (*see* Fig 2.14), though the distance between the rows varies considerably.

There are also several triple stone rows, such as Challacombe and that on the south slopes of Cosdon, known locally as the 'Cemetery', and one multiple or 'complex' example at Corringdon Ball. Within these groups the character varies greatly, and there are no rules as to what the average stone row consists of. To date, the most useful analysis of these rows is Emmett's detailed study of 1979, from which the following statistics are extracted. The maximum length exceeds 3400m, which is the single row

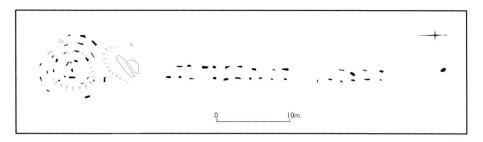

Fig 2.17
Plan of the Shoveldown
double stone row on
Chagford Common (part
of) and the multiple ring
setting, which forms the
terminal (RCHME 1:100
scale survey).

on Stall Moor; and all the recorded examples in excess of 500m are single rows. The majority are much shorter, averaging about 100m. Few of the stones used in Dartmoor rows are tall, with the exception of Stalldown and parts of the Hingstone row (*see* Fig 2.24). For several stone rows, the stones stand barely proud of the ground, such as Langston Moor and Sharpitor, and for the majority they are less than 1m tall, although many rows have particular stones that are notably taller than the average for that row, as at Hingston Hill, where the stones closest to the terminal cairn at the west end are much taller than the other stones in the row.

It would appear that whatever the function of these monuments, the individual groups or communities who built them adapted the basic concept to suit their own requirements and the unique location and the materials available. Possibly, the amount of available manpower may have influenced the size of the stones and complexity of the monument, but several of the rows could have been constructed by as few as two or three individuals.

Although the dating for stone rows generally remains imprecise, and in view of the Cut Hill evidence needs to be reappraised, their late Neolithic/early Bronze Age date has long been assumed by their association with a series of other types of ceremonial and sepulchral monuments, including round barrows, cairns, ring cairns and cists (*see below*). These may form terminals at one end of the row, or they may be located near by. Several of the stone rows terminate with a standing stone or 'menhir' at one end, such as the three rows at Drizzlecombe (Fig 2.16), as well as Shovel Down and Langstone Moor. These would seem to give focus or precedence to one end of the row, but there is currently no way of telling if the menhir preceded, was an original feature of or was added to the stone row. It is more common to find sepulchral remains forming the terminal of a stone row, in the form of round cairns (Fig 2.17).

Round barrows and cairns

This group of monuments marks a distinct departure from the chambered tombs of the early Neolithic in both design and concept. Chambered tombs were usually communal mausoleums, which served as the resting place for an unknown number of anonymous individuals, represented only by their bones, whereas some round barrows offer us our first indirect contact with specific individuals, who were interred in them, often with a range of artefacts representing the material aspects of their lives. But although round barrows do represent change, they are still following a tradition of burial under a mound. Indeed there are indications that some round cairns represent a transitional form in that they have vestiges of chambers or entrances, redolent of passage graves found in Ireland and the Isles of Scilly and datable to the late Neolithic. Other sites within this category, namely the ring cairns, have demonstrated that human interment may be completely absent; so as a group the cairn includes a diversity of round stony features of which the main variations are discussed below (Fig 2.18).

Round barrows and cairns are the most numerous prehistoric monuments in Britain, with 30,000 examples having been recorded

Fig 2.18
Diagram showing the
transitional nature of artefact
and monument chronology in
terms of the Neolithic and
Early Bronze Age.

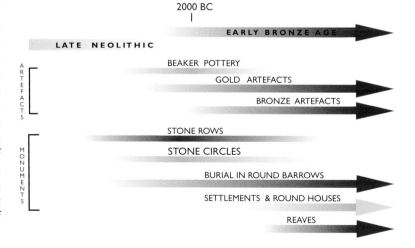

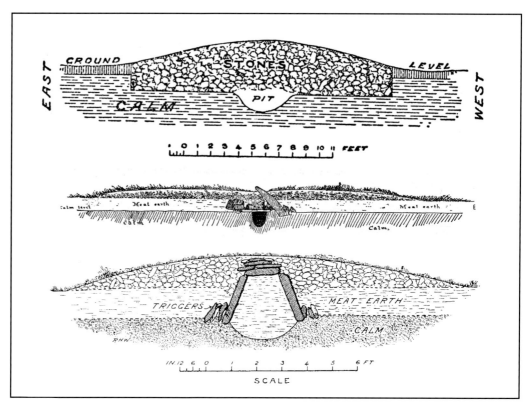

(Last 2007, 1), and there are about 700 recorded on Dartmoor. They also have the longest tradition of excavation of any class of archaeological monument, 'barrow digging' being documented as long ago as 1178 (Grinsell 1953, 110), although in Devon it is believed that the first such intervention was in 1324, possibly at the Chapman Barrows on Exmoor (Bar Comm 1886). It was Dean Jeremiah Milles of Exeter, President of the Society of Antiquaries, who first undertook archaeological fieldwork on Dartmoor barrows in 1752 on Mardon Down (Grinsell 1978, 87), and the literature of the early 19th century has frequent anecdotal references to the opening of barrows, though with few reliable accounts of the finds. Spence Bate's report (1872, 549–57) on his finds at Two Barrows, Hameldown is the first to provide any details of the barrow itself and the digging methodology (*see* chapter 1).

The significance of barrows to the 19th century investigators is highlighted by the existence of a Devon Committee on Barrows, appointed by the Devonshire Association in 1878, formed specifically to investigate these numerous monuments. Their work continued until the 1950s, resulting in a very detailed body of data and several excavations. Although many unscientific excavations of barrows took

place through the 19th century, by the end of it a more methodological approach had developed, with several excavations on Dartmoor by the Barrow Committee and the DEC, producing details not only of the graves and their contents, but also the construction of the barrows (Figs 2.19 and 2.20). The results of all the DEC's excavations have been usefully collated and summarised by Grinsell (1978, 85–180) and by Butler (1997, 275–7). Unfortunately the

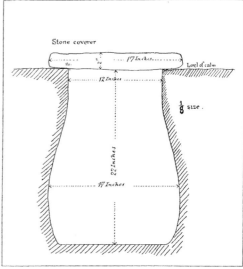

Pit under Cairn near Hemstone Rocks.

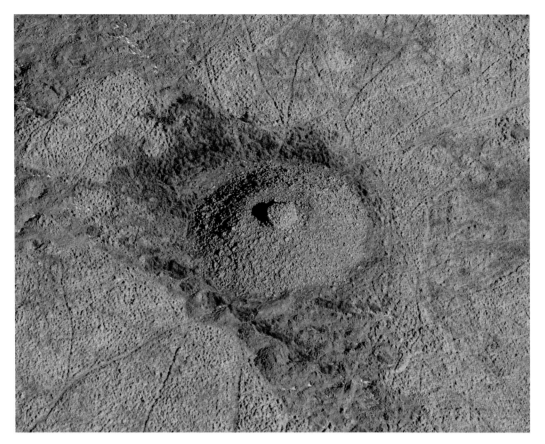

Fig 2.21
Aerial view of the
re-fashioned Eastern White
Barrow with a central
'pudding basin' mound
imposed on the flattened
remains of the cairn. Note
how the surrounding area
has been disturbed by post-
medieval tinners' pits (NMR
24580/007; (© English
Heritage. NMR).

evidence from Dartmoor barrow excavations peters out soon after these committees lost their momentum, with little further work taking place after 1910, until a group of cairns was excavated on Shaugh Moor in 1977 in advance of their destruction by clay dumping (Wainwright *et al* 1979, 10). This work, so far, is the only excavation to provide radiocarbon dates for prehistoric cairns on Dartmoor, which, when calibrated, produced a range of dates within the Early Bronze Age. Our understanding of the Dartmoor cairns is supported also by more recent excavations and studies elsewhere in the UK, right up until the present day, which offer a huge body of comparative data.

The term 'barrow' may be defined as a mound of earth or stone, usually covering one or more inhumations or cremations. On Dartmoor, where the majority of these monuments are constructed mostly from stone (Fig 2.21), they are often described as 'cairns', particularly on OS maps, although several earthen barrows also survive on the moors. The rocky terrain, thin soils and underlying granite geology of Dartmoor would nevertheless have prevented construction of some of the large elaborate earthen examples found in Dorset or Wiltshire,

but that same stone provided a material that facilitated local variants in style. It is unlikely that many Dartmoor cairns had pronounced ditches, but if they did they have silted in the several millennia since their abandonment.

In early studies, cairns were considered only as mounds used to cover a burial and little regard was paid to the physical characteristics of the cairn itself. Variations in appearance were often put down to robbing and interference in the post-prehistoric period. More recently, however, studies have revealed a huge diversity in the form, size and construction of cairns beyond a simple mound of stone and earth, and various attempts have been made to categorise them, which are recommended reading for more detailed reference (Grinsell, 1978; Turner 1990). But for the present purpose of description there are essentially six basic forms: round cairns (large and small); embellished round cairns; ring cairns; ring settings; and multiple rings.

Round cairns (large), including tor cairns

Grinsell coined the term 'prestige cairns' to describe these often very large stony heaps sited in ridgetop and hilltop positions, which

Fig 2.22
A large, though heavily
disturbed, stony, tor cairn
on Rippon Tor
(photo: Phil Newman).

are clearly located to be visible from the surrounding landscape. The fabric of these cairns is moorstone boulders, usually of a manageable size, collected from the surrounding area – so a supply of loose stone in the locality was a prerequisite to the building of these monuments. The cairns may have an overall spread of 40m but many are much smaller. Most have been heavily interfered with over time and their original profiles lost, now standing no higher than 3m at most. Some have been re-fashioned in the historic period, such as Eastern White Barrow with its rather too perfect, pudding shaped structure rising out of the spread remains of the main barrow (Fig 2.21). The interference and modification to these cairns continues to this day with some visitors constructing additional smaller cairns and shelters within the fabric of the large cairns (*see* Fig 2.28), an activity which is to be discouraged. The haphazard rubble-heap appearance of many of these cairns today (Fig 2.22), following centuries of interference, may belie their original appearance, and one excavated example revealed that it was built of stones slanted upwards (Bar Comm 1905). This cairn also contained a central cremation pit, but no dates have been retrieved from any of these cairns as yet and, although highly likely, there is no certainty that they all have associated burials beneath them. Large cairns are almost always located on hilltops

(but see Giant's basin below) and were probably deliberately sited as eye-catching features, perhaps following the tradition of the Neolithic long barrows.

Round cairns (small)

This is the most common form of cairn. These simple mounds of stone and earth, with distinctive dome-shaped profiles, have no outward signs of embellishment and may be as small as 3m in diameter, but may be up to 10m. They may be sited near to and associated with ridge-top cairns, but equally may be found on lower ground and in groups. These cairns have, with only a minute number of exceptions, been dug into at some time in the past, usually leaving an untidy hollow gash in the centre. As a result a central cist or burial pit has often been exposed (*see below*).

Included in this group are entrance graves, which although rare on Dartmoor are nevertheless present. These are round cairns with evidence of an entrance or stone-lined passage leading into the mound from a point on the periphery. This entrance is a feature they share with the chambered tombs, though they are assumed to be later, and may represent a variation and continuity of the Neolithic tradition of tombs that remained unsealed and could be re-entered. Entrance graves may therefore be among the earliest of the round cairns on Dartmoor; but as with most of these early monuments, information from modern excavations and radiocarbon dates are lacking. These sites are more common in Cornwall, and in particular on the Isles of Scilly, where more than 50 have been recorded (Barnett 1982); but as yet few examples have been recognised on Dartmoor. The most convincing example is the Watern Hill 'King's Oven' cairn, though several other possible examples, all heavily disturbed, have been identified by Butler (1997, 157). This 17.5m diameter mound, though now considerably reduced in height, has a short, stone-lined passage on the north-east side. The hilltop location and relatively large proportions of the Watern Hill cairn may hint at the possibility of other likewise located round cairns having similar features, though currently obscured.

Embellished round cairns

This group includes both mounds of stone or earth encircled by spaced stones forming a perimeter (encircled cairns), and flat-topped mounds (platform cairns), with a 'kerb' of upright contiguous stones. Some are found in similar locations to the plain round cairns, with similarly placed central cists, but this group is also the most common form to be associated with stone rows (eg Drizzlecombe, Hartor, Cosdon, Yartor). Among the largest and most impressive is that on Hingston Hill (Figs 2.23 and 2.24). The cairn has been badly disturbed with a large central hollow providing evidence

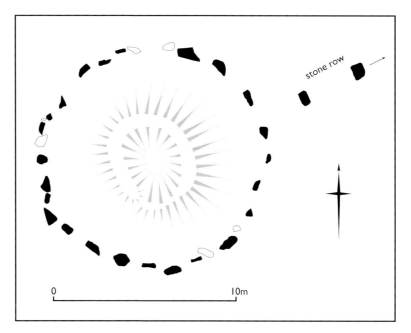

Fig 2.23 (top)
Plan of an 'encircled cairn' on Hingston Hill, surveyed at 1:100 scale. The stony central cairn is much disturbed but would once have been much larger. The stones were re-erected by the DEC in the 1890s.

Fig 2.24 (above)
Hingston Hill 'encircled cairn' and single stone row (photo: Phil Newman),

Fig 2.25 (left)
A partially robbed probable platform cairn with central cist, also robbed, near Houndtor (NMR DP082123; © English Heritage. NMR).

for the presence of barrow diggers in search of a central burial, and the raised mound survives to a reduced height. Surrounding the cairn is a circle of spaced upright stones, all less than 1m tall, with an internal diameter of approximately 12m; these stones were re-erected by the DEC in the 1890s, but the overall impression of a raised mound, albeit diminished in size, surrounded by a circle of stones at the head of an impressive stone row, is still to be appreciated.

A different variant can be seen near Hound Tor (Fig 2.25), where a cist is surrounded by a circle of contiguous stones. Although not complete, this kerb circle probably retained a flat-topped mound of earth, of which only vestiges survive, once covering the cist and its burial.

On Pinchaford Ball, a much despoiled cairn has a 16m diameter circle of contiguous stones surviving as the only evidence of a similar type of cairn, the fabric of which has been almost totally removed, a large depression in the centre demonstrating the extent of interference at the site. This too was likely to have been a platform cairn, though no evidence of a cist survives (Fig 2.26).

Many of these cairns were very much smaller, such as that at Hawns, with a 2m diameter kerb (Fig 2.27), and Yar Tor 'Money Pit' (Fig 2.27), with a slightly elliptical kerb of up to 3m in diameter. Both contained cists set into mounds,

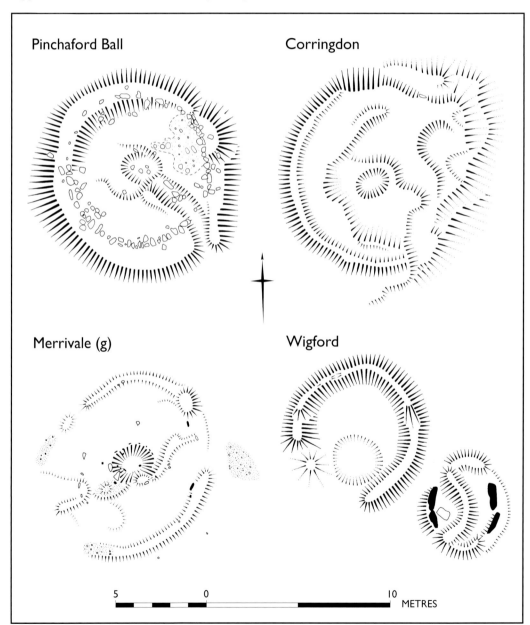

Fig 2.26
Earthwork plans of round cairns. The fabric of the two ring cairns at Merrivale and Corringdon has been heavily disturbed, but at Wigford Down much of the earthwork appears to have survived. A second smaller cairn with vestiges of a kerb is located only a few metres to the south-west. The Pinchaford cairn, also heavily robbed and spread, was probably a platform cairn, surrounded by a masonry kerb, some of the stones from which survive in situ.

Pinchaford Ball

Corringdon

Merrivale (g)

Wigford

5 0 10 METRES

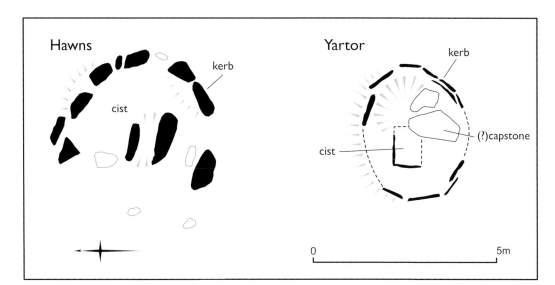

Fig 2.27
Kerbed cists at Yartor (Money Pit) and Hawns. Both examples have been disturbed and stones have been robbed. Yartor comprises thin edge-set slabs of granite forming a kerb surrounding a rectangular cist, much of which is now missing. Vestiges of a probable cairn survive (not illustrated), although now very spread, and earthfast stones set with it may represent remains of a retaining circle. Only the two side slabs survive on the cist at Hawns and 50 per cent of the kerb is now missing (EH 1:100 scale surveys).

and the Yar Tor example, which forms the terminal of a stone row, appears to have been set into the centre of a fairly large mound, now very spread, with an outer circle still in place.

Ring cairns

This group includes earth or stone circular embankments defining a central space, which may or may not contain other visible features, such as a small mound or a cist or a pit burial. The banks often have openings, such as those on Stall Down (Fig 2.28) and Wigford Down (Fig 2.26), which are suggestive of entrances. The ring in some cases has evidence for a stone kerb on one or both sides of the bank. At Merrivale (Fig 2.26), a short distance south of the stone rows, a heavily disturbed ring cairn comprises a low stony bank, effaced in places, with a central pit, which certainly indicates an unrecorded excavation in search of the burial. Three earth-fast stones on the inner rim of the bank may indicate the sole trace of a stone kerb.

A notable characteristic of ring cairns is that they seldom occur isolated and are usually either paired with other cairns of different forms or are part of a group. The only modern Dartmoor round cairn excavation, undertaken in 1977, focussed on a group of six cairns on Shaugh, which included two poorly preserved ring cairns, neither of which had any evidence of interment (Wainwright *et al* 1979, 10–33).

Ring settings

These comprise a ring of upstanding stones, defining what appears to be an unaltered space, though often accommodating burials or

Fig 2.28 (previous page)
Aerial view of a ring cairn (lower), and large round cairn (top) on Stall Down. The ring cairn has a diameter of approximately 24m (NMR 24098/045; © English Heritage. NMR).

Fig 2.29 (right)
A ring setting at the edge of Soussons Forest. The circle of upright stones, which was re-erected by the DEC in the 19th century, surrounds the remains of a central cist (NMR DP082163; © English Heritage. NMR).

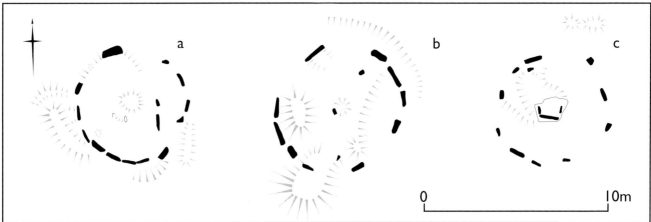

Fig 2.30 (above)
Plans of small ring settings on Lakehead Hill, showing the re-erected stones of the circles and vestiges of probable denuded cairns (grey). Cairn 'c' has a cist with capstone in situ (see Fig 2.31; RCHME 1:100 scale).

Fig 2.31 (right)
Restored ring setting with central cist at Lakehead Hill (photo: Phil Newman).

cremations contained within cists, or pits. Some certainly represent the embellished cairns described above, now denuded. Beside the road at Soussons, surrounded on three sides by conifers, is one of the clearest examples (Fig 2.29), the stones of which were re-erected by the DEC. The circle has a diameter of 8.6m and an apparently level interior. Two sides of a central cist remain in place, although the cover stone is missing and the chamber is silted. There is no surviving evidence that the cist was ever covered by a cairn. Three smaller settings survive on Lakehead Hill, all variously 'restored' (Fig 2.30). These are all circles of thin, edge-set stone between 6m and 8m in diameter. One of the circles contains a fine cist (Fig 2.31), with all four sides *in situ* and its slab stone replaced by the restorers. Only a few metres away there is a second circle of similar appearance but with no cist. A shallow indentation in the centre may indicate the activities of treasure seekers and the undulating ground in and around the circle could indicate vestiges of a cairn. A further circle of this type survives only a few metres to the north. Much is missing but enough survives to reveal its similar attributes.

Multiple stone rings

These monuments comprise thin slabs of stone set on edge and arranged into concentric circles. Of the two recorded Dartmoor examples, both have four circles and are at the head of a stone row. The Shoveldown example (Fig 2.32), which has an outer circle diameter of 8.5m, forms the terminal of a double stone row and appears to have once been covered by a cairn with remnants of the mound still present. The Yellowmead circle (Fig 2.33) is much larger, the outer circle being 19m in diameter, and there is no evidence that a cairn ever covered it. The stones of the central circle are almost touching, giving the impression of a chamber, but it lacks an entrance. This monument was subject to fairly extensive restoration in 1921 by the Rev Hugh Breton, and its accuracy is often questioned. Breton recorded several stones near the circle to the south-west, which he considered to be parts of a stone row leading towards the monument.

Cists and burial pits

Barrows and cairns, when excavated, have often revealed the remains of an inhumation or cremation. The remains of the individuals

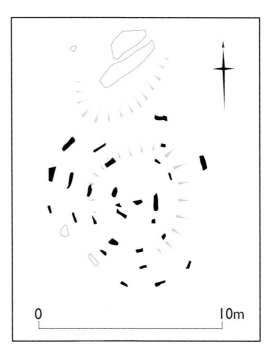

Fig 2.32
Plan of the multiple ring at Shoveldown (RCHME 1:100 scale survey).

0 ⊢──────────────────────┤ 10m

Fig 2.33
Aerial view of the Yellowmead Fourfold multiple stone ring. The outer ring has a diameter of c 20m (NMR 24898/024; © English Heritage. NMR).

Fig 2.34
Stone cists, all three of which were excavated in the late 19th or early 20th century. Thornworthy (top) near the waters edge of Fernworthy Reservoir. The rectangular chamber, made from granite slabs, was covered by a single capstone, now displaced. The chamber measures approximately 1m long × 0.6m wide and 0.5m deep. It is encircled by an earth and stone ring cairn, not shown. Lakehead (centre) this cist was reconstructed by antiquaries in the 19th century 'too drastically' according to Lesley Grinsell (1979). The interior of the chamber measures approx 1.3m × 1.2m; it is encircled by a stone kerb and forms the terminal of a short stone row. Crow Tor (lower) has its displaced capstone to one side and measures approximately 1m × 1.2m (photo: Phil Newman).

were interred either in a simple burial pit or within a cist. A cist, for which the antiquarian term is 'kistvaen', comprises a stone box recessed into the ground, with two parallel long sides of granite slabs and end pieces set between the sides, and the whole structure covered by a single large slab (Fig 2.34). Many cists are associated with cairns, either centrally within a ring cairn or buried beneath a mound; but for a good number of cists no trace of a cairn survives, so it is possible that some were originally only lightly covered by earth. The size of the cist itself varies greatly: on the north slope of Down Tor a group of three cists are all very small, the smallest being 0.5m × 0.3m and could only have contained a child inhumation or a cremation. Larger examples such as Lakehead (1.7m × 1.2m) or Merrivale (2m × 0.8m) could have easily accommodated an adult crouched inhumation. However, of the known cists and of those excavated, only a few have provided any human remains.

One intriguing observation made by Worth, when summarising the findings of the Barrow Committee, is that with only a tiny number of exceptions, the longwise orientation of cists lies between north and west, although there is no obvious explanation for what must have been a conscious decision on the part of the builders (Spooner and Russell 1967, 178–9). Although cists are found in other areas of the UK, their number on the granite moors of Dartmoor, with more than 180 recorded, and of Bodmin Moor, where 58 are known (Johnson and Rose 1994, 39), is far greater than on other upland zones of south-west England. Although there are many cairns and barrows recorded on Exmoor and on the Quantock Hills for example, only two cists have been recorded on the former (Riley and Wilson-North 2001) and none on the latter (Riley 2006). Burial or cremation pits, without the stone lining, have been found at several excavated Dartmoor cairns, including Hameldown, Hurstone Ridge and Hemstone Rocks, the last comprising a bell-shaped pit with a stone covering slab (Fig 2.20).

The multi-phase nature of barrows and cairns

Before the days of scientific excavation techniques, it was often assumed that a barrow, of whatever design, represented a single event, being the grave constructed around an individual who had died. Although it has long been known that additional interments were sometimes placed into the cairn at a later date, the monuments themselves were seen as single phase structures, where the differing elements were assigned to building style rather than to phasing. As data from excavations have accumulated, it has become apparent that the structure of many barrows underwent a series of modifications. One study of excavated barrows in southern England, where reliable radio-carbon dates have been retrieved, demonstrated multiple phases within the structures, extending over a period of several centuries, and up to 1,000 years in one case (Garwood 2007, 33). These phases may have included enlargement or embellishment of the monument, or changes in funeral rite, and often resulted in the deposition of 'new' types of material goods.

Although the number of archaeologically excavated cairns on Dartmoor is limited, several sites explored by the Barrow Committee and others, including Spence Bate, provide probable evidence for phased construction. Two Barrows at Hameldown, for example, has the outward appearance of a mound but Bate's section drawing shows that beneath this was a peripheral stony ring with a small central cairn (Bate 1872). This demonstrates the potential for a cairn of outwardly uncomplicated appearance to be the product of a sequence of events rather than a single building phase, and it seems likely that the more complicated examples, such as stone settings and embellished cairns, are products of more than one phase of construction (Fig 2.35).

The funerary function of cairns is likely to have been only one of several uses for these structures, which may help explain the changes to their fabric. Indeed, the excavated ring cairns on Shaugh Moor failed to provide any evidence of human interment, and had no apparent funerary role. A metaphor often used to explain the potential for cairns and barrows to have had much broader meaning, is the English parish church; if excavated by someone unfamiliar with the Christian religion, they would be overwhelmed by evidence of burial and funerary monuments and may conclude that a church was nothing more than a

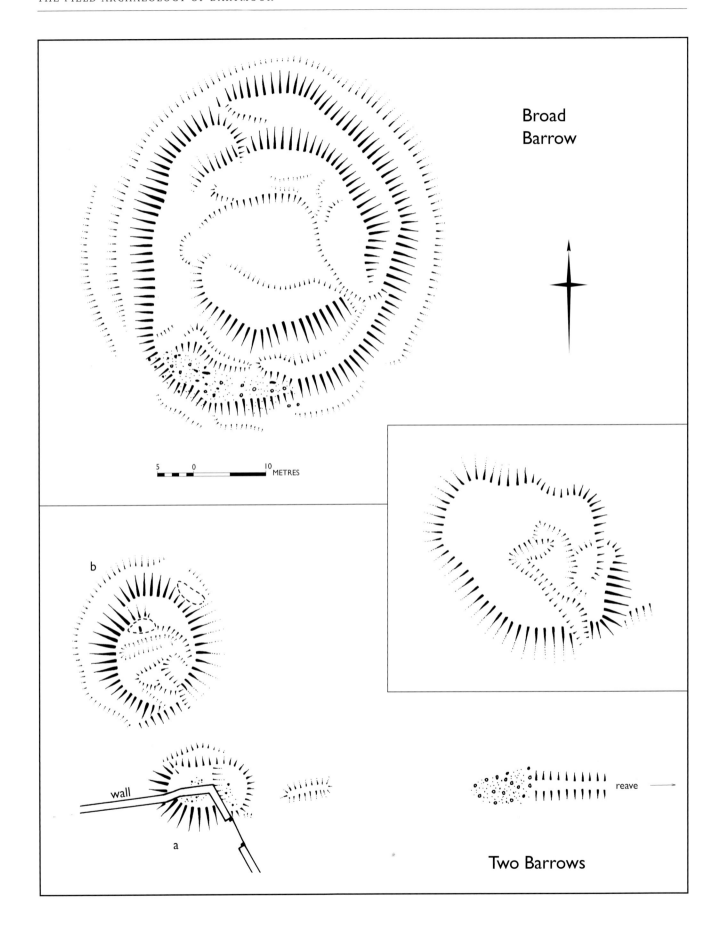

Broad Barrow

Two Barrows

mortuary, while being unaware of its main functions as a place of worship, ceremony and the central social focus of a community. Similarly, the changing liturgical practice that lay behind modifications in the church's structure would not necessarily be obvious in the surviving fabric. The multi-phase nature of cairns, including the imposition of interments, changes to the fabric and the addition of embellishment, may thus be explained as having wider meaning for the community that built and maintained them, beyond the single function of burial.

Groups, alignments and cemeteries

Although cairns often occur singly, it is more usual to find them in identifiable groups. These may be closely spaced clusters, usually termed 'cemeteries', or they may be more spatially separate but within an identifiable locality, such as the watershed of a river, or other topographically defined spaces. Alignments of cairns frequently occur along the crests or ridges, often with highly conspicuous profiles, and visible from lower ground and nearby hilltops of similar altitude.

Fig 2.35 (opposite) Earthwork plans of cairns on Hameldown. Broad Barrow is among Dartmoor's largest hilltop cairns with a diameter of just under 50m. At Two Barrows the southern cairn 'a' sits on the line of a reave, which was later adopted as a post-medieval field boundary. Cairn 'b' is the site of Spence Bate's excavations of 1872, which led to the discovery of the Hameldown Pommel (RCHME 1:100 scale survey).

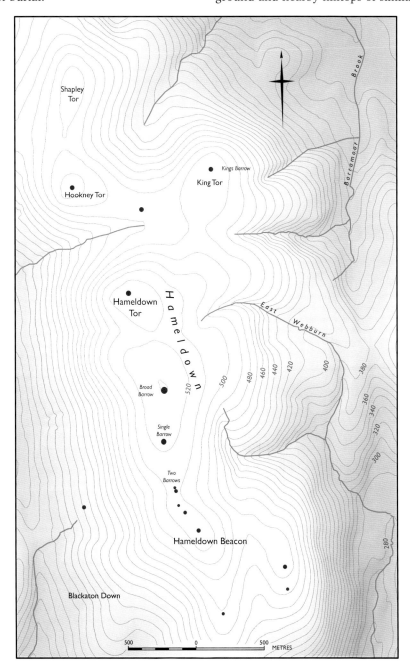

Fig 2.36 Digital terrain model of Hameldown showing positions of barrows on the highest points of the ridge (height data licensed to English Heritage for PGA through Next Perspectives™).

Fig 2.37 (overleaf, left) Digital terrain model showing long barrows, round cairns and ceremonial monuments on southern Dartmoor, including Western Beacon, Ugborough Beacon and Corringdon Ball. Plan includes EH and OS survey data (height data licensed to English Heritage for PGA through Next Perspectives™).

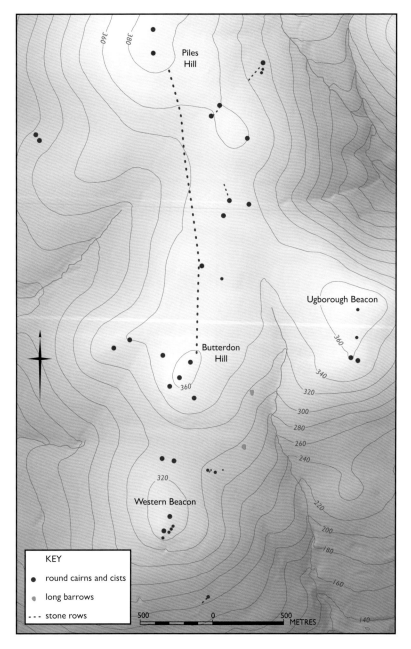

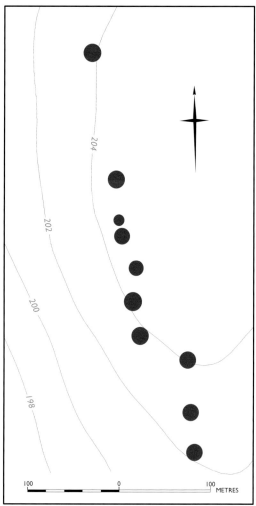

Fig 2.38 (above, right) Simplified plan showing an alignment of round cairns near the summit of Crownhill Down, just outside the National Park (height data licensed to English Heritage for PGA through Next Perspectives™).

What we know of the general chronology of round cairns suggests that these groups may have been established over many generations, perhaps continuing the tradition of a community and its enduring association with a place, which was strengthened by the spiritual presence of ancestors, the memory of whom is continued through their funerary monuments. The eye-catching locations were chosen deliberately to symbolise this association, both to members of the group and to outsiders, serving as potent reminders of territory, place and the enduring presence of communities.

A particularly fine cairn alignment runs along the ridge of Hameldown (Fig 2.36), a large hogsback of land, which rises abruptly from the surrounding moorland to 532m OD and extends north–south for 4km, incorporating several granite outcrops. It is the largest and most conspicuous topographical feature in the Widecombe area. Thirteen cairns are located along the ridge, including the excavated 'Two Barrows' (Fig 2.35) and others with evocative modern names such as 'Broad Barrow' (Fig 2.35) and 'Kings Barrow', and although their profiles have been somewhat diminished by the forces of attrition, their former impact can be imagined by the modern observer. On Hameldown the cairns are widely spaced, but in other places the alignments are much closer together; on Crownhill Down (Fig 2.38) a relatively straight alignment of 10 cairns, staggered in two sections, runs just below the western crest of the hill. In this case the cairns are in places spaced as little as 4m apart.

Clusters of cairns, as opposed to alignments, also occur on hilltops. On Western Beacon, Dartmoor's most southern upland promontory, which overlooks the South Hams and from where the south Devon coast and the Plym estuary is visible, there is a group of six closely spaced, large, stony cairns in an apparently random cluster. They may, however, have associations with other cairns on nearby hilltops at Ugborough Beacon and Butterdon Hill (Fig 2.37).

Round cairns, artefacts and the dating of Dartmoor in prehistory

The term Bronze Age has its origins within the Three-Age System, defining the period dominated by bronze technology, and, like the Neolithic, the term is difficult to use outside the field of artefact studies because different elements of human activity changed at different rates. The introduction of a new material, bronze in this case, did not mean that burial, ceremonial and domestic aspects of a community's existence changed at the same moment, although the presence of the new metal may have been among the agencies of cultural change. But many cultural elements of the period we know as the Early Bronze Age were developing long before bronze arrived on the scene. Barrows, cairns and the funerary practices associated with them were one such

element of this transitional period. Frustratingly, as has been remarked several times above, the establishment of a chronology for Dartmoor's prehistoric archaeology is hampered by a shortage of radiocarbon dates; although the Shaugh Moor excavations (Wainwright *et al* 1979) provided a fine cluster of very close dates of *c* 3723 ± 30 BP (1747 cal BC), the single location of the cairn group means the dates they provided cannot yet be seen as typical for the whole of Dartmoor. For the majority of Dartmoor's round cairns, it is the few datable finds from early excavations that are used to place the remaining monuments into a chronology, based almost entirely on associations (*see* Fig 2.18).

A list collated by Jeremy Butler shows that 130 archaeological interventions have been recorded taking place at Dartmoor cairns between 1797 and 1977 (Butler 1997). Although many of the investigations produced little or no useful data owing to environmental conditions of the site, the ineptitude of the excavators or a failure to record their findings, enough material was retrieved for a very basic insight into Dartmoor's place in the context of British prehistory.

Among the pottery artefacts found in Dartmoor cairns was a number of vessels of a type known as 'beakers', which date to a period commencing *c* 2500 BC. These ceramics are found over much of Britain and indeed parts of Europe, where they are believed

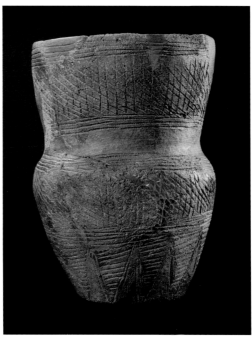

Fig 2.39 (far left)
A Beaker urn retrieved from a cairn on Watern Down, excavated by the DEC in 1897, now housed in Plymouth City Museum. The vessel stands 250mm high (NMR DP099378; © English Heritage. NMR).

Fig 2.40
A Beaker urn decorated with comb-stamping. Found in a small burial mound ESE of Fernworthy stone circle (see Fig 2.42), excavated in 1898 by the DEC, now Housed in Plymouth City Museum. The vessel stands to a little over 180mm high (NMR DP099387; © English Heritage. NMR).

Fig 2.41
A collared urn retrieved
from a cairn on Hurstone
Ridge, excavated by the
DEC in 1901, now housed
in Plymouth City Museum.
The vessel stands to over
480mm high (see Fig 1.7
for size comparisons)
(NMR DP 099389;
© English Heritage. NMR).

to have had their stylistic origins. Fine examples were retrieved from Watern Down (Fig 2.39) and Fernworthy (Fig 2.40), both of which have been successfully reconstructed, with other fragments coming from cairns at Lakehead, Thornworthy and Langcombe. Beakers are important chronological markers; they are the first pottery type to have been deposited in graves, unlike Neolithic pottery, which is nearly always retrieved from domestic or non-funerary ceremonial contexts. They are also associated with the differing burial rite, of crouched inhumation in cists or graves under round barrows or cairns. Other artefacts associated with beakers include, carved jet and amber, flint arrowheads of the distinctive 'barb and tang' variety, and items of metal, both gold and copper alloys, including bronze. Such evidence, which at first sight appears to indicate major and sudden cultural changes, led earlier researchers towards an invasion or migration hypothesis, believing that a large number of so-called 'Beaker Folk' emigrated to the British Isles from Europe, where beakers are also common, and displacing the indigenous population. This concept has now been largely rejected and archaeologists today are inclined to view the change as cultural diffusion or a migration of ideas and styles linked to small-scale movement of people.

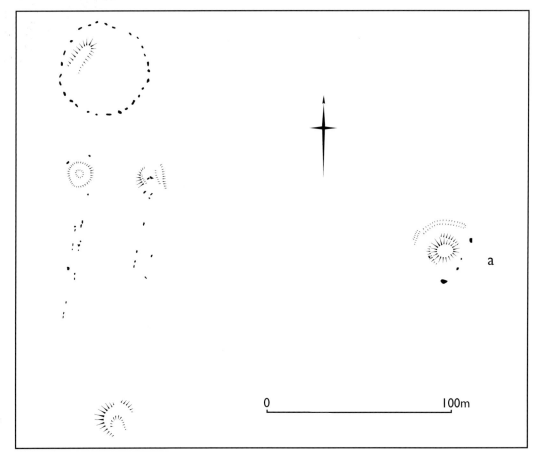

0   100m

Fig 2.42
A cairn sanctuary associated
with a stone circle and
double stone rows at
Froggymead, Fernworthy.
The cairns and rows have
been badly disturbed and the
stone circle re-erected by the
DEC. Excavations of cairn 'a',
in 1897 resulted in the find
of a beaker (see Fig 2.40).

Although beaker burials are the first to be associated with metalwork finds, not all of them actually contained metalwork. At Fernworthy a bronze 'knife' was recovered alongside the beaker, but at Watern Down or any of the other Dartmoor beaker sites, no metal finds were noted. This may be due to survival, but generally an absence of metals could be seen as evidence of an earlier beaker burial before the general availability of metals. Where beaker burials have provided radiocarbon dates elsewhere in Britain, collectively they suggest the 'beaker period' commenced c 2500 BC, with beakers continuing to be deposited as late as 1800 BC (Quinnell 2003, 1), spanning the late Neolithic into the Early Bronze Age. Dartmoor's earliest round barrows therefore may date from this time, and although only five beakers have been recorded, all but the Fernworthy example were retrieved from cists under either plain or embellished round cairns; so it is possible that many similar cairns of this type, with their cists now exposed, once contained burials of the beaker period.

The Hameldown bronze dagger, found by Spence Bate at Two Barrows in 1872, was of later date than the beaker burials, its type being defined as of the Camerton-Snowshill group, from a period of rich burials sometimes containing gold and generally referred to as the Wessex phase in southern England, c 1750 BC–1550 BC. The amber pommel with its gold pin decoration, may be slightly earlier (Quinnell 1994a, 59). The cairn from which this was retrieved, described above, had origins as a ring cairn, later earthed over into a mound, and the artefacts were found in a burial pit, along with burnt bone, covered by slabs. One other important cairn find was that of a 'collared urn' (Fig 2.41), excavated by the DEC from a pit within a small cairn on Hurston Ridge (see Fig 2.19). This form of pottery, dating from 2000 BC and a little later, when found in barrows and cairns, was nearly always used as a cinerary urn to contain cremated bone.

From this somewhat meagre collection of artefacts, and what is known of the phased construction of cairns elsewhere, it can be postulated that Dartmoor's round cairns had origins possibly as early as 2600 BC, and continued to be constructed, maintained and sometimes adapted or modified for differing burial rites until maybe as late as 1450 BC.

Association with stone rows and sanctuaries

Many round cairns have associations with stone rows. The most frequent occurrence is where a cairn forms the upper terminal of a row. Examples exist at Hingston (see Fig 2.24), Wotter (see Fig 2.14), Hartor and Drizzlecombe (see Fig 2.16) and Fernworthy (Fig 2.42), all of which demonstrate this combination particularly well. There can be no certainty as to whether the cairn or the row was built first, but where two or more rows with cairn terminals exist in the same location, as at the last three examples, the pre-existence of the cairns would at least provide a rational explanation for the starting point and direction of the rows. A slightly different situation occurs at Merrrivale (Fig 2.43), where two parallel double rows run approximately east–west. The northern row has remains of a terminal cairn on the eastern end, but the south row has a small cairn placed centrally, interrupting the continuity of this very straight double alignment. This strongly suggests that the cairn was added to an existing stone row. For the rows that have no terminal feature associated with them, of which there are 12 on Dartmoor (Emmett 1979, 98–9), it cannot be assumed that these terminal features did not exist, although equally there is no reason to assume that one did.

Although all these observations are a little imprecise, what is certain is that the terminal cairns and rows, by their association, have to be considered as two parts of a single monument and therefore in contemporary use during part or all the cultural period to which they were associated. By the same reasoning, where stone rows appear to be the focus for a group of cairns, known as a 'sanctuary', it may be assumed that a succession of later cairns was placed there because of the pre-existence or association of the other monuments in the group, suggesting very strongly that these places fulfilled sacred, funereal and ceremonial roles over many generations.

Additional cairns are frequently placed in the vicinity of stone rows but, unlike the terminal cairns, do not appear to form part of the monument. At Drizzlecombe (see Fig 2.16), the three stone rows each have a cairn at the upper terminal and a menhir at the lower; there are also numerous additional cairns in the vicinity, most of which are small, but also near by is the exceedingly large Giant's Basin,

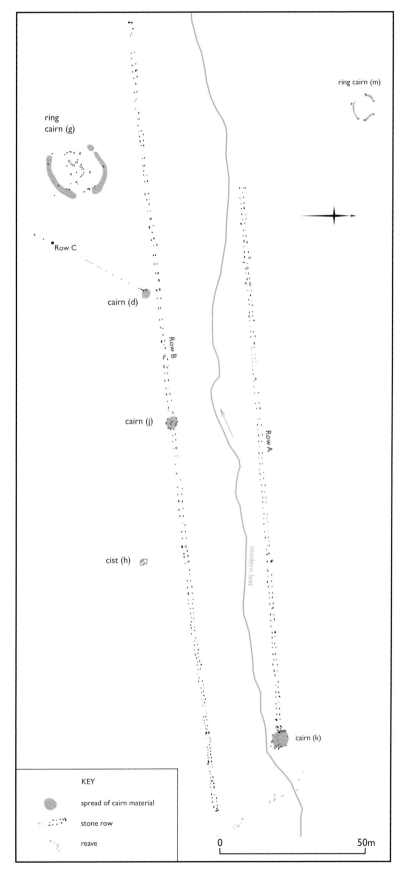

ring
cairn (g)

Row C

cairn (d)

Row B

cairn (j)

Row A

cist (h)

modern leat

cairn (k)

KEY

spread of cairn material

stone row

reave

0   50m

an unembellished round cairn of 22m in diameter. (It has had its core dug away leaving a hollowed out centre, hence the name.) At Fernworthy three double stone rows, two with terminal cairns, are associated with a stone circle and several other cairns, including that from which the Fernworthy beaker was recovered (a on Fig 2.42).

Merrivale, the favoured site of the antiquaries, continues to be the most illustrative and best known of these 'ceremonial' landscapes or sanctuaries (Fig 2.43), sitting on a more or less level shelf with views across the western borders of the moor and Cornwall, but overlooked by the higher upland of the north moor. In addition to the two double stone rows (A and B), a small single row (C) with a terminal cairn (d) runs off to the south-west and a small stone circle (e) and standing stone (f) are located only a short distance south (not illustrated). Apart from the centrally placed (j) and terminal (k) cairns mentioned above, there is a fine but badly disturbed example of a ring cairn (g) beside the row (see Fig 2.26), as well as an isolated cist (h) with vestiges of its cairn still visible. The very large capstone was damaged in 1860 when a local stonecutter removed the central section to be used as a gatepost, much to the indignation of the antiquaries of the time (Crossing 1912, 95). A number of smaller cairns are also located in the vicinity (m), but the existence of an alignment of cairns to the south-west, depicted by Butler (1994) and Gerrard (1998) are difficult to agree with.

These associations however, cannot provide a date for the origin of a stone row. If the excavated contents of associated cairns can be dated, as at Fernworthy, it proves only that the cairn was in use at a certain moment in time; either or both could have much earlier origins.

Summary

Clearly, the modern investigator of Dartmoor's landscape archaeology needs to be aware of the many changes to the early prehistoric monuments over the millennia. Despite their age being measured in thousands of years, even 150 years ago these sites looked very different. Firstly, there were more of them, many having since been destroyed as a source of stone as farm enclosures increased; and those that survived this onslaught have often been the subject of 'restorations', in some cases of dubious authenticity, while others were subjected to 'modification' to make them more aesthetically pleasing to the gaze of a distant viewer. The practice of barrow digging in search of treasure extends far back in time but an over enthusiastic frenzy of archaeologically motivated excavations in the 19th century has also left many of the barrows despoiled and open.

Change is equally evident as part of the life cycle of these monuments in the period when still serving their prehistoric communities. Cairns continued to be constructed, maintained and modified to accommodate changing burial rite and ceremonial practice, while combinations and concentrations of monument types suggest enduring trans-generational links to favoured places in the late 3rd and 2nd millennia BC. Cairns served as terminals for stone rows, ring settings around cists may have started life as open stone circles, or may have been added to pre-existing cairns and several cairns that started out as ring-shaped monuments were buried to form round cairns.

Burial and ceremonial monuments, however, form only part of the landscape evidence for prehistoric Dartmoor; by the middle centuries of the 2nd millennium BC, the archaeological evidence becomes dominated by the remains of houses, settlements, farming and land division, although the barrows and stone monuments continue to be important and are inextricably linked with these developments. This association leads on to the next theme for discussion.

Fig 2.43 (opposite) Simplified plan of the Merrivale stone rows and cairns that make up part of the ritual complex. Based on an RCHME 1:100 scale survey (reduced).

3

Settlement and land division in the 2nd millennium BC

The environment and vegetation of Dartmoor underwent further change in the Neolithic period as did the human response to it. The pollen record shows that patchy clearances like those by the long-barrow builders continued for ceremonial and burial monuments, including the stone rows and the earlier large cairns. For example, the pollen evidence from Cholwichtown stone row strongly suggests that this monument had been built in a clearing, and raises the question: was the clearing created specifically for the stone row, or was the building of such stone monuments a response to the existence of a growing number of clearings? Unfortunately, the later pollen evidence is not as good as that for the Mesolithic and early Neolithic periods, and it is therefore uncertain how the landscape altered so radically from one of woodland to one of open moorland, at least above the 200m contour. However, the growth of 'blanket' peat, which had been developing since the 6th millennium BC, and the gradual descent of the tree line, perhaps exacerbated by browsing animals, explains the more open, less tree-covered terrain that existed by the 3rd millennium BC or earlier. The existence of peat is an indication that heathland species had come to dominate the upland flora by this time. Samples from Cut Hill indicate that peat development occurred here by the early to mid-6th millennium BC (Fyfe and Greeves *in press*).

Andrew Fleming postulated a plausible concept to describe this uncertain contribution of human intervention to Dartmoor's landscape during this period: he suggested that early farmers were 'responding to the increasingly open landscapes' of their predecessors, who had begun the process of clearance in the previous millennium (Fleming 2008, 200). Although there is little archaeological evidence and the chronology of this transition is imprecise, it was against this background of a changing environment that domestication, settlement and the use of the upland for purposes other than just ceremony and burial became evident on Dartmoor in the 2nd millennium BC. This does not rule out the possibility that such activities had already been occurring, but the more enduring stone hut circles and enclosure walls of this period are the earliest field evidence to survive.

There are three distinct elements that combine to make up the 2nd millennium BC landscape of Dartmoor. First there are the remains of round houses or 'hut circles' (as labelled on OS maps). These were the dwellings of the upland inhabitants, comprising circular, stone-walled structures with conical timber and furze roofs, of which only the stone element survives. These hut circles are occasionally isolated, but are more often found in dispersed groups, 'neighbourhoods' or larger settlements. Second, in some cases groups of hut circles are surrounded by walled enclosures, which form part of a patchwork of similar enclosures, some containing hut circles, and some not. Other groups are unenclosed. Third, there are reaves. These are stony linear banks that appear to divide up large zones of upland into coaxial strips in an apparently organised scheme.

The hut circles and settlements, enclosures and reaves are closely associated and clearly represent single elements of a complex and dynamic period of landscape development. At the same time, ceremonial monuments and round cairns continued to have an important role.

Hut circles

Note: In the following discussion the term 'hut circle' is used in preference to 'round house' when referring to the archaeological remains, the latter term being more appropriate to describe what hut circles once represented rather than what survives. Hut circle is the traditional term favoured by former Dartmoor writers and will be familiar to all who use Ordnance Survey maps of the area. Also, there is no certainty that all hut circles were used as houses.

Collectively, the hut circles are Dartmoor's superlative prehistoric asset (Fig 3.1). Stone hut circles are common elsewhere in Britain, especially in uplands like Bodmin Moor or the Cheviots, but nowhere else can the remains of *c* 3,500-year-old buildings be seen in such

abundance and in such an excellent state of preservation than on Dartmoor. According to Butler (1997, 141) there are 4,000 surviving examples. The huts are individually interesting, and show a large variety of types, sizes, construction techniques and landscape associations.

Unlike barrows, which had been a target for the curious since medieval times, hut circles remained largely undisturbed until comparatively recently; but as archaeology developed in the 19th century, inevitably,

Fig 3.1
Stone hut circles on Dartmoor: (top) Merrivale (NMR DP 055108); (lower) Wigford Down (NMR DP099178) (© English Heritage. NMR).

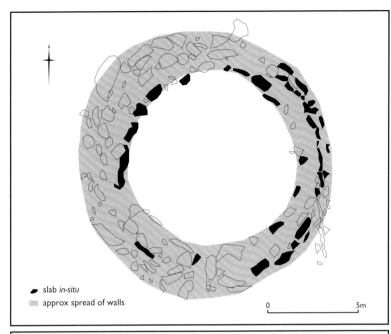

slab *in-situ*

approx spread of walls

0   5m

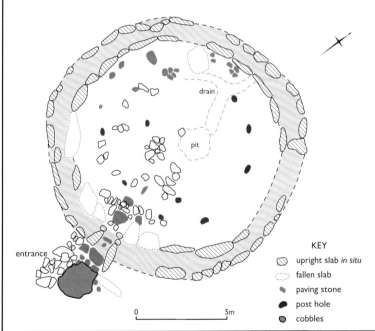

drain

pit

entrance

0   5m

KEY

upright slab *in situ*

fallen slab

paving stone

post hole

cobbles

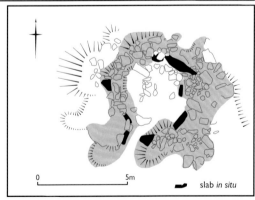

0   5m

slab *in situ*

excavations of Dartmoor's hut circles began. The Dartmoor Exploration Committee (DEC) undertook the majority of these excavations: between 1893 and 1906 more than 200 individual huts were excavated (*see* chapter 1). The work concentrated on many of the larger settlements where, in some cases, every hut was dug, including Grimspound, Watern Oke, Langston and Broadun. The quality of excavation varied, but, considering the scale of this work, on the whole the results were far short of what might have been produced in more expert hands, and the full potential of the many excavated sites was lost. Nevertheless, substantial information was retrieved from the numerous finds, including stone tools, domestic equipment, for example querns for grinding grain, and pottery, although not abundant.

Aileen Fox undertook a mid-20th century excavation campaign. She excavated Round Pound near Kestor in 1951–2 (A Fox 1954), followed by a rescue dig on Dean Moor in advance of the creation of the Avon Reservoir in 1954–6 (A Fox 1957). These were the first major excavations on Dartmoor using what we would today recognise as 'modern' techniques, using adequate recording methods and post-excavation analysis. More work followed in the 1970s on Shaugh Moor, where Geoffrey Wainwright directed excavations, which included an entire enclosure containing five hut circles in an area earmarked for clay waste tipping (Wainwright and Smith 1980). Andrew Fleming undertook research excavations on Holne Moor (Fleming 2008, 92–118), which focussed on the relationship of hut circles with the parallel reaves, and at Shapley Common, Alex Gibson revealed the potential for these sites being occupied much later than previously suspected (Gibson 1992, 119–46).

Hut circles consist of ruined stone walls, constructed in a circular plan, which supported the lower edge of a timber roof. The roof would have comprised wooden poles fixed to form a cone and supported on a ring of uprights poles set back from the centre. Smaller timber cross-members, interwoven withies and a covering of whatever vegetation was available to form a thatch would have completed the structure.

Hut circles are distributed widely over Dartmoor. Although they are less common in some parts of the moor, they are absent only in the very highest uplands. Other hut circles also survive around the moorland edge.

For example, at Hammerslake near Lustleigh a group of particularly large, robustly built huts survives on the wooded eastern slopes of Lustleigh Cleave at c 250m above sea level.

Although excavation exposes the walls of these sites in fine detail, the structures can often be appreciated by simply examining some of the better surviving examples as they lie in the field. The huts survive as distinct circles of stone, partially covered by turf. They often have clear interiors levelled into the slope, as few were built on perfectly level ground. The internal diameters vary dramatically between 2–3m and up to 14m (in the case of one unusually large hut near Sharp Tor). Hut circle walls have mostly tumbled to form stony turf-covered banks or rings of earthfast slabs, but individual stones often remain *in situ*, revealing construction details.

The hut builders used four basic construction methods for the walls:

1 A double stone ring of edge-set upright slabs placed to form concentric rings c 1m apart, providing vertical, flat interior and exterior wall faces. The space between the rings was filled with smaller stones and perhaps soil. Particularly fine examples can be seen on the south-east slopes of Vag Hill, Merrivale (Fig 3.2) and at Throwleigh Common.

2 Often there is only a single stone ring, where it is likely that no outer face existed, being substituted by a coursed wall or by a thick stony bank to serve the same purpose as an outer stone ring. This construction method is clear on one of the Grimspound huts, excavated by the DEC in 1894 (Figs 1.5 and 3.2).

3 Some huts have fully coursed walls, where stones were carefully laid one upon the other to form a dry-stone structure. This technique is less easy to observe on undisturbed huts, but was particularly clear at an excavated example on Holne Moor (Fleming 1988, fig 44).

4 A fourth method, employed on the excavated examples at Shaugh Moor (Figs 3.3 and 3.4), comprises interior and exterior coursed facings with a random stone fill. It is possible that many hut circles of this last type survive, but in their current state have the appearance of random circles of turf-covered rubble.

Some earlier writers surmised that the various constructional techniques represent chronological advancement in building method, making it possible to differentiate between early and late examples. But any number of other factors may have been more influential in this, not least that the chosen building style was to some extent governed by the stone available locally. Most hut circles survive within the granite zone, where there is a choice of large flat slabs, but on western Dartmoor, around Whittor, there is less choice, hence the apparent random nature of hut circle construction in this district. Here, smaller pieces make up the fabric of the walls. It also is likely that certain huts, usually the smaller, poorly constructed, unenclosed examples, were intended for less enduring purposes, perhaps as seasonal dwellings for graziers visiting at only certain times of year, rather like 'sheilings' in the Scottish highlands. Conversely, the larger, robustly built huts were probably intended for longer periods of occupation or use.

All hut circles had a single entrance, formed by an opening in the wall (Fig 3.5). These are frequently still discernable as gaps in the stony banks and upright stone door jambs often survive *in situ* or leaning on one or both sides of the opening, as at Merrivale. Most surviving entrances open towards the south-east, but this is not universal. It seems likely that such positioning represents the optimum to avoid the excesses of the upland weather, or perhaps

Fig 3.2 (opposite)
Plans of hut circles. The Merrivale hut (top), has in situ slabs surviving from the inner and outer wall linings (from an EH aerial photogrammetric survey); Round Pound hut circle at Kestor (centre), based on Fox's excavation drawing, is of similar construction with inner and outer slabs in situ. The post holes (red) represent the positions of upright posts that supported the conical roof (© The Devonshire Association, with permission). The smaller hut at Grimspound (bottom), which was excavated in 1894 by the DEC, is here represented by a modern earthwork plan.

Fig 3.3
A hut circle exposed during excavation at Shaugh Moor, showing the walls to have been constructed from small pieces of stone, laid in a dry-stone fashion (© Plymouth City Museum and Art Gallery).

Fig. 3.4
View of the enclosure at Shaugh Moor, excavated in the 1970s, showing the enclosure wall and five huts circles fully exposed (© Plymouth City Museum and Art Gallery).

Further examples possibly remain unrecognised, or perhaps timber or wattle structures served this purpose at other hut circles.

Hut circles were frequently refashioned and reused after their initial occupation. The excavation on Holne Moor revealed that a well-built, though smaller (2.5m) hut circle, had been constructed within a much larger one (Fleming 2008, 102). Other examples are in a group of huts near Yestor Brook on Walkhampton Common. Excavations at Shaugh Moor revealed a number of occupational phases in which existing walls were thickened (Wainwright and Smith1980); and at Shapley Common the stone buildings were found to have had timber precursors (Gibson 1992).

Artefacts and dating

The acidic soil on Dartmoor effaces quickly any organic material deposited in hut circles, so the only artefacts to survive are of stone, and occasional pottery and charcoal. Nevertheless, these materials provide much insight into the lives of the hut dwellers. Food was sometimes cooked in pits, on heated river cobbles, or by boiling it in water heated by such stones or 'pot

to capture the maximum amount of sunlight inside the hut circle. A number of possible social reasons have also been suggested to explain the other variants, including privacy and social interaction (Gerrard 1997, 39). Some excavated hut circles at Grimspound and Shaugh Moor had an L-shaped stone porch or weather wall extending at 90° from the entrance, offering even greater protection from wind and rain, or perhaps greater privacy.

boilers' placed in ceramic pots. Fragments of cooking pots and many pot boilers have been recovered from hut circles. At Dean Moor, quern stones were found, used for grinding cereals into flour, together with whetstones for sharpening metal blades. Numerous flint and chert tools, including scrapers for preparing animal skins, and flake blades, used for butchery, have also been retrieved.

Altogether, our knowledge of hut circle construction and of some of the occupants' domestic activities has increased, but the poor survival of organic material has excluded enough radiocarbon dates to provide an accurate chronology. However, some dates were retrieved from the Shaugh Moor and Shapley Common excavations and when all the dating evidence is stacked up, including that from pottery, it becomes clear that the stone hut circle format was in use from the early 2nd to late 1st millennia BC. The radiocarbon dates from Shaugh Moor place the earliest occupation of the hut circles at between *c* 1800 and *c* 1600 BC, but interestingly they also demonstrate that each hut was occupied, either continuously or intermittently, for several centuries, and that the overall structural sequence for the settlement was up to 1,000 years. The site was only finally abandoned during the Early Iron Age. For other hut circles, such as those excavated by the Dartmoor Exploration Committee (DEC) in the 1890s, the only dates are derived from the pottery.

Some of the first ceramic fragments retrieved by the DEC, found at Yestor Bottom and at Raddick Hill, were of a type now known as the

early Trevisker series, named after an archaeological site in Cornwall from where it was first classified. This is a form of domestic pottery found widely in south-west England, for which extensive radiocarbon dates from excavated Cornish sites provide a secure date range commencing in the middle and later 2nd millennium BC. An example from Raddick Hill (Fig 3.6) has been restored and is now on display in Plymouth City Museum. Only one sherd of Trevisker was retrieved from the Shaugh Moor enclosure excavation in the 1970s, although sherds of a type of domestic pottery known as a biconical urn were found, and a range of dates was also retrieved from radiocarbon samples. Together this material suggests a period of occupation at this site between 1800 BC and 800 BC (Wainwright and Smith 1980, 119). Most recently, excavations of a hut circle in 2009 at Bellever provided Trevisker pottery with a date range between 1500 BC and 1150 BC (Quinnell 2009) and radiocarbon dates from charcoal inferring that the building was occupied from 1610 BC to 1400 BC, then abandoned by 1420–1260 BC (Fyfe and Head 2009).

Generally, from the excavated evidence it is safe only to say that Dartmoor's first hut circles date from about the early to mid-2nd millennium BC, but that there is a strong possibility that unexcavated sites may prove to have earlier origins. The possibility that timber houses were used long before building with stone must also not be overlooked. Clues that round houses were still being built, or at least maintained and occupied, in the later prehistoric period come from Kestor. Here, in the 1950s, Aileen Fox found fragments of a type of pottery known to be of late Bronze Age–Early Iron Age date (A Fox 1954). At Shapley Common, radiocarbon dates suggest that a stone house, occupied in about the 1st and 2nd century BC, had a timber precursor that was in use probably only a couple of centuries earlier (Gibson 1992).

At the time of writing, results of research excavations of a hut circle at Teigncombe are awaited. Preliminary results suggest that pottery contemporary with the use of the hut circle was Trevisker Ware, with some Iron Age material in overlying contexts (H Quinnell pers com).

Until more evidence of this type becomes available, statements about the earliest occupation and period of occupation of round houses on Dartmoor cannot be straightforward.

Fig 3.5 (opposite, bottom) A stone hut circle near Trowlesworthy Warren. Note the upright, in situ door jambs on the far side of the hut (NMR DP099143; © English Heritage. NMR).

Fig 3.6 An urn of Trevisker style, retrieved during an excavation of a hut circle on Raddick Hill in 1896, now housed in Plymouth City Museum. The vessel stands to more than 300mm high (NMR DP099393; © English Heritage. NMR).

Settlements

Fig 3.7
Earthwork plan of
Grimspound, an enclosed hut
settlement. EH 1:500 survey.

Although a few Dartmoor hut circles are isolated examples, the vast majority have associations with others in groups or settlements. Such settlements comprise three or four huts up to large villages of as many as 76, as at Standon, and 90, as at Watern Oke (*see* Fig 3.14). Most settlements also have some association with enclosures, being either fully enclosed, partly enclosed (ie with some huts within an enclosure and some outside, or with interconnecting plots), or in neighbourhood groups associated with reaves (*see below*).

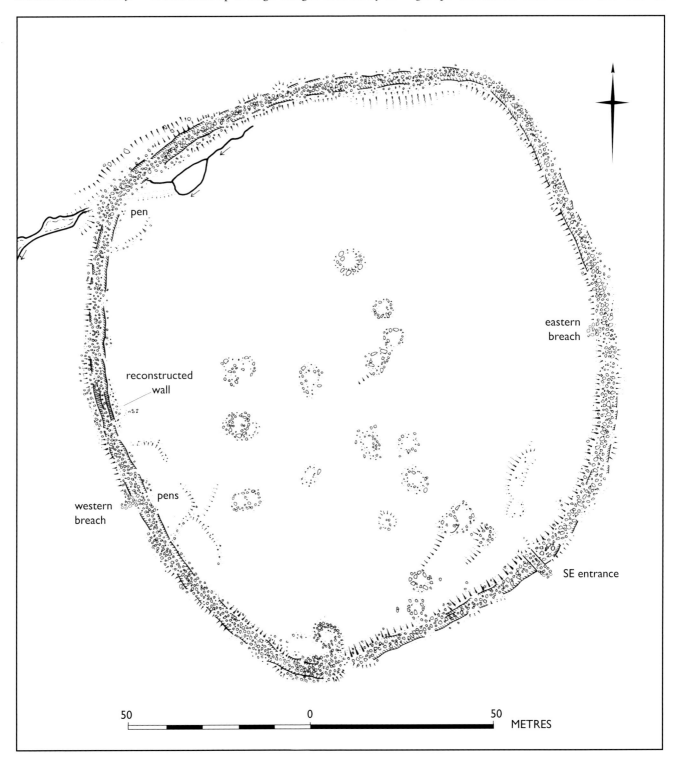

pen

eastern breach

reconstructed wall

pens

western breach

SE entrance

50 0 50 METRES

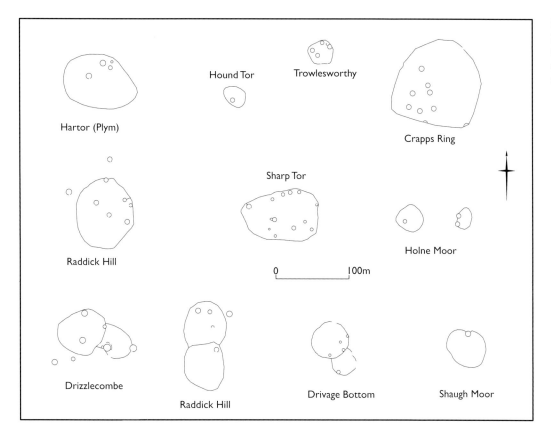

Fig 3.8
Thumbnail plans of single
enclosed settlements (top);
simple aggregated, double
enclosed settlements (bottom).

There are a few settlements, however, where no features survive other than the hut circles, such as near Deadlake in the Walkham Valley and the Dart below Rough Tor. There is the possibility that timber fences were used, but to what extent is unknown. All of these categories offer intriguing implications in terms of settlement growth, development and duration, if, as is quite obvious, the majority of settlements were an evolutionary product of developing social groups.

More generally, these settlements collectively pose similarly profound questions regarding the occupation, management and tenure of the uplands in the 2nd millennium BC.

Enclosed settlements

Grimspound (Fig 3.7), apart from being Dartmoor's most known and visited prehistoric settlement, is a good example of a single-enclosure settlement or 'pound' where 24 hut circles were impounded by a substantial sub-circular, 1.45ha enclosure wall. It is possible that some or all of the hut circles pre-date the enclosure; this was the case at Shaugh Moor, a much smaller example, where excavation revealed that structures had existed for 100 years or more before the enclosure was added

(Wainwright and Smith 1980, 110). A second small example at Shaugh Moor shows that an existing single hut circle was incorporated into the wall of an enclosure added later (Fig 3.8).

The walls of the enclosure at Grimspound are not typical, being of massive proportions between 2.5m and 3.5m thick with stone facings inside and out and a rubble infill (Pattison and Fletcher 1994). Only a few Dartmoor enclosures are this robust; most are of much slighter construction and usually contain fewer hut circles, such as the small groups in the Avon Valley near Huntingdon (*see* Fig 3.20) and in the Plym Valley near Hartor (Fig 3.8). Typically the enclosure walls survive as low, turf-covered stony banks of 1–2m wide, rarely standing to more than 0.5m high, and often partly disguised by covering vegetation. But occasionally they incorporate large upright or edge-set boulders and large tumbled pieces of stone, providing clear, well-defined remains (Fig 3.9).

Grimspound has a 2m wide entrance on the south-east segment of the enclosing wall, which was fully exposed and reconstructed by the DEC in 1894, when, possibly, the proportions became exaggerated. The excavations at Shaugh Moor (*see* Fig 3.4)

Fig 3.9
Ground photo of
typical upstanding
prehistoric
enclosure wall –
this example at
Trowlesworthy
(NMR DP099158;
© English
Heritage. NMR).

revealed that the enclosure did not have an entrance but possibly just a simple stile, suitable for the passage of humans rather than of animals. Entrances, with a few exceptions, are not easily identified in enclosure walls, and it seems likely, given the lack of access for animals, that the purpose of at least some enclosures was to keep animals, both wild and domesticated, away from the living space.

Aggregated enclosure groups

Many settlements, once enclosed, continued to evolve through the addition of more enclosures, often also containing stone hut circles, though sometimes not. The 'founder' enclosure acted as a nucleus from which a progression of houses and boundaries developed as piecemeal additions, representing growth of a community and its changing spatial needs. Often the growth developed to no more than a second enclosure, as at Ryders Rings (*see* Figs 3.12 and 3.13), Raddick Hill or Drizzlecombe (*see* Fig 3.8), but frequently expansion continued, forming spread clusters of amorphous enclosures, each tacked onto the walls of, and filling spaces between, the existing group (Fig 3.10). In some cases two or more nuclei expanded to meld into a single cluster, as at Roundy (Fig 3.11), where three separate free-standing enclosures (a–c) were assimilated into the expansion, though they need not have had contemporary origins. At Legis Tor, at least ten phases can be recognised on even a basic survey plan (Fig 3.11). This settlement may

Fig 3.10
Aerial view of aggregated settlements near Avon Dam (NMR 24579/034; ©
English Heritage. NMR).

Fig 3.11
Thumbnail plans of
complex aggregated
enclosed settlements.

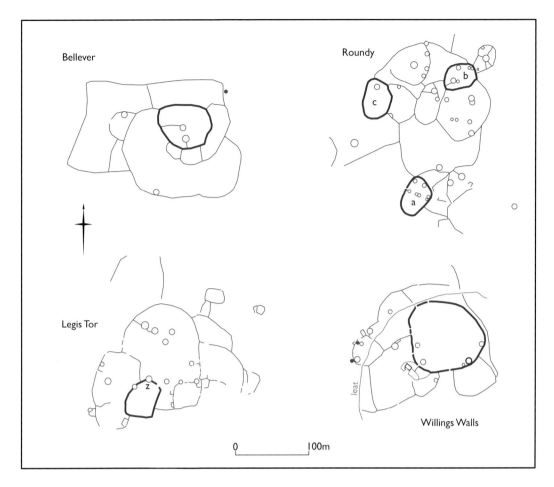

have originated as a group of huts, or possibly
even one hut (z), onto which the first enclosure
of 0.17ha was attached. Further enclosures
were added, including one large one of 1.04ha;
some internal partitioning also created
additional cells. Perhaps the clearest example
is on the northern slope of Bellever Tor (Fig

3.11), where the founder enclosure sits at the
centre of at least nine separate elements of
outward expansion.

There is a striking variation between the
robustness and scale of some enclosure walls, as
noted at Grimspound, but at Ryders Rings,
Shaugh Moor (see Fig 3.23) and Crapps Ring

Fig 3.13 (opposite)
Earthwork plan of Ryder's
Rings near Avon Dam, an
aggregated settlement of
two enclosures (EH 1:500
survey).

(*see* Fig 3.8) similarly large-proportioned walls are present, leading early writers to refer to them as fortifications or ramparts. Possibly these sites were occupied longer than others, and were improved more frequently, but an explanation of their strong enclosures is not obvious, other than perhaps to impress onlookers from other communities by their strength.

Ryders Rings (Figs 3.12 and 3.13) is a complex and very different enclosed settlement to most. It has robust walls, of a similar scale to those at Grimspound, and it is likely that the earlier enclosure (a) was built around several pre-existing huts. This is evident by the shape of the north wall, which deviated to join two of the huts near an entrance. It is also unusual because the eastern wall of the primary enclosure (a) was modified into a series of pens, after the second enclosure (b) was added. These pens are unusual too – few other settlements have them – and there are a further 11 pens, and vestiges of others, attached to the interior of the secondary enclosure (b). They seem a too large to have been roofed, so it is probable they were for penning livestock.

Partitioned settlements

Some hut settlements are unenclosed, but have connecting walls between individual huts. This is a different approach to the arrangement of space around the houses, and shows no apparent need for an outer enclosure. Standon Hill (Fig 3.14), a settlement on the western side of Dartmoor above the Tavy Valley, and one of the largest hut settlements, has such an arrangement. Although it is unlikely that all the hut circles belong to the founding group, it is clear in all cases that the adjoining walls are a secondary feature, built between existing hut circles. There is also the possibility that timber or wattle fences were used where no stone wall survives, explaining, perhaps, why a series of huts to the south appear isolated with no connecting walls.

Watern Oke, a similarly large settlement spread along a south-west slope of the upper Tavy, has fewer dividing walls between the closely grouped houses. Why these settlements evolved in this different way is uncertain, but it is notable that the majority of the large examples of this type are located on the north-western side of the moor, an area conspicuously lacking coaxial reaves, which dominate the 2nd millennium landscape on the eastern side.

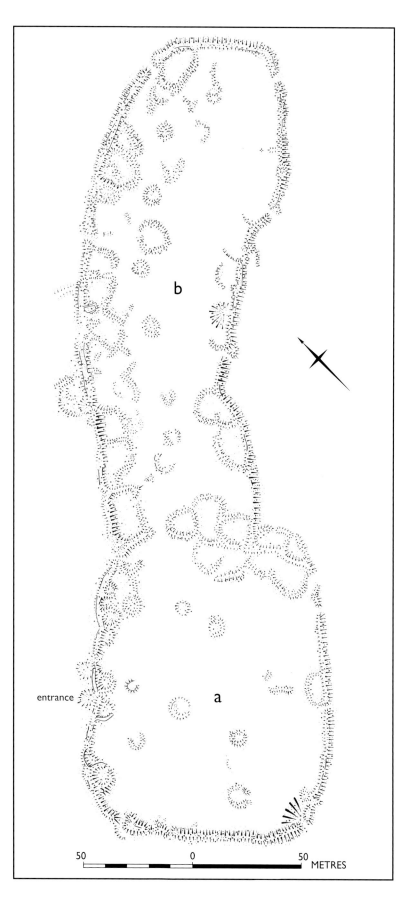

Fig 3.14
Thumbnail plans of open
(ie unenclosed) settlements.

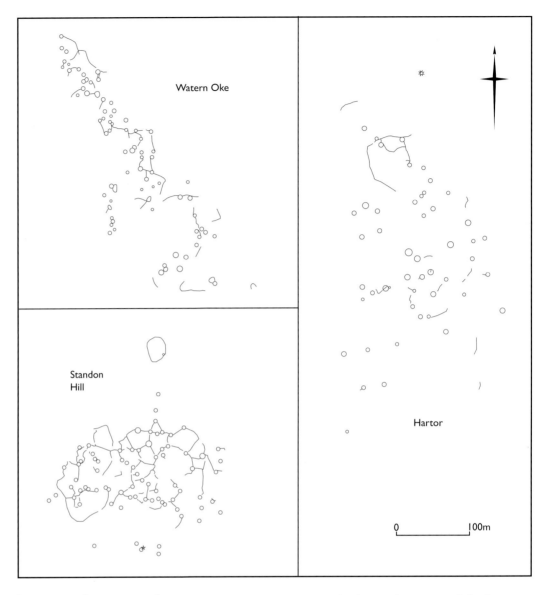

Reaves and reave settlements

In contrast to the amorphous forms and apparent piecemeal development of the settlements, the land divisions, known on Dartmoor as 'reaves', appear orderly and planned. Reave is a local term that describes linear earth and stone banks, or ruined former walls, that transect areas of the moor. Reaves follow straight and mostly undeviating alignments, often at odds with the topography. Collectively they form coaxial systems made up of blocks of parallel reaves following a common axis (Fig 3.15). In some places reaves bind the various threads of the prehistoric landscape, although at other places they appear to stand alone and separate from the prevailing evidence of settlement and enclosure.

Curiously, despite being one of the foremost elements of Dartmoor's prehistoric landscape, and forming striking field remains that are observable even to a beginner in field archaeology, the 2nd millennium date of the reaves has only been recognised since the 1960s. Indeed, the story of the discovery of their date itself adds a fascinating dimension to them, as told in detail by Andrew Fleming (Fleming 1988).

Several early 19th-century antiquaries, including Northmore and Mason, noted the reaves and had begun to understand their implications; but by 1830, with the publication of Samuel Rowe's seminal paper on Dartmoor's antiquities, the prevailing theory was that the reaves were trackways or tracklines rather than walls, boundaries or land divisions.

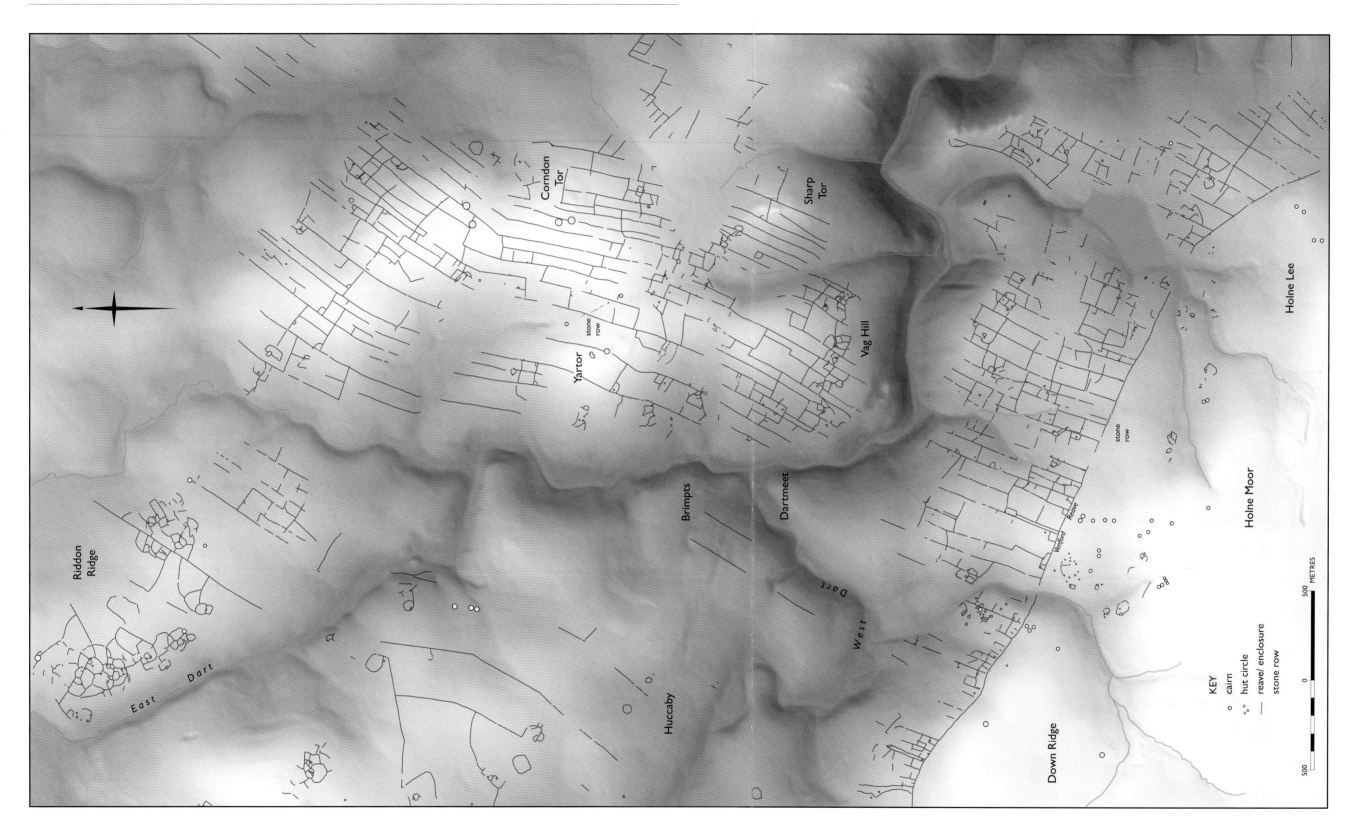

Fig 3.15
Digital terrain model showing the valleys of the East and West Dart, overlain with survey data
from the Dartmeet and Holne Moor parallel reave system, including prehistoric settlement, coaxial
reaves and cairns (height data licensed to English Heritage for PGA through Next Perspectives™).

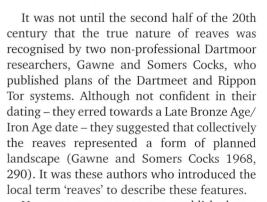

Fig 3.16
Aerial view of Sharpitor
showing the Walkhampton
Common Reave deviating
slightly as its course
traverses the outcrop of the
tor. A second reave branches
to the south-east (left) from
the outcrop. On the north
slope of the tor there is a
small open settlement and
an enclosure (NMR
24901/011; © English
Heritage. NMR).

In 1889 Robert Burnard, later to become a prominent member of the DEC, even went as far as to suggest that one particularly well-defined reave, which runs approximately east–west across the moor near Postbridge, was part of a route extending from Exeter to Tavistock and Cornwall beyond. He concluded that this route, then known as the Great Central Trackway, represented a portion of the Fosse Way (Burnard 1889, 431–6). This idea soon became the conventional wisdom to the extent that 'Ancient Trackway' was the term used to describe reaves on Ordnance Survey maps as recently as the 1960s, although on modern maps they are accompanied by the descriptor 'Boundary Work'.

It was not until the second half of the 20th century that the true nature of reaves was recognised by two non-professional Dartmoor researchers, Gawne and Somers Cocks, who published plans of the Dartmeet and Rippon Tor systems. Although not confident in their dating – they erred towards a Late Bronze Age/Iron Age date – they suggested that collectively the reaves represented a form of planned landscape (Gawne and Somers Cocks 1968, 290). It was these authors who introduced the local term 'reaves' to describe these features.

However, reaves were not established as a formal component of the Dartmoor 2nd millennium BC story until a full-blown research project took place. In the 1970s and 1980s Andrew Fleming led a university team to study reaves and to establish their date, extent and importance. It is thanks to Fleming's publications that we have not only a grasp of their significance and implications, but also have a nomenclature with which to discuss them (Fleming 1978, 1983, 1988, 2008).

The reaves are similar in construction to the enclosure walls surviving as turf-covered stony banks. Some are of subtle appearance, and when covered with peat and vegetation survive in profile only as slight rises in the ground, with the occasional stone protruding. Others however, have the appearance of ruined walls, visible for great distances across the moor. The Great Western and Walkhampton Common reaves, for example, both run across Sharpitor (Fig 3.16) and can be seen easily when driving from Princetown to Yelverton in a car. Originally they may have formed the bases of hedge banks, as animal barriers, but it is unlikely that any were built up to become high walls.

As boundaries, reaves offer a great contrast to other prehistoric enclosures and fields. Collectively it is their regular and apparently planned layout that sets them apart. Individual reaves are for the most part straight: they traverse the landscape, sometimes over considerable distances, often showing little regard for the topography or the usefulness of the land, running across the contours of hills, transecting deep river valleys and ascending to the summits of hills and tors, often over difficult, rocky terrain. Where arranged into blocks or systems, they run in parallel, following a common axis – hence Fleming's term 'coaxial' – and the reaves within a coaxial system can be seen to be conforming to a single

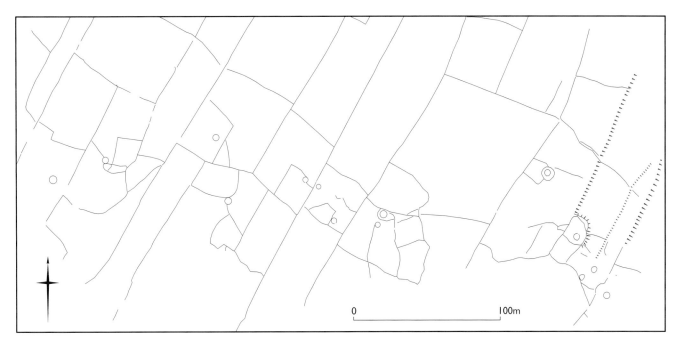

Fig 3.17 (above)
Simplified plan showing reave settlements on south-facing Vag Hill, part of the Dartmeet reave system. Some of the enclosure walls were refurbished in the post-medieval period when the area was used as a rabbit warren. Other post-medieval features have been omitted for clarity.

Fig 3.18
Aerial view of the Holne Moor reave system near Hangman's Pit, looking south. The coaxial reaves can be seen running from bottom left to top right, halting at the terminal reave that runs at 90° to it. Also visible in the foreground is a series of medieval and post-medieval leat channels, including Wheal Emma, which is traversed by the road, and disused tinworks (NMR 24102/013; © English Heritage. NMR).

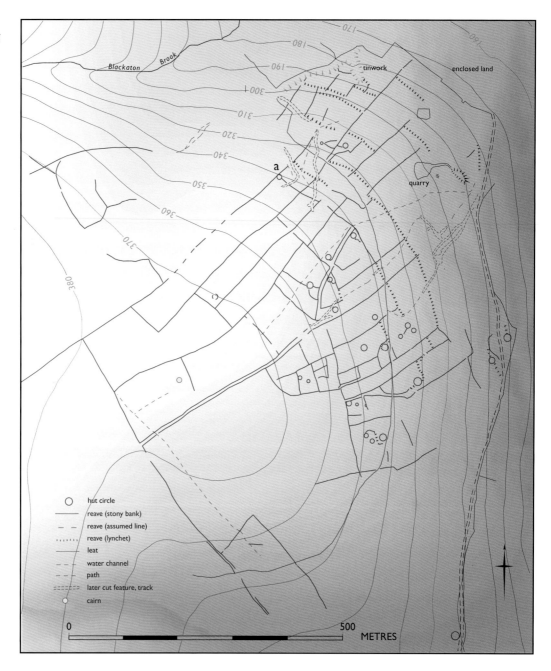

Fig 3.19
Topographical map showing the Throwleigh Common parallel reave system and hut settlement (height data licensed to English Heritage for PGA through Next Perspectives™).

○ hut circle
—— reave (stony bank)
- - reave (assumed line)
······ reave (lynchet)
——| leat
- – water channel
- – path
======= later cut feature, track
○ cairn

0   500
                     METRES

axis (Figs 3.17–3.19). These strips are often partitioned by shorter reaves set at 90°, referred to as transverse reaves. Arrays of coaxial reaves will, in some examples, be halted at a common transect where meeting a 'terminal' reave, which runs at right angles to the system. The Venford Reave on Holne Moor is a prime example (*see* Fig 3.15).

Fleming considered these terminal reaves to be boundaries between the areas defined by reave systems on one side and the undivided moorland, which he believed was used as an area of pasture, on the other. Although the

spaces created between individual coaxial reaves could, in some cases, be referred to as 'improved' land, free of stone, others were not, because their surfaces were left uncleared. It is debatable therefore whether much of this ground contained crops and it is more likely to represent a controlled grazing regime, or perhaps a system of tenure. Cultivation probably took place in the smaller plots in the vicinity of the reave settlements (*see below*).

Beyond the pasture land defined by the terminal reaves, in some parts of the moor an additional class of reave can be identified, apparently delineating the boundary between pastures associated with the reave systems and an area of the high moors. These Fleming termed 'contour' and 'watershed' reaves, because of their apparent adherence to the prevailing form of the terrain over which they run. He suggested that the central zones of the moor, which they defined, offered further delineation of areas of summer pasture. The Great Western Reave, so named by Andrew Fleming, is perhaps the best example, running across Walkhampton Common near Leeden Tor. Although major sections of the reave are missing on the ground, this reave may have been continuous, between this point and Whittor, traversing Merrivale and Roos Tor, a distance of over 10km (Fleming 2008, 55–67). However, the contour reaves are not a universal component of the reaves systems and it is possible that those that do exist represent incomplete schemes, as is suggested by their missing elements.

The zones beyond the terminal reaves at places like Holne Moor (*see* Figs 3.15 and 3.18) and Shaugh Moor frequently contain the more piecemeal type enclosures, settlements and hut circles described above, and whose apparent organic appearance seems to have little in common with the orderly design of the reaves. But there are also many huts and settlements within, and specifically associated with, the coaxial systems, referred to here as reave settlements. The huts of the reave settlements are spatially more dispersed than some of the other types of hut groups – compared with the dense arrangement on Standon for example (*see* Fig 3.14); but although not quite as intimately located, what Fleming termed 'neighbourhood groups' can be recognised, where hut circles appear concentrated into discrete zones within a reave system. At Throwleigh Common (*see* Fig 3.19), a small compact reave system on the north-east fringe of the upland, 24 hut circles are dispersed among the compartments of the system. Some stand alone, away from any of the reaves, whereas others are touching the reaves. Several have short ruined walls or banks that extend from the side of the hut circle back to the nearest reave, creating small enclosures abutting the reave. One hut (a on Fig 3.19) is built into the junction of two reaves.

In other places the hut circles are more integrated with the reaves, where additional small walls have been incorporated into the system to provide them with a courtledge, or perhaps cultivable plots. On Holne Moor and Dartmeet, many of the houses have adjoining walls extending in two directions linking them to the nearby reaves and creating smaller enclosures (*see* Figs 3.15 and 3.17). The hut circles associated with reaves are often among the larger examples. This is certainly the case at Kestor, Throwleigh Common, Corndon, Wigford Down (*see* Fig 3.1) and at Holne Moor where there are many massive huts.

Fleming identified numerous individual 'coaxial systems' and made two crucial observations about them: first, confirming Gawne and Somers Cock's research, that each system appears to be designed, following an overall scheme that dictated orientation and extent; second, that each system is a self-contained and separate entity. These observations pose the obvious question that if all the various systems were broadly contemporary, does this individuality mean that each was created by a separate group of people? Having raised these issues Fleming went on to discuss more profound anthropological questions: Were these groups in conflict, competing for space? Or was there a more amicable arrangement, and if so, was there some sort of hierarchy or central authority able to organise the scheme on such a large scale?

Since this initial research was published there has been much reassessment. In a re-examination of the origin of reaves, Johnston (2005, 1–21) has suggested that the systems are not as planned as they at first appear, and that their origins lie within artificial alignments that already existed in the landscape, such as trackways or areas of clearance. For example, several excavated reaves have revealed the existence of precursors as ditches or as timber fences. Following the construction of one linear reave, others could have been added in a piecemeal manner, but following the axis already laid down, so rejecting the concept of planning, particularly in terms of a moor-wide scheme.

Whichever interpretation one favours, there is still a great deal that we do not know about the reaves. Most of the problem stems, once again, from our lack of dating for prehistoric Dartmoor. Fleming believed that the reaves have origins *c* 1700 BC, based on the evidence from his excavation on Holne Moor, but there is insufficient data on the pace of the growth of reave systems and over how long a period they developed. There is also no real evidence on

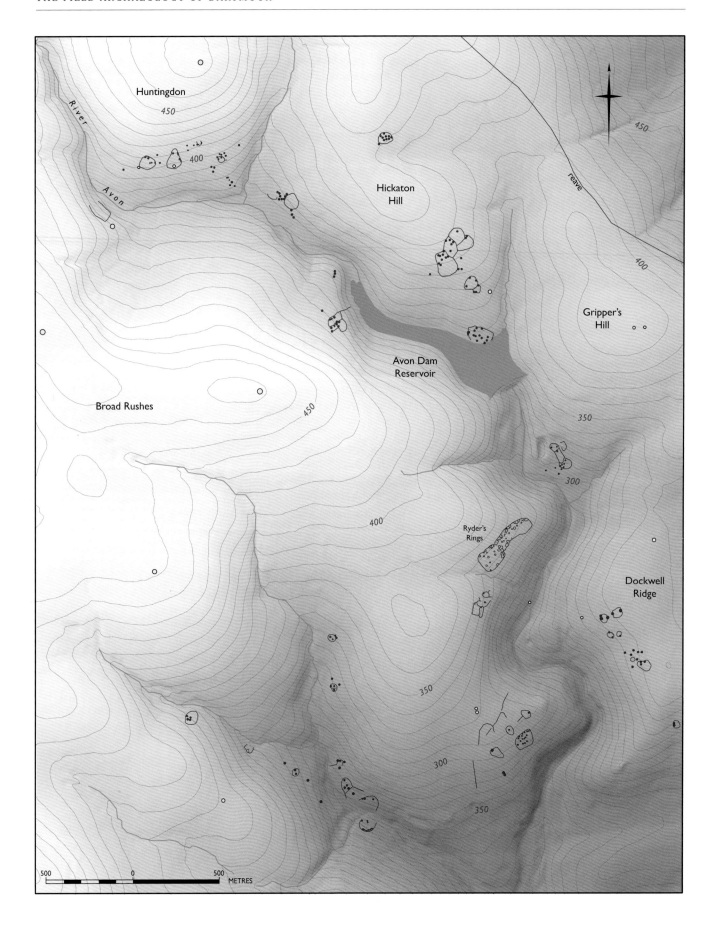

Huntingdon

450

River

400

Avon

Hickaton
Hill

450

reave

450

400

Gripper's
Hill

Avon Dam
Reservoir

Broad Rushes

450

350

300

400

Ryder's
Rings

Dockwell
Ridge

350

350

300

350

500   0   500   METRES

whether the majority of the hut circles in the reave settlements pre-existed the reaves or were added to them. In one or two examples it was the former, as at the Throwleigh hut circle built into a T junction, but for most sites the relationships between the huts and the reaves are ambiguous.

A likely scenario could be that houses and reaves were two components of a single process: some of the houses predated the reaves in their area and were incorporated as the reaves were constructed, whereas others were added as the community and its infrastructure developed. The part played by timber in the layouts of these systems must not be underestimated. Wooden fences certainly preceded the stone reaves in places and the potential for many small sections of hitherto archaeologically undetected wooden fencing, augmenting the reaves, is also considerable.

One of the most significant issues surrounding the reaves is their relationship with other types of 2nd millennium settlement: aggregate, open and enclosed. Their totally different character could imply the existence of communities with a different economic strategy, social order or lifestyle to the occupants of settlements associated with reave systems; or possibly they

represent chronologically separate episodes of activity within discrete areas, or perhaps more widely. It is conceivable that settlements isolated from the major reave systems were those of pastoralists – graziers who maintained flocks sufficient for their needs within the locale of their settlement. For example, the Avon Valley (Fig 3.20) is an almost reave-free zone, but contains many enclosed and aggregate settlements along its slopes, such as Ryders Rings (*see* Figs 3.12 and 3.13). Wainwright and Smith (1980) even considered that the excavated Shaugh Moor enclosure was occupied seasonally rather than permanently. In other areas, however, such as Riddon Ridge (Fig 3.21), the aggregate system clearly had a more interesting and intimate relationship with reaves, where some appear to have evolved independently of the reaves to be incorporated later, while others were attached to the reaves at an early stage in their growth. At Holwell (Fig 3.22) a reave and a small elliptical enclosure represent early elements in the sequence, followed by the infill of small rectangular enclosures; but which phase the two hut circles represent is uncertain. Near by, at Emsworthy Rocks (Fig 3.22), an enclosed settlement of seven hut circles utilised

Fig 3.20 (opposite)
Prehistoric settlements in the Avon Valley: topographical map showing the river and its tributaries. Note there is only one reave on this part of Dartmoor, running south-west from Puper's Hill (source: EH survey plans and NMP Dartmoor Sheet SX 66 SE/ SX 66 NE; height data licensed to English Heritage for PGA through Next Perspectives™).

Fig 3.21
Plan showing prehistoric (red) enclosures, reaves and medieval (green) banks on Riddon Ridge. Hut 'a' began as an isolated hut circle, which was incorporated into a small enclosure. A second enclosure was added, followed by a curvilinear section of wall joining to the reave. Two further enclosures were then added. Hut 'b', also free-standing, formed the centre point for three small enclosures that surround it, which were later joined back to the reave to form additional enclosures. The primary enclosure associated with hut 'c' joined back to the reave in its first phase and subsequent additions followed the same scheme. A cross reave joining the enclosure corner at 'd' back to the fragmentary reave to the north-west – a later addition – demonstrates that elements of the coaxial system continued to be added after the imposition of attached aggregate enclosures. To the north-west a large system of huts and aggregated enclosures appear to be associated with only one short section of coaxial reave (e).

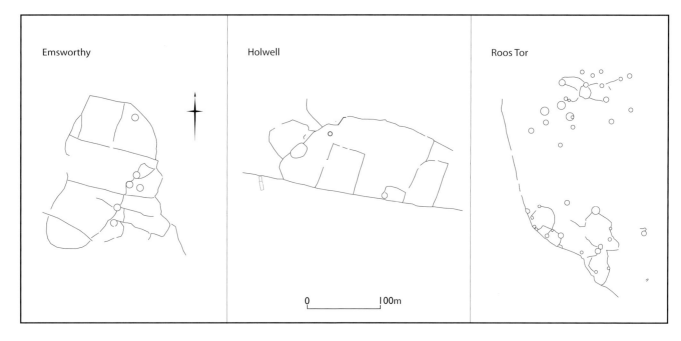

Emsworthy

Holwell

Roos Tor

0   100m

Fig 3.22
Thumbnail plans showing
settlements associated with
reaves at Emsworthy,
Holwell and Roos Tor. In
some cases the latter may
have been disused before
being incorporated into
the settlements.

sections of previously abandoned reaves, cutting east–west across the interior. At Roos Tor (Fig 3.22) a series of small, irregular enclosures appear to have been added to one side of the reave on the north but, interestingly, not on the south side. Not far from the site of the excavated enclosure on Shaugh Moor, is another more substantial example containing two hut circles (Fig 3.23). At first sight, the Shaugh Moor enclosure appears to have had reaves added to it, leading off in three directions. However, a slight linear earthwork that runs across part of the interior is likely to be a continuation of one of the reaves and

tends to suggest that this enclosure, in its surviving form, post-dates the building of the reaves, although they probably remained in use after it was built.

Finally, the upland of Dartmoor and its reaves should not be considered different to the hinterland, for there is good evidence that reaves systems once extended off the moor, and although in most such areas they have been superseded by the more piecemeal medieval enclosures, occasionally the patches of parallel reaves can be seen to have been incorporated into the later fields as at Kestor, Brent Fore Hill and Butterdon Down. Elsewhere in Devon,

Fig 3.23
Aerial view of the large
enclosed settlement at
Shaugh Moor. Ground
evidence suggests the
enclosure overlies an
earlier reave, although
other elements of the
reave system appear to
be later (© West Air).

isolated patches of prehistoric field systems, with a striking similarity of form to the reaves, survive at Dainton, Ogwell, Torbryan (Gallant *et al* 1985, 23–37) and Deckler's Cliff in the South Hams (Newman 2003). In fact, since Fleming originally brought reaves and the concept of prehistoric land divisions to the attention of the archaeological world in the 1980s, similar evidence has been recorded in many areas of Britain, particularly in southern England, but also Pembrokeshire and East Anglia (Fleming 2008; Yates 2006). These later discoveries demonstrate that although Dartmoor has by far the best preserved evidence, reaves should be seen as part of a much wider phenomenon and an integral component of life and the landscape in the Middle to Late Bronze Age and beyond in Britain.

Dartmoor in the 2nd millennium BC

Although there is a shortage of chronological detail from excavations, it seems almost certain from the field archaeology that Dartmoor was not a static landscape in which particular types of houses, settlements or forms of land use were favoured for a certain period of time, to be superseded by others. Neither is a single explanation appropriate for the whole of Dartmoor, because separate regions of the moor produce different evidence. A more accurate description of the 2nd-millennium BC Dartmoor would be of a landscape in transition – dynamic and continually evolving on a scale that would not be seen again until the medieval period nearly 1500 years later. One thread of continuity is the hut circles, as many generations of Dartmoor dwellers chose to build and live in round houses, as elsewhere in Britain; the hut circles at Shaugh Moor were over 1,500 years old when the excavated house on Shapley Common was occupied, so there is the potential for massive societal and demographic change in that period. Much of this change is not yet visible to us in the archaeological record, but would certainly have influenced the way people interacted with their landscape.

The evidence for a human presence at *c* 2000 BC is limited to the stone rows, round cairns and perhaps the stone circles. As yet, domestic sites are not known from that early, but we may speculate that timber buildings could have

marked the first phase of settlement, starting perhaps with scattered groups of huts. People began to build circular dwellings with stone foundations, probably not long after 2000 BC, although the earliest dated examples are approximately 1600 BC. House platforms, of the type found elsewhere in Britain such as the Cheviots, representing the remains of timber round houses, are extremely rare on Dartmoor. Those that exist, such as Borro Wood, are likely to be of Iron Age date. However, there is no reason why many of Dartmoor's stone huts did not have timber precursors – indeed Fleming's work has demonstrated this to be so. Some of these settlements might have only been used seasonally, as temporary bases for groups leading a transhumant existence, taking advantage of summer grazing for their livestock or exploiting a range of upland resources.

Other settlements certainly became permanently occupied. A diversity of enclosure options were developed by these communities, depending perhaps on their farming strategy, or possibly issues of security. Some remained partly open, as at Langstone (Fig 3.24), while others became completely enclosed by stone reinforced banks or walls, such as Ryders Rings (*see* Figs 3.12–13). Another group continued to expand into complex aggregated settlements like Legis Lake (*see* Fig 3.10). Of course there is also great potential that timber or wattle fences and enclosures also played a major role in the settlement construction, even though the excavated evidence is meagre. As yet, there is no way of knowing what triggered the decisions by individual groups to adopt the various layouts of these settlements.

In some parts of the moor, coaxial reave systems apparently formed a contrasting component within the settlement process, dividing up large tracts of land in association with different, separate hut groups. Collectively the reaves could represent agreement by a large organised group on issues such as territory,

Fig 3.24
Thumbnail plan of Langstone Moor, a settlement layout that includes open and enclosed elements.

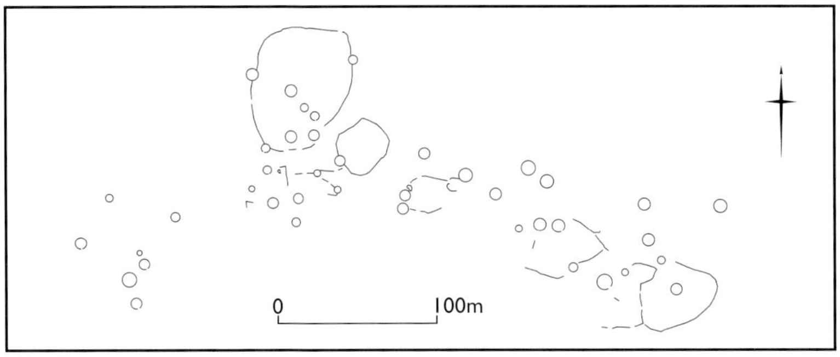

tenure, grazing rights and farming methods; or perhaps reaves were an imposition by certain groups over others at a time when land resources were at a premium. The argument by Fleming that each reave system was built as an entity is compelling, but the synchronous arrival of the Dartmoor systems is not yet proven.

It is difficult to understand what beliefs people held 4,000 years ago, but it is clear that a continued spiritual presence of the ancestors was important. Their remains were deposited in round cairns, often at eye-catching locations, and perhaps reinforced ethnic identity by enduring association within the place they lived. Although construction of round cairns began in the late Neolithic, dating from pottery and metalwork shows a continuous cycle of cairn building, refurbishment and maintenance extending into the middle of the 2nd millennium BC.

Some ceremonial monuments also continued to have a role. In many places the reave builders respected the stone rows of their predecessors and avoided crossing them. For example at Holne Moor (see Fig 3.15) and Hurston Ridge the reaves run parallel and close to the stone rows. Even where stone rows are crossed by reaves, the rows survive and were not robbed of stone, perhaps indicating that their meaning and value had not been lost to the reave builders. For example at Fernworthy (see Fig 2.14) the reave crosses the row at approximate right angles, and at Shoveldown the reave cuts a fairly harmless course between the rows. At other places, for example Merrivale (see Fig 2.43) and Drizzlecombe (see Fig 2.16), the presence of the ceremonial landscape must surely have influenced the choice of location for the settlements. Although perhaps not always fulfilling their original function, whatever that was, it seems that the stone rows were respected enough to be left alone as the landscape developed for other purposes. It would be interesting indeed to know if these earlier monuments had the same cultural resonance for the reave builders as they had for the stone row builders.

The introduction and use of metals, in particular bronze, was an important factor in 2nd millennium BC European society. On Dartmoor it was particularly relevant because tin, a constituent of bronze, was once found in abundance here. Some scholars (eg Price 1985, 129–38) regard it as self-evident that Dartmoor tin was exploited in the Bronze Age, and it seems likely. However, it does not necessarily follow that the settlement, agriculture and economy of Bronze Age Dartmoor was wholly to support the exploitation of tin; only that metallic resources probably played a role in the occupation and evolution of the landscape.

The chronological details for the end of this period of intense activity and apparent prosperity on the uplands are even less clear than those for its beginning. Fleming believed that the reaves had an active life of only 3–400 years before decline and abandonment (ie by c 1300 BC–1200 BC), accelerated perhaps by climatic change to a wetter environment (Fleming 2008, 141). Recent palaeoecological research to some extent supports this interpretation, showing that Dartmoor's climate was certainly wetter after 1395 BC (Amesbury et al 2008, 94). It is not certain from the current evidence when the more general retreat from Dartmoor occurred and how long it took. Indeed, there is also no reason to suspect that this 'retreat' was total, and it seems unlikely that the area was completely abandoned, regardless of climate or perceived marginality. Needless to say, any change would be gradual.

Although some meagre evidence has been retrieved, such as a radiocarbon date suggesting late occupation of one of the hut circles on Shaugh Moor in 600 bc [871 cal BC] (Wainwright and Smith 1980, 110), there is little sign of continuous human presence on Dartmoor into the 1st millennium BC. However, as Amesbury et al (2008) have noted, settlement abandonment does not necessarily equate with landscape abandonment; perhaps the evidence has simply been elusive.

4

The Iron Age and Romano-British periods, c 750 BC to AD 410

Following the more intense activities of the Early and Middle Bronze Age in the 2nd millennium BC, there has been, until recently, a puzzling scarcity of archaeological evidence for the occupation of the uplands of Dartmoor in the subsequent millennium, particularly during the later Bronze Age. It is not until the Iron Age, towards the end of the 1st millennium BC, that there is evidence for the next major developments within the Dartmoor landscape, and these occurred mainly around the peripheries of the moor with the arrival of the hillforts. However, recent archaeological discoveries are changing perceptions of the

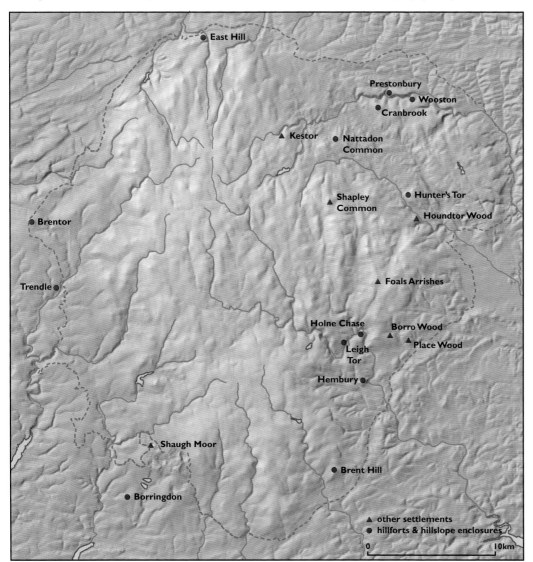

uplands in the Iron Age too, and although there remains little evidence for Late Bronze Age occupation on Dartmoor, human presence during that period cannot be precluded either.

The Iron Age, the last technologically defined period of British prehistory, lasted from c 750 BC to AD 43 and ended with the coming of the Romans under Claudius. As in earlier periods, material culture changed gradually from Late Bronze Age to Iron Age and it is an accumulation of observed changes over time that marks the differences in the archaeology between the two periods. The Iron Age is, therefore, best understood as a development of the Bronze Age rather than as a completely different epoch. Some aspects of life changed while others did not. For example, iron became the foremost material for metal artefacts and brought a major change in the manufacture of weapons as well as edged tools for working the land, for woodland tasks and for building in timber. Bronze was still used to make many other artefacts, but the evidence for ironworking sites is more common as iron became progressively more important. There were also new forms of ceramics at domestic and funerary sites, in some cases more refined and more decorated. New forms of burial were introduced in the British Iron Age, but examples have seldom been recorded in the West Country and so far they are unknown on Dartmoor (Fig 4.1).

The most striking change in the landscape evidence for much of Iron Age Britain is the increased number of defended settlements. A need, or perceived need, for security or to convey strength to others began to pervade society, which suggests major changes in political interaction between social groups and resulted in the building of robust, enclosed settlements and hillforts.

Hillforts did not suddenly appear fully formed, and many investigations of them have demonstrated that they evolved from much simpler enclosed settlements during the transitional period from the Late Bronze Age to the Early Iron Age. For the people living in these places and elsewhere, life revolved around working the land and rearing livestock, based at settlements with domestic lifestyles that have more similarities to Bronze Age life than they have differences. The first written records about Britain's people are by the Greek writer Strabo, who describes them as '… war mad, high spirited and quick to battle but otherwise straightforward and not of evil character'. The written accounts provide the first evidence of tribal territories or kingdoms in Britain, in the period immediately before the Roman invasion. The Dumnonii dominated the region of Devon and Cornwall. Strabo describes them as 'so beyond the pale of civilisation that they minted no coins of their own' (Manning 1976, 16).

The Iron Age on Dartmoor

Less than 60 years ago, one of the West Country's leading archaeologists of the time, C A Raleigh Radford, wrote: 'No settlement that can be attributed to the Iron Age or the succeeding Roman period, has yet been identified on Dartmoor' (Radford 1952, 75). Radford was the last survivor of the Dartmoor Exploration Committee (DEC), and although he had joined long after its main period of activity in the 1890s and early 1900s, the task had fallen to him to summarise the DEC's work in the light of a further half-century of archaeological discovery in Britain. It is therefore no surprise that he should have come to this conclusion: the DEC's excavations still provided the only excavated archaeological evidence available and the DEC excavators had indeed failed to uncover, or perhaps to recognise, any evidence of the Iron Age in the course of their work. In Radford's view, this apparent lack of an Iron Age presence on the upland had been due to deteriorating climate, which had gradually prevented cultivation and lead to a retreat from Dartmoor. Settlement, he believed, had transferred to a series of hillforts around the peripheries of the moor, which were some of a large number of similar sites dominating the Iron Age landscape throughout Devon.

Even before Radford's time it had been one of Dartmoor's most profound archaeological enigmas that, following the intensity of activity in the 2nd millennium BC, archaeological evidence of human presence on the uplands declined to a barely perceivable level in the later Bronze Age and Iron Age. The significance of climatic changes as a probable contributing agent of these changes has been much debated.

After c 1000 BC, the climate deteriorated as the Sub-Boreal phase, with its relatively warm, dry weather, changed to cool, wet conditions in the Sub-Atlantic phase. So it is known that the climate was generally getting wetter, and that

it was probably more difficult to grow crops. This evidence has led to theories that Dartmoor was abandoned as a place of permanent settlement. Environmental archaeologists have warned, however, that abandonment of an entire upland as a result of climatic change is too much of a generalisation (Casseldine and Hatton 1994, 44). It is probably better to consider localised incidents, such as single lean growing years, as responsible for individual desertions, which combined over an extended period of decline, perhaps lasting centuries.

Since Radford's evaluation, several new pieces of evidence have come to light. Only one year before Radford's publication Aileen Fox had begun excavations at Kestor. Fox's work concentrated on several hut circles, including Round Pound, a particularly large example contained within a concentric enclosure (Fig 4.2). Among the finds was evidence of iron smelting in the Round Pound hut itself, and there was pottery that Fox dated to the Iron Age (Fox 1954, 52–3). Fox naturally assumed that the settlement and field system were also of Iron Age date, and noted the similarity between the field system and those found elsewhere in England, believed to be of the same period and

known as 'Celtic Fields'. However, at Kestor, these are now understood to be reaves and, as discussed in chapter 3, have origins in the 2nd millennium BC. Modern interpreters therefore consider Kestor to be a Bronze Age settlement that was still occupied or was reoccupied in the later Bronze Age and the Iron Age. The iron smelting may be something of a red herring, however, and may not have been associated with any of the known occupational phases of the site. This conclusion is based on the impracticalities of working an iron furnace in a low-roofed building and the fact that the iron working evidence was undated. It seems most likely that the ironsmelting took place in the shell of a building that had already been abandoned (Silvester 1979, 178). Further evidence of Iron Age habitation came from among the finds of a hut circle excavation at Metherall in the 1930s by R H Worth. Some of the pottery, not fully understood at the time, is now also believed to be Early Iron Age (Silvester 1979, 179). During Wainwright's 1970s excavations at Shaugh Moor, the same enclosure that provided evidence for the origins of the site in c 1600 BC also produced pottery and other artefacts suggesting that the buildings were

Fig 4.2
Aerial view of the large hut circle at Kestor, excavated by Fox in the 1950s. (NMR 24093/011. © English Heritage. NMR).

re-occupied during the Middle Iron Age (after *c* 300 BC). One artefact found was part of a rotary corn grinding quern of a type believed to have been introduced no earlier than the 5th century BC (Quinnell 1994b, 78), though more typical of 300 BC or later.

Important, more recent evidence for Iron Age occupation of the Dartmoor upland comes from Gibson's excavations at Shapley Common. Before work began Shapley Common was assumed to be a Middle Bronze Age landscape, and Gibson hoped to add to knowledge of 'reave-associated settlement' (Gibson 1992, 19–46). Quite unexpectedly, however, the excavators discovered that a crudely built stone hut circle dated to *c* 100 BC and had a timber precursor that may have been occupied about a century earlier. Although the radiocarbon dates for the early phase are not totally straightforward and rely on some interpretation, all the pottery from Shapley Common conforms to the Glastonbury style, a type found widely across the West Country and dated Middle to Late Iron Age (Quinnell 1994b, 78).

Although the evidence of Iron Age domestic sites is isolated and fragmentary, the material thus far discovered contradicts Radford's suggestion that upland Dartmoor was unoccupied in this period. This recent evidence also suggests that some hut settlements with origins in the 2nd millennium BC were either still occupied or were reoccupied during the Early Iron Age. It is often the case in archaeology that once a small piece of evidence unexpectedly begins to unravel an enigma, more evidence quickly follows as archaeologists learn what to look for. It seems almost certain that future excavations of hut settlements will reveal further Iron Age material of the type found at Shapley Common; it is also highly likely that Iron Age material would have been completely overlooked in early excavations of hut circles in the pre-radiocarbon dating era, hence the poor overall quantity of the evidence we do possess. The excavations at Bodrifty in western Cornwall provide an insight into what might be unearthed in future Dartmoor excavations. Here, stone hut circles, whose structures closely resemble those of Dartmoor, provided a good sample of pottery spanning the period from the 6th to 1st centuries BC (Cunliffe 2005, 279).

Despite possessing a limited, if increasing, knowledge of domestic Iron Age sites, there remains a shortage of evidence about human interaction with the Dartmoor landscape and what economic part it played during the whole of the Late Bronze Age to the Romano-British period. How did Dartmoor fit into the economic strategy and perception of the period in general, not only of those living in the immediate area but also of people in the hinterland and lowlands of Devon?

Hillforts and hillslope enclosures

The hillfort is the characteristic, and to the majority of people perhaps the most familiar, landscape evidence from the British Iron Age. Typically, hillforts survive as massive single or multiple earthwork ramparts, comprising steep banks and low ditches, formed into large enclosures of several hectares. Elevated locations were chosen, where the natural topography could be sculpted and strengthened by earthworks to form an impressive-looking edifice that may have served a number of functions, including defence and settlement.

There are various hillfort forms common in many areas of England and Wales where suitable locations exist, with the exception of north-west England and parts of the Pennines. The term includes several types of defended enclosure. Some of the more massive and better-known examples are in the south of England where Maiden Castle, Hambledon Hill (Dorset), South Cadbury, Ham Hill (Somerset) and Danebury (Hampshire) are familiar to many. These are all extremely large multivallate (with multiple ditches) hillforts with complex entrances. Further west in Devon and Cornwall, however, hillforts of this size and complexity are less common. In east Devon only Hembury (Payhembury) and Woodbury can be considered of moderately large proportions. The majority in the county are small, with single ramparts and simple entrances and these can be more appropriately termed 'hilltop enclosures'. Other sites fall into the sub-category of multiple-enclosure forts with widely spaced ditches enclosing pasture surrounding the fort, which is sometimes on a hilltop and sometimes on a slope. Devon is well endowed with these smaller forts and although the term hillfort is too grand to describe many of them, it is used here loosely to include all hilltop and hillslope defended enclosures.

There are 12 hillforts, within Dartmoor National Park, but it is notable, and a cause for debate, that all are located around the peripheries of the moor rather than on the upland, (*see* Fig 4.1). Indeed, on distribution maps of Devon's hillforts (ie A Fox 1996), Dartmoor appears as an empty void in a county where their distribution is otherwise spatially consistent with the area and its topography.

A similar pattern exists at Bodmin Moor in Cornwall, where two strongly defended sites are well away from the upland (Johnson and Rose 1994, 48), and at Exmoor, where seven hillforts mostly lie around the moorland peripheries, commanding major river valleys (Riley and Wilson North 2001, 57). It is clear that the West Country's uplands were considered differently in the late prehistoric period compared to earlier times.

This apparent encirclement of Dartmoor's uplands by hillforts led one early researcher to interpret them as strategically placed fortifications built by 'Iron Age Invaders' to check raiders moving along the valleys. The indigenous population, in his view, still resided on the upland under the control of these 'invaders' (Brailsford 1938a, 457). The peripheral distribution of the hillforts also contributed to Radford's theory that these sites became occupied after a retreat from the uplands (Radford 1952, 75).

As the largest and most impressive ancient earthworks in Britain, hillforts were among the first sites to come to the attention of early antiquaries; but they could only guess at their age, and, because their construction was considered too advanced to have been built by the pre-Roman population, they were often given names like 'Caesar's Camp', when believed to have Roman origin, or 'Danebury' reflecting a belief that they were even later and of the Viking period. On the earliest county map of Devon, by Donn in 1765, several hillforts are depicted, including Denbury near Newton Abbot (with the annotation 'Danish Encampment'), Hembury (Buckfastleigh) and Wooston on the Dartmoor borders; and despite many omissions, the inclusion of those depicted indicates their importance as features of the historic landscape in the mid-18th century (Ravenhill 1965). By the early 19th century, writers such as Lysons (1822) were rejecting the idea that the 'ancient encampments' of Devon were Roman or Viking, but were 'constructed by the Britons', of the period now known as the pre-Roman Iron Age.

Barrows had offered early excavators the often illusory promise of a quickly attained prize for a morning's work, and hut circles, even when approached with some academic purpose could be excavated fairly swiftly. A hillfort, however, was a very different proposition for the antiquaries. They are much larger and more complex; they required much greater resources to excavate them; and there was the problem of where one should start and what questions might be answered by excavating them. On a national scale the excavation of several large hillforts began in the 19th century: Rev Warre at Worlbury in 1851, Pitt River's (and others) at Cissbury in the 1870s, Mortimer Wheeler at Maiden Castle the 1930s and more recently Barry Cunliffe at Danebury in the 1970s and early 1980s. Despite these major projects rural hillforts have still received much less attention and resources than many other types of archaeological site.

In Devon, excavations at Hembury (Payhembury) and at Woodbury have been on a moderate scale. On Dartmoor, small-scale excavations have been carried out at Cranbrook (DEC 1901, 130–5) and East Hill (Brailsford 1938b, 86–91).

Probably because of the constraints of excavating these sites, much more archaeological effort has gone into earthwork survey as a way of understanding the extent and complexity of hillforts. The Ordnance Survey had quite coincidentally initiated this trend by including hillforts on their maps from the earliest editions in the 1800s. The OS owed

Fig 4.3
The first-edition Ordnance Survey earthwork plan of Hembury hillfort, Buckfastleigh.

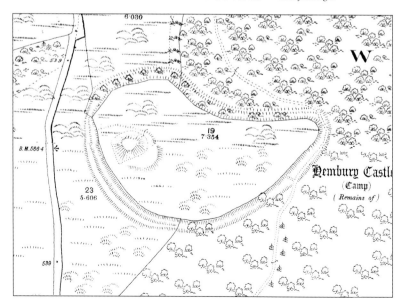

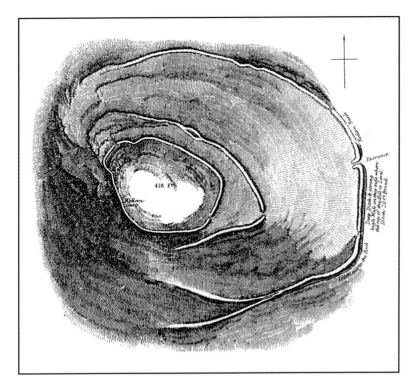

Fig 4.4
An engraving entitled
'Prestonbury Castle, a British
Camp, Dartmoor' published
by Sir John Gardner
Wilkinsons, J Brit Archaeol
Assoc 1862.

its existence to mapping for military purposes, hence its title; fortifications and strategically located defendable earthworks such as hillforts, which could serve for artillery in the future, were an important feature of their maps. By the 1880s, when the much larger-scale 25-inch county 1st edition maps were being surveyed, the level of depiction was such that plans of the major hillforts could be little improved at that scale today, although of course much of the small detail is missing (Fig 4.3). Gardner Wilkinson, P O Hutchinson and others also made useful records of these sites: Wilkinson drew a fine plan of Prestonbury Castle in 1862 (Fig 4.4) and Hutchinson made sketch plans of many Devon hillforts in the mid-19th century, although regrettably none of those around Dartmoor (Butler 2000).

Dartmoor's hillforts

Location (*see* Fig 4.1)

There are 12 hillforts within the National Park, distributed unevenly around the periphery. There are clusters in the Teign Valley and on the south-east side near Buckfastleigh; and outliers on the south, north and west of the moor. All the hillforts have commanding views, whether over particular topographical features, such as river valleys, or of large areas of countryside. Some views are more restricted than others.

Cranbrook and Prestonbury both have 360° vistas providing striking views of their surroundings, including sight of each other, as they are on opposite upper slopes of the Teign Valley (*see* Fig 4.16). Hembury is sited on the end of a ridge overlooking the land to the south-east, the lower Dart Valley and towards the South Hams, although today these views are largely obscured by trees. Hunter's Tor resides on the northern tip of a long ridge where the topography falls away steeply on three sides. East Hill sits on the edge of the north Dartmoor escarpment with its back to the moor, overlooking the lands around Okehampton and the Mid-Devon Culm Measures beyond to the north.

The reasoning behind choices of location for Wooston and Holne Chase castles are less obvious. Woosten (*see* Fig 4.16) comprises a complicated set of earthworks that extends down the south slopes of the Teign Valley, the main enclosure occupying a flattish spur of land half way down the slope with views along the valley. Holne Chase is a promontory of high ground formed by the meanderings of the River Dart, which runs around three sides. Curiously the hillfort builders chose not to place it on the highest part of Holne Chase but on a lower, slightly sloping plateau. Although overlooking the Webburn Valley, views from it are restricted and it is questionable whether its position was actually chosen for strategic reasons.

Of all the Dartmoor hillforts, Brentor perhaps occupies the most strategically useful location and, in today's terms, has the most striking perspective, with views of the near vicinity on all sides. More distant views are of the western Dartmoor escarpment and parts of the central north moor, from Sourton Tor in the north to Eylesbarrow in the south; of parts of the Tamar Valley to the south-west, and of Bodmin Moor and Kit Hill to the west; north, beyond the northern tip of Dartmoor, of large areas of mid-Devon's low-lying Culm Measures, including even more distant views of Exmoor; and south to Plymouth Sound and the English Channel. Brentor is best known to modern visitors to Devon for the small church of St Michael de Rupe, originally built in the 12th century but rebuilt in the 19th, which sits on its summit and is a prominent landmark in the western part of the county and in east Cornwall.

Construction: ramparts and entrances

The main elements of a hillfort are its rampart earthworks, which may enclose or partly enclose a defined space, or conform to the natural topography, to establish a perceived level of security. Most commonly a rampart comprises a high linear bank, formed of earth excavated from a ditch running parallel to it. The height of the bank and the depth of ditch combine to form a steeply sloping obstacle to those attempting to cross it. Excavations at some hillforts throughout Britain inform us that inner banks were often reinforced with timber, either as a box rampart (where the earth bank is faced with timber front and rear) capped with a walkway and parapet, or as a 'glasis' (in which a timber palisade extends

vertically from the top of a simple ridge of earth that forms the rampart). After abandonment the timbers of both variants decomposed, causing the ramparts to slump; two thousand years of weathering and erosion smoothed over the earthworks to give the banks a rounded appearance, and the ditches have silted up to only a fraction of their original depth. This 'classic' form is visible at Hembury (Fig 4.5), Holne Chase (Fig 4.6) and Cranbrook (Fig 4.7).

Entrances were a potential weak point in the defensive circuit of a hillfort. Excavated examples such as Danebury (Cunliffe 1986, 76) show that their builders incorporated strong timber structures to compensate for this weakness, often complimented by additional external earthworks, such as a barbican.

Fig 4.5
Earthwork plan of Hembury Hillfort., located on the south-eastern end of a ridge overlooking the River Dart to the east and Holy Brook to the west. The feature on the west side of the interior is believed to be the remains of a 12th-century motte and bailey castle (see chapter 6). This site lies within National Trust land with free access (RCHME 1:1000 survey; height data licensed to English Heritage for PGA through Next Perspectives™).

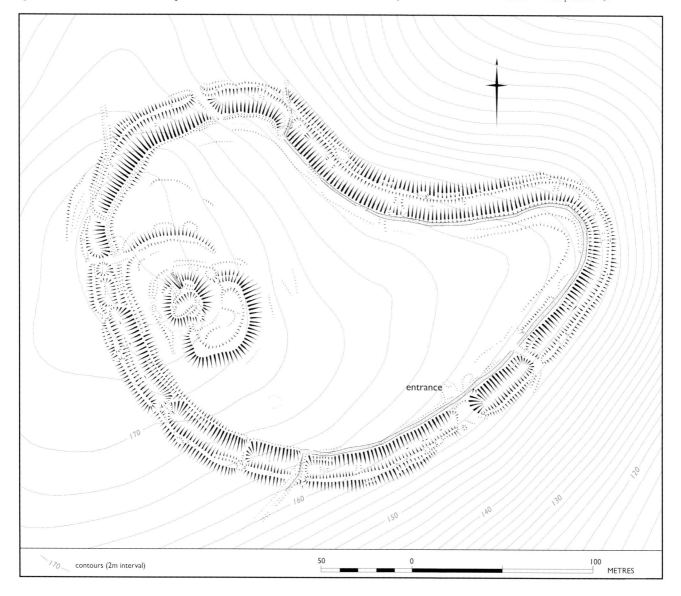

entrance

170

contours (2m interval)

170   160   150   140   130   120

50   0   100
METRES

Fig 4.6
Earthwork plan of Holne Chase hillfort, not located on a hilltop but on shelf of land below the summit. Note that there is no automatic public access to this monument (RCHME 1:1000 survey; height data licensed to English Heritage for PGA through Next Perspectives™).

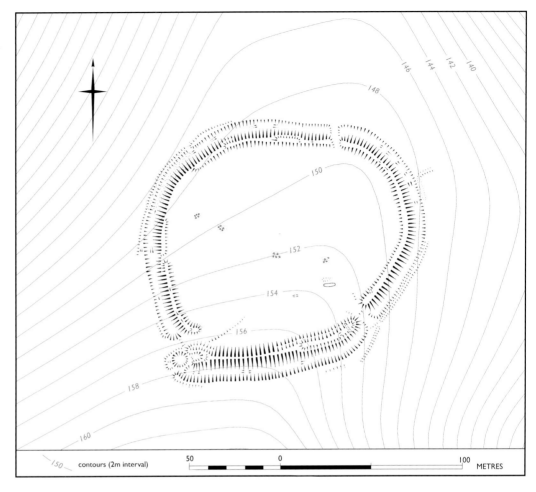

contours (2m interval)   50   0   100 METRES

As the point of entry, these areas were also the obvious location for architectural display. The only Dartmoor example to have any external earthworks is Brentor (Figs 4.8 and 4.9), but the majority have a simple causeway across the ditch with an opening in the rampart to accommodate the gate. At Hunter' Tor the entrance has been strengthened by turning the rampart inward (Fig 4.10).

Hembury (Fig 4.5) sits on the end of a ridge where defences do not follow the contour of the hill, giving the 2.8ha interior a slight slope; however they do roughly follow the form of the topography, with the north-west rampart cutting off the ridge and providing the hillfort with an interesting kidney-shaped plan. Despite several later breaches, the ramparts have a consistent appearance for the whole of the circuit. The total width of the combined banks and ditch is on average 24m. The 14m-wide ditch, which survives more than 3m deep in places, is reinforced by a rampart or bank on the inside and a smaller bank or 'counterscarp', running around the outside. The probable

entrance, visible by a simple causeway across the ditch, is on the south-east side. A slight dip in the ground, visible in places just beyond the inner bank on the interior, is probable evidence of additional earth scooped out and used to heighten the bank. The rampart was in part re-used in the medieval period to form the base of a hedge-bank. A large earthwork on the western interior is believed to be the remains of a small motte and bailey castle, probably of 11–12th century date (*see* chapter 6).

Holne Chase (Fig 4.6) is smaller than Hembury, enclosing *c* 1ha. It is sited on a shelf of gently sloping ground. The defences form a roughly oval-shaped enclosure comprising a rampart and ditch, with vestiges of an exterior counterscarp in places. The average total width of the defences is 15m but this increases markedly on the southern section to 20m, where the rampart stands to 4m high and the ditch 4m deep. This is the most exposed section of the hillfort, being overlooked from the slope above, and would certainly have been the side from which the site was approached. The site has two original entrances, one at each end of the more massive bank on the south side. Both are simple passages through the defences, although the rampart on the south-west entrance has been used as a source of quarry material, making it appear more complex than it actually is. At both entrances the banks kink inwards towards the interior (Riley 1995, 91–5).

Cranbrook (Fig 4.7) sits on the summit of a gently domed hilltop overlooking the Teign Valley and encloses an area of c 2.6ha. Previous writers note that the defences are incomplete, with parts of the circuit on the north sector consisting only of lines of boulders marking out the proposed course of the rampart and its external ditch (Silvester and Quinnell 1993, 27). The other three quarters of the circuit, however, are in place and are quite extensive,

including a second ditch extending around the south and south-western sides. There are two entrances, on opposing sides of the ramparts, represented by openings in the rampart with causeways across the ditch; on the east side both terminals kink inwards, so the gate would have been slightly set back from the main alignment of the circuit.

Similar observations have been made at Hunter's Tor (Figs 4.10 and 4.11), the most complex of the Dartmoor multiple-enclosure forts. Hunter's Tor's defences show at least two, but possibly three, development phases; and earlier and later remains of agricultural activity extends the hilltop's chronology even further. The earthworks of the main site comprise three elements: the inner (a), central (b) and outer (c) ramparts, none of which have

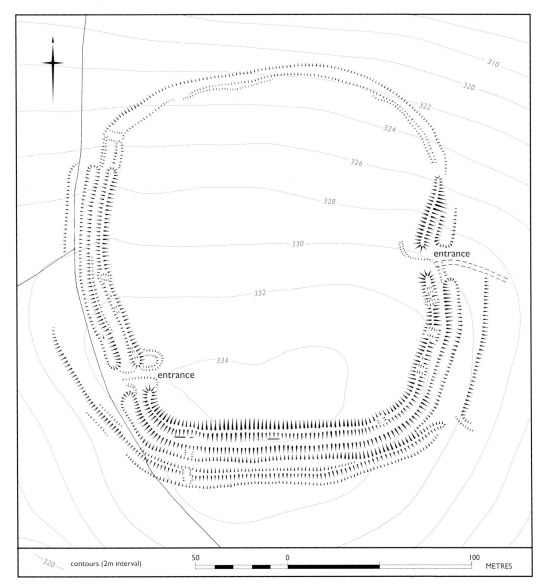

Fig 4.7
Earthwork plan of Cranbrook Castle, one of three hillforts overlooking the Teign Valley – sited within Access Land (RCHME 1:1000 survey; height data licensed to English Heritage for PGA through Next Perspectives™).

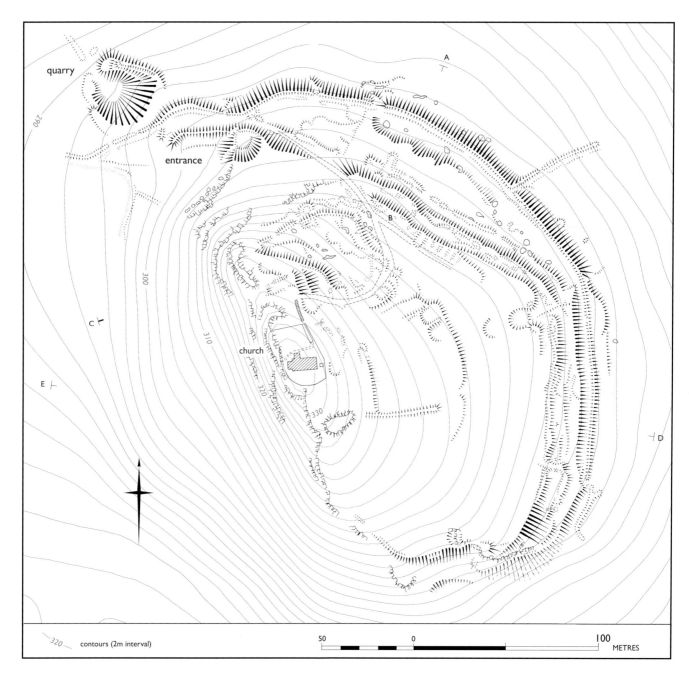

quarry

entrance

church

contours (2m interval)

50   0   100

METRES

Fig 4.8
Earthwork plan of Brentor
showing the large
incomplete curving outer
rampart on the north-east
side and the steep slopes to
the west; access is on a
permitted path (EH 1:1000
survey; height data licensed
to English Heritage for PGA
through Next
PerspectivesTM).

the proportions of Hembury or Holne Chase. The inner and outer ramparts, although uneven in shape, are approximately concentric and of similar style and construction, whereas the central rampart is offset to the south and of stonier makeup. The entrances of all three, however, are aligned.

Although slight, the inner circuit appears complete and could have supported a timber palisade surrounded by a shallow ditch. The outer rampart is the most imposing, but has a moderate ditch on the outside (which has been ploughed out on the east side). This outer

rampart does not form a complete circuit, for there is no trace of anything on the same scale on the western side, where the hillslope falls away steeply.

The central rampart sits at odds with the other two, lying between them but not concentric with either. It represents a separate phase, almost certainly later. Its entrance has in-turning walls forming a passageway into the inner enclosure. Unlike the inner and outer ramparts this is a stone-faced bank redolent of the 2nd millennium enclosures so common elsewhere on Dartmoor, particularly on the

Fig 4.9
Aerial view of Brentor
(NMR 23449/23; ©
English Heritage. NMR).

higher moors. There is no reason why stone-faced banks would not continue to be in use, particularly if, as is clearly the case at Hunter's Tor, the soil is thin and the ground very stony, especially on the steep western side. Like Cranbrook, the defences at Hunter's Tor appear to be incomplete (*see below*), although the entrance area appears to be all in place.

The western half of Brentor (Figs 4.8 and 4.9) comprises very steep slopes defined at the top by a line of precipitous rocky outcrops capped by the tor. The eastern side, though

moderately steep, has fewer outcrops, and today comprises grassy slopes. The building of the ramparts was clearly an attempt to utilise the natural defences on the west side by adding artificial defences on the east side to secure that side of the tor. The tor was probably much valued from early times for its commanding views (*see above*), giving it strategic value for its occupants.

The rampart is unusual on two counts: firstly, it is located near the bottom of the slope, whereas it is more normal to secure only the

Fig 4.10
Aerial view of the hillfort on
Hunter's Tor showing its
location at the northern end
of the Lustleigh Cleave spur
(NMR 24896/003;
© English Heritage. NMR).

upper sections of a hill; secondly, although the artificial bank that forms the rampart is substantial, (up to 5m high), there is no outer ditch – it was constructed by quarrying material from just within the rampart, and piling it onto the bank below to steepen the natural slope (Fig 4.12). Thus the rampart appears very large from the outside, though on the inside it stands only 1m high. It was later adapted into a field wall by facing the interior with stone to

Fig 4.11
Earthwork plan of Hunter's Tor hillfort, a multi-phased hilltop enclosure (EH 1:1000 survey).

Fig 4.12
Section drawing of Brentor showing the profiles of the ramparts.

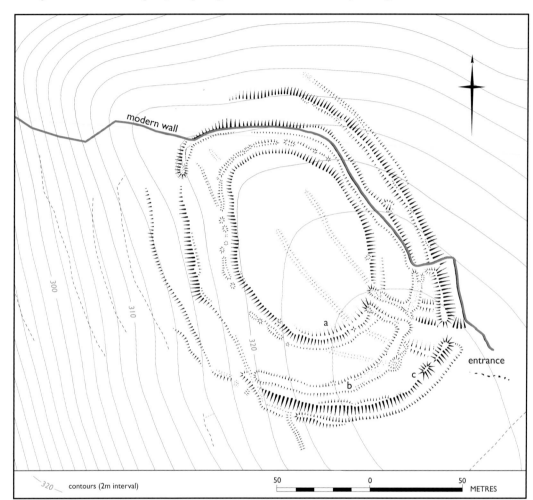

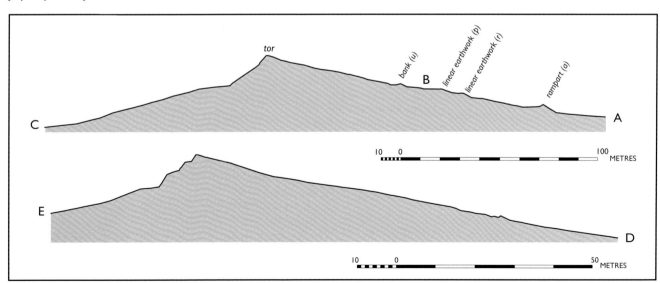

form a hedge bank. This rampart was, however, not completed and it extends for only 216m along the contour at the base of the hill before halting abruptly. Its course was only later completed when the field wall builders adopted it, probably in the medieval period. A second, straighter pair of apparent earthworks on the interior of the fort are considered to be ramparts by some writers, but this is unlikely as these appear to be quarrying scars. They have no bank or ditch and are very uneven in character. The entrance on the north-west side comprises two banks or hornworks projecting at 90° from the rampart, forming a slightly curved passageway up to the gate area.

At Prestonbury the natural topography was also used to advantage (Fig 4.13). It sits at the summit of a precipitous curving gorge formed by the junction of the River Teign and one of its tributaries. This fort overlooks Fingle Bridge and much of the Teign Valley. The river flows more than 200m below. The ramparts are of a different character at this hillfort, and the term 'hillfort' may be something of an overstatement. 'Multiple-enclosure fort' is more accurate. It comprises an oval enclosure with a series of spaced outworks on the eastern side. None of the ramparts are particularly formidable and there is no trace of any ditches, although these may have silted in following many centuries of ploughing in this artificially stone-free area.

Borro Wood, near Ashburton is not strictly a hillfort, rather a hillslope enclosure (Fig 4.14). Its prehistoric date has been doubted, but survey has revealed it to be a good candidate for a 1st millennium BC settlement. Nevertheless, there is no dateable evidence, so this interpretation remains only a possibility. It once had a strong stone 'wall' enclosing 4.1ha of sloping ground on the valley side of the River Ashburn, although the stone has been much robbed. Within the enclosure are a number of circular earthwork terraces cutting into the slope, possibly house platforms that are the positions of former timber round houses.

Function and discussion

Danebury hillfort in Hampshire was occupied for more than 500 years (Cunliffe 1986).

The excavated evidence leaves little doubt that warfare and defence were high on the agenda of those who built and resided within the hillfort. However, more recent interpretation of these larger sites also emphasises their role as central, high-status places for communities. The apparent defensive appearance of the ramparts was a means of projecting strength rather than serving a primarily marshal purpose, although capable of doing so if required.

It is also clear that people of the Iron Age were essentially pastoralists and farmers. Much of Devon's evidence for the Iron Age suggests people living in either open settlements, as at Kestor, or in lightly defended hillslope enclosures, like Milber Down near Newton Abbot. Several multiple-enclosure forts, usually termed hillslope enclosures in the south-west,

Fig 4.13
Aerial view of Prestonbury hillfort. Note that there is no automatic public access to this monument (NMR 24574/011; © English Heritage. NMR).

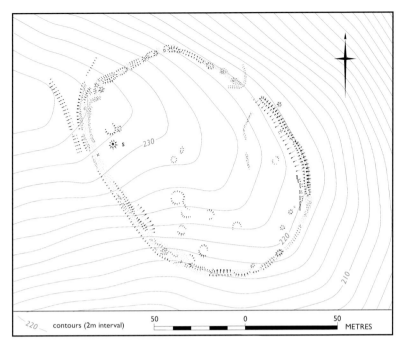

Fig 4.14

Plan of Borro Wood, a small hillslope enclosure on the southern edge of the moor near Ashburton. A number of circular platforms on the interior of the enclosure are likely to be the site of platforms for timber-framed round houses. Note that there is no automatic public access to this monument (EH 1:1000 survey; height data licensed to English Heritage for PGA through Next Perspectives™.).

including Milber Down (A Fox 1952, 1–22), have widely spaced ditches and are generally accepted to have been for the security of livestock, and occupied by people who, if not wholly passive, were not conspicuously bellicose. The primary purpose of massive ramparts, may have been to influence the perceptions of onlookers regarding a community's success and capabilities, but it is clear from the field evidence that most of the Dartmoor examples cannot be seen in the same league as the strongly defended, high-status sites found in other parts of Britain, such as Maiden Castle, South Cadbury and Danebury.

At Cranbrook, Hunter's Tor and Prestonbury the defences are slight and the ditches did not represent a great obstacle to a determined attack force. Even at Hembury, with its moderate ditch, the surviving material of the rampart suggests that it was not of great height. Holne Chase, sited well below the summit of the hill can hardly be termed a strategic stronghold, despite the outward display of strength seen in the south rampart. These were not so much bases for warfare, but places of security, more suited to the task of providing protection for property, people and livestock against lesser dangers.

For Dartmoor's hillforts we possess excavated evidence of the interiors only at Cranbrook (DEC 1901), but investigations elsewhere in Britain demonstrate that they were populated with large round houses, usually timber. At Hembury

and the Boro Wood enclosure, circular depressions more than 5m diameter in diameter indicate the probable position of such structures, but without excavation we can only guess at the location and numbers of these houses at most sites. At Danebury, which is larger and more complex than any hillfort in Devon, there was evidence not only of many dwellings within the hillfort, but also of craft buildings for metalwork and pottery. There were also many iron tools for agriculture, animal bones and a massive capacity to store grain in deep pits (Cunliffe 1986). Danebury, however, is in a well-drained chalk region and such pits are unlikely to have existed on Dartmoor's poorly drained geology, where digging a pit of any depth usually results in it quickly filling with water. Many hillfort excavations have also produced numerous small rounded pebbles, believed to be slingshot – a number were found at Cranbrook during excavations in 1900.

One unresolved issue is the incomplete nature of the ramparts at five of Dartmoor's hillforts: Hunter's Tor, Brentor, Cranbrook, East Hill, Nattadon. Of these it is notable at Hunter's Tor and Cranbrook that although the circuit of the rampart appears unfinished, the areas around the entrances are much more complete than at other sections, a point first noted by Silvester and Quinnell (1993, 17–31). To these may be added Brentor, where although hornworks strengthen the entrance, the main rampart is incomplete. Hunter's Tor also has more elaborate earthworks by the entrance, together with an external ditch, giving an impression of strength not consistent with the north-west side, which appears to rely on the steepness of the hillside to compensate for the lack of a ditch. At East Hill, although not a true hillfort, a curving rampart delimits a prominent corner of ground at the summit of the very steep East Okement Valley on the west side, providing a prominent defensive position (Fig 4.15). However, the bank and ditch appear to terminate, falling far short of the lip of the slope on the west side, beyond which no trace of the feature survives. Despite later ploughing, which would have damaged the rampart, the complete lack of an earthwork suggests that the bank and ditch were never completed, and might indicate that the line of defence beyond that point was constructed of timber only.

What lies behind these anomalies is intriguing. Possible explanations include the idea that in a society where visible displays of strength were all important, the natural and artificial fortification of settlements was essential for communities to succeed. Projects of this scale depended on the human resources available, which may have been limited, and construction had to be prioritised. The entrance and main approaches were the favoured starting point for construction, perhaps because they were considered the premier component in any visual scheme the builders were attempting to impress on outsiders. Why these works were apparently never completed could depend on a number of factors, including the failure of a community to muster the necessary resources, or a cultural shift where the need for such defence or the impression of strength was no longer a priority. One intriguing possibility is that places like this were never intended to present anything other than a facade and that

ramparts did not need to be completed to be effective as long as they appeared to be strong. The parts of the earthwork circuit considered less important visually, may simply have comprised timber palisades of which no trace survives on the surface, in which case the term 'incomplete' only applies to the earthworks as they appear today; the timber palisade may well have been complete.

Why this phenomenon should be so widespread on the peripheries of Dartmoor is harder to explain and would no doubt be a fruitful focus for further research. It is not restricted to Dartmoor, however, for 'incomplete' hillfort earthworks have been recorded elsewhere: most famously at Ladle Hill in Hampshire, believed to be unique at the time it was published (Piggott 1931, 474–85), and at Elworthy Barrows in Somerset (Feachem 1971,

Fig 4.15 Earthwork plan of East Hill, a small defensive earthwork overlooking the East Okement Valley (EH 1:1000 survey; height data licensed to English Heritage for PGA through Next Perspectives™).

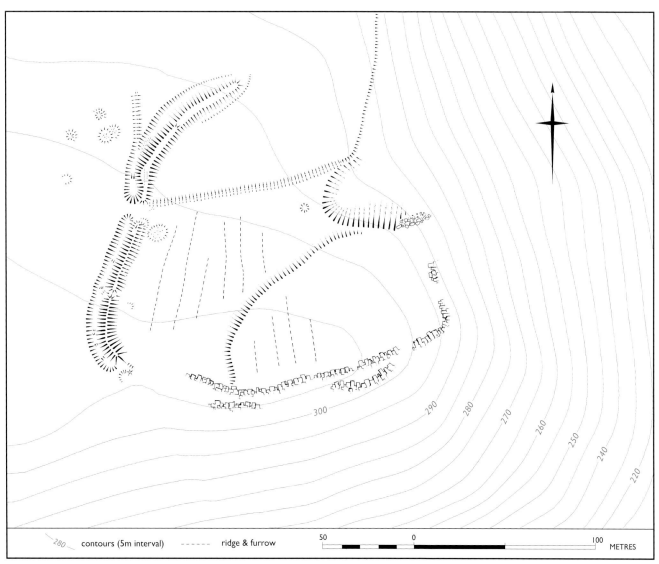

280 contours (5m interval)   - - - - - -   ridge & furrow

50   0   100   METRES

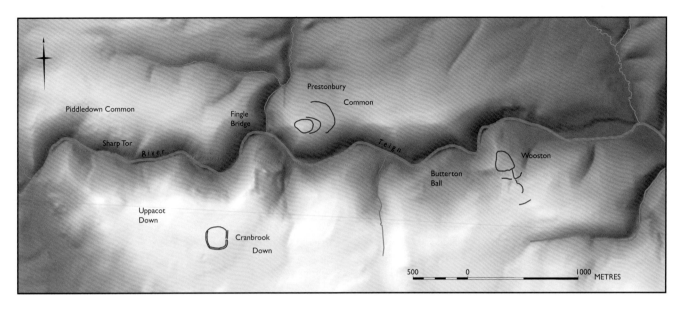

Fig 4.16
Digital terrain model of the Teign Valley showing relative locations of Prestonbury Cranbrook and Wooston hillforts (height data licensed to English Heritage for PGA through Next Perspectives™).

26), Shoulsbarrow in North Devon (Silvester and Quinnell 1993, 27–8) and a recently recognised site at Bicknoller in the Quantock Hills in Somerset (Riley 2006, 60). Indeed nationally, unfinished hillforts, or at least incomplete constructional phases of hillforts, may be regarded as fairly common.

Some disagreement exists over the precise sequence of events at Cranbrook Castle, where the line of boulders suggested by Silvester and Quinnell to be a 'setting-out bank' (1993, 17–31) has been interpreted by Collis (1972, 216–21) as an earlier enclosure that was in the process of being strengthened when it was abandoned. Collis believes that the structure is rather too substantial to have been a setting-out bank. If Collis is correct, this would accord well with the idea that the surviving evidence of many hillforts represents the last phase in a sequence of upgrades and rebuilds, which commenced with a simple hilltop enclosure having origins possibly as early as the Late Bronze Age. At Cranbrook therefore, perhaps the remains reflect incomplete improvements rather than an incomplete hillfort.

Despite a lack of excavated evidence, it is reasonably certain that all these sites have origins in the mid- to late-1st millennium BC, the period covered by the Iron Age. Apart from excavations by the DEC in 1900 (DEC 1901), which unearthed sherds of pottery now known to be of Early Iron Age date (Silvester 1979, 181), this dating scheme is based entirely on our knowledge of hillforts elsewhere. Smaller, lightly defended hillforts such as the sample surrounding Dartmoor, are generally found to

have been occupied during the earlier part of the period from 750 BC to 400 BC, although exceptions are of course likely. However, many hillforts are sited on hilltops where there had been earlier activity. Hembury (Payhembury) in east Devon, for example, began life as a Neolithic causewayed enclosure, which is not an uncommon form of precursor for a hillfort.

The contemporary occupation of all of Dartmoor's peripheral sites within the Iron Age is less certain. For example, the Teign Valley may have been synchronously occupied at the three closely located hillforts that overlook the river, but they could equally have been temporally separate within the 300- or 400-year time span that they are thought to have been occupied (Fig 4.16).

The Romano-British period 43–410 AD

Politically, the Iron Age in Britain ended with the Roman invasion of 43 AD. Although the political, social and tribal order underwent a period of turmoil, the usual caveats apply with regard any changes in the archaeology of the landscape. No doubt a sudden 'alien' presence increased the types of goods and artefacts that came into circulation, beyond that which is known to have arrived through trade in the pre-Roman period. For this reason the term Romano-British (RB) is normally used to reflect the continuity of British Iron Age culture when fused with the increasing influences of Rome during this period.

Without excavated material, we cannot know when individual hillforts became abandoned. Many of the larger hillforts in Dorset and Hampshire, where excavated, have proved to have been occupied until the 1st century BC. Some are believed to have served as refuges at the time of the Roman campaign under Vespasian after the invasion of 43 AD, although this is based on somewhat meagre evidence. Although quite recently a Roman coin, identified as a copper *As* of the early 2nd century AD was found at Hunter's Tor (oral inf DNPA), it is not currently known for certain if any of the Dartmoor hilltop sites were still occupied that late.

In Devon as a whole the Roman invasion is poorly represented archaeologically, compared with other parts of Britain. The county town of Exeter is a Roman foundation, its origins in the 1st-century AD fort. Although a few other small military forts are known in the county, including several recent discoveries, the evidence is scattered between north, mid and east Devon. Dartmoor, in south Devon, and the South Hams are currently blank areas for evidence of the Roman army (Maxfield 2000, 78). There is a cluster of these camps around Okehampton, including an earthwork at Sourton Down, just off the moor, believed to be a fortlet, although its date is not yet proven. A Roman road skirts around the top of Dartmoor and some fragments of Roman building material of uncertain origin were excavated at Okehampton (Higham *et al* 1982, 27). On the upland itself, however, Roman evidence is restricted to the occasional find of coins, as at Hunter's Tor.

Clearly it would be unwise to declare that Dartmoor witnessed no human presence in the Romano-British period, but the problem is that there is no landscape evidence of activity; neither have any excavations produced anything substantially Romano-British in character. It is known that the Romans were interested in tin, and a trade in Cornish tin was recorded by the Greek chronicler Diodorus Siculus (Book V, 22) in the 1st century BC. It would make sense for them to have exploited the rich deposits of Dartmoor too, particularly as they did not have to go so far west to procure it. Sampling of river sediments off the moor has offered some support for the suggestion that tin was worked on Dartmoor in the Romano-British and post-Roman periods (Thorndycraft *et al* 2004, 219–36), but how this might be manifested in the field archaeology is yet to be established.

Once again we are reliant on other areas of Devon to provide some insight into the way people were living and interacting with the landscape. Excavations reveal that small enclosed farmsteads continued to be the main sites of occupation well into the 1st century AD and beyond. At Rudge, near Morchard Bishop, a hillslope enclosure with a timber palisade and outer ditch provided evidence of occupation from the late 1st century AD (Todd 1998, 148). It was a settlement in which people of five centuries earlier would have felt quite at home. From the excavation of a small rectangular enclosure near Stoke Gabriel in the South Hams came evidence that it was occupied from the 1st to 4th century AD (Masson Phillips 1966, 3–34).

Towards the end of the RB period, an increased level of insecurity among the population is often cited as the reason for the re-occupation of many earlier 'defendable' sites, such as hillforts. Most famously, South Cadbury in Somerset has been associated by some with Camelot, or the power base of King Arthur (Alcock 1972), when excavations there in the 1960s demonstrated that it was a centre of some significance in the early centuries of the 1st millennium AD (Barrett *et al* 2000). High Peak, an earthwork site in east Devon, was certainly re-occupied in the 5th century AD (Pollard 1966, 35–59), which confirms that this behaviour was occurring in Devon too. It must be remembered, however, that only a fraction of Devon's large earthwork sites, including hillforts, have been scientifically excavated, so there is potential for discovering that such activity was more widespread.

For the narrator of Dartmoor's prehistoric past, following the almost frenzied period of activity on the uplands in the 2nd millennium BC, the dearth of evidence of such intensity in the later prehistoric period provides an enigma, although the peripheral hillforts partly fill this void. It is to be hoped that that future excavations of domestic sites, such as Gibson's work at Shapley Common, will provide further evidence for late-1st-millennium occupation of the upland. In the meantime, based on the evidence available, it appears that Radford's suggestion of a retreat from the uplands on the basis of a lack of evidence for that period may yet prove to be groundless.

Part Two
The medieval and post-medieval landscape

5

Early medieval Dartmoor, AD 410–1066

There was substantial demographic upheaval in southern England in the years following the Roman exodus. As the Saxon (English) settlers advanced westward in the 5th and 6th centuries, a similar migration of the indigenous population from the south-west took place toward Brittany, although it is not certain if these two movements were linked (Todd 1987, 239). These demographic changes caused a transition from the Dumnonian or 'British' political establishment and culture as the indigenous population migrated, or were assimilated into the emergent English society. However, by the 8th century, settlement patterns and agriculture, and their affect on the rural landscape in Devon, Cornwall and parts of western Somerset had developed a regionally distinctive character, which was to be sustained through much of the medieval period (Rippon 2007, 121).

Devon shire came into existence in the 8th century as part of the West Saxon kingdom of Wessex. Many towns were founded across the county, most of which survive today. The establishment of the Christian church began in England during this period, and the invasion and influence of Danes in the mid-9th century created a culturally fluid age. It is ironic, therefore, that rural activity in early medieval Devon is poorly represented archaeologically. Most knowledge of the period comes from urban excavations. The lack in the archaeological record of a native rural pottery industry in the West Country until the later Saxon period makes it difficult to comment on the culture and chronology of the material culture from excavations. It may be that timber and leather goods were used rather than ceramics, but, of course, rarely survive in archaeological contexts. Finds of imported pottery from the Mediterranean and North Africa, however, provide evidence of exotic trading links and are of great importance in the absence of local material.

Inscribed memorial stones found at Roborough Down, Sourton and other locations around Dartmoor indicate probable 6th-century Christian activity (Pearce 1978, 29). It has been suggested that these stones are evidence of ownership or control over land and therefore attest to the existence of an elite; also, that it was these elites who maintained the trade links with the Mediterranean (Rippon 2007, 113–4). However, these artefacts tell us little of the lives of people using the moorlands during these times and what, if any, Dartmoor's economic role was for the people of Devon.

The early medieval period on the Dartmoor upland has so far proved to be the most illusive archaeologically and, like the Iron Age, the majority of material evidence, like the memorial stones, comes from the peripheries of the moor. In lowland Devon, several forms of evidence suggest that some of the Romano-British enclosed settlements, including hilltop sites, remained occupied into the 5th and 6th centuries (Grant 1995, 97–108), while the landscape remained mostly open and subject to small-scale cereal cultivation (Rippon 2007, 113). On the uplands, however, palaeo-environmental research reveals that grasslands were maintained to a level that suggests human exploitation of the area included sustained animal grazing over a several centuries (Gearey et al 1997, 204). The extent or permanence of domestic settlement is unknown in the early medieval period, but may have been restricted to seasonal occupation associated with summer grazing. There is some evidence of domestic settlement from excavations at Houndtor, but it is illusory and more convincing evidence is awaited (Beresford 1979) (see below, chapter 7).

Historians identify a considerable decline in the county's population after the migration period noted above, leaving much previously cultivated land vacant (Hoskins 1954). It seems reasonable to conclude that for those who continued to live in Devon, and any new settlers, the Dartmoor uplands, where it has always been harder to make a living from farming, were not the first choice for settlement. This does not, however, exclude the uplands as a place for summer grazing, which was probably Dartmoor's principal agricultural role.

During this period, however, exploitation of Dartmoor for tinworking probably began to increase in importance. There is no documentation to confirm that tin was being worked in Devon before 1156, but as a valuable commodity occurring in abundance on Dartmoor it is unlikely to have been overlooked. Maddicott (1989) suggests that Exeter and the *burh* (an Anglo-Saxon fort or fortified town) of Lydford, on the western edge of Dartmoor both enjoyed a high level of prosperity in the 10th century owing to profits from the tin industry. There is, however, no archaeological evidence for 12th-century or earlier medieval tinworking. Perhaps this is only a matter of time and more excavation, as the knowledge of alluvial tin extraction extended back to pre-Roman times (Penhallurick 1986).

Lydford

Dartmoor is surrounded by several small historic country towns (*see* Fig 0.1): Ashburton, Buckfastleigh, Chagford and South Brent are within the modern National Park, but also Okehampton, Tavistock, Bovey Tracey and Ivybridge, which are all close to its borders. All survive as places of residence and commerce. Although founded on the sites of much earlier settlements most received their charters in the 13th century and grew substantially in the 19th century (Timms 1980, 99). Apart from occasional glimpses into their pasts through the character of surviving medieval buildings, or through archaeological excavations in advance of development, their origins are not always obvious. Tavistock, for example, evolved from a small settlement associated with a Benedictine abbey founded in the 10th century (Finberg 1969, 2). The only remains of the abbey to survive upstanding are architectural fragments from the later medieval abbey buildings and part of the precinct wall and gatehouse. These vestiges were absorbed into later buildings of this thriving town after the 16th-century dissolution of England's monasteries.

Lydford (Fig 5.1), on the far west side of Dartmoor, is an exception among these peripheral settlements. It is surely among Devon's most historically and archaeologically interesting settlements. It certainly existed before the 10th century, and therefore probably predates all of Dartmoor's larger medieval settlements. However, while other towns thrived in the high medieval period Lydford's importance was already waning. Limited developments within the settlement in later centuries provide a legacy of earthworks and a street plan that survive from Lydford's earlier medieval occupation.

Lydford's church, built between the 13th and 15th centuries, is dedicated to St Petrock, a Welsh saint who founded many West Country churches in the 5th century. Thus, Lydford may also have been founded in the 5th or 6th century, although Petrock cannot be associated with Lydford historically and the theory needs to be viewed with caution. The cults of Celtic saints often enjoyed revivals long after their own time and such a dedication could have been made much later (Preston-Jones 1994). Nevertheless, archaeological excavations at Lydford in the 1970s yielded fragments of imported Mediterranean pottery of a type that suggests some post-Roman occupation, so Lydford might have been a successful small settlement long before the 10th century (Saunders 1980). Indeed, results of recent geophysical survey to the north-east of the village revealed what the surveyors interpreted as ploughed-out early defensive works, likened to a promontory fort (Belcher and Birchell 2008). Such forts often have prehistoric origins and although the site is not part of the main settlement it may represent an as yet undated antecedent.

Llidan was first recorded in the *Burghal Hidage* of 919. This document, concerned with the period towards the end of the 9th century, lists a particular form of fortified town called a 'burh'. The *burhs*, of which 33 are listed in the *Hidage*, were set up in Alfred's reign, the Anglo Saxon King of Wessex, *c* 890 as part of a network of defensive strongholds during a time of Viking raids. The intention was to ensure that no part of Wessex was farther than 20 miles (32km) from a fortified centre and three other *burhs* existed in Devon at Exeter, Pilton (Barnstaple) and Halwell (later replaced by Totnes). Lydford was the most westerly in the network.

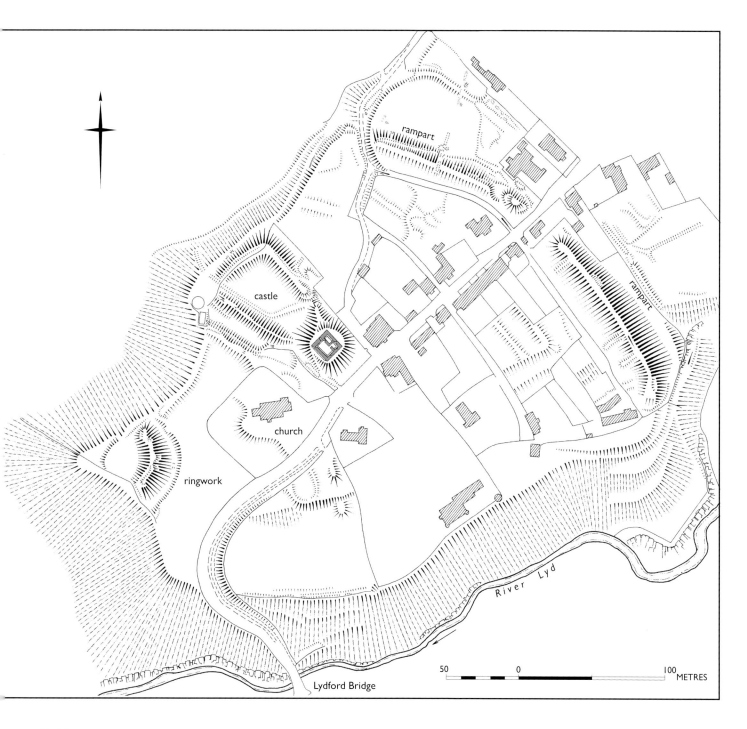

50   0   100 METRES

Fig 5.1
Earthwork plan of the Anglo Saxon burh at Lydford, showing the rampart or
'town bank' traversing the north-eastern end of the promontory. The small
11th-century earthwork castle is located at the western end of the plateau
and the later Stannary gaol sits north-east of the church (see also Fig 6.1).

Note the similar alignments of the modern garden plot boundaries and
footpaths, which may have fossilised the original grid-like layout of the
10th-century burh (based on an EH 1:1000 earthwork plan with hard detail
derived from Ordnance Survey 1:2500 scale map).

103

Fig 5.2
Aerial view of Lydford from the north (NMR 2158/01; © English Heritage. NMR).

Lydford is a complex place, with elements embedded in its layout from more than 1,100 years of continuous occupation. It survives today as a sizeable village. Evidence of the Anglo-Saxon *burh* resides alongside an 11th-century earthwork castle, a later stone tower with origins in the late 12th century (*see* section 3.2) and St Petroc's, Church a fine stone-built church of the 13th to 15th centuries. The post-Roman, Mediterranean pottery mentioned above, suggests much earlier occupation.

The *burh* is located on a promontory, formed by the confluence of the precipitous upper end of Lydford Gorge along the east side, and an equally steep tributary valley on the west (Fig 5.2). These topographical features provide natural defences on three sides. Before the construction of Lydford Bridge sometime before the 15th century, and of the modern road, approaching the settlement from the south and west would have been hazardous on such steep slopes, even impossible in places. The summit of the promontory is a plateau with a slightly rounded profile that extends some distance to the north-east. Fortifying this place was simply a matter of constructing a massive rampart to truncate the plateau between the two valleys, and the earthworks of these fortifications survive on either side of the road as the village is entered from the north-east.

The ramparts comprise spread, turf-covered banks. The southern bank is more massive, up to 30m wide at the base and 4m high. The northern bank, slightly smaller, has been heavily disturbed in places. There are no visible external ditches, although two earlier writers claim they existed (Todd 1987, 279; Haslem 1984, fig 88). Shallow ditches of less than 1m deep were found when the site was excavated in the 1960s but any deeper ditches were filled in or silted up long ago (Addyman 1997). It seems unlikely these excavated ditches would have been any deeper, given that there is so little trace today.

Several archaeological excavations have taken place at Lydford and its Saxon *burh* defences have been traced around the lip of the natural escarpments of the promontory. A low bank was discovered with an external stone revetment, but there is little upstanding evidence of it today (Saunders 1980). Its diminutive proportions suggest that the defences relied mainly on a substantial timber palisade to enclose the plateau.

One of the key elements of King Alfred's *burhs* is the layout of the streets that subdivide their interiors into grid patterns. This element reflects planned layout, implying that these were 'new' settlements rather than evolving ones, including Lydford. The layouts are much more pronounced at *burhs* with more regular ground plans, such as Wareham (Dorset), but at Lydford fragmentary elements of the street plan are likely to have become fossilized into modern surviving features, such as the two hedged pathways that run in parallel across the town's interior and other more modern boundary features that appear to maintain a similar orientation. The positions of any entrances or gatehouses has not been established for certain, although tradition is that the modern house name of 'South Gate' in the eastern corner of the rampart preserves the location of a gatehouse. The gap where the modern county road breaches the north east rampart is another possible entrance location. Abandoned trackways, cutting across the escarpment obliquely towards the summit, on the north and south sides may also once have marked the positions of entrances.

For most of the two centuries leading up to the Norman Conquest of 1066 Lydford was a thriving town. It had its own mint – a sure sign of status in Anglo-Saxon England – and silver pennies from the reign of King Ethelred II (976–1016) were minted here. The peace was broken, however, in 997 when the Anglo-Saxon Chronicle records that the town was the last inland point in a Danish raid, stating: '... they entered the estuary of the Tamar, and so up until they came to Lydford. There they burnt and slew everything they met.' (Garmonsway 1972, 131). Some scholars interpret this passage to mean that the population of Lydford successfully resisted the attack (Hoskins 1954, 53; Timms 1985, 20; Todd 1987, 279), but taken more literally the passage might suggest the Danes were triumphant.

Lydford retained some of its status after the Norman Conquest, serving as the site for two successive medieval castles (*see* chapter 6). One of these was the Stannary Gaol, holding miscreants punished under the laws of the Stannary Courts (*see* chapter 7), but in commercial terms the town itself declined in importance after the 14th century. Although still a market town it was eclipsed by Launceston and Okehampton and soon became something of a backwater. By 1300, only 48 burgesses are recorded and by 1600 the number of houses had dwindled to 16 or 18. In 1795, one observer describes Lydford as 'wretched remains' consisting of '[a] few hovels' (Cherry and Pevsner 1989, 548). By the time the Tithe Map was surveyed in the 1840s the enclosed part of what was now only a village, originally the *burh*, had more or less taken on the layout of today.

Lydford's prolonged decline is one of the keys to its archaeological importance, beyond the intrigue of the upstanding remains. Large areas of the *burh* interior and parts of the exterior, where extra-mural settlement may have occurred, survive modern development and are likely to contain informative archaeological remains. The village enjoyed a short revival in the 19th century when several local mines were active, and the railway made the village more accessible to the outside world. Most of the extant domestic buildings within the *burh* and the extended settlement date from this period.

The search for archaeological evidence of contemporary early medieval settlements on and around Dartmoor remains mostly unfruitful. Greeves suggests that poorly understood and undated earthworks on the slopes of Brentor, within the Iron Age ramparts (*see* Figs 4.8 and 4.9), are evidence of 'Dark Ages' structures (Greeves 2003b). This is an appealing idea, but morphologically the earthworks are difficult to interpret in this way and some may be explained as geological features. Some of these earthworks are certainly manmade, but they could have resulted from an annual three-day Michaelmas fair held in Brentor between 1231 and 1550 (Newman 2004, 15). Although more recent than the Brentor fair, a bi-annual sheep fair in Yarnbury, Wiltshire left substantial earthworks of sheepfolds.

More analysis is needed at Brentor before an early medieval date can be claimed with certainty. Nevertheless, Preston-Jones's study (1994) of Cornish churchyards reveals that some 1st-millennium BC defended sites were adopted for early Christian churches, and Brentor's 12th-century church of St Michael de Rupe on the summit may be another example, revealing pre-12th-century Christian activity.

6

Castles and status around
medieval Dartmoor

The early medieval defences associated with the *burh* at Lydford are the only site of any strategic significance on or around Dartmoor dating from the end of the Iron Age up to the 11th century, but in the wake of the Norman Conquest five additional defended sites came into existence. The West Country possessed no massive medieval castles on the scale of some in Wales, Northumberland or southern England, a fact that reflects its less eventful strategic history in the Middle Ages. Nevertheless, there are several fine smaller-scale examples in Devon and Cornwall.

Modern researchers have challenged the traditional view of castles serving a solely strategic role and focus on their wider contexts as centres of lordship, manorial administration and seigniorial residences. The role of the castle also changed during the course of the Middle Ages, developing into grand lordly residences as expressions of power and wealth (Creighton and Freeman 2006, 104–22). Although early 20th-century scholars considered castle building in England as purely of post-Norman Conquest origin (Armitage 1912), further studies have shown that a number of small-scale defended seigniorial residences were built before 1066, influenced by traditions originating in France. However, it is unlikely that any of Dartmoor's five medieval castles – two at Lydford, plus Okehampton, Hembury, and Gidleigh (in private land) – have a pre-Conquest foundation date.

Lydford Norman castle

Within the compound of the Lydford *burh* are the remains of two medieval castles (*see* Fig 5.1). The earlier of these is a small earthwork, set into the rampart on the south-west tip of the promontory, overlooking the Lyd Valley and commanding the interior of the *burh*. It consists of a substantial crescentic bank with an external

ditch, and annexes one corner of the pre-Norman town (Fig 6.1). It was possibly much larger, but has been eroded, as it sits at the top of a precipitous slope. This part ringwork, which would have accommodated a timber palisade similar to those of the Iron Age hillforts, is believed to have been erected soon after the Norman Conquest in the late 1060s. It seems likely that its location was chosen because of Lydford *burh*'s existing strategic and administrative importance, and to utilise an existing defensive position; possibly also as a deliberately belligerent statement by its Norman builders. Although the castle is not mentioned in Domesday, it was recorded that 40 houses had been destroyed at Lydford since William's arrival in England (Thorn and Thorn 1985, 100b). The Domesday entry may be explained by the imposition of the castle within the *burh*, where space was required to build it (Hoskins 1954). These events have been interpreted as part of a deliberate, coordinated scheme to suppress centres of population associated with pre-Norman governance by being unnecessarily intrusive and by slighting the earlier, indigenous fortifications and settlement (Creighton 2006, 110).

This earlier castle was occupied only briefly, and was probably abandoned before the installation of a later castle in the 12th century (Saunders 1980, 127). The earthwork bank is up to 25m thick at the base and stands to a maximum height of 5m from the bottom of the ditch, which is on average 3m deep. In the 1960s P V Addyman excavated a large portion of the ringwork's level interior and cut a transect across the bank and ditch. Although the full results have not been published, preliminary reports record the remains of five timber and earth rectangular buildings in the interior. All the buildings had been burnt to the ground and more than 5cwt of charred grain was retrieved, associated with sherds of 11th- and 12th-century pottery (Wilson and Hurst 1965, 196).

Fig 6.1
Earthwork survey of the
castles and church at Lydford
(EH 1:1000 survey).

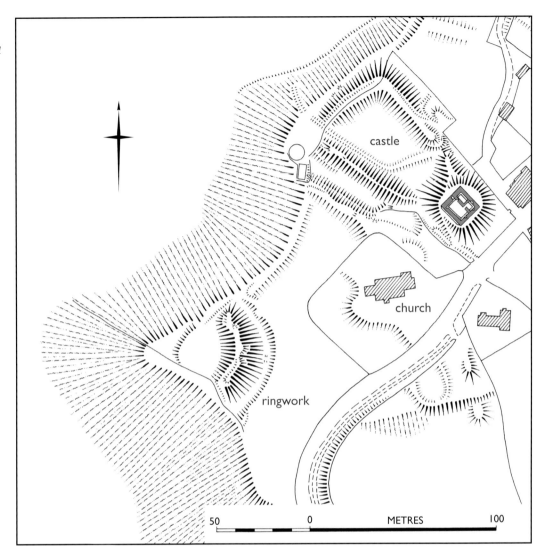

The Stannary gaol

Less than 100m north of the Norman ringwork is a second castle of very different character. It is a square stone tower or 'keep' rising from an earthen mound or 'motte', and has a roughly rectangular bailey attached to the west side. The keep has origins in 1195 as a gaol, although alterations and enlargements documented in the late 13th century also reflect Lydford's role as the judicial centre for the Stannaries, the legislative body responsible for the tin industry (*see* chapter 8). At this later time the building served as the Stannary gaol. Lydford's role as a centre for justice and administration for the Forest of Dartmoor and the Stannaries is apparent in the late 12th and 13th centuries by its association with Hugh de Neville and William de Wrotham; both were keepers of the castle for a period

and served the dual roles of administrating and enforcing Forest and Stannary laws on behalf of the king (Saunders 1980, 135).

The interior of the keep and parts of the bailey were the target for extensive research excavations in the 1960s by Andrew Saunders for the Ministry of Works (Saunders 1980). The first phase in the structural history of the site was an immensely strong square tower, built in 1195. A second phase in the late 13th century indicates that the castle was gaining importance as a Stannary gaol; this work involved demolishing the upper section of the tower, then adding two more storeys. The exterior was surrounded by an earth mound to make it look as though the keep is standing on a motte, although the basement of the tower is in fact sunk into it. The narrow bailey was added in the remaining space between the motte and the western boundary of the *burh*.

It is a much debated enigma why what was essentially a purpose-built gaol was given the outward appearance of a defended castle. The gaol remained in use through much of the medieval and post-medieval periods, but a report in 1650 describes it as in disrepair. Although repairs were undertaken twice in the 18th century, by the early 19th century its condition was again in decline.

The tower is 14.5m square with walls up to 2.1m thick. The earthen motte is 45m by 35m. The excavations revealed that a ditch of approximately 4.5m deep once surrounded it, although no earthwork evidence of this survives. The bailey comprises substantial but very spread earth banks enclosing an area c 60m × 40m. The southern rampart ditch is up to 10m wide, with precipitous sides cut into solid rock. This rather out-of-proportion ditch may have served as a quarry and a source of stone for parts of the keep.

The Hembury motte and bailey

A small, well-defined earthwork signifying the remains of a motte and bailey castle survives within the interior of the Iron Age hillfort at Hembury (see Fig 4.5). Like the early example at Lydford, this earthwork is not documented. It is traditionally known as 'Dane's Castle', but its likely construction date is first half of the 12th century. This was during the so-called 'Anarchy', or civil war, of King Stephen's reign (1135–41), when many unlicensed or 'adulterine', and mostly undocumented, castles were built. Although such reasoning is used to explain the existence of many similar undocumented examples from this approximate period, there is absolutely no evidence to confirm these origins for Hembury. Therefore this explanation must be considered only one possibility, although it would help explain the lack of documentation. Creighton and Freeman (2006, 112) offer the alternative suggestion that Hembury was created to serve for hunting, presumably on Dartmoor, as did Okehampton Castle (see below) on a much grander scale at a later date.

The location of the motte and bailey within the earthworks of an existing hillfort suggests that the hillfort ramparts were used as an outer line of defence. Whether the ramparts were refurbished, and to what extent, or if timber buildings associated with the motte and bailey were built within the ramparts, is not known.

The castle is situated on the western summit of the hillfort interior and the motte is a central, grass-covered mound with encircling ditch and bank. The motte, which originally had a standard pudding-basin profile, has a central excavation 1.5m. deep, causing it to have a hollowed appearance. It is almost perfectly circular at its base, c 32m in diameter, rising to an oval top measuring 19m × 11m. An enclosing ditch is 0.8m deep. Of particular significance are the remains of a kidney-shaped outer bank on the south-east side, enclosing an area of up to 18m beyond the mound, giving the appearance of a small bailey. Although slight, this feature provides the main clue to these earthworks' identity as a motte and bailey, which would once have supported a timber palisade.

Okehampton castle

Dartmoor's largest and most impressive castle is Okehampton in the West Okement Valley, south-west of Okehampton. It is one of Devon's largest castles and the only one mentioned in Domesday Book of 1086 (Fig 6.2).

This castle has a much more complex history than others around Dartmoor. Its structural remains and earthworks reflect its changing roles over many centuries.

Higham (1977, 11–14) discusses the castle's early documented history and its principal occupants in detail and Endacott (2003, 32–5) researched its later years. Baldwin de Brionne, who by 1071 was Sheriff of Devon, established the castle between 1068 and 1086. The castle formed the caput, or central manor, of his estate. Following a series of successions among Baldwin's descendents, the castle and the estate passed through marriage to Reginald Courtenay in the 1170s. Courtenay's son Robert married the daughter of the Earl of Devon, a title that Robert later secured. The castle remained in the possession of the Courtenay Earls of Devon until 1538 and it was during the Courtenay family's tenure that much expansion and improvements were made, particularly during the 14th century when the castle was used as a base for hunting in Okehampton deer park. The estate was broken up and the castle lost its importance after the death of Henry Courtenay, the ninth Earl, who was beheaded in 1538. It had no recorded role in the English Civil War, at which time it was probably unoccupied. Sydney

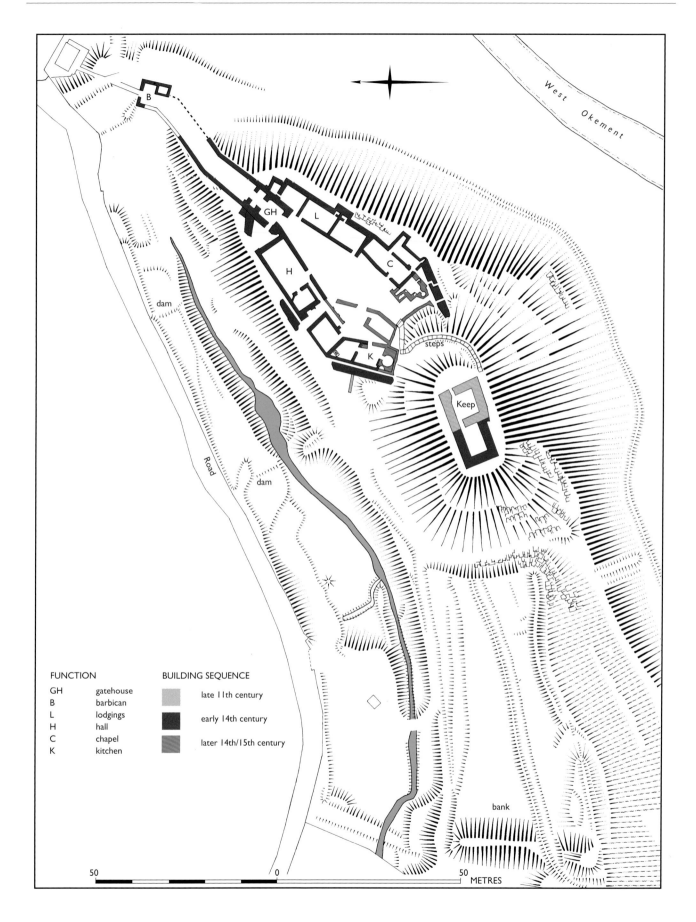

West Okement

B

GH   L

H   C

dam

Road

dam   K

steps

Keep

bank

FUNCTION

GH   gatehouse
B   barbican
L   lodgings
H   hall
C   chapel
K   kitchen

BUILDING SEQUENCE

late 11th century

early 14th century

later 14th/15th century

50   0   50
                                         METRES

Simmons, a wealthy businessman, owned the castle in the early 20th century. He instigated conservation work on the ruined buildings and set up a preservation trust before the site passed to the Ministry of Public Building and Works in 1967. The castle has been in the care of English Heritage since 1984.

The various elements of Okehampton Castle's structures and earthworks reflect alterations and growth that can be chronologically defined. Excavations in the 1970s recovered much information. All the buildings were surveyed, their functions clarified and a dating framework established, suggesting five major structural phases between the 11th and 16th centuries. Higham (1977) and Higham et al (1982) give more detailed descriptions of the castle buildings.

The castle is situated on a short, steep-sided spur of land above the north bank of the West Okement River. Along the north side runs the old A30 road, following the route of a much earlier road. This positioning would have given the castle a commanding position over this important route as it passes along the base of a steep slope approaching the outskirts of Okehampton town.

The earliest earthwork is likely to be the linear bank and ditch traversing the neck of the spur to the west of the motte. The ditch is 6.5m wide and up to 3m deep; the bank averages 11m wide and is up to 3m high. Higham's excavations failed to unearth any datable material from this earthwork, but it is possible that it represents a prehistoric cross-ridge dyke, a common form of land boundary often associated with 1st millennium BC occupation of an area (Probert 2004, 14). Interestingly, the excavators also retrieved fragments of Roman building material, although no Roman structural remains were found. The nature of any Roman activity at the site is speculative and remains inconclusive (Higham et al 1982, 27).

The motte forms the earliest element of the medieval castle and is likely to have been constructed in the later 11th century. It comprises a massive mound with sloping sides, occupying the highest point of the spur and utilising the steep, natural slope on the south side to gain additional height. Its footprint is sub-rectangular (70m × 55m), with rounded corners, and it stands 28m high above the flat field to the south. A deep rock-cut ditch flanks the western edge of the motte. A corresponding ditch on the eastern

end was backfilled during latter modifications to the bailey, and was revealed only through excavation (Higham 1977). A much ruined rectangular stone keep sits on the flat summit and had two identifiable construction phases: the square structure on the east end, with its arched entrance, was built in the 11th century, onto which an annex was added to the west side in the early 14th century.

The bailey sits at the north-east foot of the motte. The imposition of the current range of 14th century buildings effaced traces of earlier components of the bailey and any buildings within it, the foundations of which were revealed by excavation. A certain amount of sculpting of the spur may also have taken place to accommodate these newer buildings, which were placed either side of a precinct. These include a chapel and lodgings on the south side, and kitchens and a great hall to the north. A gatehouse at the north-east end of the precinct is approached from outside by a walled causeway leading up from a barbican to the far north-east. A curtain wall, now partly demolished, provided security for the north range, extending from the eastern flanks of the motte. On the south side of the precinct, a similar section of curtain wall fills the gap between the motte and the buildings, while the remainder of the south side is enclosed only by the exterior of the lodgings and chapel – not a truly defensive wall.

A series of sunken earthworks runs along the entire northern side of the castle. Although much disturbed in the 19th and 20th centuries, these earthworks are likely to represent a series of shallow ponds, separated by cross dams. The ponds would have served a dual function: enhancing the aesthetic appearance of the castle's northern aspect when approached from the road, and possibly providing farmed fish for the table. Curiously, however, the latter is not supported by the midden evidence from Higham's excavations, which produced many fish bones, but all of marine rather than freshwater species (Higham et al 1982, 135–8).

The late 11th-century castle appears to have been located to take advantage not only of the strategic possibilities of the spur – giving control and access to the main route to and from the west – but also to claim any traditional local significance that the site already possessed. The castle served as the shrieval centre of the Devon estate at this time, although it was never the main residence of any

Fig 6.2 (opposite) Large-scale earthwork plan of Okehampton Castle showing the major surviving earthworks and the footprints of the buildings with probable building sequence. On the north side of the castle, now occupied by the modern course of the stream, vestigial earthworks suggest the remains of a series of dams and ponds to manage the water supply, although these were radically altered when the side was landscaped in the early 20th century.

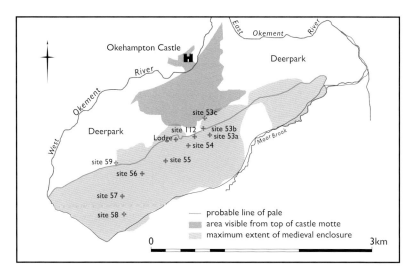

Fig 6.3
Map of Okehampton Deerpark showing the limit of the emparked land, defined by the probable pale, and the extent of enclosed lands associated with the deserted settlements (see chapter 7). Also shown is the result of a viewshed analysis, which demonstrates the potential for, and the constraints of, hunting being viewed as a spectacle from the castle (after Probert 2004).

incumbents of that role. During this phase the motte and the earlier keep were built and it is assumed that an associated bailey also existed, although its precise character is not known. The castle maintained its strategic role into the 12th and 13th centuries, and was strengthened by the addition of a curtain wall.

A major reappraisal of the castle's potential occurred in the 14th century as security became less of a priority in the West Country, and the role of segnioral castles generally developed into one of high-status residences of the aspirational lordly class who owned them. The 14th-century programme of reconstruction not only upgraded the level of comfort in the domestic accommodation but also enhanced the visual aspects of the castle in order to project the image of a fortification through a veneer of martial architecture. The guiding principle of these alterations was to create an imposing aspect to those approaching the castle along the route to the north, featuring the gatehouse, the barbican and the curtain wall extending between the gatehouse and the motte, and aesthetically enhanced by the ponds and dams. Landscaping in the 19th century partly effaced these water-management features, but vestiges of the dam earthworks survive. By comparison, the southern aspect has an austere, utilitarian appearance: high walls punctuated by garderobes, clearly not designed to shape first impressions, as the north-side aspect clearly was.

Okehampton Castle demonstrates well how the role of castles in medieval England did not remain static. Their inception as imposing centres of power in the 11th century probably reflect William the Conqueror's need to be seen to exercise control through his barons, as, for example, at Lydford. In later centuries, however, the roles of individual castles became much broader, often developing into well appointed high-status residences. In the case of Okehampton the strong keep of the 11th-century motte was a visible reinforcement of those in control. When its strategic importance declined, it found new purpose as a lordly residence for Courtenay and a base for hunting forays.

Courtenay's choice of Okehampton to build such a residence is linked to the imparkment of a large piece of land on the lower slopes of moorland south of the River Okement, to serve as a deer park from *c* 1292. The position of the castle provided easy access to the adjacent deer park (Fig 6.3), while also perhaps making the hunt a visible spectacle for an audience at the castle, especially from the motte. The deer park covered a strip of land of *c* 390ha, bounded on the north side by the West and East Okement rivers and on the south by a pale, which follows a SW–NE course between the West Okement, and a point on the Moor Brook (Probert 2004). Today the pale comprises a series of disjointed linear earthworks, partly disguised by later activity, but as a whole defines an outer boundary for the deer park and probably once supported a deer-proof fence. A number of deserted medieval settlements are amid the deer park and adjacent to the south of it. Their presence, with associated enclosure and cultivated areas, has created a complicated series of chronological relationships between the various elements. These are discussed by Probert and are summarised in chapter 7.

The specifics of how the deer park functioned are not known. Apart from the pale, few features of the landscape can be described with certainty as elements of the deer park, but its physical presence, known from documentary sources and confirmed by field evidence, provides a clearer landscape context for the castle. It explains the character of its 14th-century development as a 'fortification' of impressive appearance and luxurious accommodation, though not particularly effective in any martial sense.

Medieval farming and settlement on the uplands

Historical context

It was during the later medieval period that the human landscape of Dartmoor began to develop its character as the upland hill-farming district so familiar today. Elsewhere in south-west England, for example West Penwith in Cornwall, prehistoric and Romano-British field systems were the seminal components of an evolving landscape (Rippon 2007, 112), which continued to owe much to the early layout. But this is not so on Dartmoor, where the landscape appears to have been largely re-made in the medieval period. Elements of prehistoric reave systems or enclosures (*see* Fig 7.11) were sometimes fossilised into the medieval working landscape, but on the whole, the patchwork of enclosed fields that is visible on large scale maps, aerial photographs (*see* Fig 7.4), and of course by ground observation, have their origin in the medieval period, together with the villages, hamlets and farmsteads that are mostly still occupied. These elements formed the foundation for all later developments, which were built onto a framework of fields first brought into cultivation or used as pasture, in some cases, before the Norman Conquest. This is very much the case elsewhere in Devon too, where the long-term trend in the character of Devon's fields rarely extends into prehistory, although isolated patches of prehistoric field systems occasionally survive (Turner 2007, 28).

Following the early medieval hiatus of settlement on the uplands (see chapter 5), even an approximate date for the re-occupation and return of a more enduring, settled population to Dartmoor and its revitalisation as a living, working landscape, eludes us. This might initially have occurred on a small scale, and is thus archaeologically obscure for the earliest re-occupation. Dartmoor's resources, including summer grazing, seasonal foods and possibly tin, may have been exploited continuously by transhumant visitors using the moor, even during periods for which there is no evidence of occupation. However, permanent domestic occupation and farming were certainly occurring on the lower and middle slopes and valleys by the 10th and 11th centuries.

One advantage of this period for researchers is its historical dimension – the trickle of documentary evidence for the early medieval period becomes a moderate flow from the 12th century. This material provides more than just dates and events associated with the material evidence of the landscape, but also contexts that broaden our understanding of the people and the social system that created it. Settlement and tenure in the English medieval period was an integral component of the manorial system, which formed the basis of the rural economy and society. Manors were allotted to individual lords by the king and the land attached to each manor was divided into areas used to support the lord of the manor – known as 'demesne' –

Fig 7.1

Map showing part of Natsworthy Manor, highlighting an area of former strip fields fossilised into later fields still in use today (based on Ordnance Survey first edition 25-inch map of 1886; additional strip partitions follow Gawne (1970), derived from documentary sources).

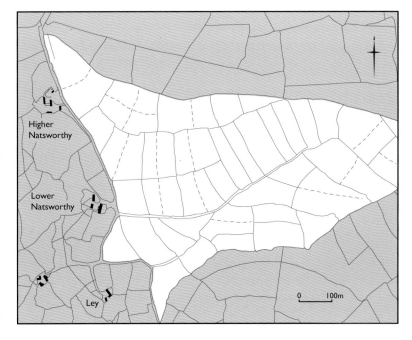

while the remaining land was held between tenants, each of whom occupied a house and a portion of land.

A useful starting point among the historical information is Domesday Book which, although compiled in 1086, was concerned with the period leading up to 1066 and describes an essentially Anglo-Saxon landscape. It refers to named places that were well established before the Normans' arrival. In many cases it is not possible to know how long they had been in existence, but it can be assumed that some at least had been founded a century or more earlier. Some familiar Dartmoor names were recorded in Domesday, including Meavy, Manaton, Hennock, North Bovey, Ilsington, Sigford, Whitchurch, Throwleigh, Buckland in the Moor and Holne (Thorn and Thorn 1985). These settlements are located around the

peripheries of the moor, although some are at an altitude of more 200m and are therefore at the interface with the uplands.

The lands of 37 Domesday manors lie mostly on the moor (Linehan 1966, 116). Unfortunately, individual tenancies attached to the manors are not named, so there is no certainty about the exact extent or location of particular settlements, when they were founded or how quickly they had evolved. The entry for Holne, as an example, is understood to represent *c* 13 unnamed farms, plus the demesne land (Somers Cocks 1970, 87). More informative is the mention of the smaller settlements and manors located on the slightly higher ground and in sheltered valleys on the very edge of the uplands. Around Manaton, apart from the village itself, there is also Neadon, Shapley, Beetor and Langstone; also

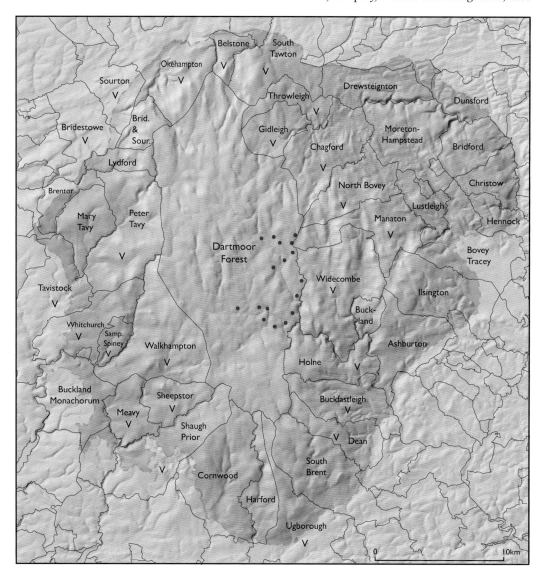

Fig 7.2

Map of Dartmoor showing the boundary of the Forest of Dartmoor and the ancient tenements within it, the Dartmoor parishes and the location of the venville parishes, each marked with a V.

Houndtor (discussed below), where two deserted hamlets survive. In the sheltered valley of the East and West Webburn River, near Widecombe-in-the-Moor are Blackslade, Dewdon, Dunstone, and Natsworthy manors (Fig 7.1). What is revealed is that colonisation of the middle altitude areas of Dartmoor was well established before the mid-11th century.

One area with a notable absence of settlements recorded in the Domesday survey is that now known as the Forest of Dartmoor (Fig 7.2), not because of the presence of trees but because it was subject to Forest Law. The area is the central portion of Dartmoor, which includes much of the exposed high ground on the north and south moors, but also the more sheltered lands around the Dart Valley near the centre of the upland. Although the boundary of Dartmoor Forest does not physically exist, apart from artefacts and topographic features between which it was delineated, it is nevertheless historically one of the most important medieval elements to appear on the modern map of Dartmoor. Its existence had a profound effect on the way Dartmoor was, and still is, managed (Fig 7.2).

It is unlikely that the central uplands of Dartmoor were inhabited in the 11th century but, like most of the unoccupied areas of moorland, had been used as summer pasture. Although Forest Law arrived with the Normans, it was not until sometime after 1066 that the entire county of Devon became subject to its influence. After lobbying by the men of Devon, and a huge payment to the crown, the county became disafforested by charter of King John in 1204, except that Dartmoor and Exmoor remained royal forests. The retention of these two districts was because both had been royal demesne.

Forest Law existed essentially to preserve hunting grounds for the king and his entourage. It included many restrictions for the inhabitants of these areas. Almost all wild animals or 'beasts of the chase' were protected, as was the vegetation, especially the trees, although this may not have been an issue on Dartmoor, where few trees existed. There were severe punishments for those who broke these laws. Assarting – clearing and enclosing land for agriculture – was also mostly forbidden, so it is no surprise that Dartmoor Forest was unihabited during this time.

In 1239 the status of Dartmoor Forest was reduced to that of a Chase: although still theoretically a hunting reserve, many of the

restrictions were lifted and it was probably from this date the earliest settlements within the forest became established. The first documented examples are Pizwell and Babeny, mentioned in accounts of 1260 (Somers Cocks 1970, 96). Later, at least from the 17th century, all such places within the former forest, are referred to as the 'ancient tenements', reflecting their medieval foundation. By 1345, there were 44 ancient tenements, most of them within the sheltered valleys of the East and West Dart and its tributaries (Fig 7.2). Precise foundation dates exist for some, including Dunnabridge (Fig 7.3), where five tenements came into existence between 1304 and 1306. Each included 19 and one-fifth acres of open moorland (H S A Fox 1994, 152).

Such increased colonisation was occurring over much of England during the 12th and 13th centuries, during a period often referred to as one of climatic optimum. Average annual temperatures were warmer and thus better for agriculture on higher ground. Within this context many more farms, hamlets and villages were added to those that already existed by 1066. There was also expansion in upland areas outside the forest, and documentation confirms that the great majority of recorded settlements existed by c 1350. One surprising source of information is a tin coinage roll of 1302–3, in which dozens of

Fig 7.3
Map showing part of Dunnabridge, which comprised five tenements when founded in the early 14th century, each having 19 and on-fifth acres. The parallel morphology of the modern field walls provides evidence of fossilised strip fields (based on Ordnance Survey first edition 25-inch map of 1886).

tinners are listed along with their places of residence. For several places on this list this is the earliest documentation. They include Bagtor, Corndon, Hurston, Scorhill, Grendon and Brimpts, to list only a few (Greeves 2003a, 9–29). Growth in this upland settlement, however, does not preclude the establishment of still later farmsteads, which continued well into the 19th century and are discussed in a later chapter.

Medieval archaeology

Compared to their interest in the prehistoric monuments on Dartmoor, archaeologists have shown interest in its medieval settlement and agriculture for a comparatively short time. While many researchers have examined the documentation on issues such as the Forest, and Commoners' rights, less have undertaken fieldwork to investigate the archaeological elements of the medieval landscape. Archaeological excavations on medieval settlements have been rare by comparison with those of prehistoric hut circles. Alfred Shorter's 1938 study of the strip fields at Challacombe (Shorter 1938, 183–9) would have been an important first step for medieval landscape studies, but the author considered the fields to be 'Celtic' or prehistoric. Not until the 1960s did Catherine Linehan and Herman French (French and Linehan 1963) follow the fieldwork tradition by examining abandoned sites in Widecombe parish. Linehan later provided the first comprehensive account of deserted settlements for the whole of Dartmoor, based on field survey and aerial photographic evidence (Linehan 1966,). In this seminal paper she lists 110 deserted sites; not all are medieval, but this work raised the awareness of their potential for study. However, the contribution of Ordnance Survey Archaeological Division investigators such as Norman Quinnell was often overlooked. Quinnell had recognised the remains and the significance of various deserted medieval settlements on Dartmoor, including Houndtor, as long ago as 1953.

The existence of these places was therefore not unknown in the early 1960s, and in fact Aileen Fox had excavated a medieval farmstead in 1956, before it was submerged by the Avon Reservoir (A Fox 1958). It comprised two rectangular buildings, including one longhouse, and a small enclosure. Surprisingly, such was the late development of medieval studies within the discipline of archaeology that this, the first excavation of a Dartmoor medieval house, took place 63 years after the first formal excavation of a prehistoric house by Robert Burnard in 1893.

Between 1961 and 1972 E Marie Minter directed an important research investigation of four deserted medieval settlements: Hutholes, Dinna Clerks and two sites at Houndtor. She excavated 21 buildings, but, sadly, died before she could write up her work. It was eventually published posthumously in 1979 (Beresford 1979). Some aspects of the conclusions have been a source of charged debate among archaeologists ever since (see below), which has somewhat diminished the importance of the overall gain in knowledge that was achieved by this work.

Between 1974 and 1976 David Austin excavated eight buildings at Okehampton Park preceding the expansion of Meldon quarry (Austin 1978), and the most recent excavation, at Sourton Down, was to 'rescue' a farmstead that was to be destroyed by the A30 road improvements (Weddell and Reid 1997). Except for Minter's work, most excavations of medieval settlements on Dartmoor have been rescue work, undertaken because of circumstance rather than design.

Although small and important field survey projects have also been published (eg Fleming and Ralph's study of Holne Moor, 1982), no integrated programme of research on the scale of the prehistoric Dartmoor Reaves project, including excavation and fieldwork, has yet been attempted to explore the medieval landscape more thoroughly. It would certainly be a rewarding task.

Much supplementary information is available from work at Cornish medieval sites, in particular the excavations in advance of flooding at Colliford Reservoir (Austin *et al* 1989); while Herring's work on fields and farmsteads on Bodmin Moor has demonstrated the potential of upland landscape investigation (Herring 2006).

The landscape of farming and settlement

The medieval economy of Dartmoor was mixed: while its foundation was quite clearly food production through arable farming and animal husbandry, there were several other means of making a living for some upland residents. Tinworking was an important industry, certainly by at least the mid-12th century, and was continuously rising in importance throughout the medieval period (see chapter 8); peat cutting and charcoal manufacture were both also in demand. There was also a thriving stone-cutting industry, supplying building stone and artefacts of granite to off-moor communities.

The management of grazing was another important medieval economic activity, which although leaving limited landscape evidence, is nonetheless significant in helping to understand how open space was perceived on Dartmoor and how it affected other activities. In the early medieval period, before substantial upland colonisation, Dartmoor had served as an area of summer grazing for the cattle and sheep belonging to residents from all over Devon. Indeed it could be argued that the regular transhumance involved led to the establishment of temporary dwellings for graziers, which later became more permanent and formed the basis for settlements (see Houndtor below). The 'customary' right of graziers continued through the late Saxon period and became more formalised following the creation of Dartmoor Forest. Following disafforestation in 1239, and the beginnings of colonisation within the Forest itself, three classes of commoners are recognisable in the documents. The occupants of the ancient tenements residing in the Forest had free grazing rights anywhere on Dartmoor including the Forest. So called 'foreigners', or householders in parishes off the moor, were allowed only to graze their animals on the Commons of Devon – that is, the commons associated with other Dartmoor Parishes – but had no rights within the Forest, unless willing to pay for it. The third group was known as 'venville' tenants. These farmers resided in certain moorland parishes that surround the forest, where a number of select farms or 'villes' were designated with the privilege of restricted grazing rights within the Forest, but only by day, and with free grazing on the Commons of Devon. The importance of summer grazing as part of the economic strategy of Devon's medieval farmers should not be overlooked, and it should be borne in mind that, even at the height of colonisation and enclosure on Dartmoor, the commons and open moorland accounted for the vast majority of the space.

However, in terms of the physical remains, the major landscape legacy from medieval times onward is largely one of agriculture, dominated by the fields worked by the residents of the farms and settlements. For the archaeologist, the evidence takes two forms: the many farms that remain occupied, which have lands still utilised for farming; and deserted settlements and their abandoned

Fig 7.4
Aerial view of Scorriton, showing fossilised evidence of narrow strip fields surrounding the village (NMR 24675/043; © English Heritage. NMR).

fields. The important difference is that the former have undergone many centuries of change to arrive at their present-day appearance, whereas the latter were frozen in time when abandoned, possibly as early as the 14th century in some cases.

Fields

Medieval farms that remain occupied today have had their fabrics extensively altered over the centuries. Buildings from their earliest phases do not survive, but the fields associated with these farms do remain, in form at least. Although walls have been refurbished and strengthened, in many cases the boundaries remain as they were when originally laid out.

Medieval field systems come in three recognisably different forms on Dartmoor. Each form has evolved from its association with diverse settlement patterns and farming practices, and depends to some extent on the date it was created. Strip fields represent the evidence of what may have been some of the earliest medieval farming, and are usually associated with nucleated settlements such as a small village or hamlet, where the division of cultivable land was undertaken communally among the tenants residing at the settlement. If the farms survived, the strip fields were enclosed by hedges or wall banks at a later date to create the fields that are often still in use today.

Dispersed settlements, comprising single farms situated within a cluster of associated fields, may have had later founding dates, contemporary with the recorded period of expansion in the 12th to 14th centuries. Their field patterns have an almost organic appearance, resulting from land being enclosed piecemeal from the open moorland to form animal pasture, although often the fields also have evidence of arable cultivation. Dispersed settlements were also sometimes associated with a mainly arable farming regime, where a single farmstead, though possibly shared between two tenants, may be identified amid a landscape of formerly cultivated fields.

Strip fields

Although visible on aerial and satellite photographs, one of the best ways to visualise strip fields, and to get some idea of their original extent, is by examining the 1st edition

25-inch to the mile OS maps of the 1880s, drafted before the 20th-century tendency of grubbing out hedge boundaries to create larger fields. In the area surrounding Scorriton there is a fine survival of strip fields, still impressive from the air (Fig 7.4) but clear also on 19th century OS maps. The layout of these strips survives because, later in the medieval period, they were enclosed by hedges and, although several strips may have been made into one field, the hedges follow the lines of former strip boundaries; hence their partial survival in the shape of the modern fields. Scorriton, though now a thriving village, was still a relatively small settlement, even as late as the 1880s, and, along with neighbouring Michelcombe, is likely to have origins as the focus of several of the 13 farms associated with the Domesday manor of Holne. Natsworthy (*see* Fig 7.1), also one of the Domesday manors, is another prime example. This south-facing boss of land would have been particularly suited to cultivation and was divided into a series of long but narrow strips, some running parallel with the contour while others run up and down the slope. Further sub-divisions appear on the Tithe Map of 1844, when apparently the strips were still apportioned separately between five holdings or tenements (Gawne 1970, 54), although many of the divisions still visible on the 1880s map, have since been removed. The strips at Natsworthy and Scorriton may have been in use before 1066, as both were recorded in Domesday Book, but at Dunnabridge (*see* Fig 7.3), where the founding date of the tenement was recorded between 1304 and 1306, a similar strip layout existed.

At Natsworthy and Dunnabridge little trace remains of the sub-divisions or individual strips that once existed, as they have been either ploughed out or eroded. However, at several farms the earthworks of the strips often survive, particularly at farms on higher ground, where the settlement became abandoned, or in fields reverted to pasture.

An exemplary survival is at Challacombe (Figs 7.5 and 7.6), associated with a hamlet of that name in the valley of the West Webburn (*see* Fig 7.16). Here an extensive system of strips survives as earthworks spread across the spur of Challacombe Down and on the lower slopes of Hameldon. Both are moderate to steep slopes and, to be cultivated successfully, the majority of the strips, together with the

Fig 7.5 (opposite) Plan showing the surviving evidence of strip cultivation and later enclosures at Challacombe. Also depicted is the extent of medieval and post-medieval tinworking as well as surviving prehistoric features (based on an RCHME 1:2500 survey).

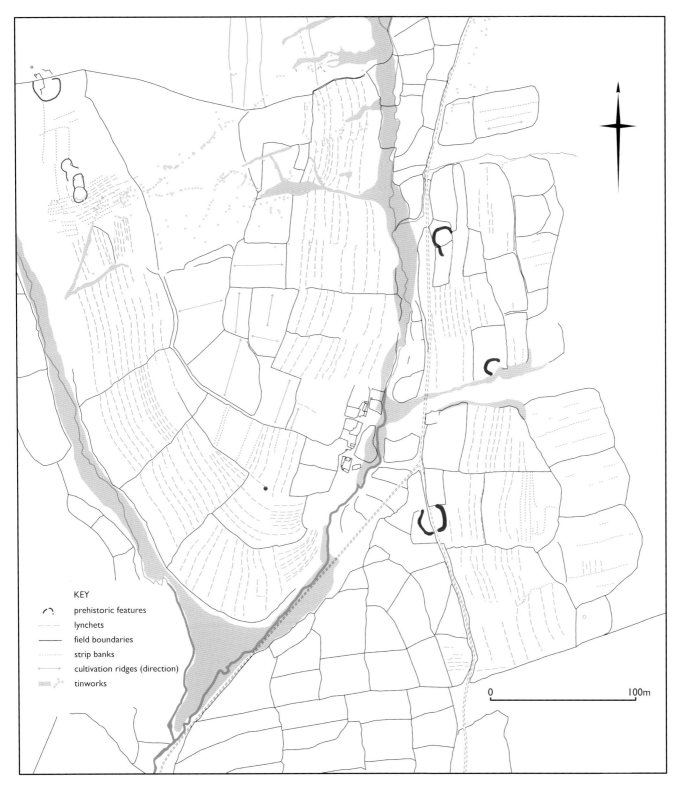

KEY

⌒ prehistoric features

‑ ‑ ‑ lynchets

──── field boundaries

········ strip banks

⟵⟶ cultivation ridges (direction)

▓··· tinworks

0 ──────────── 100m

plough teams that cultivated them, needed to follow the contour of the hill. The result of ploughing each strip separately, possibly over many centuries, was that the soil gradually crept downslope, stopping at the bottom edge of the individual strips (at the lower limit of the ploughing), which was probably defined by a fence or hedge. Here a shallow scarp or 'lynchet' formed, separating each strip from the next one. To keep the strips or 'landscores'

Fig 7.6
Aerial view of the eastern
flank of Challacombe (see
Fig 7.5) showing the
earthwork lynchets that
divided the hillside into
cultivated strips (NMR
18696/27; © English
Heritage. NMR).

Fig 7.6
Aerial view of the eastern
flank of Challacombe (see
Fig 7.5) showing the
earthwork lynchets that
divided the hillside into
cultivated strips (NMR
18696/27; © English
Heritage. NMR).

Fig 7.7 (opposite)
An early RAF aerial view
of Blackaton. The
earthwork remains of a
village are in the central
portion of the image,
surrounded by strip fields,
some of which were being
eroded by agricultural
actively when this
photograph was taken in
the 1960s (RAF 63992
July 1964).

at a manageable length, they were arranged into named blocks, and at Challacombe several of these blocks went by the name of 'Ware', eg, 'Overgang Ware', 'Roe Ware', 'Mill Ware' and 'Long Ware'. This is known because they are set out in a document of 1787, which, remarkably, demonstrates that the apportionment of the land at Challacombe was still undertaken on the strip basis, with tenants of the three surviving Challacombe farms, (North, South and East) each having land dispersed within the Wares (Bonney 1971, 83–91). By this time each block or 'Ware' had been enclosed by a wallbank (Fig 7.6).

Due to a lack of modern ploughing over much of Challacombe, the evidence of the strips has survived almost intact. The strips comprise a series of sloping terraces, each defined on the bottom edge by a lynchet. With good low sunlight, these show up particularly well, as also do the cultivation earthworks that run lengthwise along some of the terraces. Lynchets of this type are uncommon on Dartmoor, many having been ploughed out since the 19th century, but with the correct light conditions surviving examples can be seen at other places on the moor, for example in fields north of Hexworthy and at Butworthy (see Fig 7.8).

Within the West Webburn Valley, Challacombe was not alone. In fact the next major settlement downstream – south – was Blackaton, where remains of a much larger deserted medieval settlement survives (Jamieson 2006). This settlement was once associated with strip fields and lynchets on Hameldown, as recorded by Somers Cocks (1970, 84), although the main evidence for it now is an aerial photograph of 1964, which shows the lynchets and strips quite clearly, before they became effaced by modern ploughing and 'improvement' (Fig 7.7).

Not all Dartmoor's arable fields were part of such extensive shared strip-field systems of the kind that existed in the West Webburn Valley. Dispersed settlements, containing one or perhaps two farmsteads, were also numerous, although the arable fields are of a similar character to those of the larger systems.

At Butworthy, east of Wapsworthy, there is a fine example (Fig 7.8), where earthwork evidence of former strips surround two separate deserted settlements. The boundaries of some survive as lynchets, while others have been built up into baulks of stones cleared from the strips. A third group of particularly narrow strips is delineated by shallow stony banks 18m apart.

In the valley of the River Plym, some notable areas of former strip fields survive on the eastern slopes of Gutter Tor and Hentor (Fig 7.9). At the latter, the fields are located on a gentle north-west-facing slope on the south-east side of the river. This area has been occupied since prehistoric times, with evidence of hut circles and enclosure dispersed over the

slopes; and from the 19th century the site was occupied by a rabbit warren. A small ruined farmstead of medieval character (*see below*) is located within the northern part of the field system, which forms the settlement focus of the fields. The strips form two adjacent blocks, one above the other, each running lengthwise across the slope, separated by stony earth baulks with silted ditches. The strips are not surrounded by stone wall banks or dry-stone walls, neither wholly or individually, as elsewhere on other strip systems at farms abandoned at a later date. The evidence at Hentor therefore provides a good example of how such areas of arable fields in other Dartmoor locations would have appeared before the onset of later enclosure.

Cultivation earthworks

In conditions of low sunlight, especially in winter, zones of closely spaced, linear earthwork ridges, each separated by a shallow furrow, can be observed covering large tracts of moorland. These features represent the remains of past cultivation where the soil has been prepared to form a tilth suitable for planting crops, and are usually referred to as 'ridge and furrow', or simply 'rig'. Most are contained within deserted fields but others appear to be on areas of otherwise open moorland. There are several variants in size

and form, and because they cannot be accurately dated from these characteristics alone there is some uncertainty about what periods they belong to. Examination of such evidence needs to be approached with caution because it is often the case that the surviving features are of a much later or earlier date than that of the field within which they appear to be contained. Even the strips created to be cultivated were subject to changes in cultivation technique, and evidence of the earlier regime may be partly or completely effaced by later activity. A good example is Okehampton Park (*see* Fig 7.23).

The earliest traces of cultivation come from the strip fields associated with the nucleated settlements, medieval hamlets, villages and farmsteads, for example Scorriton, Natsworthy and Challacombe. All of the Dartmoor manors recorded in Domesday possessed one or more ox-drawn ploughs, and these were undoubtedly key to the cultivation of the elongated strip fields. Unlike the sloping grounds described at Challacombe (above), on lesser slopes strips are usually arranged to work with the topography, so that the plough teams travelled along gentler gradients.

The plough type used at about the time of Domesday, known as the fixed mould board, turned the earth to only one side of the furrow and could only plough adjacent furrows if travelling in the same direction for both. A wide strip of ground would be ploughed by proceeding along one edge of a pre-defined oblong area and returning along the other edge in the opposite direction; eventually the opposing furrows would meet in the centre. On gentler slopes and level ground, repeating this operation over decades would result in the formation of ridges with an arched profile, slightly higher in the centre and separated by distinct furrows

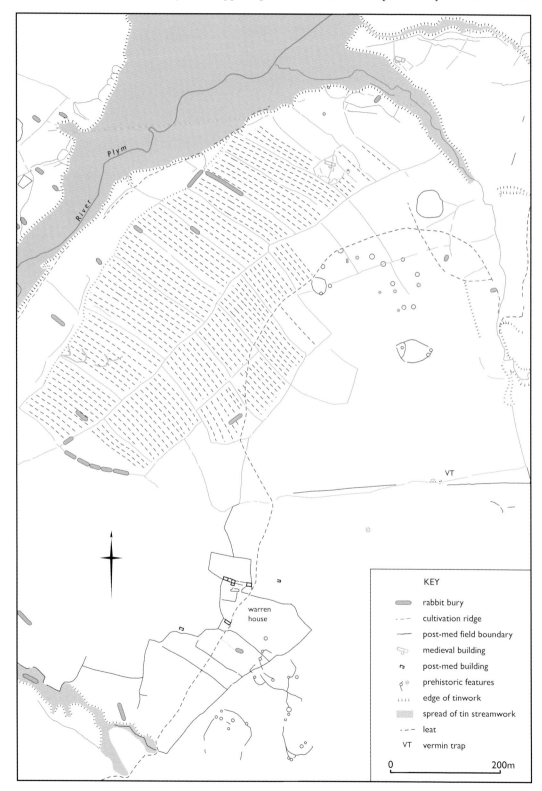

Fig 7.9
Plan of Hentor Warren in the Plym Valley. A series of strip fields containing cultivation ridges are associated with one, or possibly two, ruined medieval settlements. The area was occupied in the 2nd millennium BC, as evident from hut circles and enclosures, and was adopted as a rabbit warren from at least 1807. A ruined house and outbuildings with enclosures, together with a number of rabbit buries, provide the evidence for this later period (based on an EH 1:2500 survey).

KEY

- 🔲 rabbit bury
- – – – cultivation ridge
- ——— post-med field boundary
- medieval building
- post-med building
- prehistoric features
- ⅲⅲ edge of tinwork
- spread of tin streamwork
- – – – leat
- VT vermin trap

0   200m

123

Fig 7.10
Aerial photograph of
Godsworthy showing feint
traces of former strips with
the inverted 'J' footprint, in
fields still being actively
farmed (NMR 24965/011;
© English Heritage. NMR).

Fig 7.11 (opposite)
Simplified plan of medieval
assarts on Yar Tor and
Corndon Tor, showing the
small irregular medieval
enclosure (green) overlying
the more linear prehistoric
reaves (red). The medieval
enclosures to the south
appear to be focussed
around a deserted
settlement comprising at
least two longhouses close
by the modern road. Several
of the fields have surviving
cultivation ridges.

defining the edges, and giving the ground surface a corrugated appearance. This evidence, often referred to as 'broad rig', is common elsewhere in Britain but rare on Dartmoor, although vestiges survive at Okehampton Park. Here feint ridges of 8–12m apart remain (*see* Fig 7.23). Another example is on Holne Moor. In both cases later, narrow cultivation ridges have disguised much of the evidence.

An 'intermediate' form of ridge and furrow, narrower than the broad rig and between 4m and 6m between furrows, is found in association either with contemporary enclosures, or, at some sites, with a series of earth and stone banks or 'baulks', which define strips. In both cases the ridges conform to the axis of the baulks or field boundaries and sometimes have a reversed 'S' or 'J' appearance in plan view. Hentor (*see* Fig 7.9), Holne Moor, Okehampton Park (*see* Fig 7.23) and Butworthy (*see* Fig 7.8) all have examples. The baulks define the edges of the strips and served as dumps for stones brought up by ploughing. At Hentor the ploughed area between the baulks is between 40m and 90m and at Okehampton the distance is commonly 35m, although some are less. Their close association with deserted settlements, which today can be confidently dated *c* 1250–1450 (*see below*), suggests that this cultivation was of similar date.

The reversed 'S' or 'J' plan is found associated with both broad and intermediate ridge and furrow, and indicates ploughing with draught animals. It was difficult for a plough team to turn at the end of each furrow, so the turn was started early, giving the ridges their reversed 'S' or 'J' shape. Examples of S-shaped ridges survive at Okehampton Park (*see* Fig 7.23); examples of J-shaped ridges are preserved in the strip and lynchet fields near Lower and Higher Godsworthy (Fig 7.10).

Narrow ridge and furrow is more widespread than other forms of cultivation, but is less easily datable and harder to designate for cultivation technique. There has been discussion regarding whether the narrow rigs on Dartmoor (Fleming 1994, 101–17) and on Bodmin Moor (Herring 2006, 78–103) are the result of ploughing or of 'lazy bed' cultivation, where raised beds were created manually using a spade. Although seemingly a very labour intensive method, raised beds are an effective and productive means of tilling the earth. The technique is particularly suited to stony ground and negates the need to own and feed draught animals if no plough is used (Herring 2006, 91).

The measurement between furrows is usually *c* 2–4m. The ridges are mostly straight. When long, their course wanders slightly, but they do not follow the inverted 'S' or 'J' form of the broad and intermediate rig. They are found in areas previously cultivated using strips, as at Hentor; and they are also found within enclosed fields that had not been cultivated before. Some examples are located within enclosures, apparently created especially to contain them, of which many examples exist on Corndon Down (Fig 7.11), Sherberton Common and Dunstone Down. Others appear to be on open moorland not previously cultivated or enclosed, such as the northern end of Shapley Common, where drainage ditches dug around the higher limits are the only form of boundary.

Lazy-bed cultivation could be a viable explanation for some of Dartmoor's narrow ridge and furrow. The straightness and narrowness of the ridges is uncharacteristic of ploughing with draught animals, and the fact that they are often tightly contained within enclosures with boundary banks would also restrict the use of the plough. The axis of the narrow rig is often across the width of the cultivated area, rather than of the length, and thus gives short ridges, even sometimes crossing the contour of quite steep slopes rather than working with them. Both of these features would be counter-intuitive in terms of the traditional ploughing techniques used in the medieval and post-medieval periods. At Corndon, for example, not only are the ridges short between two parallel boundaries, but they also run uphill and utilise a field where two sides taper into a point, resulting in extremely short ridges (Fig 7.11). In contrast, some very large swathes of land are involved; on Sherberton Common, where a number of abandoned rectangular fields contain narrow rig, there is also an open area of 10ha to the north with ridges of up to 285m long. It seems more credible that this would be the result of ploughing rather than of lazy beds. A possible compromise explanation, but far from satisfactory, is that the ground was originally broken by ploughing, then the 'beds' maintained by people with hand tools.

There has been a tradition in Dartmoor literature that narrow rig is the result of a single episode of cultivation borne of necessity during the Napoleonic wars of the early 19th century (Fleming 1994, 103). However, it is likely that most if not all are much earlier, as they are frequently overlain by later

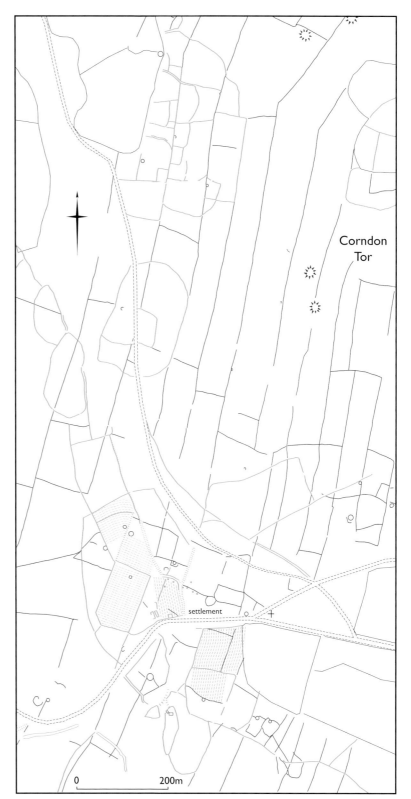

Corndon Tor

settlement

0   200m

landscape features, which themselves pre-date the Napoleonic period. North of Headland Warren, for example, several large swathes of narrow rig have been transected by a leat associated with tinworks of probable 16th or 17th century date (*see* Fig 8.13). Fleming also cites several similar instances (Fleming 1994). It seems more likely, therefore, that this form of cultivation was in use in the late medieval and post-medieval periods, and even as late as the 18th century.

Crops and livestock

Dartmoor has always had a climate that is cooler and wetter than the lowlands of Devon, even during the so-called 'climatic optimum', and within the areas suitable for cultivation, the soils are thin and poor. Growing cereal crops is challenging in such conditions, and it seems unlikely that wheat and barley were planted on the upland farms. In fact, rye and oats – less demanding grains – were grown in preference over much of Devon and Cornwall, where the two crops were favoured for making bread and beer (H S A Fox 1991b, 303). It is probable that these two formed the mainstay of medieval arable production on Dartmoor.

During the 14th century there was a shift from arable cultivation towards livestock production. Again, this was a general trend that occurred sporadically throughout Devon and Cornwall, and elsewhere in England. It might be expected that this shift was more momentous in the upland regions, where grain growing was already at the margins of viability, and was susceptible to decreased demand. However, Fox argued that demand for foodstuffs on Dartmoor remained buoyant because the itinerant population of peat cutters, animal grazers, stone workers and tinworkers. A complete abandonment of cereal growing did not happen suddenly, and mixed farming endured through the later Middle Ages, although eventually the trend towards livestock farming resulted in the enclosure of arable fields and conversion to pasture (H S A Fox 1991a, 159). The enclosure of arable fields elsewhere in Devon began *c* AD 1250, but as is apparent from Challacombe, strip fields were maintained at some places long after the medieval period. It appears likely that it was a drawn out process that depended on the viability of the holding and the number of remaining tenants. The evidence of narrow rig shows that cultivation continued intermittently through the Middle Ages and into the post-medieval period on Dartmoor.

Enclosed fields

Many Dartmoor fields were taken in from the commons, or 'assarted', solely for the purpose of creating enclosed animal pasture and for producing winter fodder. The enclosures were usually associated with the dispersed settlements; single, isolated farmsteads, often referred to as 'ringfence' farms to express the fact that the farm and its associated land was a single unit with an outer boundary. Such farms were in contrast to larger settlements with integrated land allotment. The occupants of single farmsteads worked the land that surrounded it, although they were often the homes of more than one tenant and their layouts reflect piecemeal growth, resembling aggregate enclosures of the 2nd millennium BC. Indeed it was not unknown for prehistoric enclosures to be refurbished and incorporated into medieval fields. At Routrundle (Fig 7.12) two small single prehistoric enclosures, one containing a hut, sit amid the later additions; and at East Deancombe farm, a much larger enclosed settlement has been re-used in a similar way (Fig 7.13). A characteristic of these farms was that, although enclosed, only a small proportion of the acreage was improved. Improvement involved clearing surface stone from the fields but was only necessary where the intention was to cultivate the land. Many of these stony fields, such as the majority of those around Routrundle, were improved in the late 19th and early 20th centuries; they are now devoid of stone and have since been ploughed. Farmsteads in the Deancombe and Newleycombe valleys offer a contrast because several remained occupied into the 20th century, until being abandoned when the Burrator Reservoir was built and all agriculture within the watershed was terminated (Hemery 1983, 114). Many fields were therefore not subject to 'modern improvement' using tractors and machinery, as their stony surfaces testify.

The practice of taking in or enclosing land for farming was not confined to the medieval period and on Dartmoor continued into the 19th century. Within the Duchy lands (the Forest of Dartmoor) occupants of the Ancient Tenements were entitled to add eight more acres to their holdings when passing the tenancy between generations. These additions are known as 'newtakes'. Such encroachments, permitted or otherwise, also continued on the commons outside the Forest, and many small

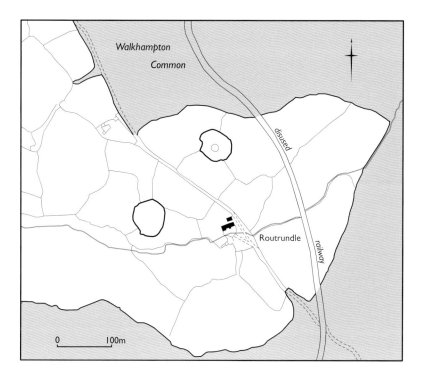

Fig 7.12
Map showing the field
layout at Routrundle, a
medieval farm 'taken in'
from the commons. The
plan highlights the re-used
circular enclosures of
prehistoric date, in one of
which a hut circle survives
(based on Ordnance
Survey first edition
25-inch map of 1886).

farms have peripheral fields that are clearly additions. On Yar Tor and on Corndon Downs (*see* Fig 7.11) there is evidence of such piecemeal assarting associated with a deserted settlement just north of the modern road. In places sections of the prehistoric reaves have been re-used to form field boundaries, but other fields have been added with no regard for the prehistoric walls, and a series of conjoined, amorphous fields extends across the saddle of the hill to the north-west. Farther north, another series of small enclosures adapted and added to the prehistoric reaves in a similar way, although it is not known with which medieval settlement they may have been associated.

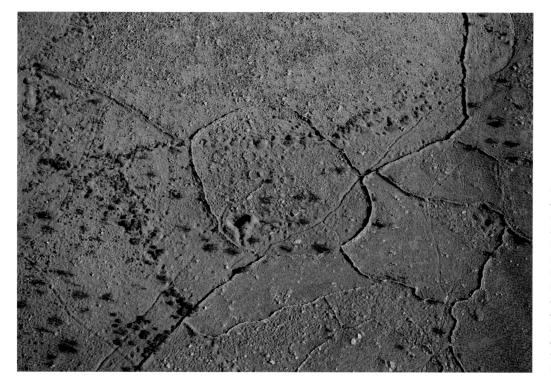

Fig 7.13
Aerial view of a prehistoric
enclosed settlement at
Deancombe, the walls of
which were fossilised when
refurbished to become part of
the piecemeal expansion of
the medieval field system.
Several hut circles survived,
although the ground within
the enclosure was badly
disturbed by later tin
workings (NMR 24897/033;
© English Heritage. NMR).

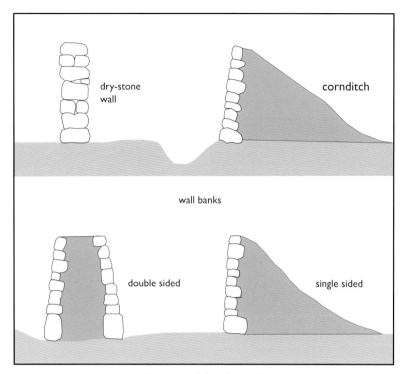

Fig 7.14
Schematic diagram
illustrating the profiles of
the main types of medieval
field boundaries.

Types of field walls

Medieval and post-medieval field boundaries vary in appearance and the variations in some cases mark approximate chronological horizons. Fleming and Ralph (1982) first applied this technique to Dartmoor as part of their detailed study of field systems on Holne Moor. They established a basic typology of

boundaries and suggested that for each form there is an approximate time span; Newman's later surveys in the Newleycombe and Deancombe valleys add additional variants (1994, 207) (Fig 7.14). The technique works best on long-abandoned walls that have not been re-furbished in the past 200 years or so.

Corn-ditches

Of the medieval walls, the most significant is the corn-ditch. This comprises a sloping bank with an external, near vertical dry-stone facing or revetment and an external ditch. Tradition has long told of how these walls were created during the Forest period, ie before 1239, and were used in the commons surrounding the Forest. They were designed to impede the King's deer from entering the enclosed lands, but should they do so, the sloping bank enabled them to return to the commons without difficulty. Fleming and Ralph's work on Holne Moor, where a good sample of corn-ditches survives, suggests that the tradition, with regard to chronology at least, was probably more or less correct and that many could indeed have originated in the Forest period. There is no reason, however, why the tradition did not continue after 1239.

Wall banks

Simpler wall banks with one or two stone-revetted faces but no notable ditch are particularly common. These represent the

Fig 7.15
A classic 'accumulated'
landscape, on an area of
currently open common
land north of Cox Tor. The
prehistoric evidence of hut
circles and sections of
enclosure is overlain by a
medieval assart, which
contains clear evidence of
narrow rig. After
abandonment of these
outfields, the boundary of
the remaining medieval
fields to the right was
consolidated with a wall
bank, which is still
maintained (NMR
24963/031; © English
Heritage. NMR).

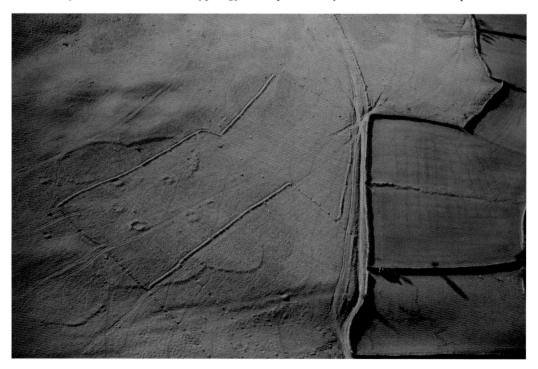

majority of boundary types, especially where the boundary has been maintained into the modern period, although many long-abandoned wall banks are on the open moors in areas such as Corndon Tor. They frequently formed the base for a hedge, following a tradition with origins in the medieval period.

Dry-stone walls

Moorstone granite, with its weathered, rounded edges and uneven shapes, is not the most suitable material for the construction of dry-stone walls, and the result is often unstable. Thus, wall banks, bonded together and strengthened by soil, were popular and endured on Dartmoor. However, when a wall needed to be built quickly, dry-stone was the easiest option, so they were often used in association with 18th- and 19th-century enclosures (*see* chapter 9); few are likely to have origins before the 17th century.

Earth banks

Earth banks are simple linear banks (Fig 7.15). They were probably originally made of turf, with a shallow ditch on the exterior. Once abandoned the banks erode and so seldom remain higher than 0.8m, and the ditches have silted up. Earth banks were commonly used to enclose cultivated land, serving both to demarcate the plots and the ditches to drain it. There is no evidence that all were associated with hedges, but some certainly would have been. Many stone-faced banks are likely to have begun life as earth banks, faced at a later date.

Settlements

The heart of the Challacombe field system was the settlement or hamlet, a cluster of individual homesteads at a shared location (Fig 7.16). What survives is termed a 'shrunken settlement' because only one tenant, based at Challacombe Farm, works all the land today, there were at least five separate holdings as late as 1613, and possibly eight in earlier times (Pattison 1999, 62). Gradually, over several centuries, the individual farms were abandoned and the fields were merged with those of the surviving farms. The foundations of abandoned buildings and the outline walls of the separate crofts survive as upstanding archaeological remains thanks to Challacombe's fairly late decline. At many other surviving settlements

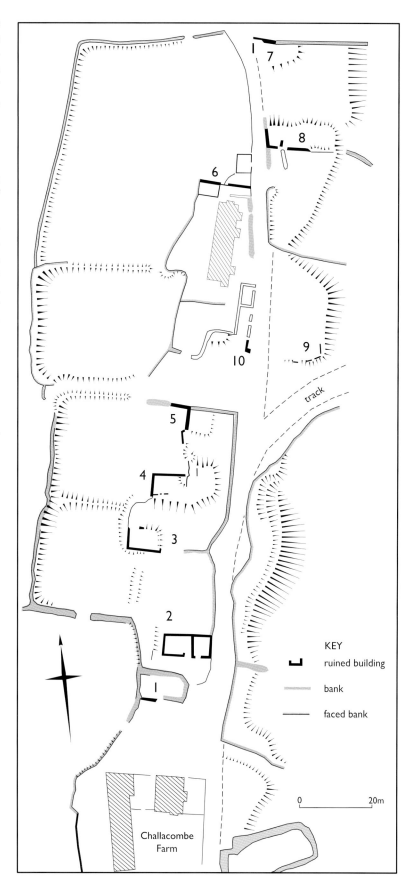

KEY

▢ ruined building

bank

faced bank

0 _____ 20m

Challacombe Farm

Fig 7.16 (previous)
Plan of the shrunken
settlement at Challacombe,
showing the currently
occupied buildings, toft
boundaries of individual
holdings and fragmentary
remains of ten ruined
buildings (from an original
unpublished survey by R
Robinson and D Griffiths;
(© DNPA, with
permission).

the shrinkage might have occurred much earlier, so effacing evidence of other houses as they became redundant. This process occurred at the majority of shared farms. Another example is Dunnabridge, where the five tenant occupants of 1305 gradually reduced to a single tenant by the 19th century.

When we look at successful farms on Dartmoor today, with fine granite buildings and well cared-for field boundaries, we are looking at places founded at least 700 years ago, though for many there is more than 1,000 years of development. Houses were rebuilt, usually on a larger scale, outbuildings and barns were added, fields were improved and expanded, and individual holdings were often amalgamated or 'engrossed' as population varied.

Deserted settlements

Some settlements were abandoned. Possible reasons are discussed below. Abandoned settlements provide important snapshots of the lives of Dartmoor's medieval residents and farmers. Of the 110 deserted settlements listed by Linehan (1966, 124), and of those recorded since her publication, about 45 can be confidently ascribed to the medieval period,

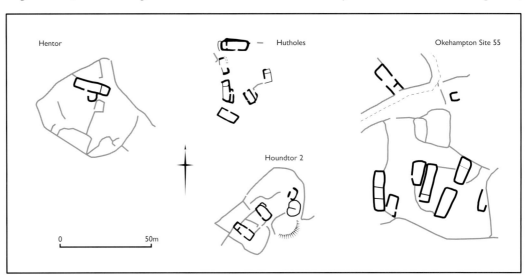

Fig 7.17
Thumbnail plans of
small deserted
settlements simplified
from large-scale surveys,
comprising longhouses
and other buildings set
within a courtledge.
Structures at Houndtor
2 and Hutholes survive
as low walls following
Minter's 1960s
excavations, whereas at
Okehampton and Hentor
the stony foundations
are turf-covered.

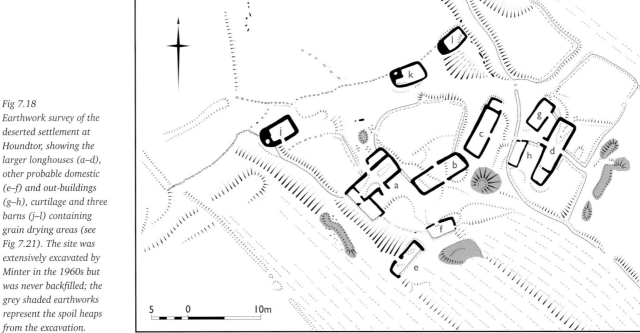

Fig 7.18
Earthwork survey of the
deserted settlement at
Houndtor, showing the
larger longhouses (a–d),
other probable domestic
(e–f) and out-buildings
(g–h), curtilage and three
barns (j–l) containing
grain drying areas (see
Fig 7.21). The site was
extensively excavated by
Minter in the 1960s but
was never backfilled; the
grey shaded earthworks
represent the spoil heaps
from the excavation.

abandoned before *c* 1500. These vary in scale from small farmsteads with one or two buildings, to hamlets such as Hutholes (Fig 7.17) and Houndtor (Fig 7.18), with between 5 and 12 buildings, to Blackaton, where remains of a possible 17 buildings have been noted (Jamieson 2006). There are also several deserted settlements known to be of medieval origin but abandoned much later, often in the 18th and 19th centuries, and where the character of the field evidence is different; these are discussed separately.

Nature of the evidence and common components

Settlement desertion also happened outside the uplands in south-west England, but the best examples have survived on Dartmoor, Exmoor and Bodmin Moor. Although within Dartmoor National Park deserted longhouses are often found in farmland that is still occupied, it is those found on the open moor that are of greater interest, often having associated unaltered abandoned field systems. Once deserted, the settlements and their land remained preserved.

Deserted settlements are dispersed across Dartmoor, although they exist mainly between 250m and up to 380m above sea level, with the majority nearer 350m. None has yet been recorded above 380m. Although it is true that most of the colonists chose sheltered valleys to locate their homes, there are exceptions, such as the single longhouse on the north slope of Down Tor, which is exposed and north facing (*see* Fig 7.22).

The majority of deserted settlements have visible evidence of only one or two buildings, although settlements with three or more are not uncommon. The larger settlements such as Houndtor, with 11, and Blackaton with a possible 17 ruined buildings are unusual. There is also a fine group of dispersed settlements in Okehampton Park, where seven small farms, each of up to eight buildings are arranged in a neighbourhood but are spatially distinct, separated by distances between 100m and 350m (see case study below).

The rectangular buildings survive only as stony earthworks, often more subtle in appearance than the hut circles of 2,000 years earlier. The most well-known of these deserted sites is Houndtor (Fig 7.18), the largest settlement excavated by Minter in the 1960s,

which is located on the south-east slopes of the tor. Its appearance, along with that of Hutholes, also excavated by Minter, is very different to the majority of deserted medieval settlements because, following the excavations, the buildings were not backfilled, consequently their walls and layouts are clear to see.

Longhouses

The most common domestic structure at these settlements was the longhouse. Archaeological evidence and standing building ruins suggest that there was a fairly standard layout, which endured on Dartmoor and in Devon for several hundred years. Longhouses were constructed from moorstone, using an unmortared technique, set against a slope into which they were terraced. They have an elongated rectangular ground plan, with average dimensions between 11m and 18m long by 2m and 4.5m wide, although extremes exist at both ends of the average. At Houndtor and at Okehampton Park, excavations revealed that the walls were not particularly high, mostly less than 1m, and this was likely to be their original approximate height; such low walls supported a timber-framed apex roof providing room for the occupants to stand up. Following a more recent excavation of a longhouse at Sourton, it was suggested that, in this case at least, the stone footings formed the base of a cob wall (Weddell and Reid 1997).

Although shared with other styles of medieval buildings, a key diagnostic feature of early longhouses is the cross-passage, a central thoroughfare across the centre of the building with a doorway on both sides. The doorway openings can be seen on the excavated longhouses at Houndtor and are particularly clear at Dinna Clerks, where return walls were probably the base of a porch. Although the houses at Hutholes and one at Houndtor appear to have only one entrance, excavations revealed that in both cases the entrances on one side had at some time been blocked up.

Traditionally, the lower level of the longhouse is believed to have housed livestock while the upper section was the family residence. The idea that livestock was kept in a 'shippon' forming part of the domestic building is supported by the presence of drainage channels running down the centre of the floor of the lower level at the Houndtor longhouses, enabling the occupants to easily clear out manure, etc. However, given

Fig 7.19
The foundation walls and interior of a longhouse at Hutholes near Widecombe-in-the-Moor, exposed during excavations by Exeter Archaeology in 1994 (photo: Phil Newman).

Fig 7.20
Low-level aerial view of a deserted settlement at Butterbury, showing typical earthwork remains of longhouses and croft walls (NMR 24960/022; © English Heritage. NMR).

the limited space in these building, perhaps only the most valuable animals, such as the oxen used to pull ploughs, or particularly vulnerable beasts such as young calves and lambs, were kept indoors, and this only when necessary and probably only in harsh winter weather. Excavations also reveal central hearths on the floor within the domestic area.

Several longhouse plans show that additional chambers were either added or included in the original construction of the building at the domestic end, known as an inner room. At Houndtor two of the excavated houses (a and d) show this clearly, as also has the main longhouse at Hutholes (Fig 7.19) and two of the examples at Okehampton. At Houndtor one of the houses (a) also has an annex built at right angles to the end of the building, with access only from the interior. It was clearly an extension of the domestic area. Others (c) have external annexes or outhouses built onto the exterior.

Other buildings, outbuildings and barns

Not all surviving ruined buildings were longhouses. Many certainly did not function as dwellings, although some smaller buildings that do not conform to the longhouse format might well have been smaller dwellings (Fig 7.20). At Houndtor, apart from the three principal longhouses (a, b and d), eight other buildings survive. At least three of these (b, e and f) functioned as houses before being used as barns or stores, including one (b) that had started life as a longhouse, in which one door was blocked when it went into use as an outbuilding (Beresford 1979, 131).

Some of the most intriguing buildings are those believed to have contained kilns for drying cereal grains, which after harvest may have remained damp due to the upland climate. Fungal infections triggered by damp in the stored grain would have been devastating. Three such grain-drying barns exist at Houndtor (j, k, and l), one at Hutholes and one at the Houndtor farmstead (Houndtor 2; *see* Fig 7.17). Others have been noted on Bodmin Moor (Johnson and Rose 1994, 90). The buildings are fairly standard rectangular structures with a single entrance, but built against one end of the interior is a flat-topped stone feature, with a hearth and a circular kiln, set side by side within it. These details are clearest on the Houndtor examples (Fig 7.21).

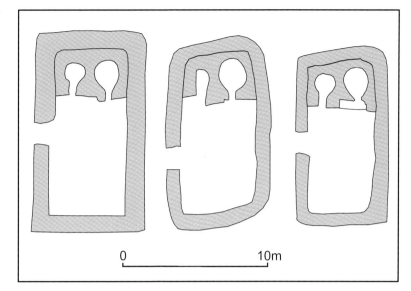

The occupation of settlements

As for prehistoric settlements of nearly 2,000 years earlier, much of the chronology of the medieval settlements has been derived from archaeological evidence, although for the medieval sites this is supplemented in one or two cases by historical documents. Thus, we do have a more precise and detailed general chronology for the occupation of settlements during the medieval period. However, documentation for individual deserted settlements is rarely complete and for most is non-existent. Often, although there is a random date from within the period a site was occupied, its founding and abandonment dates are obscure. Fortunately, pottery from all the excavated Dartmoor medieval settlements (Dean Moor, Houndtor 1 and 2, Hutholes, Dinna Clerks, Okehampton Site 59 and Sourton Down) has been subject to a collective re-appraisal by the West Country ceramics expert John Allan, who has looked not only at the individual finds, but has made important connections with their places of manufacture and distribution zones. Dating of this pottery is now far more precise than when most of it was first excavated. Some forms are closely datable. An absence of some pot types and a presence of others leads to the conclusion that the pottery post-dates *c* 1200 and that the settlements excavated so far were established from *c* 1250 (Allan 1994, 145). This dating agrees with the documentary evidence for expansion into the uplands. Probable milder climate encouraged

Fig 7.21
Ground plans of the three 'barns' at Houndtor deserted settlement, equipped with grain-drying kilns (based on Minter's excavation drawings published in Beresford 1979).

Fig 7.22
Aerial view of a single,
isolated, deserted longhouse
on the north slope of Down
Tor (NMR 24900/009;
© English Heritage. NMR).

colonisation of places that were formerly less attractive, and is contemporary to the earliest occupations in Dartmoor Forest.

The evidence for earlier occupation at these sites is controversial and is not supported by pottery evidence. At Okehampton Park, Austin recorded a timber building phase that predated that of stone, but he did not consider it to be earlier than the 12th century, immediately preceding the stone building phase. At Houndtor, however, Minter excavated the feint remains of three much smaller sunken huts that predate the longhouses and which she interpreted as 'sheilings', evidence of temporary settlement by graziers visiting the moor for summer pasture. These timber buildings were undated but supposed by Minter to be post-Roman (ie after 410), although buildings of this type are known from elsewhere as late as the 13th century (Beresford 1979, 112). More controversial is Minter's claims that the 13th-century stone longhouses at Houndtor and Hutholes had a sequence of turf-built predecessors, dating from 700–800 onwards, based on the excavated evidence of a series of shallow stakeholes. This idea is firmly rejected by Austin (1985, 71–9), and a re-excavation of

Hutholes in 1994 (see Fig 7.19) failed to retrace the stakeholes that Minter cites (Gent 2007, 35–82). This controversy is unlikely to be resolved in the short term, but informed opinion currently doubts the existence of the stakeholes or suggests alternative explanations for them.

Desertion and shrinkage

The archaeological evidence is also crucial to understanding the abandonment of these farms and settlements in the medieval period. Allan's work on the pottery suggests that desertion occurred by 1450 at all the excavated sites, although some, including Hutholes, could have been deserted by 1350 (Allan 1994, 145).

The causes of shrinkage or abandonment are one of the fascinations of deserted settlement study. Why did some survive the medieval period and remain thriving today while others did not, lasting in some cases only a couple of centuries or less? Authors discussing this topic often refer to Dartmoor as 'marginal'. Because of its height above sea level and wetter climate some forms of agriculture, particularly cultivation, are more challenging, so it follows that during climatic downturns life on Dartmoor becomes more arduous. When climate is fair and population is rising it is reasonable to expect increased occupation of marginal lands, as is concluded for 13th- and early 14th-century Dartmoor. Conversely, with deteriorating climate, retreat from uplands is expected. It is also suggested that epidemics such as the Black Death of 1348–9 was responsible for a major demographic upheaval in England, severely depleting the population, but also broadening the opportunities for those who survived. As climate worsened it is not surprising that take-up of newly available lowland farms would be at the expense of the less rewarding uplands.

But this broad-brush explanation may not be wholly correct. Individual holdings may have been abandoned for a number of reasons, either to do with matters of tenure, or perhaps no one wished to take over the occupancy when a tenant died. As discussed in chapter 4, evidence from the late 2nd millennium BC suggests a similar scenario; so it is probably wise not to imagine a mass exodus of entire families from their homes because life on Dartmoor had become too arduous. If detailed information were available, it would probably reveal a different explanation for each desertion, but set against a common backdrop of change.

Perhaps it is more sensible to see these combined factors as only part of complex circumstances. As Harold Fox observed, the medieval economy of Dartmoor was not dependant solely on arable farming; there were several alternative livelihoods, including tinworking, peat cutting, pastoral farming and granite cutting, all of which kept the Dartmoor economy buoyant and its people busy (H S A Fox 1994, 166). Summer grazing in particular would have remained viable, even during periods of wetter climate. Perhaps, therefore, the term marginal is not applicable to the residents of medieval Dartmoor, as they adapted to the varied opportunities offered by their environment; and the term only applies to arable cultivation when Dartmoor is compared to lowland areas of Devon such as the South Hams. Following the Black Death in 1348–9, only one in four of the high moorland farms within the forest was abandoned or engrossed (H S A Fox 1994, 167), a number that would surely have been much higher if the area was truly marginal.

That said, some settlements were so located as to test the potential of the environment to the limit. On the north side of Down Tor, a single ruined longhouse attached to an enclosure wall is probably a settlement that was abandoned before it developed further (Fig 7.22). Although settlements thrived on the south-facing slopes of this valley, this exposed north-facing house would have had little winter sunlight, overshadowed as it is by the tor. Of the recorded deserted settlements, that to the south-west of Birch Tor is the highest on Dartmoor at 380m above sea level (*see* Fig 8.12). The field system appears to have been a natural extension of the Challacombe enclosures in the Redwater Valley, but taking in moorland at a slightly higher altitude. There is a series of irregular enclosures, some containing faint evidence of lynchets. At the centre of the fields is a ruined settlement comprising the foundations of two longhouses. It is likely that more buildings once stood here but have been destroyed by tinworking after abandonment.

Okehampton Park: a case study

Okehampton Park is an area of medieval landscape that illustrates many of the elements described above (Fig 7.23). It is at the northern end of Dartmoor National Park, just south of the town of the same name. Ten earthwork sites, of which the majority are medieval settlements, are dispersed within an area of open ground on the upper valley of the Okement River. They formed the focus of a landscape survey by the English Heritage archaeological survey team in 2003–4 (Probert 2004). This area is particularly interesting because in 1292 Hugh Courtenay, lord of nearby Okehampton Castle, changed the status of part of the area to a deer park (*see* chapter 6).

The settlements, or perhaps more accurately, farmsteads (which for the purpose of this discussion retain Linehan's 1966 numbering system), are dispersed laterally along the contour at on average 325m above sea level. All are superficially similar in appearance, comprising clusters of earthwork remains of between two and eight buildings each, with small, attached curtilage, associated larger fields and areas of cultivation. Site 53 (Fig 7.24) consists of a trio of such

KEY

⚏ medieval buildings

medieval field system

broad ridge and furrow

intermediate ridge and furrow

baulks

narrow ridge and furrow

18th-century field banks

◇ 18th-century building

19th-century field banks/ walls

modern track

Site 53C

Site 52

Site 53B

Site 112

Site 55

Site 54

Site 53A

Site 56

cairn

Site 57

camp

Site 58

Site 111

Black Down

500   0   500 METRES

Fig 7.23
Plan showing the medieval settlements, field systems and former cultivated areas within Okehampton Park (surveyed detail overlain onto Ordnance Survey 1:10 000 base map data).

Fig 7.24 (opposite)
Large-scale earthwork survey of one of the deserted settlements (Site 53) at Okehampton.

farmsteads located in a neighbourhood group, but sites 54–8 are more discrete.

Site 52 stands out as different to the others: the earthworks demonstrate several phases of construction, possibly including an initial phase as a farmstead. Later, however, an L-shaped stone building, possibly of two storeys, was constructed, the masonry evidence reveals a higher status structure. Although previously considered to have been both a chapel and a leper hospital, it is now is thought that it could originally have served as a hunting lodge associated with the deer park.

Of particular note at Okehampton Park are the trackways that run between the field enclosures. Although surviving most clearly near the deserted settlements, they served not just these farms but also as routes for grazing live-stock from lowland settlements to and from the commons. On the wooded slopes of the Okement River are vestiges of earthwork shelves and linear hollows representing early tracks to the moor. Within the cultivated areas, however, the tracks comprise shallow linear hollows flanked by the banks of the enclosures and lynchets.

particularly cultivation, are more challenging, so it follows that during climatic downturns life on Dartmoor becomes more arduous. When climate is fair and population is rising it is reasonable to expect increased occupation of marginal lands, as is concluded for 13th- and early 14th-century Dartmoor. Conversely, with deteriorating climate, retreat from uplands is expected. It is also suggested that epidemics such as the Black Death of 1348–9 was responsible for a major demographic upheaval in England, severely depleting the population, but also broadening the opportunities for those who survived. As climate worsened it is not surprising that take-up of newly available lowland farms would be at the expense of the less rewarding uplands.

But this broad-brush explanation may not be wholly correct. Individual holdings may have been abandoned for a number of reasons, either to do with matters of tenure, or perhaps no one wished to take over the occupancy when a tenant died. As discussed in chapter 4, evidence from the late 2nd millennium BC suggests a similar scenario; so it is probably wise not to imagine a mass exodus of entire families from their homes because life on Dartmoor had become too arduous. If detailed information were available, it would probably reveal a different explanation for each desertion, but set against a common backdrop of change.

Perhaps it is more sensible to see these combined factors as only part of complex circumstances. As Harold Fox observed, the medieval economy of Dartmoor was not dependant solely on arable farming; there were several alternative livelihoods, including tinworking, peat cutting, pastoral farming and granite cutting, all of which kept the Dartmoor economy buoyant and its people busy (H S A Fox 1994, 166). Summer grazing in particular would have remained viable, even during periods of wetter climate. Perhaps, therefore, the term marginal is not applicable to the residents of medieval Dartmoor, as they adapted to the varied opportunities offered by their environment; and the term only applies to arable cultivation when Dartmoor is compared to lowland areas of Devon such as the South Hams. Following the Black Death in 1348–9, only one in four of the high moorland farms within the forest was abandoned or engrossed (H S A Fox 1994, 167), a number that would surely have been much higher if the area was truly marginal.

That said, some settlements were so located as to test the potential of the environment to the limit. On the north side of Down Tor, a single ruined longhouse attached to an enclosure wall is probably a settlement that was abandoned before it developed further (Fig 7.22). Although settlements thrived on the south-facing slopes of this valley, this exposed north-facing house would have had little winter sunlight, overshadowed as it is by the tor. Of the recorded deserted settlements, that to the south-west of Birch Tor is the highest on Dartmoor at 380m above sea level (see Fig 8.12). The field system appears to have been a natural extension of the Challacombe enclosures in the Redwater Valley, but taking in moorland at a slightly higher altitude. There is a series of irregular enclosures, some containing faint evidence of lynchets. At the centre of the fields is a ruined settlement comprising the foundations of two longhouses. It is likely that more buildings once stood here but have been destroyed by tinworking after abandonment.

Okehampton Park: a case study

Okehampton Park is an area of medieval landscape that illustrates many of the elements described above (Fig 7.23). It is at the northern end of Dartmoor National Park, just south of the town of the same name. Ten earthwork sites, of which the majority are medieval settlements, are dispersed within an area of open ground on the upper valley of the Okement River. They formed the focus of a landscape survey by the English Heritage archaeological survey team in 2003–4 (Probert 2004). This area is particularly interesting because in 1292 Hugh Courtenay, lord of nearby Okehampton Castle, changed the status of part of the area to a deer park (see chapter 6).

The settlements, or perhaps more accurately, farmsteads (which for the purpose of this discussion retain Linehan's 1966 numbering system), are dispersed laterally along the contour at on average 325m above sea level. All are superficially similar in appearance, comprising clusters of earthwork remains of between two and eight buildings each, with small, attached curtilage, associated larger fields and areas of cultivation. Site 53 (Fig 7.24) consists of a trio of such

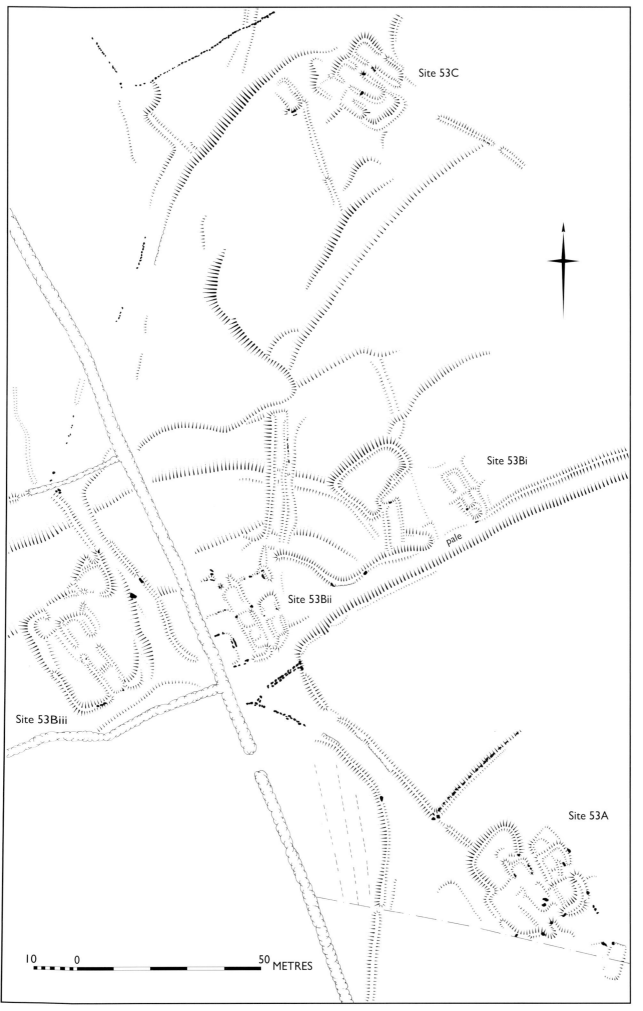

Site 53C

Site 53Bi

pale

Site 53Bii

Site 53Biii

Site 53A

10   0   50 METRES

137

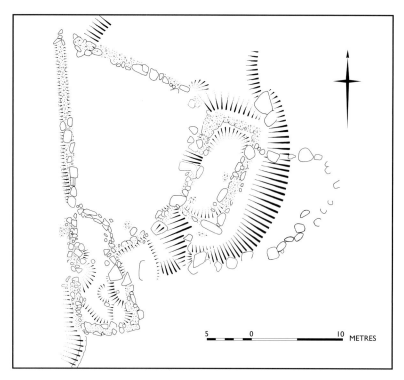

5   0   10   METRES

Fig 7.25
Large-scale plan of Hawns, a small deserted settlement in the Valley of Broadall Lake, probably abandoned in the 19th century.

Between 1976 and 1978, site 59 was excavated by David Austin, in advance of expansion at the Meldon quarries (Austin 1978, 191–240). The archaeology revealed the remains of a group of eight buildings with stone foundations, some of which had timber precursors. Much pottery was recovered, but at the time, was not precisely datable. Austin came to the perfectly reasonable conclusion that the excavated site, along with all the others, were abandoned as a result of the area becoming imparked in the 1290s when the deer park was created and a programme of human clearance had occurred. This was not an uncommon occurrence in medieval England. However, Allan's more recent analysis of the pottery has demonstrated that this site was probably not deserted until the 15th century (Allan 1994, 145). Without excavating all nine of the settlements, it has to be assumed that all had a similar chronology, and therefore most survived the early stages of the deer park creation.

In the past, there also has been some uncertainty over the extent of the deer park. The boundary of the park is not described in any surviving medieval documents. It was formerly believed to be bounded on three sides by rivers and to extend as far south as the large dry-stone wall that marks the limit of enclosed land today. This delineation was first recorded on Donn's map of Devon in 1765 (Ravenhill

1965, maps 6a and 6b), long after disparkment in 1538, and has been accepted by all subsequent writers. However, recognition of the earthworks of a probable pale suggests that the park was substantially smaller and confined to the immediate slopes of the Okement Valley; the majority of the settlements and much of the cultivated land therefore falls outside the park (Probert 2004, 89–92). Abandonment as a result of imparkment was therefore possibly restricted to sites 53b and 53c – which lie north of the boundary – although definitive evidence is lacking. What is particularly important about this group of settlements is their setting within, and association with, a contemporary landscape of agriculture containing all the elements described above. Vestiges of an earlier phase of broad rig survived changes in cultivation that resulted in areas of intermediate ridges and strips defined by baulks, which are the dominant surviving remains. Finally, probably during the 17th or 18th century, cultivation resulting in straight narrow ridges was adopted, obliterating the earlier forms in places. Although not precisely dateable, these changes in ploughing technique testify to sustained, though probably intermittent, cultivation associated with the deserted settlements. The area is now open moorland.

Later desertions

Of the total number of the deserted sites of 13th-century or earlier foundation, not all were deserted during the 15th century (Linehan 1966, 124); many survived and were refurbished or completely rebuilt in the 16th and 17th centuries, and not deserted until the 18–20th centuries. On the south of the moor, for example, Hawns was probably the home of 'Richard ate Haghene' in 1330 (Gover *et al* 1969, 271), and a succession of documentary references confirm that the site was probably still occupied until at least 1825 (RCHME 1998). The surviving ruins represent the buildings that were in place at abandonment, which may be rebuilds of the 16th century, not 14th-century structures. There are two buildings conjoined by the walls of a small, enclosed yard, which is itself attached to the walls of a large field. The structural remains (Fig 7.25) differ from those of deserted 14th- and 15th-century, entirely stone-built structures, which tend to endure as stony

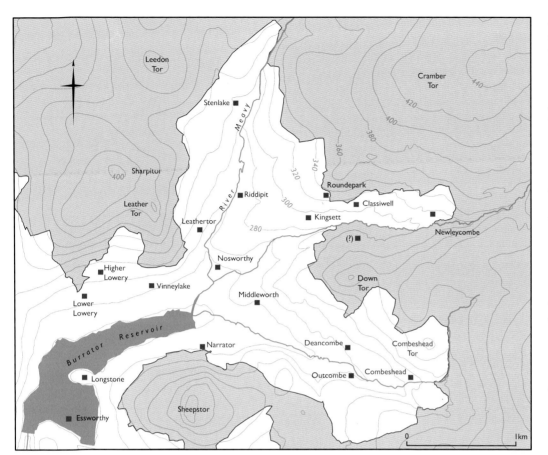

Fig 7.26
Map showing the location of deserted farms and the outline of abandoned farm enclosures, within the Meavy Valley and the catchment of Burrator Reservoir. Most were in existence by the 13th century, and were still occupied through much of the 19th century, although by the end of that period several had been abandoned. Those that survived into the 20th century were forced into abandonment following the construction of the reservoir. One exception is the single unnamed longhouse on the north slope of Down Tor (see Fig 7.22), which was probably abandoned several centuries earlier. Green shading depicts the open moorland of the commons (based on Ordnance Survey first edition 25-inch map of 1886).

earthworks, and survive as upstanding, though partly collapsed walls. It is not possible to say what function each of these buildings served, but it is likely that one was a dwelling and the other a shippon or barn.

The highest concentration of late-deserted farms survives in the Meavy, Newleycombe and Deancombe valleys on south-west Dartmoor, where 16 sites have some remains, mostly ruinous or badly damaged (Fig 7.26). Some of the farms were abandoned in the early 19th century, but the last tenants of others were not evicted until the area formed the catchment for Burrator Reservoir, built in 1898. Several of the farmhouses, including Deancombe, Kingsett and Middleworth had been rebuilt since the 1840s (Wakeham 2003, 156–7). Nearly all the farms were first documented in the 13th and 14th centuries, and historical evidence supports continuous occupation for up to 600 years before abandonment (Newman 1994, 209–23; Greeves 2003a, 16).

Newleycombe and Classiwell (Fig 7.27) are two of the best preserved of the early 19th-century desertions, although neither has any upstanding buildings as do Middleworth or Vinneylake.

Both are isolated settlements, located within their original field systems. Newleycombe (Fig 7.28) is first documented in 1303 (Greeves 2003a, 21), and therefore clearly had earlier origins, probably in the 13th century. Classiwell would have had a similar if not earlier, founding date. Despite early origins, their ruined buildings are different from those of medieval longhouse settlements, although it is notable that both sites are dominated by one long building, which could represent rebuilt longhouses. Only excavation would confirm this. Both farms have small courtyards that open onto narrow lanes lined by wall banks. The long rectangular farmhouses are one room deep and face the yard on a long side. Newleycombe has a collapsed porch at one end, evident from in situ granite doorjambs. Both farmhouses have several small outbuildings, either attached to the farmhouse as at Classiwell, or elsewhere in the yard at Newleycombe. There is a fireplace built into a central wall at Newleycombe and at Classiwell there is a 16th- or 17th-century style double-chamfered window mullion on the ground amid the ruins, which strongly suggests an approximate period for its rebuilding.

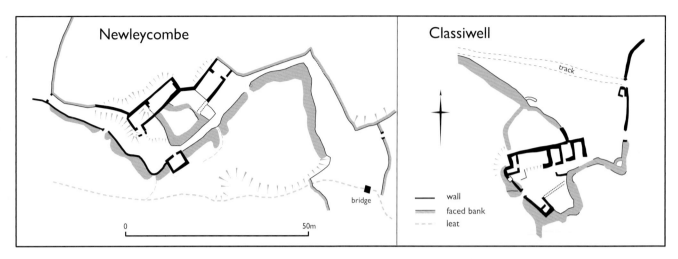

Newleycombe   Classiwell

track

bridge

0   50m

—— wall
—— faced bank
- - - leat

Fig 7.27
Simplified plans of the
deserted farmsteads at
Newleycombe and Classiwell
in the Newleycombe Valley.
Although the farms are
recorded from the early 14th
century, the remains reflect
rebuilds dating probably
from the 17th to the 19th
century. In 1839, although
Newleycombe was
abandoned, Classiwell was
still occupied, but was
deserted before 1900.

Fig 7.28
Low-level aerial view of the
ruined Newleycombe Farm
(NMR 24899/041;
© English Heritage. NMR).

Conclusion

Settlement and assarting of the upland in the early medieval period strongly suggests a return to Dartmoor following an apparent absence of permanent occupation for much of the late-prehistoric and post-Roman periods. Settlement in the low-lying areas appears to have been firmly established from about the 10th century, perhaps earlier, but expansion into the uplands became more apparent in the 13th and 14th centuries, especially as the Forest of Dartmoor became available to settle after 1239. However, the mixed economy of Dartmoor continued to rely on summer grazing on the open moorland, the vast majority of which remained unenclosed common land to which residents of upland farms, border parishes and, to some extent, residents elsewhere in Devon had rights to graze animals. People began to live in stone-built rectangular buildings in farms, hamlets or villages surrounded by fields taken in from moorland wastes and supporting crops or animals.

As some settlements became permanent, others failed and were deserted. The underlying cause of abandonment was probably a combination of changing demographics and climatic deterioration in the 15th century, but desertion mostly, though not always, affected places of marginal farming potential, either on high ground, poor soils or poor location.

But Dartmoor's record of medieval farming is mainly one of success. Much of what was current in the 12th to 15th centuries remains today. Farms, fields, trackways and farming infrastructure frequently remain occupied or in use, providing a living landscape of medieval origin. Although buildings were replaced, field walls refurbished and farming practice changed, in places the basic framework of the landscape is much as it was 700 years ago. Change was of course inevitable within this period and many elements of the current landscape are much newer. These are discussed in later chapters.

8

The medieval tin industry, 1150–1700

Context

Of all the evidence for human activity on Dartmoor, none have left such striking, visible and widespread remains as the tin industry, which has radically altered areas of the landscape wherever the search for and extraction of this important metal occurred. Tin is present in only two counties in England, Devon and Cornwall, and although the history and culture of the latter is dominated by metal mining, in Devon the industry is often overlooked; this, understandably, is due to the much smaller scale of the industry in Devon in the 19th and 20th centuries, when Cornish tin mining was still active. Today the perception of how important tin was to the economy of Dartmoor is partly lost, the industry having been abandoned for almost a century; but in the Middle Ages in particular, it was the most important non-agricultural activity, generating wealth for tinwork owners, income for the tinners – many of whom were Dartmoor residents – and revenue for the crown.

Unrefined tin is known as black tin; when smelted it is called white tin. Smelting produces a bright silvery metal that is highly valued for its low melting temperature and for its resistance to corrosion. It is, however, fairly soft and quite brittle, so is seldom used on its own, rather as a constituent in alloys since probably the early 2nd millennium BC, when it was first combined with copper to produce bronze. The production of bronze, however, requires only a proportionately small quantity of tin, and by far the greatest demand for the metal, from the Roman period until the late 18th century, came from the manufacture of pewter. Today, pewter is made from tin with copper, antimony or bismuth, but in the medieval and early post-medieval periods most pewter was a straightforward combination of tin and lead. It was used on a

massive scale for table and household wares, being an attractive but substantially cheaper equivalent to silver. The demand for tin from pewter producers was in decline in the late 18th century, but it was replaced by the need of it for the tinplate industry, which began on a large scale in the 1720s and rose exponentially into the 19th century.

Ever since a serious interest in Dartmoor's past first developed, during the 19th century, many have speculated that tin was worked in prehistoric times; an idea that is made all the more compelling by the fact that there were Bronze Age inhabitants on Dartmoor who might have recognized the presence of the tin deposits and were aware of the significance for making bronze. Likely though this may seem, so far no archaeological evidence for prehistoric tinworking has been discovered on Dartmoor itself. This is curious considering that a good deal of evidence has been retrieved from Cornish tinworks that confirm the existence of a prehistoric tin industry (Penhallurick 1986, 173–224). Most of the evidence from Cornwall consists of artefacts that were retrieved by 19th century tinners when reworking 'ancient' tinworks, and this seldom occurred in Devon, where tinworking was restricted mostly to underground mining by that time. Recent examination of Dartmoor's river sediments away from the moorland has provided radiocarbon dates suggesting that wastes from tinworking processes were being deposited in the rivers in both the Roman and post-Roman periods (Thorndycraft et al 2004), although as yet there is no information to indicate where precisely the tinworking was taking place and no tinworks of this period or earlier have been identified.

The first documentary evidence that a Devon tin industry had become established, is the pipe roll of 1156 (Finberg 1949), from which it is clear that the industry was already in existence. One writer has suggested that the prosperity of 10th-century Saxon Lydford, on the western edge of Dartmoor (see above) was built upon wealth generated from tin (Maddicott 1989), although as yet this plausible idea relies solely on interpretation of the historic record, rather than on specific written details or on archaeological evidence.

The Stannaries

A rise in the importance of tin in the 12th century is confirmed by the first 'stannary' charter for Devon and Cornwall in 1201, issued by King John (Pennington 1973, 15). The charter confirmed the customary privilege of 'tin bounding', which allowed the tinners to search for tin wherever they pleased, and to divert water supplies as they needed them; it also removed the tinners from common law and henceforward all matters of justice concerning tinners and the tin industry would be under the jurisdiction of the Lord Warden of the Stannaries, a crown appointee who presided over the stannary courts. The stannaries were the several districts that made up the tin mining region of Devon and Cornwall from which the industry was presided over and administered. After a charter of 1305, Devon and Cornwall were dealt with separately and by 1328 Devon had four stannaries, centred on the towns of Ashburton, Tavistock, Plympton and Chagford (Greeves 1986, 147). On certain days of the year an event called 'coinage' took place at these towns, when finished tin was assayed, taxes were paid on it and tin traders could buy the product. Details of several coinages at Ashburton and Tavistock, and the tinners who attended, are known from documentation (Finberg 1949, 155–84; Greeves 2003a).

Crockerntor

Since the early 14th century the Devon stannaries held parliaments or 'Great Courts' on Crockerntor, a granite tor on central Dartmoor, which represents a common point not far from where the boundaries of the four Devon stannaries converge. Each stannary elected a number of persons who had associations with the tin industry to represent them at the stannary courts. Here, all legislative affairs connected with the tin industry were dealt with through the enactment of laws and

the hearing of grievances. Between 1474 and 1786, 13 Great Courts were recorded, although details of others may have eluded us (Greeves 1986, 145).

Crockerntor was among the first historical places to catch the attention of early writers on Devon and its history. In 1630, for example, Risdon described the tor: 'A high rock called Crockern Torr, where the parliament for stannary causes is kept; where there is a table and seats of moorstone, hewn out of the rocks, lying in the force of all weather, no house or refuge being near it.' (Risdon 1810, 222)

In Risdon's day Crockerntor was still in use for this purpose, so there is no reason to doubt his description. Later the site of the 'Tinners Parliament' is also marked on Benjamin Donn's map of Devonshire 1765 (Fig 8.1), such was its significance. We know that the Great Courts were grand affairs. One account of 1710 describes up to 12,000 people attending, with 'abundance of booths, good victuals and drink … and nothing is wanting to make a fine show' (*DC* 9 June 1710). However, the granite furniture described by Risdon, if it existed in the form that he claimed, was removed sometime before the 1790s when both Swete (Gray 2000) and Polwhele (1793–1806) reported their absence. The useful stones, were probably removed and dispersed for various purposes long before, and there is a tradition that the so-called 'Judge's Chair' at Dunnabridge, a large stone bench with a canopy built into the wall of the pound, was made up from components taken from Crockerntor, which is possible. Quite recently, however, a more likely candidate for a granite chair was discovered near Crediton, with record of its removal to there in 1855 (Marchand 1995, 7).

Growth and decline

One of the administrative tasks undertaken by stannary officials was to compile statistics on the output and price of tin. Although incomplete, these figures demonstrate that once established, the Devon tin industry rose in importance, with output increasing on a steep upward trend between the mid-13th century and 1524, at which date it reached a peak of more than 470 thousandweight (564,000 lbs or 255,826 kg). Thereafter, the decline was as steep as the rise, with occasional small blips, but by the start of the Civil War in 1643 production had reached zero. During a slight renaissance between 1673

Fig 8.1
Crockerntor and the site of
the Tinners' Parliament
from Benjamin Donn's map
of 1765.

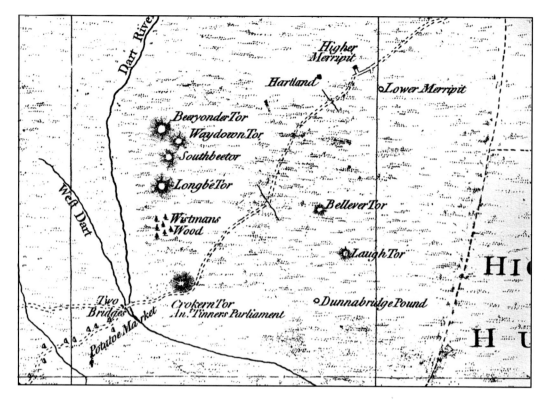

and 1726, insignificant quantities of tin were produced, and by 1750, the last date for which figures are available, the level of production was back to zero (Lewis 1908, 252–7). Although production recommenced in the late 18th century, it was on a much-reduced scale compared with the medieval period and is dealt with in chapter 11.

Tinworking and archaeology

The archaeological study of tinworking has an unusual pedigree compared with either prehistoric or medieval Dartmoor studies. Since the 19th century antiquarians had been curious about certain aspects of Dartmoor's archaeological remains, namely the 'blowing houses' or blowing mills where tin was smelted. These were often referred to as 'Jews Houses' by antiquaries and early writers. Other aspects of the industry were neglected, however. General interest was restricted mainly to speculation on the possibility of the 'ancient' origins of tinworking rather than on paying attention to the archaeological remains (eg Polwhele). This attitude changed only as late as the 1980s, when the potential for study of tinworks and other aspects of the industry's archaeology began to be realised (Greeves 1981a).

One of the first writers to note the antiquity of blowing houses was Anna Eliza Bray who, in 1836, described 'Phoenician smelting houses' near Dartmeet (1879, 254). These are certainly the buildings at Week Ford, just downstream from Dartmeet, one of which is a ruined blowing mill (*see* Fig 8.17). The Phoenician connection was part of a long-held but misguided belief that people from Lebanon in the Middle East, had traded for tin in Devon and Cornwall and had great influence within the industry here. This theory, like theories about the Druids, has remained rather persistent in West Country lore, but has now been firmly discredited (Penhallurick 1986, 123–31).

The first published note about a blowing house was in 1866. John Kelly correctly identified a building below Yealm Steps as a smelting site on the basis of artefacts that he observed to be mouldstones used for casting molten metal, although he considered them to be contemporary with the prehistoric evidence he had also recorded in the area (Kelly 1866). Only a few years later, the blowing mills cited by Bray at Week Ford, were examined by R Burnard, using a technique that he himself referred to as having 'cleared' the site (Burnard 1887–90). This was several years before Burnard's campaign of excavations at prehistoric settlements and barrows, described in chapter 1. Burnard went on to recorded several other blowing houses in the 1890s (Burnard 1891), however, most of his contemporaries showed little interest in these mills. The exception was R H Worth, who almost single-handedly recorded the majority of the known tin mill sites that are in the record today. He carried out fieldwork over about 50 years in the last decade of the 19th century and the first half of the 20th (Spooner and Russell 1967). Despite the growing fascination of Worth and one or two others with tin mills, their archaeological significance was not widely appreciated even as late as the 1950s. In the mid-1950s, as Aileen Fox undertook rescue excavations of prehistoric and medieval settlements at the Avon Reservoir site (*see* chapter 3), a particularly fine blowing house was also threatened by the reservoir but was not 'officially' excavated. It was left to a group of enthusiasts to retrieve what information they could before the site became submerged (Parsons 1956). Fortunately the structure of this mill survives and is occasionally visible at times of drought (*see* Fig 8.25).

Although 'industrial archaeology' became popular during the 1960s (*see* chapters 10–13) and some attention was paid to Dartmoor tin mining, it was not until the 1980s that conventional archaeological approaches were applied to 'early' tin extraction and smelting. During the construction of the Colliford Reservoir on Bodmin Moor, Cornwall between 1979 and 1983 a tin mill was discovered, and excavated, accompanied by fieldwork and survey examining the site's medieval context, including its tinworks (Austin *et al* 1989). This was followed in the 1990s by the excavation of a Dartmoor blowing mill, where five seasons of work took place between 1991 to 1996. The results of the latter are not yet published.

However, our knowledge of medieval and post-medieval Dartmoor tinworks, where the ore was extracted, still relies mostly on detailed fieldwork, survey and contemporary documentary accounts, which have been researched and summarised by Gerrard (2000) and others.

Tinworking

The oxide of tin, cassiterite (SnO_2), is a crystalline substance. Along with other metallic ores it is found in veins or lodes in narrow fissures in the granite and metamorphic country rock of Dartmoor and its hinterland (*see* Introduction). Underground tin lodes can be exploited by opencast methods or by mining, and indeed they were from the post-medieval period to the early 20th century. For the medieval tinners however, there was a more immediate and easily exploited source of tin in the form of 'stream' deposits. These had been laid down during the Permian and Triassic periods following the intense weathering of what were outcrops at the time, causing fracturing and erosion in the country rock and any metalliferous lodes running through them. The weathered rock was broken down to gravel-sized pieces, which storms, flooding and gravity moved downslope into river valleys and other low-lying areas. Such deposits in stream- and riverbeds are called 'alluvial' and are subject to further sorting and concentration by water, creating pure tin deposits. Where the tin settled in dry valleys and low-lying folds in the topography, the deposits are known as 'eluvial'. Although tin in eluvial deposits is less sorted, the process for exploiting both types has left similar field evidence.

Once discovered, the main tasks for the tinner were to remove any silt covering these deposits and to separate the valuable cassiterite from waste materials such as feldspar, quartz and mica – collectively known as 'gangue' (pronounced 'gang') – that had settled alongside it. This was achieved by taking advantage of the different specific gravities of the cassiterite (between 6.8 and 7.1) and the gangue (typically between 2.5 and 2.9) (Gerrard 2000, 60). When introduced into moving water the tin and the gangue become separated. Abandoned streamworks reflect this process and comprise many hectares of disturbed ground containing water channels and dumps of waste material.

Streamworks

The study of tin streamworks on Dartmoor is in its infancy. However, Sandy Gerrard, who carried out a detailed study of Cornish tinworks, has also published field surveys of streamworks in Dartmoor's Meavy Valley (Gerrard 2000), and a few surveys have been conducted by the Dartmoor Tinworking Research Group (DTRG), though most remain unpublished (but *see* Fig 8.8). The most intensive fieldwork has been done on Bodmin Moor in Cornwall, where the results of many large-scale surveys are available

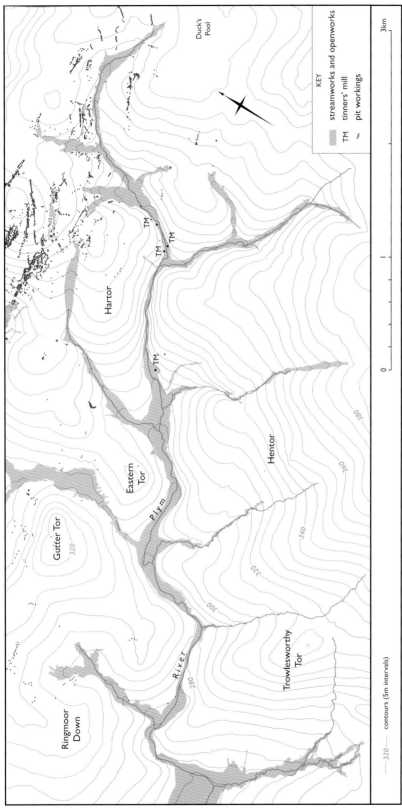

Fig 8.2

Simplified map, based on EH 1:2500 surveys, showing the extent of medieval and post-medieval tinworking in the valley and tributaries of the River Plym (height data licensed to English Heritage for PGA through Next Perspectives™).

(Herring *et al* 2008, 36–50). English Heritage's surveys on Dartmoor have so far been limited to a map scale of 1:2500, which has been helpful in defining the extent of the workings and the nature of their water supplies.

Abandoned streamworks are found in most areas of Dartmoor, particularly in the upland and especially in river valley alluvial deposits, but they may also be found extending up hillsides or located within any topographic feature where weathered tin deposits had originally come to rest. Alluvial tin was often discovered within thin ribbons of ground along stream- and riverbeds. As a result, workings sometimes occupy an entire valley floor from near the river source to the edge of the moorland, and in some cases beyond. Survey of the Plym Valley revealed that the alluvia of the river and all its upland tributaries have been worked by streamworking (Fig 8.2), covering more than 160ha. Similar evidence can be seen in most of Dartmoor's rivers and streams on aerial photographs of the Doe Tor Brook area and of Newleycombe Lake for example (Fig 8.3). Some workings are truly massive, such as those along more than 3km of the East Okement River or at the head of Doetor Brook at the area known as Dick's Pits. Other workings are comparatively small, reflecting more limited deposits, but whatever the extent, most river valleys on the uplands of Dartmoor have been affected by streamworking (Fig 8.4).

Streamworks vary in depth, reflecting the nature of the tin deposits and the extent of overburden originally covering them. They may be up to 5m, although most are shallower. The limit of each streamwork is defined by a steep scarp cut into the moor's natural landforms in marked contrast to the softer contours of the surrounding moorland, (Fig 8.5). Each streamwork is unique in form, dictated by the nature of the tin deposit and by is surrounding topography. However, certain components of the working technique are always present. Tinners usually worked systematically, their aim being to remove as much tin as possible from the working area while leaving behind most of the waste. Unfortunately, no early writer recorded details of the techniques used in tin streamworking and there is a risk that those writing on the subject in the 18th and 19th centuries – such as Pryce in 1778 and Hitchens and Drew in 1824, both discussing Cornish streamworks – were referring to more developed techniques. It seems certain,

Fig 8.3
Aerial view of the Newleycombe Valley showing the alluvial workings of the valley floor, openworks extending across the valley sides and pitworks that exploited tin lodes across the open ground (NMR 24899/027; © English Heritage. NMR).

Fig 8.4
Simplified map showing the extent of medieval and post-medieval tinworking on the upland region of central southern Dartmoor. The streamworks, with few exceptions, follow the courses of rivers and their tributaries (based on RCHME and EH 1:2500 and 1:10 000 surveys; height data licensed to English Heritage for PGA through Next Perspectives™).

however, that the essential principles used remained the same, although with variations indicated in the layouts of the sites.

One of the most common forms of field evidence, with several variants, is the result of washing a vertical workface with an artificial stream of water, then dumping the waste material in parallel linear heaps downslope of the working area (Fig 8.6). The operation commenced at the lower end of the chosen

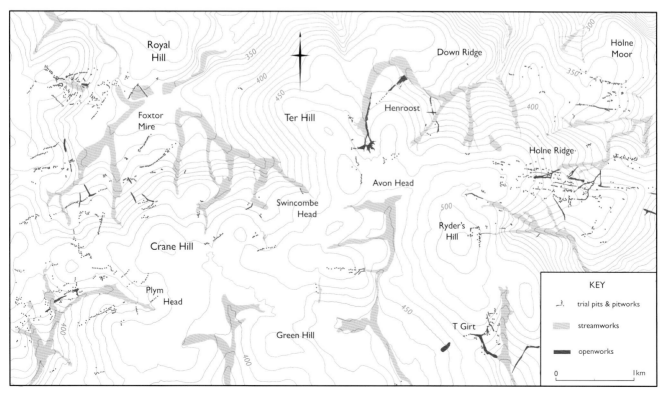

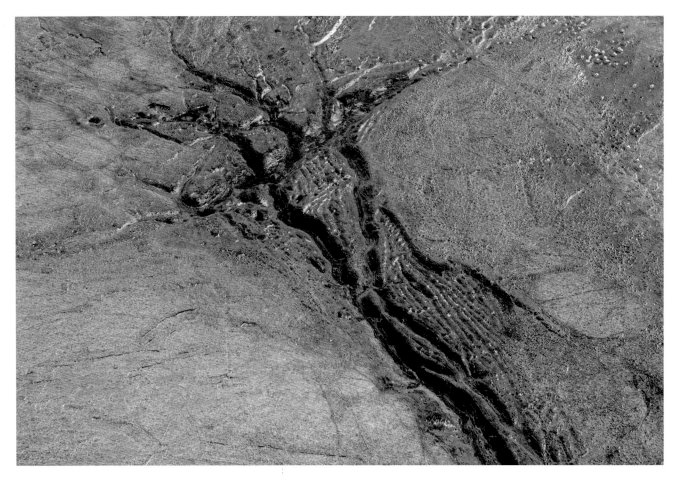

Fig 8.5
Aerial view of tinworks at the head of the O Brook at Skir Gut. The deep gully of an openwork in which tinners have followed a tin lode, has cut through the tyes and waste heaps of an area of an earlier streamwork. Within these streamworks the parallel waste heaps appear to be in separate zones following both the long axis of the working and at 90° to it (NMR 24577/010; © English Heritage. NMR).

Fig 8.6
View of interior details at Brim Brook streamwork showing the steep scarp defining the edge of the working and two oblique dumps with stone-faced retaining walls (stillings). The hollowed reedy area to the right of the image is the silted tye where the water ran through to wash the tinstone (see Fig 8.7; photo: Phil Newman).

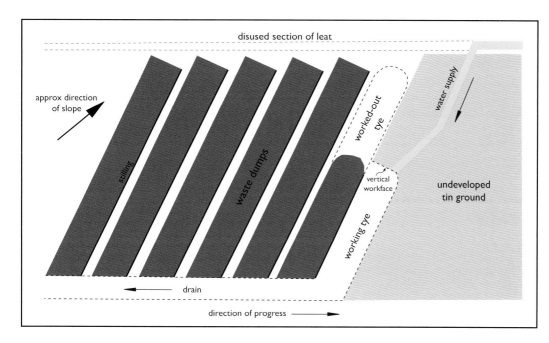

disused section of leat

approx direction of slope

stilling

waste dumps

worked-out tye

water supply

vertical workface

working tye

undeveloped tin ground

drain

direction of progress ⟶

Fig 8.7
Schematic diagram of the most commonly surviving streamworking methods, of the type found in Brim Brook (Fig 8.6) and Beckamoor Combe (see Fig 8.8), showing how an artificial water channel was diverted into the tin ground, washing the ore and waste down into a channel or 'tye'. Large lumps of waste were formed into a low wall (stilling) behind which waste gravel was dumped.

location and progressed up the slope. Having removed the turf and topsoil, a vertical face was cut within the tinground and a stream of water was diverted to the top of it (Fig 8.7). Ground previously loosened with a pick was then subjected to a controlled cascade of water that caught both tin and gangue in its flow, to deposit them into a channel at the bottom of the face called a 'tye'. The tin would sink more rapidly than the gangue, which was carried along the channel by the steady water flow; the tin and some larger pieces of waste could then be shoveled out of the tye for further sorting. Boulder-sized waste was removed by hand and used to construct a low revetment wall along the lower side of the tye, known as a 'stilling'; this was used to retain the smaller waste, which was sorted and deposited behind the wall. The workface would gradually move uphill, as tinground was removed, until eventually it became necessary to commence a second waste dump, constructed over the site of the first tye. Work continued in a fresh, parallel tye. So it went on, gradually working up and across the slope until all the tinground was worked over. Often, the terrain would enable tinners to approach the work systematically and the physical remains within the streamwork comprise arrays of parallel linear spoil heaps, retained by stillings, each with a parallel tye. However, as the stillings were usually built directly over the redundant tyes, the latter are mostly buried beneath the waste.

There are several variations in the layout of streamwork remains, often found within a single tinwork. The most common is an arrangement of short tyes set at right angles to the prevailing axis of the tinwork, giving a rib-like effect. A particularly fine example survives at Brim Brook (see Fig 8.6), and others can be seen at Beckamoor Combe (Fig 8.8). Often the tyes follow the axis of the tinwork, in which case they were much longer and sometimes had much higher waste heaps than the cross-axis examples. Skir Gut (see Fig 8.5) presents a good example of both types, as also does Dry Lake (Fig 8.9). At Hartor streamwork, which was examined by Gerrard, he has suggested that the longer tyes represent the earlier activity and the shorter examples are later (Gerrard 2000, 69). The remains of other streamworks have a less organised interior, with apparent random dumping, and where interpretation of the original progress of the work is more challenging. Several explanations may be appropriate: for example many streamworks could have been reworked long after the original remains were laid down, thus doubling their complexity. Gerrard (2000) identified examples of this through survey in both Devon and Cornwall. A second consideration is that overburden and waste were often dumped into old tinworks and this would sometimes have been done in a fairly random fashion.

Some large areas of streamworks, especially those near the sources of streams and rivers, have been partly or totally overwhelmed by

Fig 8.8 (overleaf)
Simplified plan of the tin streamworks at Beckamoor Combe, showing earthwork reservoirs and channels on the exterior of the working to supply the water, and several areas of parallel waste heaps (adapted from a 1:500 scale survey by the Dartmoor Tinworking Research Group; © DTRG, with permission).

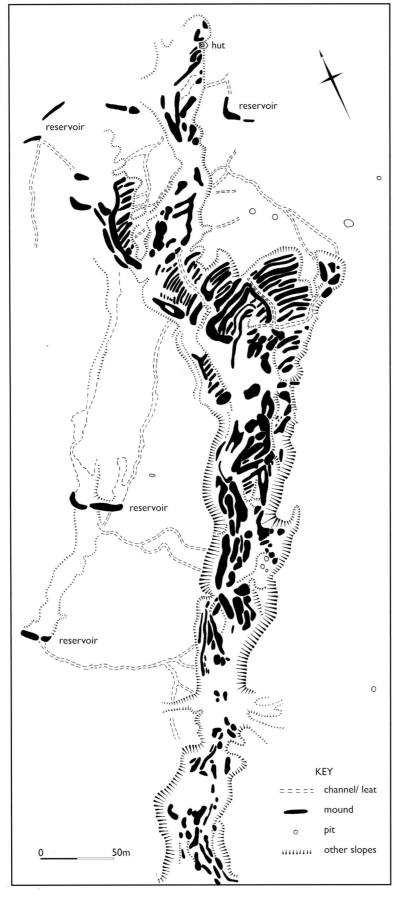

reservoir

hut

reservoir

reservoir

reservoir

reservoir

KEY

= = = = = channel/ leat

━━━ mound

o pit

ıııııııı other slopes

0   50m

mire. At the head of the River Walkham, for example, the only visible evidence of the streamwork is the scarp that defines the limits of the working, for the basin that was hollowed by it and all evidence of the activity itself are disguised by the deep mire that now overlies it.

Tin lodes

The date when tinners turned their attention to extracting tin directly from the lodes is uncertain, but on Dartmoor it had occurred at least by the late 15th century (Greeves 1981b, 142). Tin lodes are located in fissures within the country rock, which on Dartmoor is mostly granite, or metamorphic shale on the moorland edge, usually referred to as 'killas'. The lodes in this district generally follow an ENE trend, but other lodes – known as 'caunter' lodes – run ESE. Together these lodes are usually referred to as E–W lodes. They were rarely perpendicular to the ground surface, but were inclined at an angle or 'underlie'. Dartmoor had relatively shallow tin lodes compared to Cornwall, especially on the granite zone, but to establish contact with the upper section of the lode and extract the tin it was necessary to dig to some considerable depth. At a later date, this was achieved by mining the ore using shafts and adits (horizontal tunnels), which enabled much greater penetration (*see* 19th-century mining in chapter 11); but in the early stages of exploration the shallow upper sections could be reached by digging either shallow shafts or in open trenches onto the 'back' of an outcrop. However, the first task was to locate the lode through a number of prospecting techniques, for some of which highly visible remains survive.

Prospecting

The practice of 'shoding' in Devon was first described in 1671 by an anonymous writer (Anon 1671, 2099–100). 'Shode' was the term given to small pieces of tin that had become detached from the main lode. The theory behind shoding is straightforward: if by digging a shallow pit, concentrations of shode could be found, then the main lode was probably not far away. By digging other pits at intervals, each pit would either produce more or less shode, and indicate to the prospector whether he was getting closer or farther away from the lode.

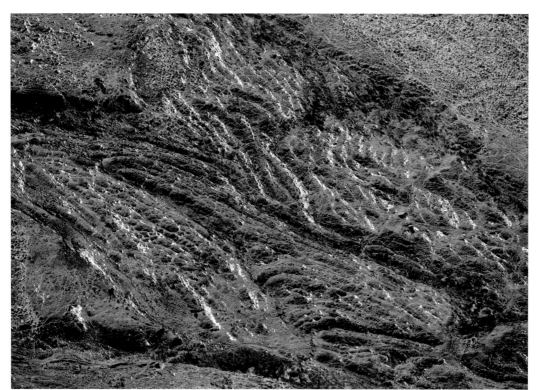

Fig 8.9
Aerial view of an area of streamworks at Dry Lake under a light powdering of snow (NMR 24577/046; © English Heritage. NMR).

Fig 8.10
Excerpt from an EH 1:2500 plan of upper Newleycombe Valley showing streamworks occupying the low-lying alluvial zone of the valley and the east–west alignments of lodeback pits running across Chance Hill.

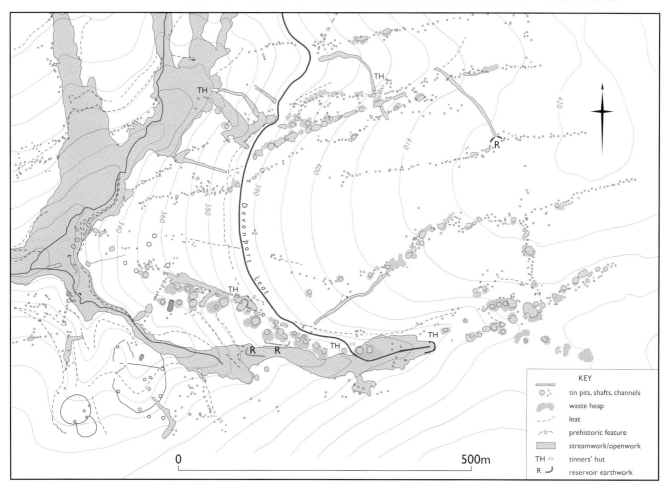

KEY

⊙ °	tin pits, shafts, channels
	waste heap
– – –	leat
⌐∘⌐	prehistoric feature
	streamwork/openwork
TH ▭	tinners' hut
R ⌐	reservoir earthwork

0   500m

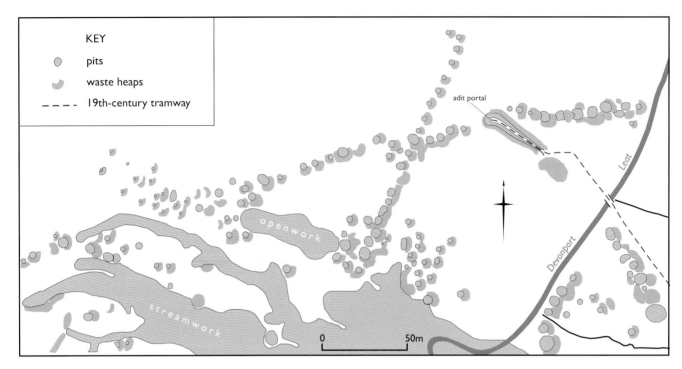

KEY

⊙ pits

◝ waste heaps

– – – – 19th-century tramway

adit portal

openwork

streamwork

Leat

Devonport

0   50m

Fig 8.11
Simplified excerpt from an earthwork survey of the Whiteworks streamworks, also highlighting the pit works running approximately east to west and north to south, and the clustered smaller trial pits.

Fig 8.12 (opposite) Earthwork survey of the upper Redwater Valley and the Birch Tor and Vitifer mining area, showing deep openworks following north-east-trending tin lodes, alluvial streamworks, various pitworks, leats and later mining remains. Also visible is a prehistoric hut settlement, a medieval settlement and medieval fields, together with components of the later rabbit warren (see Fig 9.3) (surveyed at 1:2500 scale).

Eventually the concentration of tin would be so high that the tinner could be confident that he was above the lode and extraction could commence. Alternatively, if the pits produced little or no shode, then the location would be abandoned, or as the anonymous writer of 1671 puts it: 'farewell to that hill'.

In 1671 the pits were referred to as 'essay hatches', that is test or trial pit, and evidence for these occurs in abundance in many areas of Dartmoor. It comprises lines or linear clusters of small, elliptical pits. These are usually 2--3m in diameter, have conical profiles, and are often heavily silted or water-filled and reedy. They have a small crescent-shaped heap of spoil on the lower (downhill) side, which is the material excavated and demonstrates limited depth. They can easily be confused with extractive pits (see below), although they are nearly always smaller and separated. Some of the clearest examples can be seen in the valley of Newleycombe Lake (Fig 8.10); also in the Plym Valley and in the vicinity of Birch Tor, Fox Tor and Whiteworks (Fig 8.11). Experimental research in Cornwall suggests that the elliptical form was the result of digging with a long-handled shovel, wide enough and long enough to dig down to the bedrock as quickly as possible with sufficient elbow room (Herring *et al* 2008, 32).

Another prospecting technique described by the anonymous writer of 1671 uses water. Water was diverted along a hillside in an artificial course called a leat, and released across the slope. This technique is frequently documented for lead mines in northern England and in Wales, where it was known as 'hushing, but this term is not recorded in association with any West Country tin mines. After a couple of days the flow of water would expose the underlying geology and any shode present. Examples of field remains for this technique are difficult to identify. It would require a copious supply of water and a relatively steep slope to be effective. Gerrard (2000, 30) has identified possible examples on Hartor in the Meavy Valley, where channels running down the hillside appear to be associated with a leat running along the contour. Similar examples exist in the Newleycombe Valley on the north slope of Down Tor, but research needs to be done to confirm that any of these are evidence of the technique described. In both cases it is likely that the leats were constructed for other purposes before being adapted for prospecting.

Pit works

Once the tinners were satisfied that they had discovered a lode, extraction could begin. Two methods were employed in the medieval and post-medieval period: The first method involved digging a series of shallow vertical shafts down to the back of the lode, for which the term 'lode-back pit' has been coined by

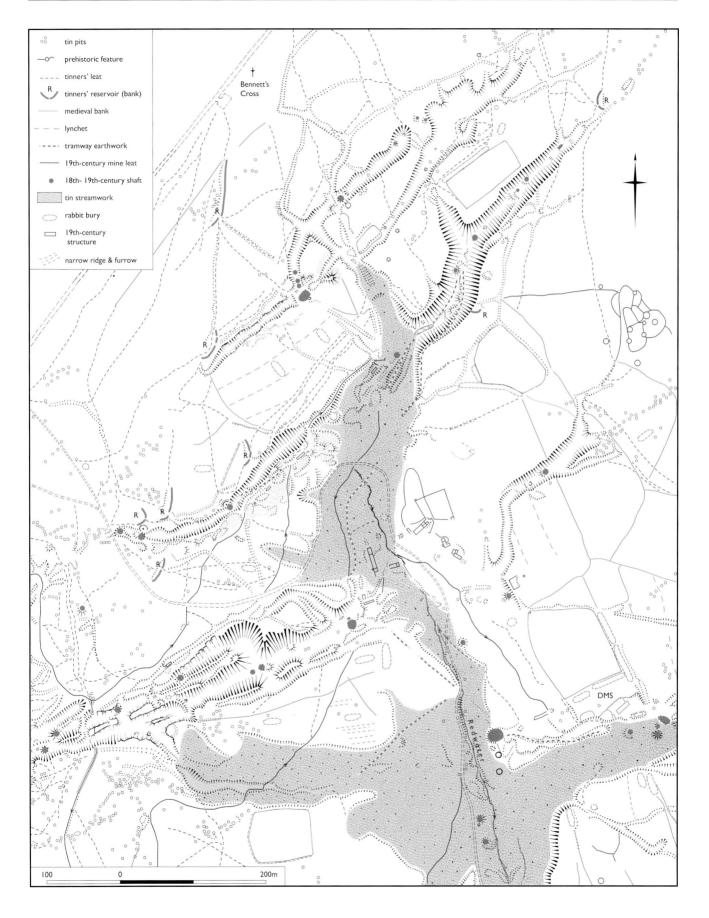

Legend:

- ○ tin pits
- ⌒○⌒ prehistoric feature
- - - - tinners' leat
- R tinners' reservoir (bank)
- —— medieval bank
- – – lynchet
- ··· tramway earthwork
- —— 19th-century mine leat
- ● 18th- 19th-century shaft
- tin streamwork
- rabbit bury
- □ 19th-century structure
- narrow ridge & furrow

Bennett's Cross

Redwater

DMS

100   0   200m

archaeologists – although this term would not be recognised by the tinners, who referred to them as shafts. This method probably had early origins and was the precursor to deep underground mining, but details of the transition and chronology from this simple technique to conventional deep-shaft mining are unknown.

As each shaft reached lode depth, the tin was worked laterally on either side until working became impractical because of waterlogging, lack of ventilation or the imminent danger of collapse. Additional shafts were then sunk farther along the lode. The field evidence is therefore a series of conical pits, following the ENE or ESE orientation of the lode. These pits are generally larger than trial pits described above and are usually closer together; they have much bigger spoil heaps, usually on the downslope side, reflecting the larger amount of waste. Often the ground between two or more pits was also removed as work progressed, creating deep trenches. Again the Newleycombe Valley has some of the most representative examples of such workings, particularly around Drivage Bottom and Newleycombe Farm (*see* Figs 8.3 and 8.10); others survive at Whiteworks and Eylesbarrow, and in many cases they were reworked later with deeper shafts. Such is the case at Huntingdon (*see* Fig 11.3) and Whiteworks (Fig 8.11).

Openworks

An alternative, and more involved, method of working tin lodes was by opencast pits or 'openworks', in which both tin and overburden were removed. These workings were often referred to as 'beamworks', many being documented in the 16th and 17th centuries, including Gibby Beam, Pipers Beam, Owlacombe Beam, athough they are alternatively known as 'gerts'. The earliest documented example is 'Joys Beam' of 1511 (Greeves 1981b, 327), and their main period of operation was between then and, probably, the early 17th century. One Cornish writer in 1748 considered opencast techniques to be ancient (Borlase 1748, 168), which suggests that they had been obsolete for a long time, even in the mid-18th century. Unfortunately no contemporary account of how these Devon beamworks were exploited has survived. The field remains comprise massive cuttings with sloping sides of up to 12m deep. Some of the

longest examples at Vitifer are 500m long and 80m wide. The interiors are mostly devoid of waste heaps, although often there is evidence of later shafts sunk into the floor of the working. It is notable that almost all beamworks are associated with alluvial streamworks, often appearing to branch off from the large streamworks of the valley floors, as at Newleycombe, Vitifer (Fig 8.12), Ringleshuttes and along the O Brook, where some of the most spectacular examples exist (*see* Fig 8.5). Their discovery and subsequent exploitation probably occurred as a follow-on process of streamworking, without the need for prospecting, and they may therefore represent some of the earliest lode discoveries. This may also explain the choice of beamworks over pit works as a working technique: the latter are more usually detached from the immediate area of streamworks, and have trial pits associated with a prospecting stage.

Water supplies

Associated with tin streamworks and openworks are the earthwork evidence for water supplies, used to divert and store water in the extractive processes. The remains comprise artificial water courses, known as leats, and small storage ponds or reservoirs sited near the workings.

Alluvial stream deposits commonly existed in valleys with rivers or substantial streams, where water procurement was simply a matter of diverting the river in a leat to the workings. Many short leats were effaced as work progressed upstream, but ones that survive are often contained within the worked area. However, for many streamworks, in particular those at greater altitude and those where the eluvial deposits were worked higher up the valley sides, there was either insufficient or no permanent local water supply. Management of the available water resources was therefore required to procure one.

Openworks always have evidence of former water supplies, usually including one or more reservoirs, but precisely what the water was used for is not known. It may have been used to wash the ore as it was dug from the ground or to remove overlying soil to expose the lode, similar to the technique described above. Alternatively, in a few cases water may have been used to remove the top section of some

Fig 8.13 (opposite) Part of a complicated 1:2500 survey plan of the West Webburn Valley showing limits of the medieval and post-medieval streamworks, openworks and pitworks, the courses of the leats and reservoirs that supplied them. Medieval and post-medieval field boundaries are also depicted. Note the cultivation ridges (green pecked line) cut by one of the leats. Later mining and prehistoric features have been omitted for clarity (see Fig 8.12 for key).

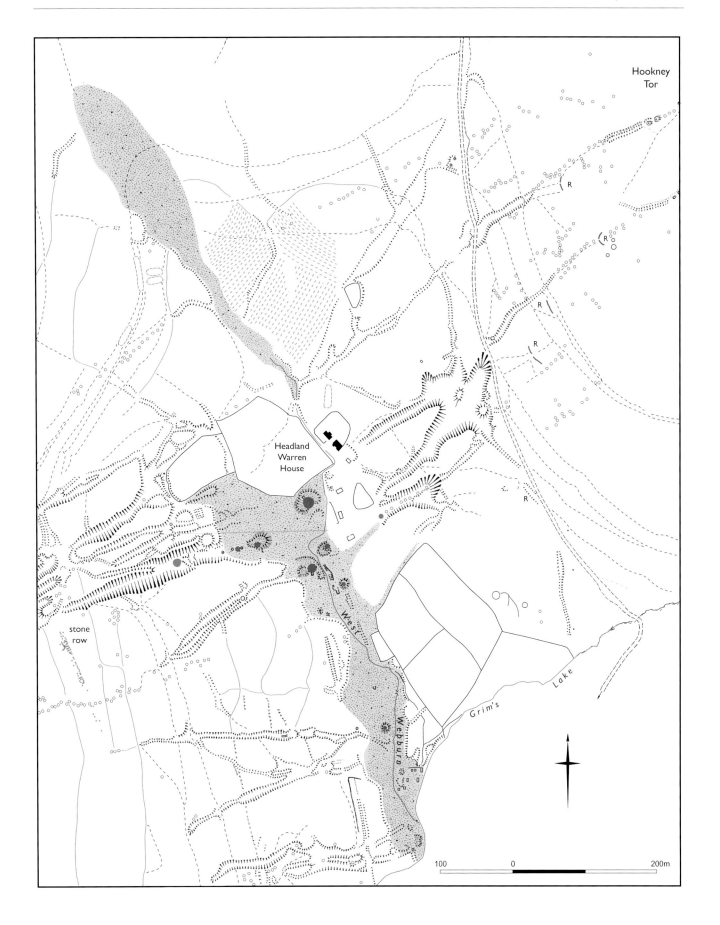

Hookney
Tor

R

R

R

R

R

Headland
Warren
House

stone
row

West

Webburn

Grim's

Lake

100   0   200m

tin lodes where it was sufficiently weathered and broken up to be worked as an eluvial streamwork, using water from leats and reservoirs. In these cases, as the tinners dug deeper and the lode became more consolidated, a different method was necessary: masses of the surrounding ground was removed from around the lode effacing the evidence of the earlier activity, with the exception of the leats and reservoirs. Thus the remains of the water supplies may not be associated with the deeper sections of the workings, but with streamworks, the evidence for which has mostly been destroyed. Examples of openworks that appear to occupy ground previously worked as streamworks are Skir Gut (*see* Fig 8.5) at the head of the O Brook, where a deep gully has incised the streamwork remains; and at Willabeam in the Newleycombe Valley (*see* Figs 8.3 and 8.10), where vestiges of streamworks are visible as well as reservoirs (see Gerrard 2000 for further examples).

Leats

Leats were used to divert water from either rivers or streams in nearby or neighboring valleys; or they acted to collect water from lesser sources high on the valley sides, such as small springs, bogs and rainwater run-off, depending on the altitude of the tinwork and the availability of a supply. At Birch Tor and Vitifer, for example, the majority of the streamworks and openworks in the Redwater Valley (*see* Fig 8.12) were supplied with water diverted in leats from the headwaters of Statt's Brook to the west (Fig 8.13), from Grim's Lake to the east or from a small tributary of the Boveycombe to the north. Often a single valley slope will have several leats at different altitudes running in parallel along its flanks. The narrow earthwork channels, usually no wider than 1m, run along the contours of the hillsides; they have small earthen banks of excavated material on the downslope side, but the channels themselves have become heavily silted over time and the earthworks are very subtle as a result. In areas of heavy vegetation they can be difficult to follow, but many can be walked along their entire length. The slight dimensions of these leats sets them apart from the many later Dartmoor leats made to supply mills, mines and other industrial processes. These latter are usually much larger, generally less silted and sometimes lined with stone.

Reservoirs

Where water was at a premium it needed to be stored, and small earthwork reservoirs were simply constructed by hollowing out a piece of ground on a moderate slope and using the excavated material to create a bank or 'dam' on the lower side, thus raising the overall depth of the hollow up to 2m in some cases. These earthworks can be found adjacent to tinworks, though usually slightly higher up the slope, so the water could run downhill. The most common format is a crescent shaped bank with a central opening for a sluice (Fig 8.14, a–d and f). Alternatively, and more simply, a section of a leat bank was sometimes strengthened and the channel deepened to form a linear pond at the end of the leat. Other variants include straight banks with stub ends at right angles or the adaptation of existing features such as disused sections of tinworks. All reservoirs have an opening in the bank to accommodate the sluice, where traces of stone may be found that once supported the timber sluice gate.

Several areas of the moor have numerous examples of such earthworks serving both streamworks and openworks. On the south slope of Cramber Tor there is a fine array of differing types, including one particularly well preserved example (Fig 8.15); and at Henroost a single openwork has four associated reservoirs arranged at differing levels, representing phases in the working of the lode. One of these reservoirs has remains of a fine masonry sluice. A complex area of openworks at Ringleshuttes has 12 good examples, and in the area of Birch Tor and Vitifer mines there are more than 30 of these small earthworks (*see* Figs 8.12 and 8.13). One of the largest reservoirs recorded is a curving, almost circular earthwork at the head of Hartor Brook, which measures in excess of 75m across (Fig 8.14, f).

One of the best places to observe tinners leats and reservoirs is along the valley sides at the head of the West Webburn (Fig 8.13), where six separate leats can be seen running from various points along Grim's Lake, which was the source of water, close to Grimspound. The leats head north-west following the contour of Hookney Tor's lower slope, where some of them supplied the openworks to the east of Headland Warren. Water was stored in a series of earthwork reservoirs from which it was diverted to where needed. Two additional smaller reservoirs, sited farther east and higher up the slope, appear to

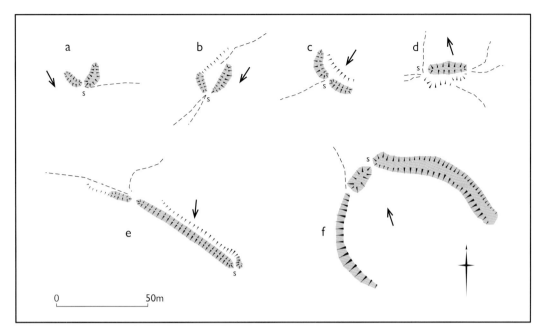

Fig 8.14
Thumbnail earthwork plans of reservoirs associated with tinworks near Cramber Tor and the Newleycombe Valley at Willabeam (a and b); Raddick Hill (c); Down Tor (d); Classiwell (e); Hartor Brook Head (f). Letter 's' denotes positions of sluice openings. Pecked lines show leats supplying water and diverting water from the sluice opening. Arrows represent approximated downhill direction of the slope.

Fig 8.15
Earthwork remains of a tinners' reservoir with central sluice opening, sited just above the Devonport Leat on Raddick Hill (photo: Phil Newman).

have stored rainwater. Three of the leats continue north-west, then traverse the land at the head of the West Webburn, cutting east through an area of cultivation ridges and crossing the boggy streamworks at the head of the river, where only one channel can be traced, although all three reappear on the west side to continue south-west towards Challacombe. On the western valley side the courses of the leats are suddenly halted by a series of large openworks, which have cut across them at a later date. It is likely

these leats were adapted to supply this episode of work. However, the channels reappear to the south continuing along the slopes of Challacombe to their final destination: a series of narrow openworks on the east slope of the hill.

The chronology of tinworks

Dating the various developments and techniques of tin extraction is still imprecise, chiefly because the dating framework, such as it exists, is dependent on documentation and the random nature of its survival. Little or no documentary evidence from the first four centuries of the industry's known existence in Devon or Cornwall alludes to tinworking methods. Archaeological analysis of tinworks is currently based mainly on large-scale earthwork surveys (Gerrard 2000; Herring *et al* 2008). Although these can provide simple relative chronologies for the different elements within individual workings, earthworks cannot provide dates. Excavation of these sites is at an early stage, restricted to one small area of streamworking (Gerrard 2000, 67–9) and archaeologically derived dates for any tinwork are lacking.

The dating of streamworks poses a particular problem. It is known that working of Dartmoor tin had commenced by 1156 and was widespread by 1200. However, reference to individual tinworks is rare for this period with no tinworks mentioned by name. The first reference to a recognisable streamwork is to 'la Dryworke' (today known as Dry Lake) on the boundary of the Forest of Dartmoor in 1240 (Rowe 1896, 290). Documentation is more common for the period between the 15th and 18th centuries, when a good number of streamworks were recorded by name, and whose locations can be identified if the name survives or is remembered – for example Owlacombe (Ashburton) in 1492, Smallacombe (Ilsington) 1525 and various works with the name Foxtor in the 16th–18th centuries (Greeves 1981b, 300–50). However, a reference in a document is rarely any help in establishing the origins of a streamwork, which could have existed long before its first record; frequently, a streamwork will be referred to in separate documents over several centuries and there is no way of knowing the extent of the activity on each of those dates. There is also field evidence for many other streamworks, for which there is no known documentation. The total working life of a streamwork before exhaustion could add up to several centuries and the earthworks may represent only a final phase of activity. There can be few examples of medieval or post-medieval earthworks in Britain that are so difficult to date with confidence. A streamwork surviving on the moorland today as archaeological remains could have origins as early as the 12th or as late as the 18th century, and the earlier it was first worked the more likely it is to have been re-worked at a later date; and it is known that a small number of streamworks continued to be re-worked into the 19th century.

The date at which the tinners began to turn their attention to tin lodes is also far from certain. This development was not recorded by any medieval writer and it has always seemed a safe assumption that as long as tinners of the 12th to 15th centuries had a plentiful supply of stream tin then the working of lodes, which required far greater expenditure of labour and capital in both extraction and processing, would not have been a priority. The documentary evidence appears to validate this notion because references to lode works are only known from the 15th century and later; thereafter references to beamworks become common until the 18th century (Greeves 1981b).

However, as references to all types of tinwork are rare before 1450, and the categories of workings are scarcely mentioned in such early documents anyway, this may be a distortion of the data. It may well be that tin lodes were discovered as a result of streaming activity, in which case the tinners continued to extract the material despite the greater effort, such considerations being cancelled out by the high value of tin. On the basis of documented examples and from comments made by 18th-century Cornish writers such as Borlase (1758) and Pryce (1778), the techniques for working lodes using beamworks was moribund by the mid 17th century. But by that time the use of shallow shafts had evolved and developed into the more modern method of mining discussed in chapter 11.

The dressing and smelting of tin

Once removed from the ground cassiterite must be put through a series of processes to convert the raw tinstone into a usable metal, including crushing and concentrating, before smelting. For tin retrieved from streamworks, a certain amount of concentration could be achieved at the extraction site, but ore from all sources, including streamworks, then needed to be transported to processing areas where these tasks could be completed before smelting. The technological details of these processes, normally referred to as 'dressing', as well as of those for smelting were not well documented in the Middle Ages, but from the 14th century in Cornwall (Gerrard 2001, 129) and therefore probably in Devon too, smelting was carried out in water-powered mills, equipped with blast furnaces, known as 'blowing' mills. Crushing and dressing took place in stamping or 'knocking' mills, which in Devon were first recorded in 1504 (Ibid, 104). The Ordnance Survey mistakenly refer to all tin mills as 'blowing houses', although many marked on OS maps of Dartmoor were in fact stamping mills. Many more examples are not marked on maps.

The number of tin mills surviving on Dartmoor is impressive. More than 80 sites with archaeological evidence survive, including 50 with structural remains. Compared with Cornwall, where medieval and post-medieval tin production was on a vast scale by comparison, there are only four surviving blowing mills and seven stamping mills with structural remains (Gerrard 2000, 108). It is known from documentation that Cornwall once possessed many more than actually survive, but Dartmoor is the major location in Britain for the archaeological resource of tin mills.

Tin mills

The structural remains of blowing and stamping mills are similar (Fig 8.16), and it was the machinery contained within them that differed. They comprised small (no larger than c 10m × 5m), roughly rectangular buildings constructed from un-mortared moorstone, nearly always granite, with walls of on average 0.8m thick. A wheelpit, reinforced with moorstone, was located on the exterior end or side of the building and housed a wooden waterwheel to transmit power through an axle to the machinery inside. The condition of these structures and their wheelpits varies greatly. Several survive as upstanding, though roofless structures, including those at Black Tor south bank and at Week Ford Mill B (Fig 8.17). For others the structures have been effaced and we know of their existence only from the finds of certain large artefacts, such as mortar stones and mould stones (see Figs 8.21 and 8.23), or residues such as slag. For a third group the walls are ruined to just above foundation level, the interiors are strewn with tumbled stone and the whole of the remains are covered by turf, such as at Blacksmith's Shop (Fig 8.18), or Mill Corner beside the River Plym.

Tin mills are always located close to a reliable water supply that could be diverted without too long a leat. Waterwheels powering Dartmoor tin mills were, without exception, overshot or pitchback – the water was delivered to the top arc of the wheel. For this reason, mills were always built at the foot of a slope and were often constructed into the base of the artificial escarpment at the edge of a tinwork,

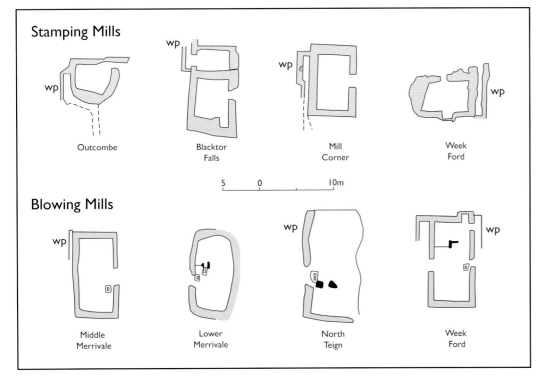

Fig 8.16
Outline drawings of tin stamping and blowing mills where field evidence survives (after Newman 1998, with permission).

Fig 8.17
Plan of the tin mills at
Week Ford on the River
Dart. Mill A has the granite
lining of a furnace (a) and
mouldstone (b) in situ,
confirming its status as a
blowing or smelting mill,
together with numerous
displaced mortarstones (not
shown). Mill B, slightly
higher up the slope, has a
well-defined wheel pit (c)
on the eastern end and a
fine stone-faced leat
embankment stands south
of the building. The lack of
a furnace and the presence
of numerous displaced
mortars (not shown)
around the mill suggest that
it probably functioned as a
stamping mill only. The
silted channels of leats
survive and once diverted
water from the O Brook,
which flows north, to the
east of the mills (after
Newman 1993).

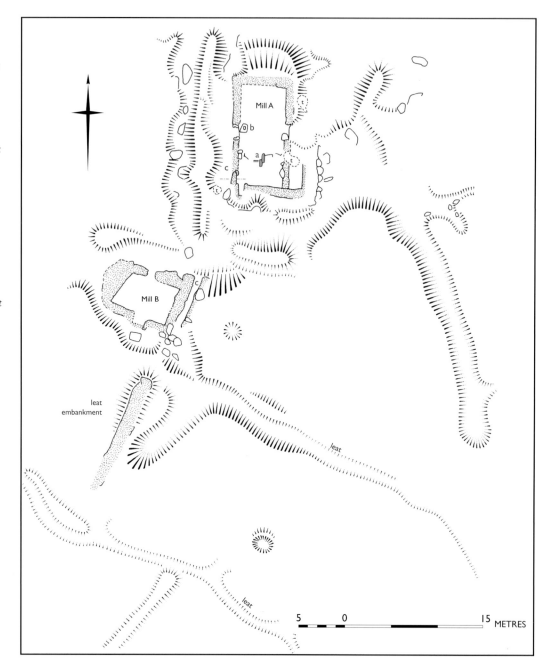

giving a sudden drop, so that water could be conducted directly to the wheel in a short wooden launder. However, where the slope was more gradual, a level-topped leat embankment, built from stone and earth, was used to regulate the height of the leat before the wooden launder delivered the water to the top of the waterwheel. Examples can be seen at Week Ford (*see* Fig 8.17) and at Mill Corner. The largest waterwheels used in these early mills had diameters of *c* 3m, and none were smaller than 2.5m, with widths or 'breast' of between 0.46m and 0.6m.

Crushing and dressing the ore

Before tin could be smelted it had to be concentrated – all the gangue removed leaving only the cassiterite. Much of the tin, especially from lode sources, was contained within a matrix of worthless rock. The easiest method to remove the waste was to crush the material to fine gravel, then concentrate the tin using the same principle of settling in water, as described above, in the streamworks.

One means of achieving this was the crazing mill, which used the same principle as corn and grist mills. It comprised two circular stones of granite set horizontally, one resting on the other. The larger stone was the stationary mill base on which the upper stone rotated and the tin, fed in a hole in the centre, was crushed to a fine sand between them. The rotating stone was probably powered by the mill's waterwheel, although none survive *in situ* to suggest precisely how. Because the tin had to be in small pieces before being introduced to the crazing mill, there is good reason to believe that they were mainly associated with alluvial tin, which was already suitably sized when extracted. It seems likely for this reason some crazing mills were in use earlier than some stamping mills, although they were often used simultaneously as part of the crushing process at a single mill site. Only three examples of crazing mill stones have been recorded archaeologically, and one of those, at Outcombe Mill (Spooner and Russell 1967, 320), has been stolen since first coming to light. The finest example is associated with the mill remains at Gobbett, where both the upper and lower displaced stones survive (Fig 8.19).

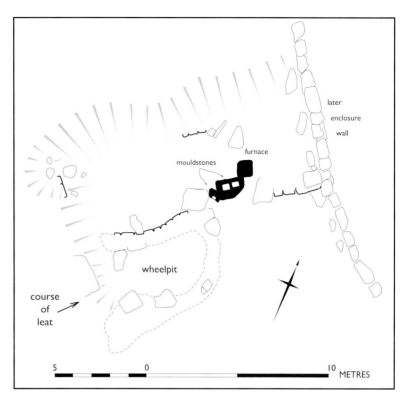

Fig 8.18 (above)
Plan of the blowing house near Teignhead Farm known as Blacksmiths Shop, surveyed at 1:100 scale. The walls are mostly ruinous and the wheel pit has been backfilled, but one upright side of the furnace survives in situ as does one complete double mould stone and a fragment of a second.

Fig 8.19
Granite artefacts at Gobbet Mill, (left) mouldstone, with rectangular hollow for the ingot; (left, below) lower stone of the crazing mill, (1.2m diameter); (below) upper stone of the crazing mill (0.9m diameter). The small holes on its upper surface would have engaged with whatever device was used to provide the motive power and rotate the stone (photo: Phil Newman).

Stamping mills

The main apparatus for crushing tin ore was the stamping mill (Fig 8.20). Stamps comprise heavy upright baulks of timber set side by side in a timber frame within which they could rise up and down freely. Protruding from each of the stamps was a peg or tappet. This engaged with a cam, fixed to an axle that extended from the waterwheel in front of or behind the stamps. As the wheel rotated, the movement of the cams forced the stamps upwards in sequence and then, as the cams disengaged at the top of the cycle, gravity caused each baulk to fall on the ore below. The lower end of each baulk was shod with iron, known as the 'stamp head', which combined with the weight of the timber would crush the ore. Although at 19th- and early 20th-century mines, massive stamp batteries might comprise dozens of stamps, in medieval and early post-medieval stamping mills, three baulks were the maximum powered by a single waterwheel, although two were most common.

This stamping technology was not restricted to the West Country tin industry, for it was also used in Europe at about the same time as its introduction in Devon and Cornwall – about the 15th century if not earlier. The basic principles of stamping mill technology changed little during the many centuries in which it was deployed, right up to the early 20th century when the industry declined (*see* chapter 11).

The earliest stamping mills crushed the ore in a dry state, but we have no way of determining from archaeological evidence if or where this method was ever used on Dartmoor. As the structural remains that we do have are more likely to date from the 16th century onwards, it seems probable that most of the surviving stamping mills would have used wet stamping, introduced early in that century elsewhere in Europe, according to one contemporary account (Hoover and Hoover 1950). With wet stamps the base of the device, where the stamps struck the ore, was contained within a box into which a controlled flow of water kept the material moving and conveyed the crushed stone through a perforated grid on the front or end of the stamps box, once broken down to the required size. Ore was fed in from behind through a coffer, making the process continuous.

The horizontal face that absorbed the downward force of the stamps was made from fine-grained granite, with a flat upper surface. The continued pounding gradually wore cupped hollows into the stone face; when these hollows reached a certain depth, they became less efficient and the stone block was replaced. Such discarded stones, called 'mortarstones', are the main artefact associated with stamping mills, and their presence near a structure confirms the mill's stamping status. The term mortarstone was coined by Robert Burnard (1887), who believed the hollows were formed

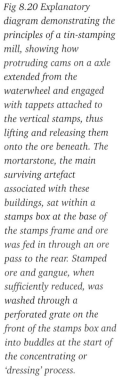

Fig 8.20 Explanatory diagram demonstrating the principles of a tin-stamping mill, showing how protruding cams on a axle extended from the waterwheel and engaged with tappets attached to the vertical stamps, thus lifting and releasing them onto the ore beneath. The mortarstone, the main surviving artefact associated with these buildings, sat within a stamps box at the base of the stamps frame and ore was fed in through an ore pass to the rear. Stamped ore and gangue, when sufficiently reduced, was washed through a perforated grate on the front of the stamps box and into buddles at the start of the concentrating or 'dressing' process.

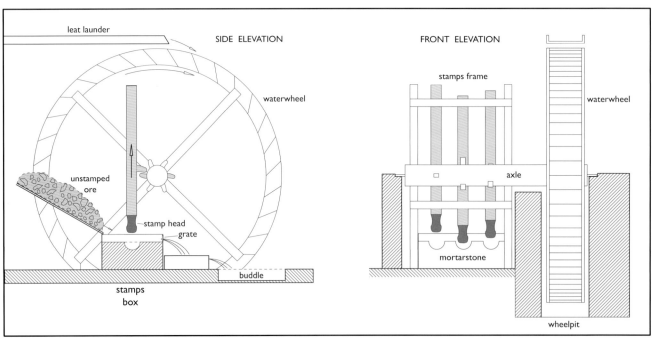

Fig 8.21 (far left)
The heavily ruined
structure of a tin
mill beside the
River Meavy near
Nosworthy Bridge.
The presence of
many mortarstones
reveals this to
have been a
stamping mill
(photo: Phil
Newman).

by hand stamping rather than by mechanical stamps. It is a misleading term as it implies that the hollows were a necessary part of the crushing process rather than a result of it.

Mortarstones are numerous at the sites of some mills: the two mills at Week Ford, for example, have 13 and 24 were found at the excavated mill at Upper Merrivale, including some built into the walls (Passmore 1998, 10–11). Numerous examples are scattered within the ruins at Nosworthy mill (Fig 8.21). At other sites there is only one, for example at the Blacktor Falls left bank mill. Occasionally a mortarstone has been separated from its original location and survives as an isolated artefact, such as the fine example built into a boundary wall at Runnage (Fig 8.22) and the triple stone at Venford (Fig 8.23). Although

in these cases the mill was likely to have been located near by, no traces of the structures are known.

Stones suitable for use as mortarstones often had more than one flat face and several examples have hollows on two or more sides where the stone has been turned in the stamps box to provide a fresh flat surface. The majority of mortarstones have paired hollows, reflecting the use of a pair of stamps; there are, however, several triple-hollowed examples where the battery contained three stamps, such as at Week Ford, Nosworthy right bank and Venford. Where four hollows have been noted, as at Horrabridge and Runnage, these appear to be two pairs of two, where a suitably large flat surface has been realigned for further use after the initial pair of hollows became too deep.

Fig 8.22 (above, top)
A mortarstone incorporated
into a dry-stone wall near
Runnage. The stone has two
sets of two hollows, caused
by realigning the stone
under the stamps after the
first pair of hollows wore
too deep to be efficient.

Fig 8.23 (above, bottom)
A large mortarstone with
three hollows at Venford.
Nothing is known of the
structure from which it was
retrieved, although it is
likely to be submerged
beneath the modern
reservoir. (photo: Phil
Newman).

Blowing mills

Fig 8.24
Large-scale plan of the
partly excavated Upper
Merrivale blowing mill,
showing the outline walls of
the main mill; two wheel
pits, one of which may be
associated with a second
mill to the south; a
collapsed furnace and the
mouldstone in situ adjacent
to the entrance (© DTRG
with permission).

Smelting was the final stage in the processing of tin. The fuel available to medieval tinners was peat charcoal, which needed a forced draught from a set of bellows to achieve the high temperatures required. In the early years of the medieval industry, limitations of the smelting technology meant that tin had to be smelted twice, the second smelting taking place within one of the Stannary towns. After 1198 a tax of 13s 4d per hundredweight (112lb or 50.8k) was levied on this second smelting in

addition to the 30d already paid on the first smelt, but in 1305 both taxes were replaced by a single tax of 1s 6¾d (Lewis 1965, 149). It is likely that the introduction of the blowing mill or 'blowing house', powered by water, had sufficiently increased the efficiency of the smelting process to enable a single smelt. In Cornwall, a 'blouynhous' was mentioned in documentation as early as 1332 (Gerrard 2000, 129) and it is likely that others were at work in Cornwall and Devon at about that time, contributing to the prosperity of the Devon tin industry in the 14th century. However, it is not until the mid-15th century that historical references are made to individual blowing mills in Devon; and reference to examples identifiable in the field come as late as 1514 when a blowing mill at Dartmeet was recorded (DRO 48/14/40/3). Many more blowing mills are recorded in the 16th and 17th century when Dartmoor tin was enjoying something of a boom (Greeves 1992, 47), but by 1719 only two survived in use in the whole of Devon, although their locations are not known for certain (Greeves 1996, 84).

Structural remains of at least 23 blowing mills survive on Dartmoor, and at least 16 sites are known from stray artefact finds (Greeves 1991). The buildings differed from those of stamping mills only in their contents, which at blowing mills comprised a blast furnace with water-powered bellows. It is worth observing, however, that most of the larger tin mills were blowing mills while the very smallest mills were usually stamping mills.

Contemporary descriptions of blowing mills and their furnaces are few, and those that do survive are from Cornish writers. Thomas Beare, for example, in 1586 (Buckley 1994, 10–18) provides some detail of how tin was smelted, but provides little description of the physical appearance of the furnace, mentioning only minor details. It was not until 1778, very late in the era of this technology, that William Pryce described the blast furnaces used by his generation of tin smelters in Cornwall. According to Pryce the furnace was constructed from moorstone 'cemented and clamped together'; it was 6ft (1.8m) tall and up to 2ft (0.6m) wide at the top (Pryce 1778, 136).

Only the bottom sections of the furnace structures survive, of which five examples are known: at Avon Dam, Blacksmith's Shop (*see* Fig 8.18), Week Ford (*see* Fig 8.17), and at Upper and Lower Merrivale (*see* Figs 8.16 and 8.24).

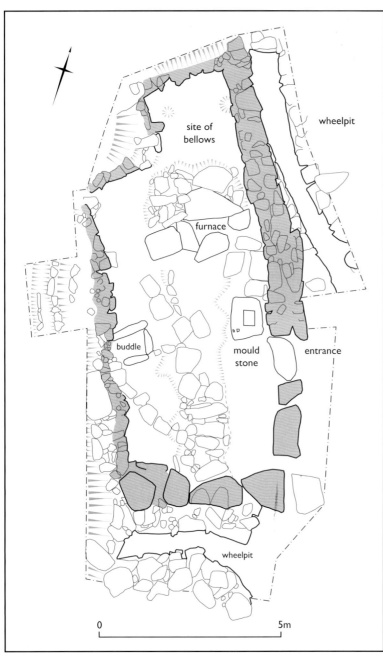

site of
bellows

wheelpit

furnace

buddle

mould
stone

entrance

wheelpit

0   5m

Fig 8.25
The interior of a ruined tin mill in the Avon Valley, showing an in situ furnace, mould stones and a double mortarstone behind the furnace. This site is now submerged beneath the Avon reservoir, but is visible during times of extreme drought (photo: Phil Newman).

Furnaces are set centrally within the floor of the building, in some cases built against a low half-wall that divides the interior into two levels. The best and most publicised example of a furnace is that at Lower Merrivale, where three adjacent upright granite slabs form an open-fronted rectangular structure, which was clearly the base of the hearth. Sitting in the bottom of the structure, slightly displaced, is a long rectangular granite block with an 8cm deep recess cut into the upper surface, forming a shallow trough. This is the float stone described by Pryce in 1778, in which the molten tin was tapped and collected at the bottom of the hearth to be ladled into moulds. Unfortunately, out of almost 40 known blowing house sites on Dartmoor, this and one other example on private land are the only recorded float stones. Even at the excavated mill at Upper Merrivale, where the entire furnace was uncovered, no float stone was identified.

The molten tin was cast into moulds to form ingots. The moulds were usually cut from substantial blocks of granite, which were capable of absorbing the heat and were located close by the furnace, usually adjacent to the mill's doorway. Mouldstones are the main artefact associated with blowing mills and, like the mortarstones that confirm status for stamping, the presence of a mouldstone is confirmation of smelting. The rectangular recesses that form the mould are on average 40cm × 30cm, in which, it was said, an ingot of suitable weight could be cast, to be hung one either side of a packhorse, although Worth calculated that the average ingot would have weighed 195lb (88.4kg) (Spooner and Russell 1967, 195). *In situ* mouldstones, survive at all three of the upper Walkham mills, as well as at Week Ford and at Blacksmiths Shop, while displaced examples are at Gobbet (*see* Fig 8.19), Avon Dam (Fig 8.25) – only visible at times of severe drought – and at the two Yealm blowing mills. There is also a number of disassociated mouldstones at various locations on Dartmoor, which imply the former existence of a blowing mill near by (Greeves 1991, 18–20).

Tinners' huts

On modern Ordnance Survey maps of 1:25 000 scale and above, numerous 'Tinners' huts' are depicted in the river valleys and beside the streams in the remoter parts Dartmoor's moorland, particularly in the higher areas of the north and south moors. Some of these structures have been marked on the map since the 1st Series OS 25-inch county series of the 1880s, although the term tinners' hut is a fairly recent appellation, introduced in the 1980s. In the only published study of these and other 'post-prehistoric' structures, the author Brian Le Messurier (1979), declined to apply such a prescriptive title to them, although he considered them to be shelters used by shepherds, peat cutters and tinners, all of whom would need refuge from Dartmoor's, at times, ferocious weather. Many of those recorded by Le Messurier were some distance from tinworks.

Within areas of streamworks, open works, – and even nestling among the spoil heaps of pit workings – small, ruined, roofless rectangular structures are frequently encountered. Such unspectacular remains, set amid the stony heaps and channels, are easily overlooked. The structures are roughly-built with low, dry-stone walls. The builders often took advantage of any man-made features that already existed as a result of tinworking, using spoil heaps and gullies to provide shelter from the wind; and in streamworks there was a plentiful supply of manageable sized stone to build with. These huts have a single entrance, no trace of any windows and we must assume that their roofs were made from timber and covered with whatever plant material was available, for example turf, furze and rushes. The quality of construction varies considerably: some are of selected stone, neatly coursed into well-built walls, such as the example at Steeperton Brook (Fig 8.26), insulated with earth around the exterior. The large example at Fishlake has an interior footprint of 6.4m × 2.4m and walls remaining up to 1m high, although the interiors of tinners' huts are frequently strewn with tumbled masonry, suggesting that the walls were higher.

Other examples appear to have been built in a great hurry and perhaps not intended for enduring use. Some of the better structures may have served as semi-permanent accommodation for people working in remote areas – for sleeping, eating and shelter. Several have fireplaces, such as that at the northern end of Beckamoor Combe. Smaller, more ephemeral structures, such as the very insubstantial huts along Fur Tor Brook, may have been used as short-term shelters or perhaps as tool and equipment stores; it is unlikely that the walls were ever tall enough for a person to stand up when inside.

Unfortunately no tinners' hut has yet been dated. Some may be assumed to be more recent, on the basis of preservation and association with 18th- and 19th-century mine remains – near Runnage for example or Drivage Bottom – but most are likely to be earlier, although how much earlier is unknown.

Although it seems likely that tinners and later miners needed shelters and that many of these structures were built to fulfil that need, it is questionable whether all such structures when associated with tinworks, were built by tinners; indeed most were built into areas of working that were already disused. The hut in a gully near Hookney Tor for example, a few meters from the road, could as easily have been built by the road builders when the Widecombe to Challacombe Cross road was constructed in the 19th century.

Fig 8.26
A Tinner's hut built into the edge of a streamwork in the upper valley of the River Taw. This building is in particularly fine condition; many other examples are ruined to foundation level (photo: Phil Newman).

9

Warreners and improvers in the post-medieval and early-modern periods

Context

Rabbit warrening was once an important component of the Dartmoor farming economy. Although ample archaeological evidence survives, attention from landscape archaeologist has been limited. In 1966 Catherine Linehan introduced the study of rabbit warrens into the Dartmoor literature and provided a useful appendix of 16 sites with general descriptions of some of the features and deserted buildings. Four years later R G Haynes provided the seminal paper to specifically address this subject, although the focus of his work was mainly the vermin traps – the stone traps used by the warreners to control stoats and weasels, for which many examples survive within the Dartmoor warrens (Haynes 1970). Haynes also provided summary descriptions of each known warren, and his work serves as a basis for subsequent writers (Gerrard 1997, 94–5; Williamson 2007). Individual warrens have rarely been the subject of fieldwork, with the exception of small articles on Beardown (Probert 1989), Headland (Newman 2002a) and the Plym Valley warrens (included in a general study of the upper Plym Valley by Robertson in 1991, but still unpublished).

Rabbits are not indigenous to Britain, and although it was formerly believed that they were introduced by the Normans shortly after the Conquest in 1066, there is now good evidence that rabbit meat was being consumed by the Romans during their occupation, although it is not known to what, if any, extent rabbits were farmed by them in Britain. It is thought, however, that the rabbit did not adapt to become part of Britain's wild fauna in the post-Roman period, and it was not until the 11th century that they were re-introduced to England on a large scale (Williamson 2007, 11). Rabbit meat was prized by the medieval nobility and the fur was used extensively for trimming articles of clothing.

The earliest warrens were therefore the property of noblemen, supplying only their domestic needs, and so were often associated with areas of parkland or within larger estates.

As consumption of rabbit meat worked its way down the social scale, however, lesser landowners began to create warrens and allow warrening on their estate lands. Warrening became a useful means of utilising marginal areas of wastes, heaths and moorland – generally unprofitable for conventional farming – and by the 15th to 17th centuries it had developed into a commercial activity, supplying meat and fur for sale. This is likely to be the period when warrening became established on Dartmoor and remained so until the 19th century, when declining demand, first for the fur then for the meat, led to abandonment of most of the warrens. Only Ditsworthy and Trowlesworthy (Fig 9.1) survived into the 20th century, though both were no longer producing rabbits by 1947 (Hemery 1983, 219). Warrens were once numerous elsewhere in England and Wales, with examples spread fairly evenly over the country (Williamson 2007, 90), but with a cluster of large warrens and so much surviving earthwork evidence on Dartmoor, it was clearly one of the more important and better known warrening areas.

Rabbits prefer soft, free-draining soils, and hate the wet. Although Dartmoor has high rainfall, its moderate, free-draining stony hillsides and soft peaty soils, make a suitable environment for rabbits to thrive. There is plenty of grassland and other vegetation, such as heather and gorse, on which they can browse. Dartmoor also has topographic advantages for warreners: rivers and streams could be used as natural barriers to stop rabbits straying into neighbouring farmlands and causing damage to crops. Many Dartmoor warrens were located on open moorland with no immediate farming neighbours, which made these area well suited for rabbit husbandry.

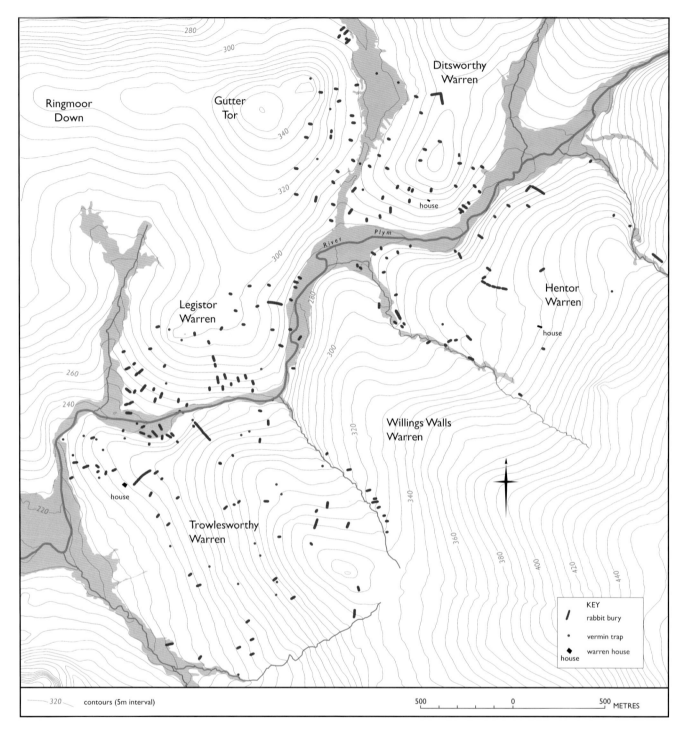

Fig 9.1

Map of the Plym Valley showing the location of the individual warrens, rabbit buries (pillow mounds) and vermin traps (based on EH 1:2500 surveys; height data licensed to English Heritage for PGA through Next Perspectives™).

The Dartmoor warrens

Twenty sites with archaeological evidence for rabbit warrening have been recorded on Dartmoor. At least one other warren, Crane Hill, is known from documentary evidence but lacks field evidence (Stanbrook 1994b). These may be divided into three groups: larger warrens, including commercial and sporting warrens; smaller warrens, with less than ten buries; and isolated single buries. The larger warrens are Ditsworthy, Legis Tor, Trowlesworthy, Willings Walls (Fig 9.1), Beardown (Fig 9.2), Headland (Fig 9.3), Vag Hill (Fig 9.4), Huntingdon (Fig 9.5 and 9.6), Merrivale and Wisman's Wood; smaller examples are Skaigh, Zeal Burrows, Sheepstor, Yalland, New House and Holne Moor. Isolated

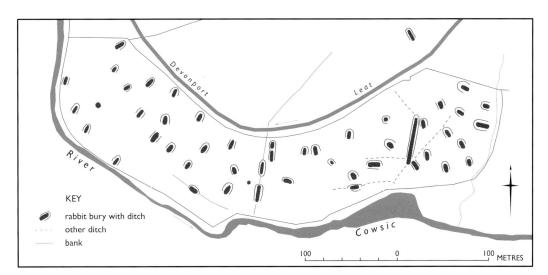

Fig 9.2
Plan of Beardown Warren near Two Bridges, a spatially compact warren of 50 buries based on an RCHME 1:1000 earthwork survey (Probert 1989).

earthworks have been identified at several locations, including Drivage Bottom, Dendles Wood, Rook and Corringdon Ball.

Earlier writers have suggested that Trowlesworthy Warren in the Plym Valley may have had 12th– or 13th–century origins (Haynes 1970, 156; Willamson 2007, 108). This

conjecture was based on documents first published in 1810 as a supplement to *Risdon's Survey of Devon,* but originally written in about 1630. More recently, detailed documentary research by Robertson has revealed that although the place name Trowlesworthy existed since at least 1272, it is unlikely to have operated as a

Fig 9.3
Headland Warren based on EH 1:2500 plan, showing rabbit buries, boundary stones, enclosures and locations of vermin traps.

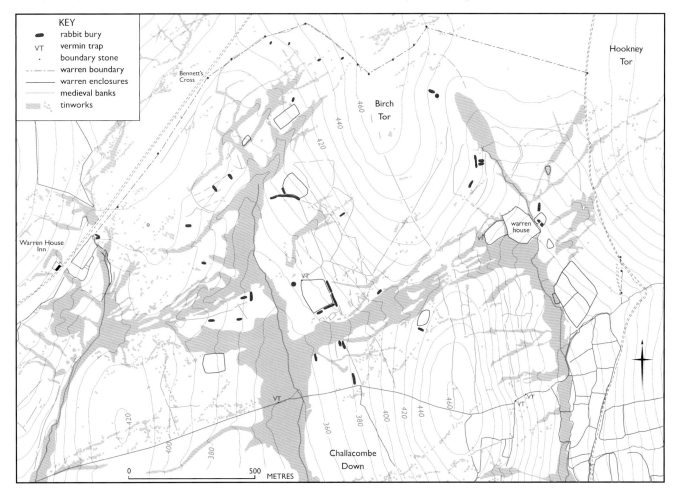

169

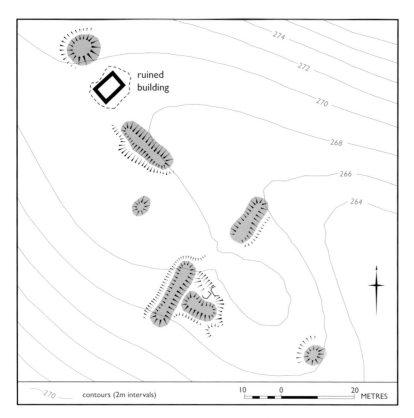

ruined
building

274
272
270
268
266
264

270 ____ contours (2m intervals)

10   0   20
METRES

Legis Warren was first recorded in 1718, but the earliest reference to Hentor is 1807 (Robertson 1991, 264). It is notable that the remains associated with the warrens of Hentor and Ditsworthy, sit amid evidence of medieval settlements, some of which are documented from the early 14th century, with extensive associated cultivation strips. It is unlikely that these two activities would have occurred simultaneously and indeed several of the rabbit buries at Hentor and Ditsworthy overlie the cultivation evidence, strongly suggesting that crop growing had ceased before the start of warrening. It now seems certain that rabbit warrening on Dartmoor has origins no earlier than about 1600, and in the Plym Valley the warrens were later conversions of farms that had for several centuries been farmed more conventionally. This is also the case at Headland and possibly at Vag Hill (Fig 9.4).

The origin and development of several commercial warrens and others known as 'sporting' warrens was during Dartmoor's 'improver period' in the late 18th and early 19th centuries. William Marshall wrote in 1796, that the rabbits could be economically viable in the 'higher weaker lands' of the West Country, and it has to be assumed that this included Dartmoor (Marshall 1796, 271). However, on his visit to West Devon Marshall found only one working warren on 'the skirts of Dartmore'. Beardown Warren (see Fig 9.2) was founded in this period during the 1790s (Probert 1989, 229), and Huntingdon (Figs 9.5 and 9.6), a large

Fig 9.4
Large- scale plan of part of Vag Hill warren, showing details of the rabbit buries.

warren until 1651 (Robertson 1991, 192). Vag Hill Warren, beside the River Dart, appears to be the earliest documented warren, entering the record in 1613 (Haynes 1970, 163); Headland Warren is first recorded in 1754 (Brown 2001, 29), but may have earlier origins, possibly also in the 17th century; and warrening is recorded at Ditsworthy in 1676 (Robertson 1991, 259).

Fig 9.5
Aerial view of Huntingdon Warren, showing the many rabbit buries on the south-east slopes of the hill and a series of drainage channels. Also in the photograph are several prehistoric hut settlements and remains of a large wheel pit associated with Huntingdon Mine (NMR 24101/044; © English Heritage. NMR).

Fig 9.6 (opposite)
Plan of Huntingdon Warren. Although surrounded on three sides by water, the warren extends to the west of the River Avon and is demarcated by a boundary wall (height data licensed to English Heritage for PGA through Next Perspectives™).

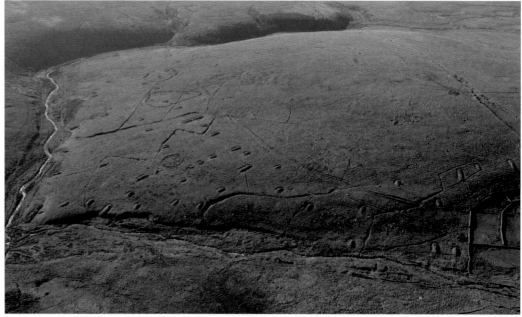

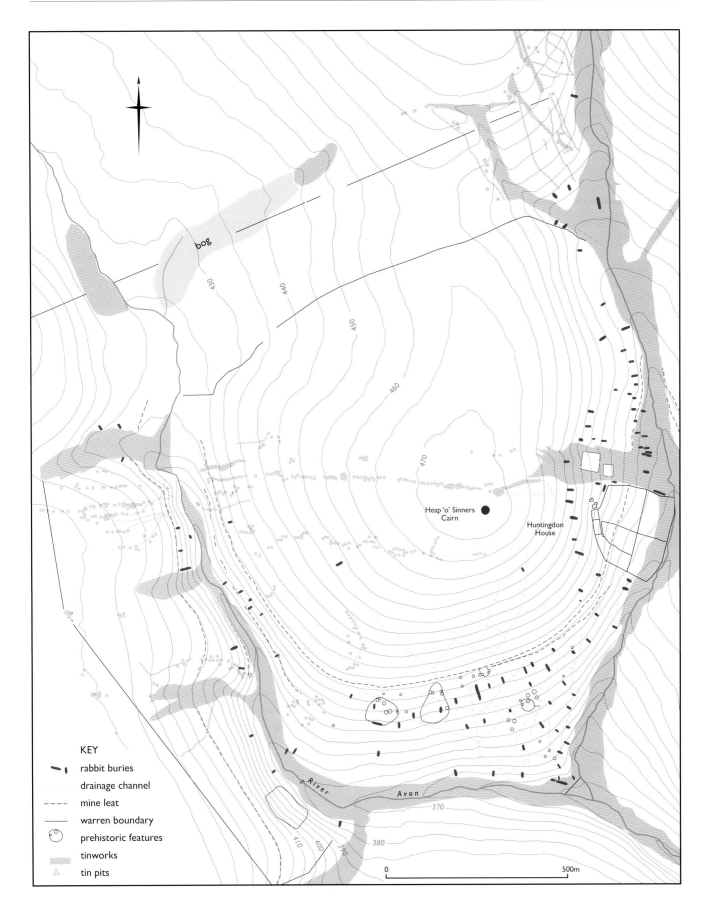

bog

Heap 'o' Sinners
Cairn

Huntingdon
House

River Avon

KEY

rabbit buries

drainage channel

mine leat

warren boundary

prehistoric features

tinworks

tin pits

0   500m

commercial warren, was created in about 1808 on land already taken in from the Forest before 1759 (Stanbrook 1994a, 82–3). The founding date of Merrivale Warren is not known, but it may have been disused by 1802 when Rev Edward Atkins Bray visited the area (Bray 1879, 270); and Wistman's Wood, a sporting warren, is perhaps the latest, which, according to Hemery (1983, 455), was established in 1895.

Field evidence

On Dartmoor, the legacy of rabbit warrening is mostly well preserved and quite easily observed, comprising predominantly the earthen mounds known as buries or 'pillow mounds' in which the rabbits were reared; the warren houses, either standing or ruined; vermin traps; rabbit-proof boundaries and ditches, and in some cases, boundary markers.

Boundaries

The boundaries of rabbit warrens needed to be strictly defined, but because this form of stock do not require walled fields, the extents of the warrens were often marked using other means. Many were bounded by rivers and streams, which provide natural barriers that rabbits would not cross. Trowlesworthy Warren has perhaps the best example of a water barrier (see Fig 9.1): the warren is almost completely encircled by the River Plym and its two tributaries, Spanish Lake and Blackabrook. Because topography makes the source of the Blackabrook only a few metres from the north side of Spanish Lake, only a short section of the boundary, an earthen bank, had to be created artificially to span the remaining gap. How rabbit-proof this would have been is questionable, and it may have been reinforced by timber or perhaps hawthorn bushes. Willings Walls and Hentor are also both bounded by the Plym on the north side and they too utilise smaller tributaries to provide additional boundaries. On the south-west sides, however, neither has a physical boundary, although Hentor Warren has a series of inscribed stones marking the limits of the property. It seems likely in these cases that a rabbit-proof barrier was not necessary where the warren opened onto the wastes of the upland, where even if the rabbits did stray, they would not cause damage. In contrast, Ditsworthy, on the north side of the Plym, relied on the river

on the south, and a substantial stone-faced bank to provide a boundary on the north-east and west sides (see Fig 9.1).

During a visit to Dartmoor by the Rev John Swete in the 1790s he passed Headland or 'Meads' Warren and reported that there was, 'no fence but a few stones piled on one another and ranged in a certain line, evidently serving to ascertain its limits than to preclude the rabbits from roving: indeed on the dry hill beyond this barrier … they appeared as numerous, as they were within the restricted line' (Gray 2000, 38).

Swete was undoubtedly referring to the series of boundary stones that delineates the lands of Headland Warren on the north and east sides (see Fig 9.3). Interestingly, many of these stones are set into the disused outer field boundary of a long-abandoned medieval farmstead near Chaw Gully. It would appear that like the Plym Valley warrens, Headland was using land previously subject to cultivation. In this case, however, the colossal impact of tinworking on the land in the medieval and post-medieval period, along with the higher altitude, had rendered it extremely marginal in terms of normal upland farming, so rabbit rearing was a viable alternative.

Rabbit buries or pillow mounds

'Pillow mound' is a term coined in the early 20th century by the archaeologist O G S Crawford, the Ordnance Survey's principal recorder of antiquities. A descriptive term was needed to distinguish the mounds from Neolithic long barrows, with which they were frequently misidentified, and the name was derived from their morphological similarity to a bolster. However, the expression describes only the shape of the archaeological remains and not their purpose, while the vernacular term for these mounds, with which most country people would be familiar, is 'bury'. The identification of rabbit buries by antiquaries should not have been a problem on Dartmoor, where many remained in use into the 20th century. Nevertheless Rev E A Bray was 'taken in' by the mounds at Merrivale Warren when he visited them in 1802, believing he had recorded 13 barrows and concluded that 'the spot seems to have been a sacred cemetery of the Druids' (Bray 1879, 230–3). This conclusion is all the more curious because Beardown Warren, with 50 buries, probably created in the 1790s, was on land owned by the Brays and he must surely have been familiar with these features. As late as 1912, William Crossing, the author of the celebrated *Guide to Dartmoor* (1912, 369), also warned against mistaking them for barrows. Elsewhere in Britain, rabbit buries continued to be archaeologically excavated well into the 20th century in the mistaken belief that they contained prehistoric burials (Williamson 2007, 38).

Several forms of buries have been identified, though all served the same purpose: to provide soft dry ground for the rabbits to burrow in and inhabit, while easing the managing and harvesting of the crop. Although rabbits are natural burrowers, there are several reasons why it was necessary to provide them with artificial mounds. Firstly, many areas of the moor are thin-soiled and rocky, with limited areas suitable for burrowing, so mounds provided both soft earth and depth. Also, rabbits prefer to burrow into a moderate slope and the flanks of an artificial mound would provide that. Rabbits also require a dry environment, as water-logging of breeding areas is disastrous. A raised mound, built into a slope surrounded by a ditch provides such a dry environment and helps prevent water from entering the burrows. It is also easier to manage the rabbits contained within buries, especially when harvesting them, done by netting the burrow openings and sending in ferrets to flush the rabbits out.

Buries are to be found located singly, in spatially separate groups, or in close clusters.

A single warren may contain all three spatial variants and there appears to be no rationale behind these layouts.

The most common or standard form is an elongated, straight-sided mound with rounded ends and a raised profile having a curving side profile and a flattish top (Fig 9.7; *and see also* Fig 9.4). These linear mounds are, with a few exceptions, aligned across the contour of a hillslope, either at right angles to it or set obliquely. Surrounding each mound is a ditch to provide drainage, although often partly silted. Mounds are as small as 8m long × 3m wide and larger examples are up to 45m long × 10m wide. Most only stand to a maximum height of 1.2m, although many are less than 1m high. Some linear buries are much longer than these standard examples: at Headland Warren, for example, where 34 have been recorded, several are in excess of 100m (*see* Fig 9.3), although these are unusual. The linear mounds were most commonly raised on undisturbed terrain, occasionally existing features were adapted for use as buries. At Headland Warren several of the mounds utilised the spoil banks of disused leats, and at Hentor a boundary bank associated with the strip fields was converted into an array of buries.

Although less common, circular buries also exist, with a base diameter of up to 15m, and are easily confused with round barrows and mining spoil heaps. Those that survive at Headland and at Vag Hill (*see* Fig 9.4) are distinguished by their well-preserved profiles and clear ditches surrounding the mounds.

Fig 9.7
A large rabbit bury or pillow mound at Trowlesworthy Warren (NMR DP099171; © English Heritage. NMR).

The most densely packed area of buries is within the five Plym Valley warrens, where a total of 211 have been recorded, and Huntingdon Warren, where 112 are contained within the single warren. Beardown has 50 mounds within an enclosed area of less than 4.2ha.

To establish how they were constructed, several buries have been excavated in recent years, although as yet none on Dartmoor (Williamson 2007, 41). Some excavations revealed that stone structures were built into the ground before the mound of earth was thrown over, forming stone-lined tunnels and chambers for the rabbits to use on first being introduced to the mound. In other cases, where the stone is more random, it may have been a means of assisting with drainage of the covering earth section. Stone revetments along the bases of buries at Merrivale and at Beardown suggest evidence of this practice.

Often associated with rabbit buries are drainage channels that cut obliquely across the slope at slightly higher altitude than the mounds. These prevented storm water from intense downpours inundating the buries. Clear examples of straight trenches with a V-profile transect the eastern slope of Huntingdon Warren, within a dense cluster of buries.

Vermin traps

As their description suggests, vermin traps were installed within warrens to control natural predators, which if not adequately controlled could seriously deplete rabbit crops. On Dartmoor the main problem would have been from stoats, weasels and possibly rats, but elsewhere in Britain polecats, wild cats and foxes were a problem. Foxes also inhabit Dartmoor and were no doubt also successful rabbit predators, but the traps under discussion were used to catch only the smaller mammals described above. Vermin traps were used at all British warrens, particularly the pre-19th-century ones, but in most regions the traps were constructed from wood and do not survive. On Dartmoor many, if not all, were made from stone and survive in abundance, providing a unique archaeological resource. R G Haynes (1970) discusses the subject and the field evidence in detail, recorded most of the known examples and constructed working models of the mechanisms.

Stoats and weasels are small, low quadrupeds that stand only a few centimetres above the ground. They therefore keep a low profile on the moorland, choosing natural dips and an obstacle-free terrain when crossing it. Warreners used this habit to their advantage by placing their traps in just such places, for example in low natural or man-made gullies, or by creating obstacles that had to be avoided, such as earth banks. To direct these animals into traps, low, stony banks with a V-plan were created between natural obstacles, such as earth-fast boulders, the bottoms of gullies, or to an apparent portal through a stone wall. These banks limited the directions the creatures could travel and funnelled them into the traps. There were usually two V-shaped banks, with the pointed ends converging on the trap, giving an X-shaped ground plan, so the trap worked for animals travelling in either direction. The trap itself was a short stone tunnel of two edge-set flat slabs and a flat cover stone. To the approaching stoat or weasel it would appear as a portal providing easy passage through the bank, but inside, a mechanism was tripped by the creature entering it, causing vertical slate shutters to fall across the entrances and trap it (Haynes 1970, 151).

The most common surviving field evidence is the funnel banks (Fig 9.8). They are particularly abundant within all the Plym Valley warrens – more than 39 are depicted on Fig 9.1, and others have been noted (Haynes 1970). The stony banks are often no higher than 0.5m, but are frequently up to 10m long. They are commonly associated with existing man-made features, such as the ruined medieval settlement at Gutter Tor, where one of the buildings and a yard wall have been adapted to form a trap. Several examples of this type of trap also survive at Vag Hill Warren on the Dart, where in all cases, the traps are disguised to give the appearance of an easy passage under a stone wall.

The traps themselves rarely survive intact: in many the edge-set side walls are *in situ*, but the cap stones are usually displaced. One where the cover stone remains, though not *in situ*, is on the south slopes of Gutter Tor, built into the base of a field boundary. The edge-set stones of the sides both have a vertical groove cut into the end of the inside face to accommodate the shutters. The cover stones have small holes, as described by Haynes to hold wooden pegs to secure the mechanism, and lie removed, to the east.

It is believed that vermin traps became less common as a means of pest control in the late

Fig 9.8
The ruined funnel walls
of a vermin trap at
Trowlesworthy Warren,
showing the opposing V
footprint of the wall
(NMR 7266; © English
Heritage. NMR).

18th and 19th centuries, for warrens established during this period have few if any recorded examples. At Headland, probably 18th-century, only four are known, and at Hentor, probably late 18th- to early 19th-century, there are only two. Four have also been recorded at Huntingdon, a 19th-century warren. At Beardown, Wistman's Wood, Merrivale and Skaigh no examples are known. Haynes has suggested that this decline in the use of vermin traps was due to the increasing availability of guns to warreners (Haynes 1970, 164).

Fodder enclosures

An unusual feature of Headland Warren is a series of six isolated enclosures – with stone walls and one with walls of stone-faced earth (*see* Fig 9.3) – distributed over discrete parts of the warren. These are referred to locally as 'Jan Reynolds Playing Cards', following a legend retold by William Crossing (1912, 318), although literary licence seems to have overlooked the fact that their forms are rather too irregular to be compared with cards. The shapes and approximate areas vary: the largest is approximately 1ha and the smallest about 0.5ha. Two of the enclosures have narrow-gated entrances, with gate posts still *in situ*. The purpose of the enclosures is debated: explanations vary between use as places to contain the rabbits (used instead of buries) and rabbit-proof areas for growing winter fodder. It has also been suggested that these enclosures were used to lure – by the promise of good things to eat inside – and entrap rabbits through a small entrance, trapping the rabbits inside or netting them as they entered.

Another account suggests that they were used as vegetable plots and fodder fields for bullocks, and not associated with rabbits at all (Newman 2002a, 22–4). However, it is known from warrens elsewhere in Britain that discrete enclosures of this type are common and were used to grow winter fodder to feed the rabbits (Williamson 2007, 71). The stone walls provided a rabbit-proof boundary, which although probably not 100% effective, made it possible to conserve the vegetation within until needed. This may explain the lack of a gate opening on the majority of the Headland examples.

Improvers and newtakes 1780–1880

Although some farm abandonment occurred after the major episode of settlement and enclosure in the medieval period, piecemeal colonisation continued in previously unenclosed and uninhabited areas of upland for many centuries. Several farms, including some that have been abandoned and many still occupied, have founding dates as late as the 19th century.

A few of these new farms were sited around the peripheries of the commons and represent expansion of the existing structure of enclosure and settlement that had for centuries been encroaching onto the moorland. On western Dartmoor, for example, the extent of 'Doter' (Doe Tor) Green was recorded in 1694 and houses were in existence there by at least 1740 (Wessex 2007, 5). This farm occupies a small peninsula of land between the Doe Tor Brook and Walla Brook, and formed a natural eastward expansion of the existing farmlands into the wastes. The site once boasted a modest two-storey farmhouse and outbuildings and was occupied until the 1950s. The outlines and foundation walls of the buildings, all now in ruins, can still be identified. Not far south of Doetor Farm is Yellowmead, another ruined farmstead probably founded sometime before 1687, and where a similar set of earthwork ruins is found (Greeves 2008, 10).

However, with the exception of the warrens, abandoned farmsteads with a founding date in the 17th and early 18th centuries are comparatively rare, and it is not until the end of the 18th century that a number of new farms and enclosures were created on the uplands, specifically within the Forest of Dartmoor. Many of these remain occupied, but several were abandoned and comparatively short-lived; their ruins represent a brave but ill-conceived period of agricultural expansion.

From the 1780s a frenzy of farm building and enclosure by a small group of wealthy landowners, usually referred to as the 'improvers', was the result of a convergence of circumstances on both Dartmoor and in England at the time. The end of the 18th century was an age of science and innovation; machines were introduced to agriculture and experiments with fertilisers, and with adaptations of livestock breeds to increase production, were seen as part of an agricultural or rural 'revolution' to match the efforts of the industrialists in the towns. From the 1780s until 1815, the country seemed to be permanently either at war or under threat of war, and it was perceived as an Englishman's patriotic duty to increase the supply of food to the nation where possible. There was also a great enthusiasm for capitalism at this time, with fortunes to be made by investment in the right opportunities. These three factors converged to provide a national context for the activities of the improvers, but developments at a local level were also encouraging change. The creation of turnpike roads and in particular the upgrading of the trans-Dartmoor route from Moretonhampstead to Two Bridges (now the B3212) resulted in the central area of the Forest around Two Bridges itself to become more accessible. Within Dartmoor Forest several of the copyhold tenancies within the Duchy lands had come into the possession of a wealthier class of farmer who had the capital and zeal to invest in improvement, and from the 1780s

several of these copyholders were given land grants allowing them to enclose hundreds of acres of moorland, although later it would prove that they had done so on dubious legal grounds (see below). Some of the most profound changes to the agricultural scene started in the Forest in this period and continued well into the next century.

Two reports on agriculture in south-west England and in Devon were published in the 1790s that reflect the spirit of improvement. The authors of both works were convinced of Dartmoor's potential. In 1796, William Marshall suggested that a series of improvements, including burning the heath, drainage, manuring and the creation of more hedges would be beneficial. Only two years earlier, Robert Fraser had argued, more radically, that the system of common pasturing of sheep and cattle, current at the time, was an inefficient and wasteful use of the land and that it should be parcelled off to new tenants and enclosed, and new villages created (Fraser 1794, 47–65). Although several of these ideas were tried, most met with failure, and Fraser's plan, although supported by some landowners, was never carried out despite almost becoming passed as an Act of Parliament.

The historical context for this phase of Dartmoor's 'exploitation' has been thoroughly researched and published by Somers Cocks (1970), and narratives for some of the individual forest farms of this period are in Stanbrook (1994a). In terms of the archaeological landscape these events were responsible for a number of changes.

Several new farms were established: Sir Thomas Tyrwhitt for example, one of the leading Dartmoor improvers who had created a suitable gentleman's estate for himself at Tor Royal, founded additional new farms at Bachelor's Hall, Peat Cot and Swincombe; the first two are still occupied but Swincombe is a ruin. Beardown was founded in the 1780s by Edward Bray, father of Edward Atkins Bray the antiquary, and other new farms were being founded near Postbridge and on the north moor at Teignhead and Manga.

The most profound change that improvers brought to the landscape was the imposition of the massive enclosures that arose through the licenses granted by the Duchy. Although arguably the improvers set out with good intentions, these enclosures had no practical

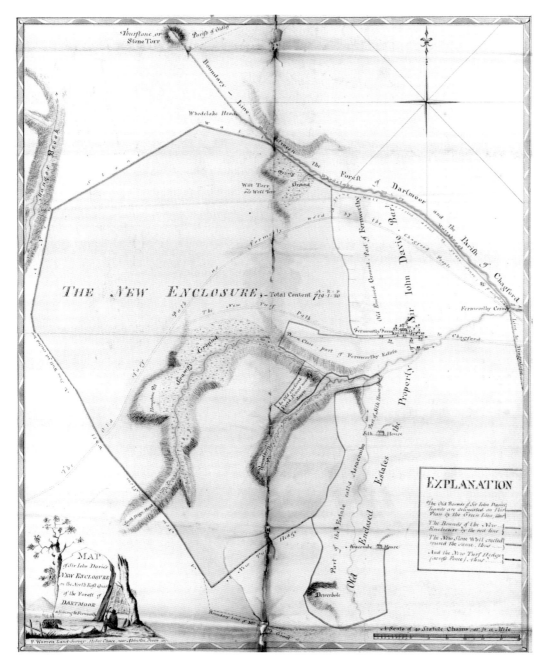

Fig 9.9
Map of 1807 depicting Sir
John Davie's 'New Enclosure',
attached to the much earlier
Fernworthy Farm (© Duchy
of Cornwall Archive, with
permission).

purpose other than to demarcate the extent of ownership, and were in effect 'land grabs'. The land within such enclosures only continued to be used for rough grazing. They were built in a hurry and the associated walls are quite different from those of earlier times. Unlike the piecemeal growth of medieval and post-medieval field systems, where small enclosures were added as a farm expanded, these new walls took in many hundreds of hectares in one action. They follow straight or gently curving lines and are most frequently of dry-stone construction. The weathered moorstone of Dartmoor is not wholly suited to dry-stone walls, which made them occasionally rather unstable and subject to collapse, but they could be built relatively quickly. Many miles of these walls were constructed north of Postbridge, west of Fernworthy and south of Princetown, creating a transect of enclosed land right across the centre of Dartmoor. The upland was effectively divided into the north and south moor tracts with which visitors to Dartmoor are familiar today. Although now sited within access lands, many are maintained up to the present.

Of the new farms created, several ultimately

Chagford
Common

Teignhead
Newtake

Manga

Teignhead

Teign

North

Fernworthy
Newtake

Thornworthy

South Teign

Fernworthy

Assacombe

Stannon
Newtake

0   1 km

Fig 9.10
Modern map of the Fernworthy
Newtake depicted in Fig 9.9
The massive newtake of 1807
dwarves the small patchwork
fields of the medieval farms of
Fernworthy and Assacombe.
The map also shows the Stan-
non and Teignhead Newtakes,
which are later additions. Red
line shows the Forest boundary
as delineated on the OS map of
the 1880s (based on OS
25-inch 1st edition).

failed, mainly due to their exposed positions on high ground – but it took over a century to happen in some cases. Teignhead Farm and Manga Farm, both above 450m OD, were created shortly after 1809. The extensive dry-stone walls enclose vast areas on the flanks of the North Teign River, and butt against the Fernworthy Newtake to the east (now subsumed by plantation) (Figs 9.9 and 9.10) and Great Stannon Newtake to the south, both also improver estates. Teignhead (Fig 9.11) was abandoned in the mid-20th century; its buildings remained

standing until the 1960s, but are now ruins, as are those of neighbouring Manga Farm.

By the 1830s the enthusiasm of the original improvers was failing, but enclosure of moorlands and commons continued throughout the 19th century, though on a reduced scale. Several more farmsteads were created particularly within the Forest. The last 'new' farm in the Forest was Nun's Cross in 1870 (Stanbrook 1994a, 60), but it was only a very small holding in terms of acreage. Outside the Forest in the border parishes areas of common

Fig 9.11
*Teignhead Farm
photographed by Robert
Burnard on 12 August 1889
(© The Dartmoor Trust).*

know and visit Dartmoor National Park today, nevertheless had a profound influence on the way the Dartmoor landscape developed from then onward: it halted the expansion of enclosed farming, preserved the remaining common lands, provided for the survival of many threatened archaeological sites and sowed the seeds for further conservation and the formation of the national park many years later.

land were also being assarted. Large examples include Merrivale Newtake, taken in *c* 1850 and Rippon Tor in the 1830s (Gill 1970, 261).

Not everyone approved of the rapid rate that the commons were becoming a dwindling resource, not least the Venville tenants (*see* chapter 7), whose rights were gradually being eroded. Enclosure was also opposed by the growing conservation movement, made up mainly of antiquaries and other gentleman who were concerned about destruction of archaeological remains that had occurred as a result of wall building and field clearance, as well as the prospect of restricted access to the land by the public. In his account of the exploitation of Dartmoor John Somers Cocks says that it was the threat of further extensive enclosure of the commons that led to the formation of the Dartmoor Preservation Association (DPA) in the 1880s. Historical research commissioned by the DPA established that much of the enclosure of land over the past 100 years had been unlawful and from that point onward enclosure on Dartmoor was halted. (Somers Cocks 1970, 261). This seemingly minor sequence of historical events, long forgotten about in the collective consciousness of those who

Farmhouses and warren houses

The remains of abandoned farmhouses and outbuildings from the 17th to 19th centuries usually reveal them to have been robustly built in granite, following a long tradition of the use of this material in the vernacular buildings of Dartmoor and its borders. However, these once fine buildings are nearly always in ruins, often the result of demolition causing the walls to collapse. The outlines of the foundations and the ground floor room layouts are all that is visible, strewn with tumbled masonry. But in some cases their former appearance can be glimpsed through photographs taken when they were standing, often while still occupied (*see* Fig 9.11). Various publications of recent years have showcased such photographs, among which Stanbrook (1994a) has assembled an interesting collection of Dartmoor Forest farms.

Deserted improver farms on the open moors include Brown's House, John Bishop's House (Fig 9.12), Swincombe, Teignhead and Manga. There is a probable 17th-century warren houses at Eastercombe (Vag Hill) and there are 19th-century examples at Ditsworthy (Fig 9.13) and Hentor.

*Fig 9.12 (below, right)
John Bishop's House in about
the 1950s (© J Boddy,
Dartmoor Archive).*

*Fig 9.13 (below)
Ditsworthy Warren House.
The house was still occupied
at least until 1947, its
survival today being due to
adoption by the military as a
bunkhouse (NMR DP099147;
© English Heritage. NMR).*

Part Three
The industrial and military landscape

10

Moorstone and granite

Eighteenth-century industrialisation

Tin extraction was probably the earliest truly industrial activity to take place on Dartmoor. However, no direct evidence of precisely when it began has yet been found. Tinworking was an ancient industry that may have origins in the early medieval period or even earlier in prehistoric times, and developed thereafter into a crucial component of the Dartmoor economy. Other medieval rural industries were important too, including peat cutting – often to supply the furnaces of the tin smelters – and stone cutting to supply building projects on and around the moor, and trade in stone artefacts.

Developments towards the end of the 18th century provided the context for industrial intensification on Dartmoor and was in step with the industrialisation elsewhere in Britain on a massive scale: the so-called 'industrial revolution'. Dartmoor, with open spaces and apparent abundant mineral and other resources attracted the attention of enthusiastic capitalists and adventurers searching for ways to exploit it. Some of these would-be industrialists were also involved in the movement towards agricultural improvement on Dartmoor, for example Redvers Buller and James Templer of Stover. A central character in this episode was Sir Thomas Tyrwhitt of Tor Royal, who apart from developing his agricultural estate and creating several new farms, was also responsible for founding Princetown in the centre of the moor, and later the prison. He also promoted the first railway to Princetown, which was to be an important factor in the development of several industries in that area. These developments are thoroughly discussed by Crossing (1989) and by Kingdom (1991).

The formation of joint stock companies to provide capital to develop industry was an important aspect of entrepreneurial activity in this period, especially mining – which did not provide instant returns – but joint capital enabled much grander enterprise. Much of this capital came from outside Devon. Tin mining was the first to enjoy a small revival, following a rise in the value of tin from the 1780s. As interest in metal mining returned to the district other metals were also prospected for. Copper had been mined in Devon on a small and sporadic scale since the early 18th century, and silver since the 13th; and by the 1790s these industries also enjoyed renewed impetus from an increase in mine adventurers exploring for the metals around the borders of the upland. From c 1820 advances in quarrying and stone-cutting techniques brought growth in the granite industry, meeting a national demand for granite in building. Transporting such heavy stone required tramways and railways, and in 1820 Dartmoor's first tramway was laid between Haytor quarries and Ventiford at the head of the Stover Canal, creating Devon's first industrial transport link from moor to sea. It was followed in 1823 by the opening of the Plymouth and Dartmoor tramway, which served the quarries on Walkhampton Common as well as the new town of Princetown (Harris 1968, 22). The new china clay industry, beginning c 1830 also required tramways. It developed on a massive scale around Shaugh Moor, Lee Moor and Crownhill Down, and is still a vibrant industry on south-west Dartmoor occupying hundreds of hectares both within and outside of the national park. Peat had been the main domestic fuel on Dartmoor since at least medieval times, and peat cutting was developed on a commercial scale during the mid-19th century. It was confined to the high moors, where the peat was at its deepest, and at Rattlebrook, on north Dartmoor, a small railway was built to move the peat off the moor.

Extractive industries were not the only industrial activity on Dartmoor in this period. Postbridge's remoteness and a plentiful water supply to power machines made it ideal as the site for a gunpowder works built in 1844. Other industries tried included ice works at Sourton between 1874 and 1876, which produced ice for food preservation as far a way as Plymouth. There were also various attempts to produce naphtha, a paraffin-like substance distilled from peat.

Although relying on different environmental resources and separate markets, all of Dartmoor's industries except china clay had one thing in common, which they shared with the agricultural improvers of the same period: they were mostly unsuccessful and they often resulted in financial ruination of the companies involved. Causes for these failures are discussed below, but two common factors were the remoteness of Dartmoor and the extra transport cost incurred as a consequence, and the misplaced optimism of the adventurers involved, which resulted in over-capitalising of enterprises that had little potential to pay a return. However, when active these industries provided a huge number of employment opportunities for the people of Dartmoor and its borders, although often only short-term. Dartmoor's economy and employment, which had for centuries been focussed on agriculture supplemented by tinning and peat cutting, shifted for a while to one that included intense industrial activity.

The study of industrial archaeology

The legacy of these abandoned industries has provided some of the most intriguing and visually striking archaeological remains on Dartmoor: massive spoil heaps associated with deep shafts (now capped) and steep quarry faces, spectacular earthworks and ruined buildings where diverse processes occurred or workers resided.

The archaeological study of past industries is today an established discipline, but its development is the most recent period specialism in archaeology. It evolved from a fascination in the subject mainly by amateurs rather than by professionals. The term 'industrial archaeology' has its roots in the 1950s and early 1960s when the priority for those pursuing it was the recording and preservation of buildings and machines at a time when, economically, the country was undergoing massive changes and the heritage of the declining industries was under great threat.

Before 1968 the only clues to much of Dartmoor's industrial past in published literature were found in works by William Crossing, who witnessed and charted the demise of some of these industries in the late 19th century and recorded it incidentally in his descriptions of Dartmoor (Le Messurier 1966; 1967), and by R H Worth, who had recorded many of the medieval and post-medieval tin mills on Dartmoor. The Haytor Granite Tramway had also fascinated some writers, probably because of its uniqueness, but their researches extended no further than what might be discovered from historical documents and their engagement with the field remains was limited to summary descriptions (Amery Adams 1946; Ewans 1964)

In 1968, however, one of the seminal books on rural industrial archaeology in Britain was published: Helen Harris's *Industrial Archaeology on Dartmoor*. She describes 18th-, 19th- and some early 20th-century industries in terms of their archaeological remains for the first time. Mines, quarries, peatworks, clayworks, leats, gunpowder mills and lesser-known enterprises such as the Sourton Tor ice works and the bottle factory at Meldon were explained in context with associated moor-wide activities. Despite the existence of more recent publications covering this topic, Harris's book remains the standard work and is in its fourth edition.

Nevertheless, in terms of conventional archaeological research techniques, beyond what might be discovered in historical documents, investigation of Dartmoor's industries is still at an early stage. Archaeological surveys undertaken by the English Heritage Archaeological Survey and Investigation team, presented here, and the work of other professionals recording buildings, such as Exeter Archaeology's work at Powder Mills (*see* Fig 13.5) and Wheal Betsy (*see* Fig 11.12), represent the bulk of the work done so far.

Granite and moorstone

Granite has been the major source of building stone on Dartmoor since the 3rd millennium BC, when the stone circles, rows and round houses were among the first permanent features to be constructed from it. Granite is a hard, enduring and attractive stone. It is unsuitable for intricate carving, but can take a polish and can withstand compression; so it is ideal for use in large buildings and bridges where enormous weight is involved. During the medieval period the people of Dartmoor used granite mainly to build their houses, but also began to export it to other areas of Devon for major building projects such as churches and large, high-status houses, particularly in the parishes around the Dartmoor border country. Granite is exceptionally hard and requires specialist techniques to cut it; it was not until the early 19th century that technology had advanced enough to be able to quarry it. Before that time 'moorstone' was the only form of granite available and accounted for all the stone used in the millennia before *c* 1800. R H Worth believed that 'granite' was a term never used on Dartmoor before it was introduced by geologists and to the residents it was always referred to as moorstone.

The term 'moorstone' refers to granite boulders that have, through geological forces, become detached from the main outcrops of the tors and deposited down the slopes as scatters of loose boulders referred to as 'clitter'. Tens of thousands of years of weathering has softened and rounded such boulders into characteristic moorstones, a familiar sight on the upland. This is the material collected by prehistoric people to build their monuments, houses, enclosures and reaves. Such unaltered moorstone continued to suffice for many Dartmoor medieval and post-medieval buildings such as the longhouses, farmhouses, tin mills and industrial buildings, randomly-built but robust, and unmortared. It was also used for facing wall banks for field boundaries. Long pieces were ideal for gateposts, and an array of everyday artefacts including apple crushers, troughs, cider presses and cheese presses were cut from moorstone blocks (Fig 10.1).

It is sobering to consider exactly just how much moorstone must have been removed from Dartmoor in the 4,000 years that it was in use, radically altering the appearance of some areas of the moor.

Granite was frequently dressed, using a hammer and chisel, to provide flat surfaces and such work can be seen on the quoins and window mullions of many Dartmoor farmhouses. Some of the finest granite structures on Dartmoor can be seen at Widecombe-in-

Fig 10.1 Moorstone artefacts: (top) a slotted gatepost at Fernworthy; (upper centre) an abandoned, part-completed trough near Hare Tor; (lower centre) an edge-runner at Merrivale; (lower) a pound stone near Holwell Tor – the latter two being components of horse-powered apple crushers. (photos: Phil Newman)

Fig 10.2
Archaeological evidence of the various cutting techniques used to cleave granite: (top) an abandoned attempt at wedge and groove stone cutting near Haytor. The stone was later cleaved in the opposite direction; (centre) the characteristic alignment of jumper holes associated with feather and tare; (bottom) longer groove of larger diameter known as 'shot holes' indicative of the use of explosives. (photos: Phil Newman)

the-Moor, where the church and church house in the square are standing examples of late medieval granite buildings made before there were any quarries. For a regular supply of faced stones for buildings of this quality, techniques were developed to cut the granite into squared or 'dimensioned' blocks. Such techniques may have been developed in medieval times and the earliest of these was the so-called wedge-and-groove method.

To cleave a stone using this technique, a line of narrow grooves is cut across the surface of the stone, each *c* 700mm (3in) deep. With the grooves running right across the cut face, wooden wedges, previously soaked in water, were forced into them, then left for a period of time. As the wet caused the wood to expand, so the granite was cleft by the simultaneous expansion of all the wedges. Archaeological evidence of this method is extremely common, though not always easy to spot without a search; but where a piece of stone has been removed, the remaining surface will have traces of the grooves still visible, although often weathered and covered in lichen. Occasionally an unsuccessful attempt at cutting a stone can be seen, such as the example near Holwell Tor (Fig 10.2), where the cut clearly failed and left the grooves intact.

Although at a later date iron wedges hammered into the grooves replaced the use of wooden ones (Stanier 1999, 53), wedge and groove was a rather unreliable and time-consuming method and at some time in the 18th century a new technique was introduced called 'plug and feather', or more commonly on Dartmoor, 'feather and tare'. The precise date when this method became more widespread is uncertain, although R H Worth claims that it was not in use until the 1790s. This technique replaced the grooves with a line of small round drill holes, and instead of wooden wedges, tapering iron plugs (tares) were used. Two thin iron strips called 'feathers' were placed into the drill hole and iron plugs forced between them. The plugs were hammered in sequence until the rock split along the line. The holes were drilled using a simple hand tool called a 'jumper' – a long, sharpened iron bar, balanced so that it could be twisted as it struck the granite when 'jumped' up and down. The tell-tale evidence of this technique is widespread in granite areas, where *in situ* granite blocks have lines of evenly-spaced semi-circular holes along the corner of one long edge, indicating that a block has been cut off and taken away (Fig 10.2).

This technique was a major advancement and increased the speed at which stone could be cut, and made the granite trade more viable. It also had a major impact on the landscape because of its widespread use. Granite areas on the edges of the moor were most favoured because the product would not need to be transported quite so far for sale. The west sides of Belstone Tors, Staple Tor, Feather Tor, Pu Tor Trowlesworthy and Haytor Downs all have extensive evidence of this activity. Often, large areas of clitter have been so thoroughly worked over that collection has resulted in a series of shallow pits where stone has been removed. Lying in the pit is the remaining stone from which the blocks were cut, each with the jumper holes clear to see. The pits and the resulting blocks that were removed, can be quite large, up to 3m long in some cases. Often there are smaller flakes of granite in a pit, indicating further working of the block after separation. For a particularly large block an inclined ramp was cut into one side of the pit to ease its removal onto a cart or sledge. Not all cut stones resulted in a pit, however, especially if the source was above ground.

Although granite quarrying began on Dartmoor in the early 19th century, moorstone continued to hold several advantages as a source of smaller pieces of stone. Firstly, the weathering of surface stone had naturally graded it by removing the softer material so that only harder rock survived, whereas at quarries, where this natural sorting had not taken place, much unsuitable stone had to be rejected . There was also the convenience of exploiting moorstone, which required a minimum of tools and investment in comparison to quarrying. Moorstone cutting therefore continued as a viable industry for much of the 19th century, especially around Pu Tor and Staple Tors on the west side of the moor. Helen Harris has written a detailed history of these moorstone workings (1981).

Granite was particularly useful for kerbs and paving in Plymouth and Tavistock, where there was much civic improvement in the mid-19th century – between the 1840s and 1890s licenses were issued to cut and remove stone from this area to meet that demand. After initial separation the kerbs, or 'setts', were dressed by craftsmen, who worked the granite on makeshift stone benches formed from a slab

of granite resting against the slope of the tor, supported on two earth-fast granite trestles. Evidence of these 'bankers', as they were known, is spread across the south and east slopes of Staple Tor (Fig 10.3), and it is thought that temporary roofs and windbreaks were erected around them for protection from the weather. Since Harris first recorded these features in the 1960s, similar examples have been recorded elsewhere in other granite producing areas of south-west Dartmoor (Dell and Bright 2008).

Fig 10.3
Sett maker's 'bankers' on the south-western slopes of Staple Tor: low stone benches at which workmen could shape pieces of granite placed on top. The openings on the bankers are between 0.3m and 0.5m wide (photo: Phil Newman).

Quarries

Although granite quarrying was possible on a small scale using only hand tools, it was not until explosives were introduced that larger quarries became possible. This development may have occurred later for the granite industry than for other stone sources because of the convenience and availability of moorstone. A small quarry was developed to supply materials for Princetown Prison in 1806–9 (Stanier 1999, 66), but the first commercial quarries on Dartmoor were opened in *c* 1820 at Haytor. Larger and more enduring quarries were later established on Walkhampton Common, at Foggintor (Fig 10.4) and at Swelltor; and smaller ones at Ingra Tor, Heckwood, Longash and Dewerstone. Even smaller quarries are also numerous, for example at Western Beacon, Trowlesworthy and Brat Tor. The last operational granite quarry was Tor Quarry at Merrivale on Whitchurch Common, which remained in work until the 1990s (*see* Figs 10.4 and 10.10).

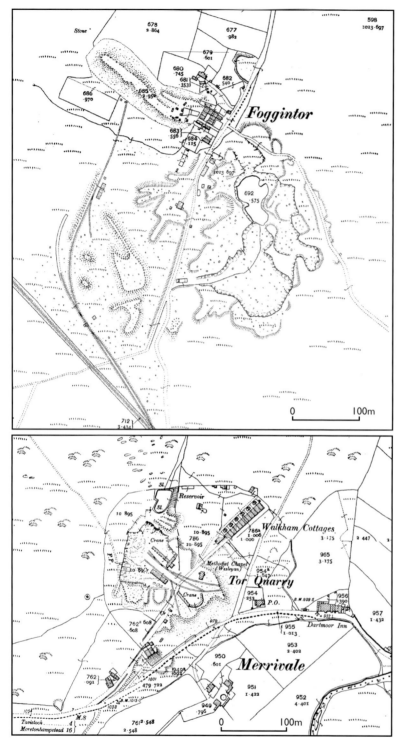

grove technique, hinting at an origin for stone cutting in this area extending back to at least the 18th century, though probably much earlier. The quarries started work shortly before 1820 when the land was owned by George Templer of Stover House, near Newton Abbot. More than 20 years earlier Templer's father James, who in the 1780s was also tenant of the ancient tenement of Bellever and was at the heart of the Dartmoor agricultural improver movement, had dug a canal through his Stover estate between Ventiford, in the heart of south Devon's ball clay district, to the River Teign estuary in order to transport the clay to a wider market. George Templer's scheme made further use of the canal to move granite off the moors from Haytor, to connect to the canal at Ventiford by a tramway, thus gaining access to the seaport of Teignmouth. Although Haytor granite was being extracted and worked before the tramway was built in 1820, it was the creation of this transport link that enabled Templer's company to expand. Other writers have explored the history of the quarries, tramway and canal, including Amory Adams (1946), Ewans (1964) and Harris (2002), and tradition has it that Templer's Haytor company was established to fulfil a contract to supply the builders of London Bridge, which is the main reason the tramway was built. By 1829 Templer was in financial difficulties and had to sell his Stover estate, but the granite company continued to operate until the late 1830s, fell into disuse for 10 years, recommenced production in 1850, and finally closed in 1865 (Harris 2002, 28).

There are five quarries at Haytor, all connected to the tramway network: Haytor (*see* Fig 10.7), Holwell, Rubble Heap (Fig 10.5), Emsworthy and Harrow Barrow. Of these, the first three are larger quarries with high quarry faces and substantial exterior spoil heaps, whereas Emsworthy and Harrow Barrow appear to be undeveloped attempts at working small outcrops. Ideally a quarry would be established on sloping ground, enabling a level access route for wheeled vehicles or a tramway to be cut into the slope, meeting the vertical quarry face at its base. Such a layout also enabled free drainage of the quarry. Three of these quarries follow this approximate format, although Holwell, which worked the eastern side of the tor outcrop, did not need an access route. However, Haytor and Rubble Heap required long level cuttings leading into the quarry area.

Fig 10.4

Ordnance survey 2nd edition (1906) depictions of the Tor Quarries at Merrivale and Foggintor, west of Princetown. Compare with the modern appearance of both in Figs 10.10 and 10.9.

The Haytor quarries

Haytor Downs, like Pew Tor and Staple Tor, has widespread evidence of moorstone extraction, covering an area encompassing Smallacombe Rocks, Pinchaford Ball, Emsworthy Rocks and Haytor Rock. This includes many examples demonstrating earlier use of the wedge-and-

The first task at these quarries was to remove any earth, called 'overburden', that covered the granite. At Holwell most of this was simply tipped down the slope in front of the area to be quarried and was later buried by quarry dumps; but at the other two, once removed, the overburden was dumped out of the way and to one side of the worked areas. The heaps can be recognised by their location and by the fact that they comprise mostly soil rather than stone (*see* Fig 10.7). These heaps include the material that it was necessary to dig from the access cuttings before the removal of any granite could start. Granite was cut from the outcrop by drilling lines of deep vertical holes down to the natural horizontal joints of the rock, then packing the holes with gunpowder, which, when detonated, caused just enough of an explosion to separate a large section without shattering it. The granite was further cut up, dimensioned and dressed using the traditional hand-tool techniques described above. The holes for the powder were also drilled using

manual borers, driven in by sledge hammers. The resulting 'shotholes' – long, deep grooves with roughly semicircular profiles left after the explosion – can be seen on unworked sections of the quarry faces and in much of the waste on the spoil heaps (*see* Fig 10.2, bottom).

Granite quarrying appears to have been very wasteful. Judging by the immensity of the spoil heaps, much of the stone was rejected, either because it was not up to standard or because blasting and cutting had spoiled the rock. At Haytor and Rubble Heap the waste stone was trammed out of the access road onto a series of long flat-topped linear dumps with rounded ends, usually termed 'finger dumps' because where several emanate from the same point they have the appearance of hands. At Holwell, with its steeper slope, these dumps are much taller and more rounded.

The granite tramway

Both product and waste were transported around these quarries, and the product ultimately shipped out on the Haytor granite tramway. Tramways had long been an integral part of industrial sites such as mines and quarries as a primary means of moving materials around, but at Haytor the tramway was novel in that granite setts were used as track in preference to iron rails or plates (Fig 10.6). This unique form, and the fact that it was the first long-distance tramway to be built in Devon (13.6km/8.5m long) make it among the most historically significant industrial monuments in the county and certainly on Dartmoor.

On Haytor Downs and near the quarries, the tramway has a main arterial route, which extends as far west as the quarries at Emsworthy

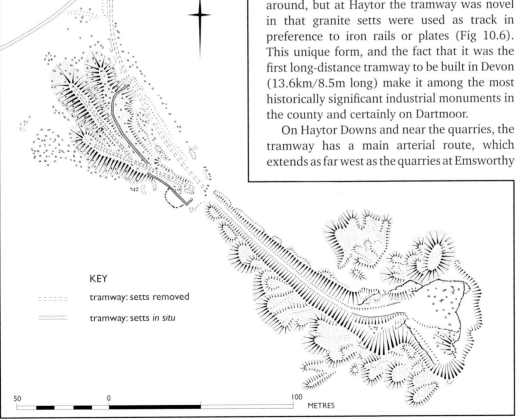

KEY

- - - - - - tramway: setts removed

———— tramway: setts *in situ*

50   0   100
METRES

Fig 10.5
Earthwork survey of Rubble Heap Quarry. A long cutting from the sunken quarry accommodated the tramway, which carried waste material onto three finger-shaped heaps. Another branch of the tramway connects to the main tramway network to transport finished blocks. Overburden from the initial phase surrounds the quarry (RCHME 1:1000 survey).

Fig 10.6
*A surviving section of the
Haytor Granite Tramway,
showing the flanged granite
rails (NMR 05049;
© English Heritage. NMR).*

Fig 10.7 (opposite)
*Haytor Main Quarry
1:1000 survey – see text for
description of quarry
features. Also visible is a
prehistoric hut circle (j)
and relict sections of reaves,
a section of a medieval tin
streamwork and a circular
earthwork (k) believed to
be a 20th-century artillery
or mortar emplacement.*

Rocks. From this, single or multiple branch lines run into the individual quarries. Sections of track can also be traced running from within the quarries and out onto the spoil heaps. Very little engineering was involved in creating the trackbeds, which mostly sit on the apparently unaltered natural moorland terrain, very simply graded to provide a level-topped profile to the bed. There is, however, a long section of embankment 1.5m high on the Emsworthy branch, an impressively high embankment runs across the old tin streamworks on the Haytor quarry section (Fig 10.6) and a substantial cutting was required for the main tramway to exit the streamwork farther up the hill. The stone setts of the tracks have survived over much of the course of the tramway, although west of Rubble Heap quarry, leading to both Emsworthy and Harrow Barrow, they have been removed, suggesting that they may have been the first sections to fall into disuse and that the setts were reused elsewhere. Each sett comprises a narrow rectangular block of granite, *c* 1m–1.6m long, but with shorter sections on the bends. Each sett has a 4cm deep flange cut along its length. The tracks were placed into parallel lines with the flange on the inside to guide the wagon wheels. The construction of this tramway was a truly

remarkable undertaking and its existence is a strong indication of how speedily granite could be cut – the whole system took less than a year to build. Over the 13.6km of tramway, even if every sett was 1.6m long, a minimum of 17 000 setts would be required.

It is possible that the use of granite rails was developed as a local solution just to move granite around the quarries, especially to deal with spoil dumping where a firm trackbed is needed to manage spoil heaps safely. The idea of creating a full-blown transport system down through the Datmoor borders using granite tracks may have developed later. A clue to this explanation is the survival of several rejected sections of trackway amid the clitter of Holwell Tor, cut from moorstone. One interpretation of this could be that some parts of the tramway were constructed before the quarries existed, hence the need to use moorstone. A second piece of evidence is a surviving section of the tramway in a small undeveloped quarry north-west of the Haytor main quarry, in a place used solely to carry wagons for dumping on a small spoil heap. This quarry, however, has no tramway connecting it to the main network, which confirms localised use of granite rails.

After abandonment *c* 1865, the Haytor Tramway tracks were extensively robbed as a source of building stone, especially in the lowland districts. At Ilsington the builders of a tin-burning house at Atlas Mine in the 1860s used setts to build walls, having prepared them by chiselling off the flanges. At Ventiford near Kingsteignton, where the tramway meets the canal, setts were used to build a bridge to carry the later Moretonhampstead and South Devon Railway in1861, the route of which partly followed the course of its granite predecessor. Many off-moor sections of the tramway survive intact, however, particularly at Lowerdown on the outskirts of Bovey Tracey and in the woods of the National Nature Reserve at Yarner.

Haytor main quarry: a case study

Little documentation concerning the specifics of the quarries or of their tramways survives, other than general references. But archaeological survey has helped establish some chronological details that agree with what little is known from documentary sources.

The Haytor main quarry is the easternmost in the complex and is closest to the modern roads (Fig 10.7). It is therefore the most visited and best known. There are two working areas: the larger (a) is earlier. It comprises a sunken working area with steep, cut faces on all sides and an original entrance (c), which enters the quarry from the east side, and through which a tramway, since effaced, carted waste material onto the three large spoil heaps to the north-east (green). A second entrance (d), which

may be later, cuts into the northern end of the worked area where another tramway carried waste stone to a single, isolated outside heap (e). There are heaps of overburden (f) on the north and south quarry exterior, and along the south side of the entrance cutting. Several earlier routes for the granite tramway serving this quarry (a) are evident on the plan

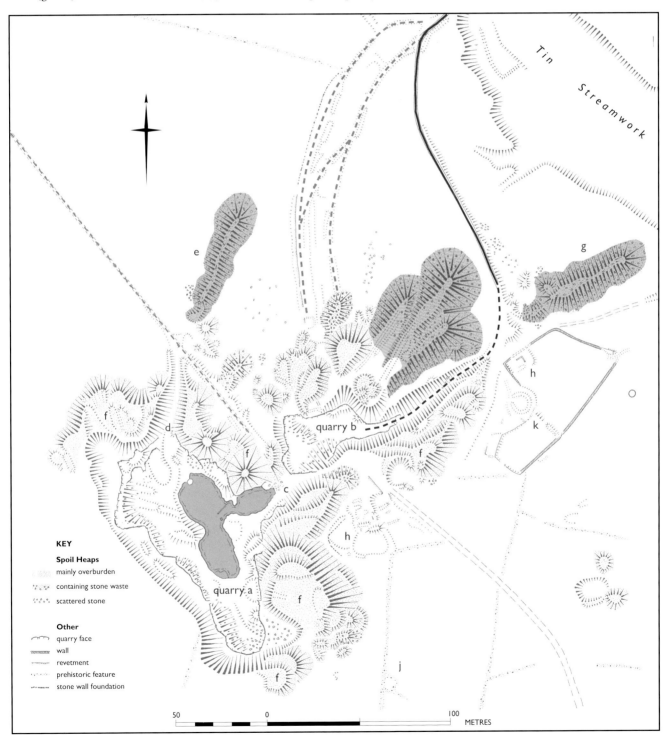

KEY

Spoil Heaps

mainly overburden

containing stone waste

scattered stone

Other

quarry face

wall

revetment

prehistoric feature

stone wall foundation

50   0   100

METRES

Fig 10.8
An engraving of 'High Torr'
granite quarry by T H
Williams, 1829. The
observer is looking south-
west towards Haytor Rock.
The buildings and
infrastructure depicted in
the foreground were later
effaced when the second
quarry pit (b) was opened
up, probably in the 1850s
(© Westcountry Studies
Library, with permission).

*Fig 10.8
An engraving of 'High Torr'
granite quarry by T H
Williams, 1829. The
observer is looking south-
west towards Haytor Rock.
The buildings and
infrastructure depicted in
the foreground were later
effaced when the second
quarry pit (b) was opened
up, probably in the 1850s
(© Westcountry Studies
Library, with permission).*

*Fig 10.9 (opposite, top)
Aerial view of Foggintor
Quarry, a large granite
quarry on Walkhampton
Common (NM 24532/004;
© English Heritage. NMR).*

*Fig 10.10 (opposite, bottom)
Merrivale Quarry on the
western side of the River
Walkham on Whitchurch
Common was the last of
Dartmoor's granite quarries
to become disused, working
up until 1997. Map evidence
(see Fig 10.4) and
contemporary photographs
show that this quarry was
the nucleus of a developing
community in the early 19th
century, with a terrace of
worker cottages and a
Methodist chapel at the site
(NMR DP055104; © English
Heritage. NMR).*

(green pecked lines) but have been blocked by later dumping (yellow), mostly of overburden, from the smaller quarry to the east (b). Upon becoming disused the granite rails were removed from the redundant branches and used elsewhere on the system, leaving only earthwork imprints of their trackbeds. It is clear that tramway courses, which enabled material from the earlier quarry (a) to be moved onto the three large spoil heaps (green), were cut by the later quarry (b), for which an additional on-site dump was created to the extreme north-east (g).

An engraving of the quarries dated 1829 (Fig 10.8) shows the earlier quarry (a) with many nearby buildings, although evidence of only a small proportion of them survives today (h). The engraver's viewpoint is to the north-east of the quarry, with Haytor Rock behind, which would place most of these buildings at the site of the eastern quarry (b) and indicate that they were destroyed by this later phase of activity. This second phase may be associated with a known period of renewed prosperity at the quarries in the 1850s. It can be deduced therefore that stone extraction from quarry (b), together with the destruction of the buildings, the rerouting of the tramway to its final course (red) and the creation of fresh spoil heaps (pink) from both quarries, all occurred on or after this date. Thus hidden

elements of the story are starting to come to light through analysis of the field evidence.

In addition to the buildings at Haytor Quarry, other Templer legacies are a series of cottages at Haytor Vale to accommodate the quarry workers and the terrace of granite-built cottages either side of the Rock Inn, which remain occupied today and form the nucleus of this now thriving Hamlet.

The Walkhampton/Whitchurch quarries

The social infrastructure that accompanied the quarry industry became far more developed at Dartmoor's other major set of granite quarries on Walkhampton and Whitchurch Commons: Swell Tor, Foggintor (Fig 10.9), Ingra Tor, Torr Quarries (Fig 10.10) and various smaller sites. Although Haytor is better known historically, the quarries of western Dartmoor were far more productive and enduring. Swell Tor and Foggintor, the largest quarries, began to be promoted as sources of granite *c* 1820, but became strong rivals to Haytor by *c* 1823 when the Plymouth and Dartmoor Railway was opened (*see* chapter 13), giving the owners access to markets in Plymouth and beyond. They continued in work for the rest of the century, after which Foggintor closed in 1906 and Swell Tor *c* 1938 (Stanier 1999, 21–2).

Fig 10.11
Red Cottages on Walkhampton
Common near Swell Tor Quarry,
as recorded by the OS 1st
edition in the 1880s. This
terrace of six quarry workers'
cottages, since demolished,
survives as a series of
earthworks, with clearly defined
rectangular garden plots.

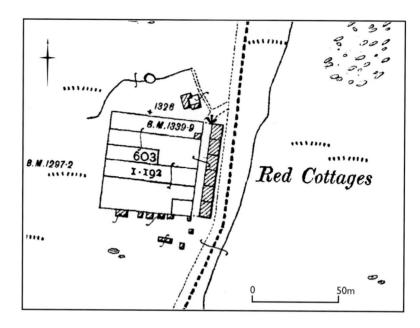

The impressive remains at both sites comprise the usual array of deep quarries with vertical faces and massive spoil heaps. They also include a number of buildings, especially at Foggintor, where foundations and ruins of several granite structures survive (*see* Figs 10.4 and 10.9) and, north of the quarries, the ruins of a terrace of cottages known as Red Cottages. Each cottage has earthwork remains of a garden plot (Fig 10.11). A much larger terrace once stood behind Torr Quarry at Merrivale, known as Walkham Cottages, but no trace of these buildings survived the later expansion of the quarry. At Foggintor, however, little has changed in the century since its abandonment.

11

Mining for tin, copper and silver-lead

Context

In the 18th to 20th centuries mining for metals was unquestionably Dartmoor's most important industry. Although never possessing very wealthy mines of the type found in neighbouring Cornwall, the economic contribution of mining in Devon was crucial for those who were able to make a living from it, especially on and around Dartmoor. Occasionally, small amounts of information are available to tell as just how crucial the industry was. For example, Williams (1862) records that in 1862 more than 1,600 people were employed in Dartmoor mines, and this must be typical for several brief periods of mining prosperity in the 19th century. From a modern archaeological perspective, the mining industry certainly left the most varied and widespread landscape evidence for the period. The remains demonstrate how the landscape was adapted and exploited to win valuable ores. They reflect a full suite of activities associated with tin, copper and lead mining and the necessary infrastructure that developed around them. Mining also provides an important social dimension to the Dartmoor story, and, together with contemporary economic activities supplies material evidence for the influences of capitalism and industrialisation, as is manifest widely elsewhere on Dartmoor in the 18th and 19th centuries.

In chapter 8 tinworking is described as a prosperous industry in the later Middle Ages; but from 1524, when production had reached its peak, output fell steeply in the late 16th and 17th centuries to nothing by the time of the English Civil War in the 1640s (Lewis 1908, 252–8). Despite a small rise in production in the late 17th century, by the 1720s tin mining was non-productive again. This was partly because the more easily worked alluvial (stream) deposits were gradually becoming depleted, while attempts to work the tin lodes using shallow shafts and openworks, had reached the limits of affordable technology within the economic constraints of the day. Accessing the deeper sections of lode required the ability to sink shafts and to drive adits through solid rock, consuming large amounts of explosives, and very often, once this was achieved, the mines would flood unless adequate pumping equipment was available to keep the lower levels water-free. Machinery was also required to haul materials out of the mines, and additional capacity and resources were needed at the ore-dressing stage because the tin lodes in question were mostly of poorer grade than stream tin and required more intensive processing.

Altogether, mining for tin was more labour intensive. It required innovative application of technology and needed greater material and economic resources than stream working or shallow-lode workings had ever required. Much of the necessary technology had been known since the 17th century, but perhaps the greatest deterrent for those thinking of undertaking a mine 'adventure' was the fact that a mine could take a long time to develop before ore could be produced – a year or more in some cases – and there were no certainties involved. The expense of developing a mine therefore was beyond the pockets of most individuals, and the few who had sufficient wealth would not risk it on such uncertainty.

It is no surprise, therefore, that many 18th-century writers referred to the Dartmoor tin industry as more or less moribund. Heinrich Kalmeter, a Swedish traveller for example, remarked in 1724, that there were only two working tin mines around Tavistock at that time, the rest having closed down (Brooke 2001, 11). It was the same story for much of that century, with occasional historical references referring to tin mines opening or in development, but generally there was very little activity by comparison to previous centuries. In 1790 a Duchy official visiting Dartmoor recorded finding only one tin mine working within Dartmoor Forest (Greeves 1980). In the 1780–90s, however, a small recovery in tin mining was inspired by a rise in the price of the metal and from then onward the industry managed a period of fragile continuity through much of the 19th century and into the early 20th. The last tin mine, Golden Dagger, closed in 1930 (Greeves 1986, 46).

By the 1790s copper mining, and to some extent lead mining, had also become established. However, these metals are not found within the granite zone of Dartmoor, rather they occur within the metamorphic

aureole that surrounds it (see chapter 1). The mines therefore are located on the peripheries of the moor, particularly on the western side around Tavistock and Mary Tavy, but also in Buckfastleigh and in the Teign Valley, the latter containing a particularly rich lead lode. Unlike tin, these metals do not occur as alluvial deposits and can only be worked from lode sources; they could therefore only be exploited once the necessary underground mining technology had been sufficiently developed to do so economically. Also, the copper and lead industries had no ancient traditions, customary rights or organised structure such as the tinners possessed in the Stannaries. It was in the rich copper mines of Cornwall, during the early 18th century, that the underground techniques of hard-rock mining advanced more swiftly and spread to

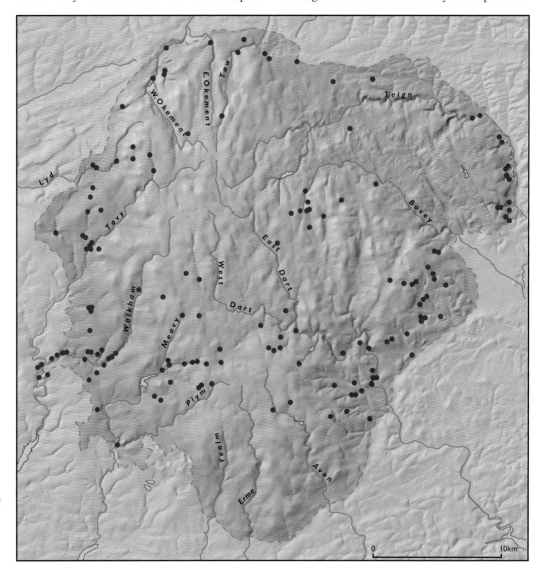

Fig 11.1
Map of Dartmoor showing the location of 18th–20th-century metal mines (tin, copper, silver-lead) within the national park where field evidence survives (height data licensed to English Heritage for PGA through Next Perspectives™).

some extent to Devon. In 1724 Kalmeter reported a small level of copper and silver-lead mining around Ashburton and Tavistock. Like tin, however, neither copper nor silver-lead was of great significance on Dartmoor and its environs in the 18th century until the 1790s, when a response to rising ore prices resulted in an intensifying of activity.

Although the improvement of pumping and explosives technologies, and the rising prices of ore offer some explanation for the progress of Dartmoor's mining industry, probably the main influencing factor was the availability of the finance, as mining 'adventurers' began to import capital from outside the county. This change allowed the establishment of many mines with potential to turn a small profit, but an additional consequence of investors' zeal to become involved in mining enterprises was that large sums of money were ploughed into the surface installations at mines of very little potential. The field evidence of many small mines shows that they were poorly developed underground, but often had disproportionate surface installations, such as dressing floors, and owe more to the unchecked enthusiasm of mine adventurers than they do to a credible mining operation.

However, many tin mines were no doubt honest attempts to make money from mining, with a good number being moderately viable and able to produce paying quantities of ore, albeit sporadically. Whiteworks (*see* Fig 11.2) is recorded working from the mid-1780s to the early 1900s (Greeves 1980) and Eylesbarrow (or Ailsborough) between 1804 and 1852 (Newman 1999); the latter was sufficiently productive to have its own smelting house between 1822 and 1831. Hexworthy was also a moderately successful tin mine, reworking an extensive area of 'old mens' workings in the O Brook Valley. Large spoil heaps and extensive heaps of dressing waste provide testament to a productive mine.

The number of productive copper mines is somewhat smaller, although Wheal Friendship at Mary Tavy was prosperous from the 1790s through much of the 19th century; and one or two smaller, less-enduring mines managed to turn a small profit from copper around the Buckfastleigh district, including Wheal Emma and Brookwood mines. Although Dartmoor's share of south-west Britain's output for tin and copper was extremely small, the number of

mines that have provided archaeological evidence is not – more than 150 separate sites survive in the National Park (Fig 11.1). The 1850s and 1860s were particularly prosperous, when many new mining companies were being promoted, although usually at the site of previously defunct enterprises.

The field evidence for 18th- and 19th-century mining on the accessible areas of the uplands is overwhelmingly for tin, although copper mines where public access exists include Yarner, Blackabrook and Virtuous Lady; and small sections of Wheal Friendship can be viewed from permitted footpaths. The following descriptions focus mainly on the tin mines of the open moorland, which may be visited safely by the public.

Field evidence of mining

In the 18th and 19th centuries the discovery of tin lodes relied less on prospecting techniques to search for fresh resources and more on the assumption that areas that had previously been worked using pitworks or openworks (*see* chapter 8) still had the potential to produce tin from even greater depths. For this reason the majority of later tin mines, with one ore two notable exceptions, were located on the sites of earlier activity. Whiteworks (Fig 11.2) is a prime example, where an array of earlier workings, including streamworks and pitworks have had the shafts, adits, leats, spoil heaps and buildings of later episodes imposed on them; and at Huntingdon (Fig 11.3) an earthwork survey has established a sequence of shallow pit workings followed by deeper shafts between the mid-18th and the mid-19th centuries. Around Birch Tor is the most spectacular collection of deep openworks anywhere on the moor, but within these old working are discrete remains of several 19th-century tin mines, including Birch Tor, Vitifer (*see* Fig 8.12) and Golden Dagger, where the shafts, waterwheel pits, leats and various buildings and features associated with mine infrastructure sit discretely amid the early post-medieval workings.

The underground techniques for tin, copper and lead mining were more or less identical: access to the underground metallic lodes has to be achieved by digging horizontal tunnels ('adits') and vertical shafts to reach the ore-bearing rock.

Fig 11.2
Aerial view of Whiteworks tin mine. This area had probably been exploited as a tin streamwork and early lode working for several centuries before attempts to establish a mine to work the lodes underground began in the late 18th century. The alignments of closely spaced small pits represent the earlier lode works and evidence of prospecting. The larger pits are blocked shafts of the 18th and 19th centuries. Several were walled-up after abandonment to preserve livestock. The ruins of several buildings survive; some are associated with the mine and others with 19th-century farming. Whiteworks Cottages, centre top, are the only buildings still standing and were originally built as miners' dwellings (NMR 24899/001; © English Heritage. NMR).

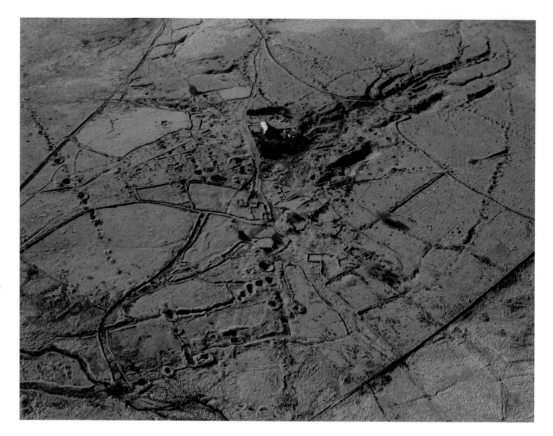

Adits

Adits are tunnels driven horizontally into the slopes of hillsides containing suspected or confirmed lodes. They served the double purpose of acting as drainage channels for water from the mine and providing horizontal access to the underground working areas. When used for drainage, adit portals are often located at the lowest possible point of terrain above river level. Most adits on the open moors have been deliberately blocked for safety reasons, or are choked with boggy vegetation, but may often be recognised by the narrow, level cuttings that lead into them, and from which water often issues. Often, long flat-topped spoil heaps with bulbous ends extend from the cutting, made up of waste transported using barrows or skips running on tramlines. Such heaps represent the material removed in digging the adit and from other underground areas of the mine.

On the northern slopes of Cudlipptown Downs, an adit was driven south into the hillside. Although its portal is now blocked, the linear cutting leading from it confirms its identity and a large flat-toped spoil mound, which extends from the end of the

gully down the slope, is indicative of waste material being trammed or barrowed from the adit (Fig 11.4).

Shafts

Shafts provided vertical access to underground sections of the mine. On the high moors nearly all shafts have been capped or fenced, and often the only way of differentiating the site of a shaft from earlier pit works is by the size of the spoil heaps, which are usually much more extensive for shaft diggings than for those associated with shallower workings (*see* Figs 11.2 and 11.3). Shafts often connected with adits to help ventilate mines, but also served other functions, such as ladder access to all levels of the mine, hauling ore and waste to the surface, and to house pumping equipment.

Horse whims

At the head of the hauling shafts stood a device for drawing large iron buckets, ('kibbles') up and down the shaft. Although some water-powered hoisting devices have been recorded on Dartmoor, the most common device was a horse gin or whim. This comprised a

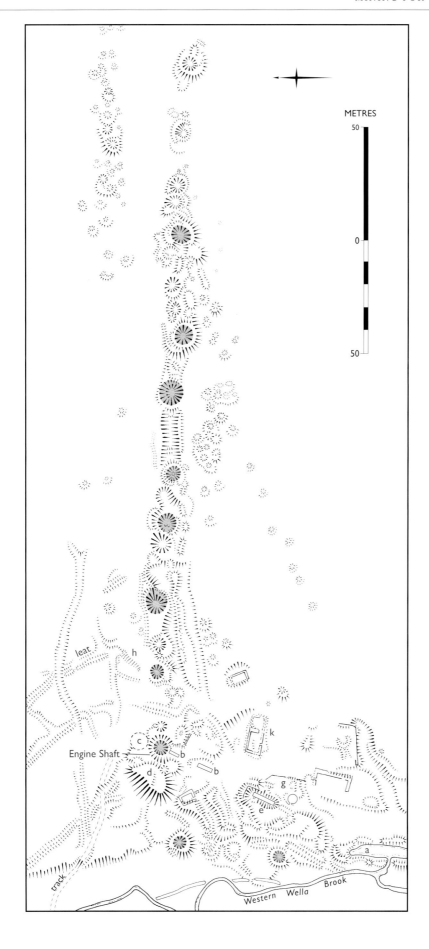

METRES

Fig 11.3
Earthwork plan of
Huntingdon Mine. An east–
west line of pit works
represents the earlier
workings, which
concentrated on the shallow
backs of the tin lode. These
transect an alignment of
even earlier, much smaller
prospecting pits which run
diagonally across the strike
of the lode. Later shafts
from the 19th and possibly
the 18th century
(highlighted) take the form
of deeper conical pits with
substantial spoil collars.
These shafts were sunk into
the earlier workings in an
attempt to explore the lode
deeper underground. The
mine was drained by an
adit (a) to the south near
the stream and a flatrod
system was used to drive
the pumps housed within
the Engine Shaft. Two bob
pits (b) survive close to the
shaft, although the large
waterwheel that powered
the system was located
farther down the valley (see
Fig 11.7). Material was
hoisted up the engine shaft
by using a horse whim (c),
including the waste dumped
on a heap adjacent to the
shaft (d). The waterwheel
depicted on the plan (e)
may have been used for
pumping in an earlier
phase, although it also
powered a stamping mill on
the north side where there
are the remains of a
dressing floor (g) with the
surviving outline of a round
buddle. A raised timber
launder conducted water
onto the wheel from the leat
embankment (h) at the
terminal of the leat.
Buildings, all ruined to
ground level, include an
office (k), as depicted on
maps of the 1860s (EH
1:1000 earthwork survey).

197

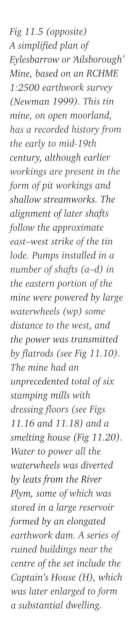

perpendicular axle with a large horizontal cable drum, known as the 'cage', mounted on the top, and sited adjacent to the shaft. It was rotated by horses harnessed to the whim, walking in a circle around the axle. The whole structure was supported by a timber frame. The cable was wound horizontally onto the cage and extended to a flanged wheel supported by a head frame sited over the shaft, down which the kibble could pass. The field evidence for these devices, usually referred to as a 'whim plat', is distinctive, although often quite subtle: a flat, circular earthwork platform of between 12.5m and 6.5m diameter, either on a raised mound – as with two examples at Whiteworks – or in a cutting forming a crescent-shaped scarp set into a slope. These plats accommodated the whim and the horse's circular route. There is often a flat stone in ther centre of the plat with a small hole in its upper surface – the 'mellior' that supported the axle. Eylesbarrow Mine (Fig 11.5) has six shafts with associated earthworks of whim plats adjacent to the shaft head; Whiteworks has three. Hauling shafts can often be recognised by the massive size of their spoil heaps, which sometimes radiate from the shaft head like fingers or take a spread, flat-topped form. Where such heaps are found, whim plats are usually not far away.

Pumping shafts

Shafts were also frequently used as a vertical route for pumping installations. When a mine penetrated to a depth below the level of the lowest adit the only route for water was to flood this lower portion of the shaft. To prevent this, pumping devices were installed. In the early days these were simple and operated by manpower or by horse whims. For deeper mines the power of a waterwheel was needed; and where very deep, steam engines were used, although more rarely on Dartmoor than elsewhere in the West Country.

Obviously in archaeological terms, the most important part of these systems was the pump itself, which was located below ground, and for the majority of Dartmoor mines, where most underground areas are inaccessible, we are never likely to view the evidence for this. However, the motive power was most frequently sited on the surface and remains of these systems often survive, and represent the main evidence for underground pumping.

It is known from documentary evidence that pumps powered by water wheels were in use on western Dartmoor at Wheal Jewel tin mine and at Black Down silver-lead mine as early as 1724 (Brooke 2001), but field evidence of these early examples has not been identified. Evidence of pumps installed from the 1790s is likely to be the earliest for which field remains survive.

The pump consisted of a vertical iron pipe, known as the 'rising main', which ran up the shaft from the lowest point in the mine (the 'sump'), to the lowest available adit through which water could be released. The water was forced up the pipe either by a plunger or by suction-lift device, activated by a reciprocating timber rod that ran down the shaft from the surface, powered by the waterwheel or, occasionally, by a steam engine. Where powered by water, the amount of water needed to turn the wheel was rarely available near the shaft, often sunk high on the side of a hill, so the waterwheels had to be located lower in the valleys where leats could be diverted to them from a river source. Power was transmitted from the wheel to the shaft through a device known as a 'flatrod', which was a series of linked iron rods supported on posts just above the ground. The other ends of the rods were connected to a crank on the axle of the waterwheel to create reciprocal motion.

Pumping wheel pits

The most notable surface evidence for a pumping installation is the ruined structure that housed the waterwheel. The wheels used were among some of the largest of their kind in Britain, with recorded diameters of up to 62ft (19m), and the stone wheel pits that housed them reflect their size. The wheel pits were sunk into the ground, partially or fully, and lined with robust masonry walling. The axles of the wheel rested on the top of the long walls, supported on large baulks of timber. They were always either overshot or pitchback wheels – the water is brought to the top of the wheel by a launder.

Although wheel pits were frequently demolished upon abandonment, especially on moorland areas, there are some notable survivors. At Vitifer, lying in a dip and set below ground level there is an intact wheel pit, one of several surviving at this mine, which housed a wheel *c* 11m in diameter to power pumps within nearby shafts. In contrast, the wheel pit at Great Wheal Eleanor stands mostly above ground and remarkably complete in a boggy, tree-covered area on the east side of Easdon Down (Fig 11.6). Belston Consols Mine, beside the River Taw, contained the largest example – just over 60ft (18.4m) in diameter and also

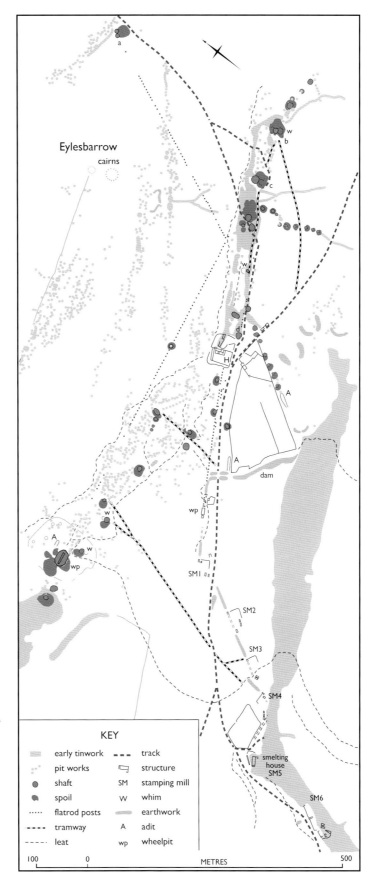

Eylesbarrow
cairns

H

dam

wp

SM1

SM2

SM3

SM4

smelting
house
SM5

SM6

KEY

early tinwork		track	
pit works		structure	
shaft		SM	stamping mill
spoil		W	whim
flatrod posts		earthwork	
tramway		A	adit
leat		wp	wheelpit

100   0   METRES   500

Fig 11.6
An upstanding and relatively intact stone waterwheel house at Great Wheal Eleanor tin mine, near North Bovey. The wheel, now removed, once powered pumps in a shaft 270m to the south-west. The structure is now surrounded by marshy ground and is engulfed in scrub. The arched opening is the exit lobby, which formed the start of the tail-race. Many wheel pits on the open moorland would have had a similar appearance before demolition and backfilling (photo: Phil Newman).

remarkably intact; although it has been recorded by other writers including Hamilton Jenkin (1981, 70) to have been 70ft (21.3m) in diameter, the interior dimension of the wheel pit is only 62ft (19m) long.

Huntingdon, like Great Wheal Eleanor, was once an upstanding wheelhouse; although mostly collapsed, enough remains to visualise its original size (Fig 11.7). At Henroost mine there is also a spectacular survivor, which although originally installed for other purposes, powered pumps 540m uphill at Hooten Wheals (Fig 11.8) towards the end of its career in the early 1900s. To the rear of the wheel pit stands a fine leat embankment, which maintained the correct height for the leat as it approached the

Fig 11.7
The ruined wheelhouse at Huntingdon tin mine in the remote valley of the Western Wella Brook. The walls of the structure once stood much higher and housed a waterwheel recorded as being of 40ft (12.2m) diameter × 5ft (1.5m) breast (photo: Phil Newman).

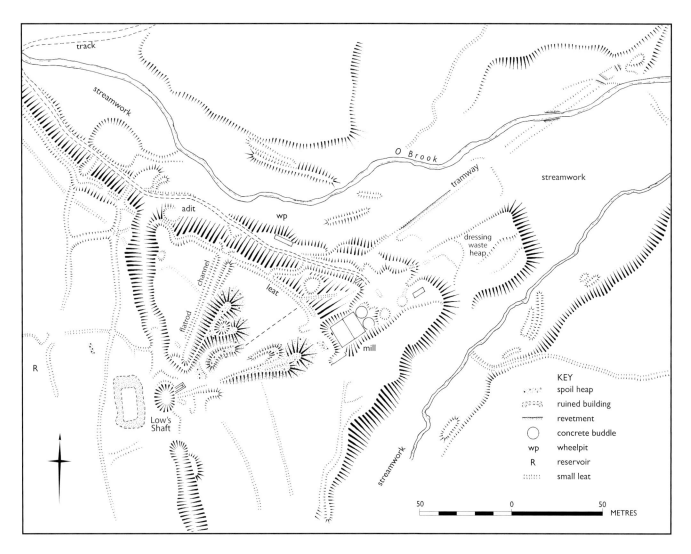

KEY

⸳⸳⸳⸳	spoil heap
⸗⸗⸗	ruined building
⎯⎯	revetment
◯	concrete buddle
wp	wheelpit
R	reservoir
⸬⸬⸬	small leat

50 0 50 METRES

top of the waterwheel. The embankment, which is reinforced with facing masonry, supported a timber launder on iron piers. A fine photograph, taken c 1905, clearly shows the wheel in motion, as well as the launder, flatrod and other features (Greeves 1986, 7). In the 19th and early 20th centuries on Dartmoor, these waterwheels would have been a common sight, more than 40 pumping wheels having been recorded. When fully operational they must have been among the most impressive and largest man-made structures on the open moor.

Flatrod systems

Although the ironwork has been removed, evidence of flatrod systems is often provided by straight linear earthwork cuttings to accommodate a straight course across the undulating terrain. These usually have a V-shaped profile and follow a direct course between the wheel and the shaft. Clear

examples survive at East Birch Tor Mine, where the cuttings run up the West Webburn Valley (Fig 11.9). At Eylesbarrow Mine, in the Plym Valley, the flatrods were supported, uniquely, on paired upright granite post, marching across the south-west slopes of the hill for more than a kilometre between a large sunken wheel pit, which housed a 50ft (15.3m) diameter waterwheel, and shafts on the east side of the hill (Figs 11.10 and 11.11).

On reaching the shaft, it was necessary to convert the reciprocal motion of the rods from horizontal to vertical, to provide the movement needed for the pumps at the bottom of the shaft, and this was achieved by a device known as a 'balance bob'. This was a braced, right angle of iron or timber fixed to a fulcrum on which it could rock; the pump rod was fixed on one end and extended down the shaft, while at the other was a counterweight to assist the wheel in forcing the weight of the water up the

Fig 11.8
Hexworthy Mine upper dressing floor at Hooten Wheals. Low's shaft, set midway along an earlier openwork, was equipped with an electric hoisting device housed in the building to the west, now ruined. Waste material hoisted up the shaft was dumped onto finger dumps near the shafthead. The underground pumps were powered by flat rods from a remote waterwheel farther down the valley. This mill and dressing floor, with round concrete buddles also powered by electricity, was one of the last to be built on Dartmoor in c 1905 (RCHME 1:500 earthwork survey).

rising main. This mechanism was retained in a 'bob pit', a masonry-lined hollow built in to the lip of the shaft. Fine examples survive at East Birch Tor (filled with rubbish) and there are several at Eylesbarrow Mine associated with the pumping shafts (*see* Fig 11.5). Bob pits were also sometimes located between the wheel pit and the shaft to accommodate additional counterweights, such as at Huntingdon where, unusually, two balance bobs were installed to give extra assistance to the wheel (*see* Fig 11.3).

Steam engines

Several mines on Dartmoor reached a sufficient depth, or at least their owners hoped they would, for a steam engine to be a more efficient option for pumping out the water – waterwheels, however large, struggled with the extra weight of the longer pump rods and the additional water at greater depth, especially if water to turn the wheel was at a premium. However, in comparison with Cornish mining districts, the total number of steam engines on Dartmoor is very small owing to the generally shallow metalliferous lodes, and the abundance of water, which made large water wheels more viable.

Beam engines work on the principle of steam, produced in a boiler, piped into the bottom of a vertical cylinder containing a piston. The piston provides reciprocal motion, which, when connected to one end of a horizontal beam (or 'bob') supported above the cylinder by a central fulcrum on top of an external wall, is transmitted vertically down a shaft by a rod connected to the outside end of the beam, thus powering the pumps. In addition to the pressure-driven piston, a condenser, recycles the exhausted steam and moves a second piston, which provides additional power to the engine. Engine houses not only contained the cylinders and condensers but served as the framework for the engine. The front wall of the building supported the beam or bob, and was known as the 'bob wall'; inside, a large solid platform accommodated the weight of the cylinder.

The best known of the Dartmoor engine houses, and certainly the best preserved, is at Wheal Betsy (Figs 11.12 and 11.13) near Mary Tavy, a mine that was in work from the 18th century, mostly for lead, although at the time this engine was installed, probably in 1868,

Fig 11.9 (opposite)
Aerial view looking along the West Webburn Valley showing the alluvial streamworks of the valley floor and the 19th-century shafts of East Birch Tor Mine sunk into the old remains. The straight linear gully that runs up the valley accommodated the flat rods of a pumping system contained within a shaft at the bottom of the image and was powered by a waterwheel farther down the valley (NMR 21582/05; © English Heritage. NMR).

Fig 11.10
Remains of the flatrod system at Eylesbarrow Mine: (top) paired granite posts running up the slope from the wheel pit near the top of the image; (lower) view from above one of the pairs showing the axle grooves (NMR DP099129 and DP099130; © English Heritage. NMR).

the mine was known as Prince Arthur Consols (Pye and Westcott 1992, 3). The surviving building is one of two engine houses recorded at this mine, the other having been demolished. The engine was used to pump the mine in the 1860s and 1870s and is sited adjacent to the now blocked Job's Shaft, which reached a depth of 142 fathoms (260m) below adit level. The main building survives almost intact, and has in recent years been consolidated in an attempt to assure its future.

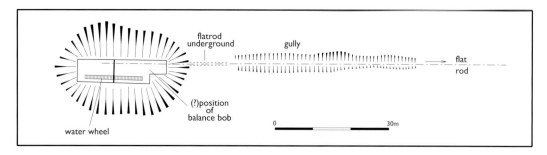

Engine houses were seldom used for pumping at relatively shallow tin mines on the high moors, but one exception was at Ringleshuttes Mine near Holne. In this case, the lack of a reliable water supply for a wheel at between 400m and 470m left the miners with little choice if they were to drain the mine. A small pumping engine house stood at the head of a shaft amid the remains of earlier openworks, but only a stump of the building survives. Its collapsed chimney remains as a linear mound of rubble across the nearby path. Today, many of Dartmoor's pumping engine houses lie on private land around the edges of the national park, although few survive in a condition anything like that of Wheal Betsy. A typical example can be seen at the site of Yarner or Yarrow copper mine within the Yarner Nature Reserve near Bovey Tracey, where the foundations of a once substantial building stand adjacent to a blocked shaft.

Ore dressing

With the revival in the tin industry in the late 18th century came more developed forms of ore dressing works. The stamping mills, as used from

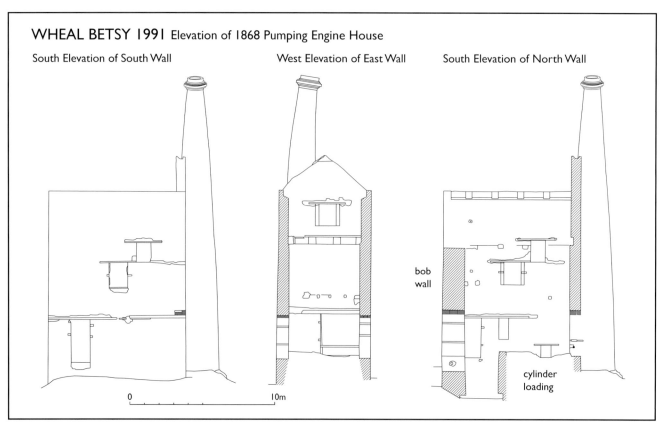

Fig 11.12
Building survey of the pumping engine house at Wheal Betsy. One of only a handful of surviving buildings of this type in Devon and the only one still standing on the open moorland. The structure, one of two engine houses built to serve this mine, housed a 60in (1.5m) pumping engine. The chimney, which was originally straight, now leans slightly owing to movement of the stonework over time, but has been consolidated by the National Trust, who now manage the site (after Pye and Westcott 1992; © Exeter Archaeology, with permission).

Fig 11.13
The engine house at Wheal
Betsy near Mary Tavy. The
image also shows the large
waste heaps of discarded
material (photo: Phil Newman).

the 15th century (*see* chapter 8), were still the favoured crushing technology, but they began to be built on a much larger scale, with more stamps designed for greater capacity; and the associated dressing floors became more extensive with large areas of the concentrating pits, known as 'buddles'. It was not unusual for a single mine to have more that one stamping mill. In some cases, where two or more exist, it is likely that one succeeded another, exemplified by Eylesbarrow Mine with six stamping mills. Documentary evidence confirms that two existing stamping mills were being refurbished and three new ones built in 1814 and that all five must have been usable at the same time (Newman 1999, 126). The remains of all survive (*see* Fig 11.16).

Where possible, stamping mills and dressing floors were located as close to the source of ore as possible as it came from the mine, to reduce the effort of handling the ore. However, these installations relied on sloping ground and needed copious water supplies to turn the waterwheels and provide additional water needed for dressing. They are therefore usually found in lower-lying ground where the water resource was most plentiful.

The layout of the stamping mills from about 1790 was more or less standard and reflects the design depicted in an illustration of a mill first published by William Borlase in his *Natural History of Cornwall* as early as 1758, and by Pryce in 1778 (Fig 11.14). Despite minor

Fig 11.14
An engraving of a Cornish
stamping mill published by
William Pryce in 1778. The
mill has a central
waterwheel with stamp
frames on either side and a
series of concentrating
devices including settling
pits and buddles. This
layout, with retaining walls
defining the back edge of
the dressing floor, remained
in use at Dartmoor tin
mines for much of the 18th
and 19th century.

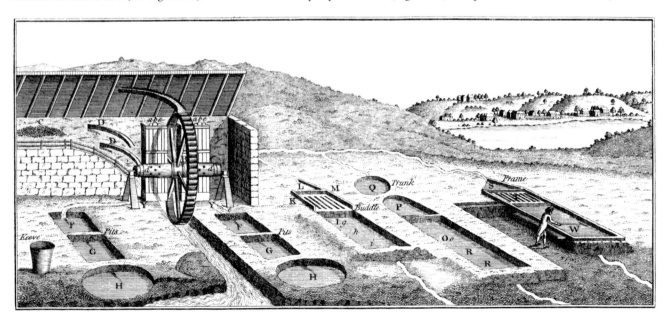

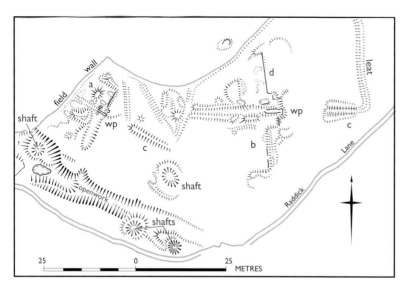

Fig 11.15
Earthwork survey of the stamping mills and dressing floors at Keaglesborough Mine. The lower, smaller mill (a) is likely to be the earlier of the two, probably dating to c 1801, although both existed by c 1830. Both have suffered some demolition, but the upper mill (b) has a very fine surviving leat embankment (c) and its revetment wall (d), which defines part of the dressing floor, is intact (EH 1:500 earthwork survey).

improvements to the technology, this layout remained in use until the early 20th century, with new stamping mills still being installed as late as the 1890s at Hexworthy Mine and in 1903 at Vitifer (Greeves 1986, 7 and 31).

The layout of these more developed stamping mills is one of an approximately rectangular level terrace cut into the hill slope with a stone revetment built to retain the slope, often with short return walls at one or both ends (Fig 11.15; *see also* Fig 11.17). The wheel pits are sunk at right angles against, or cutting into, the revetment. They project into the levelled area, either at one end of the terrace, or centrally, depending on the configuration of the stamps. The stamps were mounted on one or both sides of the wheel. These were not buildings as such, for they were open along one side, although they were often covered, either with thatch or with corrugated iron (at later sites), where the entire working area was enclosed. Farther up the slope and aligned with the waterwheel a leat embankment was raised to the correct height to deliver water to the top of the wheel by a wooden launder; like their predecessors of the early post-medieval period, the wheels were always of either pitchback or overshot design. Although most were much smaller than pumping wheels, there are exceptions: at New Vitifer Consols a 60ft (18.4m) diameter waterwheel was installed between 1871 and 1875 (*Mining J* 18.02.1871; 01.05.1875) to power both pumps and stamps. Although demolished, earthworks with vestiges of stone *in situ* survive.

The ore was fed into the stamping mill from behind, which worked on the same principle as the earlier examples described in chapter 8.

The vertically reciprocating stamps lifted then dropped onto the ore by the action of a water-powered rotating axle. The main differences were that there were more stamps and that the individual stamps were larger. The stamp batteries were usually arranged in multiples of four or six, with anything up to 48 stamps being recorded later in the 19th century, while earlier in the century it was usual to have only four, on one or both sides of the wheel. The crushed ore was washed through a perforated grate in the stamps box and allowed to settle in a series of pits below, and where the water flow kept the waste material moving while the heavier tin sank. Once these settling pits were full, the tin was removed and the process was continued in a further series of pits known as 'buddles', also set within the dressing floor area.

In the early 19th century buddles were rectangular, as depicted in Pryce in 1778. The shallow pits were sunk into the ground within the dressing floor area and lined either with stone or timber or both. The floor of the buddle was a slightly inclined plane and the stamped tin was introduced to the upper end in a stream of slow-flowing water. The tin settled near the top, or 'head' of the buddle and the waste was transported to the 'tail'. When the buddle was full, the material was roughly separated into grades, then removed for further treatment. From the 1850s, round or centre-head buddles were introduced and became increasingly popular for the rest of the century and into the 20th century, as they gradually replaced rectangular buddles. The process was the same as that with rectangular buddles, although the sunken trough of the buddle itself was circular. A circular buddle's inclined base radiated from a central cone, where the pulped tin and water were released. A set of rotating sweeps continually passing over the pulp kept the material on the surface moving and stopped the water forming into streamlets.

Contemporary photographs of many of these and other complexities of the dressing processes and associated equipment survive, and have been published (Greeves 1986; Hamilton Jenkin 1974). Reference to them can assist greatly in understanding the field remains and is recommended further reading.

Field remains of more than 70 stamping mills with associated dressing floors have been recorded on Dartmoor, including at least

57 on the accessible moorland areas. They reflect chronological variations from the 1790s to the early 20th century.

Eylesbarrow Mine has six separate dressing floors (Fig 11.16), spaced out in a sequence descending the slope of the Drizzlecombe Valley. This group associated with one mine is unique on Dartmoor, yet the field remains survive in excellent condition. There is one double mill (Fig 11.17), ie originally having stamps on both sides of the waterwheel, and five singles, where the stamps were on one side only; this includes one associated with a smelting house described below. The two earliest of the Eylesbarrow mills were in place by 1805, and include the double mill, which is the lowest in the sequence and mill number 4, a single mill. The wheel pits on all the Eylesbarrow mills survive, but, like most wheel pits on the open moorlands, they have been partly demolished and backfilled as a 'safety' precaution. Their masonry outlines survive, however, although the interiors are filled with tumbled stone and earth. The largest of these is approximately 8.5m long × 1m wide. One, however, has a surviving upstanding wall on one side with a rectangular opening through which the wheel axle passed, indicating that this wheel stood quite high above ground level. Adjacent to

Fig 11.16
Simplified plans of the stamping mills and dressing floors at Eylesbarrow Mine. Mills SM1–4 had a single stamp frame on one side only of the wheel pit, whereas SM6 had a larger waterwheel with stamps on both sides and an enlarged dressing area of commensurate capacity (based on 1:500 scale earthwork surveys; after Newman 1999).

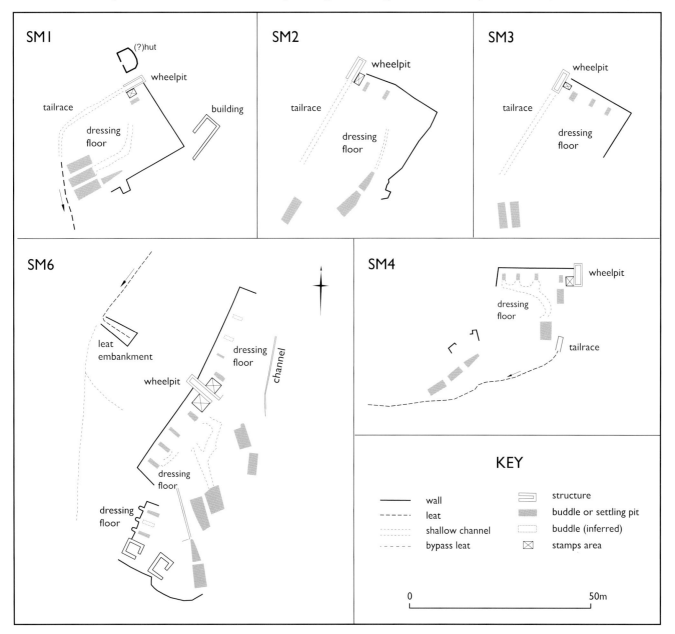

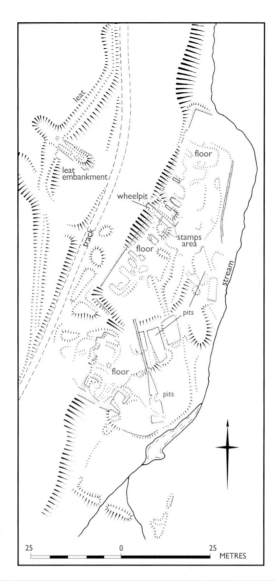

Fig 11.17
Earthwork plan of the largest of the Eylesbarrow stamping mills (SM6) (see also Fig 11.16). The now ruined wheel pit sits centrally at the edge of the dressing floor, with stamps areas set either side containing a series of rectangular pits called buddles. Further concentration of ore took place in the small structures and dressing floor to the south (see Fig 11.16 for interpretation) (RCHME 1:500 earthwork survey).

Fig 11.18
Remains of a round buddle at Golden Dagger Tin Mine. This example probably dates from the early 20th century (photo: Phil Newman).

the wheel pit is a masonry-reinforced platform which accommodated the stamps, probably only four on all the single mills at Eylesbarrow, and to one side of the stamps area the settling pits are located. These have survived at all six of the mills, but are particularly well preserved at number 6 and at number 3, where flat slabs of granite used to line the pits remain in place, and sluice openings in the lower end are visible.

Buddles can be identified at all six of the Eylesbarrow mills, but again they are clearer on some than others. Mill number 6, the double mill, has the most visible buddles, surviving as hollow rectangular earthworks located three each side of the wheel pit on the level area defined by the revetment wall. This mill also possesses a number of additional features not usually found at all such mills: a series of supplementary buddles and small buildings on the south end of the site, and several larger pits, all of which formed part of the dressing process.

Other examples of the earlier mills, dating from *c* 1800 to 1840, can be seen at Wheal Katherine, near Crane Lake, farther up the Plym Valley, and at Keaglesborough, where two survive close by (*see* Fig 11.15) – the upper, larger of these is exemplary for its surviving revetment walls, which remain to a height of 1m, and for its well-preserved stone-lined leat embankment standing a few meters behind the wheel pit. Subtle remains of a small, compact stamping mill can be seen at East Hughes Mine in the Newleycombe Valley.

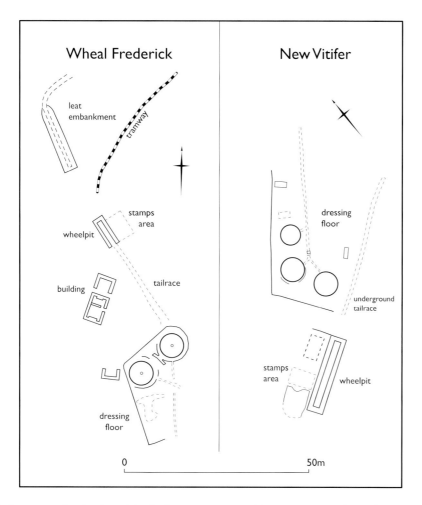

Fig 11.19
Simplified 1:500 plans
showing the layout of
stamping mills with tin
dressing floors having
round or 'centre head'
buddles at Wheal Frederick
and New Vitifer Consol.

Unusually for a moorland mine, this site has an intact wheel pit, and a clear range of buddles that survive as rectangular earthworks.

Many of the later dressing floors that survive on Dartmoor have round or 'centre head' buddles, including several on the open moors and access lands. It is likely that some of the first round buddles were constructed from timber and thus only survive as subtle, distinctly circular earthworks. Later, when stone and concrete were used to form these apparatus they usually survive much better (Fig 11.18), as at Golden Dagger. At Hexworthy Mine the layout of the dressing floor, built in the 1890s, shows some continuity with the earlier design, but with the circular buddles on the dressing floor to one side of the stamping mill. A slightly different layout existed at New Vitifer Consols (Fig 11.19). This mine was operating in the 1860s, and reflects the variation of the later layout, in which the three round buddles are contained on a dressing floor that is separate from the stamping mill sited just above. Despite some stone robbing, stone linings surrounding the trough define the circular forms of the buddles, and the vestiges of the central cones survive as raised mounds. Other places where round buddles survive are Gobbet Mine, with two surviving earthwork examples, Huntingdon Mine and Steeperdon Mine, where there are single examples at each.

Smelting

Following the slump in tin production after the 1720s, most of Dartmoor's remaining smelting houses fell into disuse. Only two were recorded in the whole of Devon by 1719 (Greeves 1996, 84). Although a small number of tin smelting houses are documented on Dartmoor in the later 18th and 19th centuries, field evidence on the open moors is restricted to the ruined site at Eylesbarrow Mine, which operated between 1822 and 1831, and which represents the last tin smelting to take place on or around the uplands. In general, the comparatively low production of tin in the county over much of

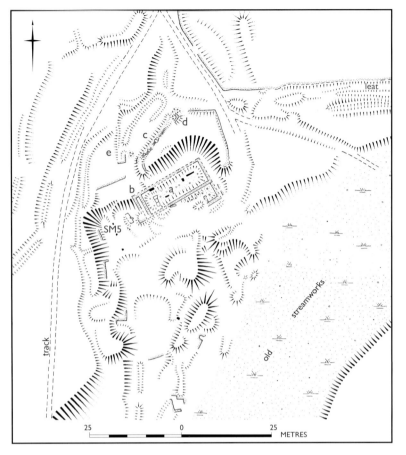

Fig 11.20
Earthwork plan of Eylesbarrow smelting house, showing the ruined structure (a) with a wheel pit (b) built into one end and the flue (c) (see Fig 11.21), leading off to the north and terminating at the base of a collapsed chimney (d). A stamping mill (SM5) is located adjacent to the wheel pit on the west side. The leat terminated at a stone re-enforced embankment (e) from where the water was channelled on a raided wooden launder to the top of the waterwheel (RCHME 1:500 earthwork survey).

a waterwheel to power the bellows, and there was a stamping mill outside the building. The blast furnace was made from substantial, faced granite blocks (now collapsed into the structure). Little evidence of the reverberatory furnace survives other than some slag-covered blocks towards the eastern end of the building, which probably represent the base of the furnace.

Outside the building, a stone flue survives (Fig 11.21), extending obliquely away from the structure and terminating at the square base of a chimney stack. The flue is made of granite, with flat slabs forming the cover.

Water supplies

The 45ft (13.8m) waterwheel at Hexworthy Mine was one of several whose size necessitated the existence of a large storage reservoir or head pond in order to maintain water capacity. The earthwork dam survives just up the slope from the leat embankment forming a terminal for the leat, which diverted water from the O Brook. Others associated with large pumping waterwheels survive at Great Wheal Eleanor, Bagtor and Eylesbarrow (see Fig 11.5). Large earthwork dams were thrown up using material excavated from the hollow that made up the pond just behind it, providing additional depth. At Eylesbarrow, the 192m long dam is lined on both sides with stone and sits along the contour of the hillside, forming a long, narrow curving pond of huge capacity. It was designed originally to supply at least four waterwheels sited below it, spaced out along the slope. At Bagtor a massive earthwork dam was constructed across the River Sig, within a disused tin streamworks. The scarped edge of the tinwork forms one side of the pond and a high linear bank form the other. Once again the capacity of this earthwork would have been considerable and it was built to supply at least three waterwheels, one of which is reputed to have had a diameter of 60ft (18.4m) (Hamilton Jenkin 1981, 134). Occasionally a dam was built across a stream, as at Steeperton Brook, where an earthwork bank extends from one side of the valley floor to the other to provide water to the wheels and dressing floors of Steeperton Mine.

Progressively larger waterwheels and the expansion of dressing processes requiring more copious supplies of water clearly presented a challenge to the mining companies for more

this period meant that smelting houses would have been uneconomical to run, so much of the tin produced on Dartmoor was exported to Cornwall or to the Tamar Valley smelters.

The Eylesbarrow smelter (Fig 11.20) was once a substantial structure and appears as a standing building in photographs taken by Robert Burnard in 1889 (Greeves 1986, 3), but is now a ruin. The layout of the structure and some of its internal features do survive, however, revealing it to have been very different from the blowing houses of a century or more earlier. Although some of the technology would have been familiar to an earlier generation of smelters, this site represents something of a transition contianing both a traditional water-powered blast furnace, of the type long used in blowing houses, and a reverberatory furnace. The latter was fuelled by coal and was introduced much later. It was found to be more effective for mined tin, while for the better quality stream tin, blast furnaces fuelled by charcoal were still preferred.

The building has a rectangular plan with internal dimensions of 17.9m × 6.1m. Attached to the western end is a wheel pit for water. The reservoirs, where installed, could store water, but actually bringing water to a site required longer leats with large capacities, and diverting water, often from multiple sources, from several miles away. The earthworks of these leat channels are much more substantive than those of leats from earlier periods, partly because they are less silted-up, but also because they are much wider and deeper. They often have moderate banks of soil on the lower side representing the material removed in digging them; and where tracks and pathways cross them, small bridges have been made across them from large stone slabs.

One of the earliest recorded of these larger leats is the Whiteworks Mine leat, which was cut in the 1780s or 1790s (Greeves 1980). The 3.7km long leat drew its main source of water from high up the River Swincombe, but it was augmented by water from several of the small tributaries that flow into Foxtor Mire. The channel follows the contour of the hillside along the north slopes of Foxtor and the Swincombe basin. Four additional leats served the mine, diverting water from the Strane River to the north of Whiteworks (*see* Fig 11.2). It is known that in 1818, two water-powered stamping mills and a pumping wheel were operating at the mine, and that by 1880 two 30ft (9.1m) diameter wheels and one of 46ft (14m) wheel were recorded. Clearly, reliable sources of water were essential at this site; hence the multiple supplies.

The Swincombe River also provided water for Dartmoor's longest mining leat, that of Wheal Emma copper mine at Buckfastleigh. This leat was dug in 1859 to supplement the mine's meagre local water supplies. The moorland section of the leat, which drew water from the Swincombe, downstream of Whiteworks, is a little over 15km long and hugs the contour across Holne Moor, following the many folds in the land, then deposited water into the River Mardle. Its substantial earthwork can be seen on the aerial photograph of Holne Moor (*see* Fig 3.18). As the Mardle descends from the moorland, after 2km, a second leat channel of 3.5km carried the water to the site of the mine; the total distance of this diversion is just over 20km.

Other major mine leats of this type are present elsewhere on the moor. The Birch Tor and Vitifer Mine leat extends for 11.5km from the East Dart below Sandy Hole Pass, supplemented by a 3.3km leat from Great

Varracombe and the North Teign River. Together these leats provided a water supply for Wheal Caroline, Birch Tor, Vitifer and Golden Dagger mines, where there were 12 waterwheels (Newman 2002b), several of which were probably operating simultaneously in the later 19th century.

Also of note are the leats which supplied the Mary Tavy mines of Wheal Friendship and Wheal Betsy, where it is recorded by one writer in 1838 that these mines combined had a total of 17 waterwheels running (Watson 1843, 55). A number of fairly short leats diverted water from Cholwell Brook, which runs through Mary Tavy, but other major supplies were brought in from streams up to 7km distant, including

Fig 11.21
Remains of the flue at Eylesbarrow smelting house, built c 1820. A chimney stack would once have stood at the end the flue, but has been destroyed, although its stone foundation outline survives (NMR DP099113; © English Heritage. NMR).

Doetor Brook. Largest of these is the Reddaford Leat, which remains in use today to bring water to a reservoir on Blackdown, associated with a hydro-electric plant at Mary Tavy. This leat has its source on the River Tavy within Tavy Cleave and runs across Nattor Down and through Willsworthy Range.

Tramways

The removal of material from deep within a mine to destinations on the surface required an efficient and rapid means to move it. Be it valuable ore on its way to the dressing floors or waste material ('dead's) on its way to the spoil tips, the universally adopted method was the tramway. Skips mounted on wheeled trolleys ran on narrow-gauge iron tramlines that could be moved by men, horses or gravity using an inclined plane. Skips running along tramlines could travel with unbroken continuity along the levels inside the mine to the surface. Alternatively, material hoisted up shafts by whims could be transferred into awaiting skips and carried away at the surface. For example, both ore and waste were raised up Lowe's Shaft at Hexworthy Mine (see Fig 11.8). The waste was then trammed onto flat-topped finger-shape dumps extending from the shaft head, while the valuable ore was carried away, on a different tramway, to the dressing floors opposite Dry Lake, until a nearer installation was built in 1905. This tramway

survives as a straight, raised earthwork running through an area of disused streamworks.

Hexworthy Mine illustrates well how dressing floors were often sited some distance from the ore source, and thus the need for tramways. Short, more localised tramways were also common. At Whiteworks Mine (see Fig 11.2) and at Birch Tor and Vitifer Mine (see Fig 8.12), for example, a number of small tramway systems served various parts of the site, although the remains are often subtle, some appearing only as well-made footpaths.

Several more ambitious and extensive tramways also survive. A clear example can be seen at Ringleshuttes, where a straight, raised embankment runs for 500m from the engine shaft down to ruined dressing floors located in old streamworks beside the Venford Brook. At Haytor Consols, an ambitious and mostly unsuccessful mine with remains spread over a large area between Bagtor and Hemsworthy Gate, the dressing floors at Crownley Parks were sited 3km from the engine shaft at Hemsworthy and a complicated tramway was constructed to link the two. Within the Bagtor newtake the earthworks are becoming lost in the mire, but near the modern road at Hemsworthy the raised tramway earthwork can be seen descending the hill towards the newtake wall (Fig 11.22). At Eylesbarrow (see Fig 11.5), the tramway earthworks survive between several of the shaft heads and the dressing floors in the Drizzlecombe Valley.

Fig 11.22
Earthwork remains of a former tramway, east of Rippon Tor, created to transport tin ore from a mine at Hemsworthy, to a dressing floor near Bagtor (photo: Phil Newman).

Fig 11.23
Ruined building foundations
at Vitifer Mine, representing
all that remains of the
former Miners' Dry, and
typical of most of the
building legacy from the
19th- and 20th-century
mining industry. In this case
the buildings were
demolished in the 1950s,
before which time the
chimney stack is known to
have been still standing. The
mound to the right of the
tree represents all that
remains of the chimney today
(photo: Phil Newman).

Other buildings and structures

Associated with mines were buildings not directly connected with the mining, but which served other purposes also essential to the mining operation. These range from workshops, such as blacksmith's and carpenter's shops; miners' accommodation, including barracks and 'drys', where clothing was dried after underground shifts; count houses; housing for the mine agents or captains; and explosives stores. On the moorland mines, neglect combined with a fairly thorough job of demolition has meant that most buildings survive only as foundation outlines strewn with rubble, and it is often difficult to define their layout or purpose. Fortunately, maps of mines drawn up when they were still in use often have these buildings annotated. Eylesbarrow Mine has a number of ruined buildings concentrated into an area near the centre of the site (*see* Fig 11.5). All are now ruins, but we can be confident of their original purpose thanks to a map of 1825. The largest was the account house, which was also the residence of the mine agent or captain. This was later extended to form a substantial

residence referred to as Ellisborough House on contemporary maps of the area. Other buildings include the blacksmith's shop, carpenter's shop, changing house, powder houses and turf house (where peat was stored) (Newman 1999, 142).

Birch Tor and Vitifer Mine is particularly fascinating for the remains of its ancillary buildings. The flattened remains of numerous structure can be traced, most of which were demolished in the 1940s and 1950s during the less conservation-conscious days of the war and post-war years. Among the structures were cottages, offices, barracks, a miners' dry (Fig 11.23) and the usual array of workshops; the fascination of the site comes in a series of photographs taken mostly in the early 20th century and published in Greeves (1986). The photographs show most of the buildings still standing, and although near the end of their lives, they were at this time still in use. These photographs thus offer a rare glimpse of how a moorland mining landscape would have appeared in the late 19th and early 20th centuries, and it is likely that scenes like these differed little for most of the previous century as well.

12

China clay

Context

Compared with the exploitation of granite and metals, china clay is a relative newcomer among Dartmoor's extractive industries, starting in the 1820s. China clay nevertheless has developed into one of the region's most successful forms of mineral exploitation; it remains productive today and Dartmoor claypits continue to produce a product of international demand. The consequence of more than 150 years of success has been profound for the Dartmoor border landscape, creating large water-filled pits, massive white spoil heaps, extensive mica (settling) dams and processing works sprawling across the lower slopes of south-west Dartmoor and its hinterland. To some, these features are not easy on the eye, especially on the border of a national park, and the industry remains the subject of a lively debate with regards the conservation issues that surround its present and future activities. Not least because of the totality of the change it causes to the visual aspect of the area, despite attempts to ameliorate the effects by landscaping the disused areas.

China clay extraction has also caused the destruction of archaeological remains; many important prehistoric sites have either been destroyed or are still threatened by the growth of the clay pits. However, it could and has been argued that the information we now possess from archaeological excavations at Shaugh Moor (discussed in chapter 3) and at Cholwichtown (chapter 2), would not have been gained had these sites not been destined for total destruction by clay working – and this to some extent offsets the destructive aspect of clay working. The conservation debate will have to be addressed by others, but, although the industry has also been responsible for the destruction of much evidence of its own past as a result of its continual need to expand, in places there are pockets of disused landscape features and structures dating from earlier episodes of clay extraction and processing; these places also deserve recognition as components of Dartmoor's historical landscape.

China clay deposits owe their existence to the decomposition of granite over many tens of thousands of years, a process known as kaolinisation, which altered the feldspars in the granite into a silicate of alumina, called kaolin – more commonly known as china clay. Although in modern times kaolin has a multitude of uses, including the manufacture of shiny and specialist papers, toothpaste, cosmetics and medicine as well as its traditional use in the production of ceramics, it was originally sought after mainly as the key ingredient in the manufacture of porcelain. In the 18th century porcelain was highly prized by the rich, but was mostly imported from the far east, although some was manufactured in England using imported clays. In the 1740s, a Devonian called William Cookworthy discovered suitable deposits at Tregonning Hill, Cornwall, which enabled an English porcelain industry to begin, based on indigenous materials, and the start of china clay working in Cornwall.

However, Cookworthy, although aware of the Dartmoor clays, had apparently rejected them as being of poorer quality to those of Cornwall. Consequently, while the industry was growing fast around St Austell in the later 18th century, it was not until the 1820s that Dartmoor's clay was, on re-examination, found to be of suitable quality.

Dartmoor clay works

China clay occurs and has been exploited on the south-west side of Dartmoor between Cornwood and Bickleigh. Most of the currently active workings lie outside Dartmoor National Park, the boundary of which has been altered

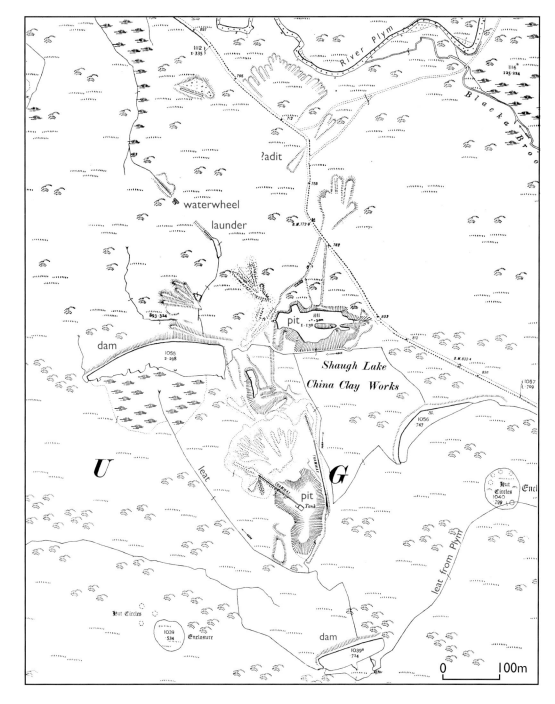

Fig 12.1
Extract from the 2nd edition
Ordnance Survey 25-inch
map of 1906 showing early
developments at the Shaugh
Lake clay works. The map
shows two clay pits, one of
which appears water-filled
and probably abandoned.
The second, to the south,
has an inclined tramway
used for hauling waste onto
a series of finger dumps.
Water for the clay extraction
process and to power
machinery was stored
behind two earthwork dams.
A small, undeveloped pit is
depicted to the north-east
and still survives, and a
waterwheel for pumping the
slurry back to surface in the
large pit is also shown.
Much that is illustrated on
this map has been subsumed
by more recent activity, but
the adit, water-filled pit and
several finger dumps remain
(see Fig 12.4). To the far
right is the prehistoric
settlement excavated by
Wainwright in the 1970s
(see Fig 3.6), which has
since been buried.

to exclude areas 'destroyed' by clay workings. Nevertheless, small areas on Wigford Down and several disused clay works lie within the park. China clay should not be confused with ball clay, which occurs on the lowlands of the Bovey Basin to the south-east of Dartmoor between Bovey Tracey and Kingsteignton. Ball clay, or 'potter's clay', is essentially a secondary deposit of kaolin that has been transported by rivers and streams from its place of origin on the upland to the low-lying valleys of the

hinterland around Bovey Heathfield and Kingsteignton. Its extraction differs from that of china clay in that it is dug from the ground in a solid form, and its use is mainly for pottery and for the manufacture of sanitary ware (Anon 2003, 3).

The earliest clay works were begun at Lee Moor in the 1830s where a number of separate enterprises established their pits (Harris 1968, 87). The area affected extends to the south-east from Cadover Bridge, and includes Shaugh

Moor, Lee Moor, Cholwichtown, Headon Down, Wotter and Crownhill Down, within which are large zones of active clay works or spoil dumping. The landscape archaeology of these pits is difficult to study because the field evidence represents rapid change, resulting in considerable effacement of earlier phases, but some idea of their progress can be gauged from early large-scale OS maps from the 1880s, 1900s and 1956 (Fig 12.1). Aerial photographs from the 1940s–1960s can also show how radically the landscape has changed through the 20th century. With so much evidence of their earlier phases now lost, it is the enterprises that failed early that can offer most to the field archaeologist, providing a snapshot of their

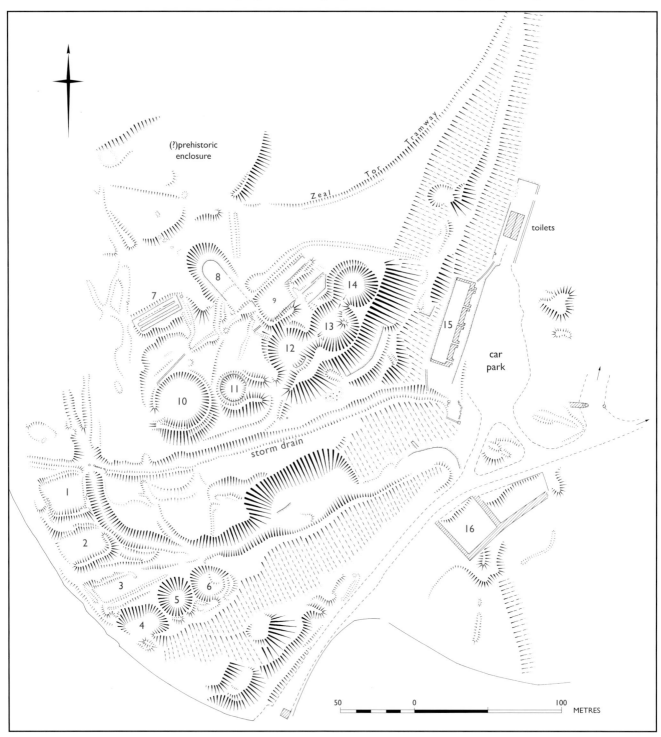

early development uneffaced by later progress. These are surprisingly few in number, but include clay works on Brent Moor at the head of Balla Brook and the remote clay pits at Redlake and Left Lake, high up on the south moor. The latter was a short-lived affair that first operated in the 1850s, and was later worked in conjunction with Redlake, where operations began in 1910 (Wade 1982, 22). Both sites have substantial remains comprising clay pits, now water filled, together with tips of waste material, ruined buildings, processing works and the Redlake tramway, which served the works and ran between the Redlake pits and Ivybridge. Two fine examples of clay processing works survive: one is at Shipley Bridge (Fig 12.2), where the Brent Moor clays were refined, and the other at Shaugh Bridge (Fig 12.3), which once served the Shaugh Lake clay works near Cadover Bridge (Fig 12.4). E A Wade describes in detail the history and aspects of the field evidence of several of these clay works, particularly Redlake (1982).

The principles of china clay extraction are quite straightforward. The kaolin itself is a fine, white powdery substance, but in its natural state is combined with small grains of minerals, such as mica and quartz (gangue), that have remained unaltered after the decomposition of the granite. The aim of the process, after freeing all this material from the earth, is to remove these unwanted gangue elements from the kaolin.

The first operation was to strip back the covering of peat and soil, or 'overburden', to expose the clay deposits. It is interesting to note that at Redlake, Left Lake and Petre' Pits at the head of the Bala Brook on Brent Moor, the clay works overlie old tin streamworks, so it is likely that the kaolin deposits were originally exposed by tinworking long before china clay working began, and possibly contributing to their discovery. In later clay works, such as Redlake in the early 20th century, as well as those still operating today, the clay ground was and still is washed away using a high-pressure blast of water through a device called a monitor. At earlier works the ground was loosened manually then washed away by water from a leat. Large stones and gravel were separated from the clay while still in the pit. At Petre's Pits, small finger dumps survive representing this material, which was dumped from hand barrows; but at Redlake the large 'sky tip' was created by using an

inclined tramway hauling the material up from the bottom of the pit, a scene captured in a photograph taken when the pits were still operating (Wade 1982, 75). Nineteenth- and early 20th-century OS maps of the Shaugh Moor area (Fig 12.1) show that much of this waste was barrowed or trammed from the pits onto 'finger' dumps, some of which have survived the later expansion of the pits. Both methods of extraction relied on an artificial water supply diverted to the site. At Redlake, two hollow reservoirs were excavated to store the water, diverted or possibly pumped from nearby sources. One relic of the early clay working at Shaugh Moor is a dry leat that diverted water from the River Plym and its tributary of Drizzlecombe, around the northern slopes of Hentor, Trowlesworthy Tor, then south to the clay works; the disused channel now terminates at the edge of a modern clay work, but it originally supplied a series of reservoirs needed for the processes (*see* Fig 12.1).

Once the clay and waste was in suspension the liquid, or 'slurry', was removed from the clay pit in a variety of ways. Where the pit was suitably situated and shallow it flowed out by gravity, utilising the sloping ground. If the pits were worked deeper, then a shaft was sunk into the bottom, connected with a level, which drained the slurry via an open adit or it could be pumped back to the surface through a second shaft. At Petre's Pits, an undeveloped site, gravity was all that was needed for the clay to flow from the shallow pits, whereas at Redlake pumping was used. One of the surviving ruined buildings at Redlake, near the water-filled pit, once housed a pumping engine. At Shaugh Lake (*see* Fig 12.1) a waterwheel depicted on the 1906 OS map is also likely to have served this purpose.

When free of the clay pit the liquid clay slurry was run into a pipeline that carried it to the processing works. Some initial stages of processing to settle out heavier waste took place not far south of the pit at Redlake, where elongated concrete tanks survive. However, the main processing works – usually referred to as 'drys' – at most clay pits, including Redlake, were sited some distance from the clay source, off the moors. This was done for a number of reasons, but was mainly to avoid carting the bulky finished product from remote moorland sites, thus requiring less expense to

Fig 12.2 (opposite) Earthwork plan of the Shipley Bridge china clay drys: 1–6, mica pits and settling tanks of the Clay Co Ltd 1885; 7, mica drag; 8, sand drag; 9–14, settling tanks; 15, thickening tank; 16, (?) collecting tank. Nos 7–16 all associated with Brent Moor Clay Co 1872–1880.

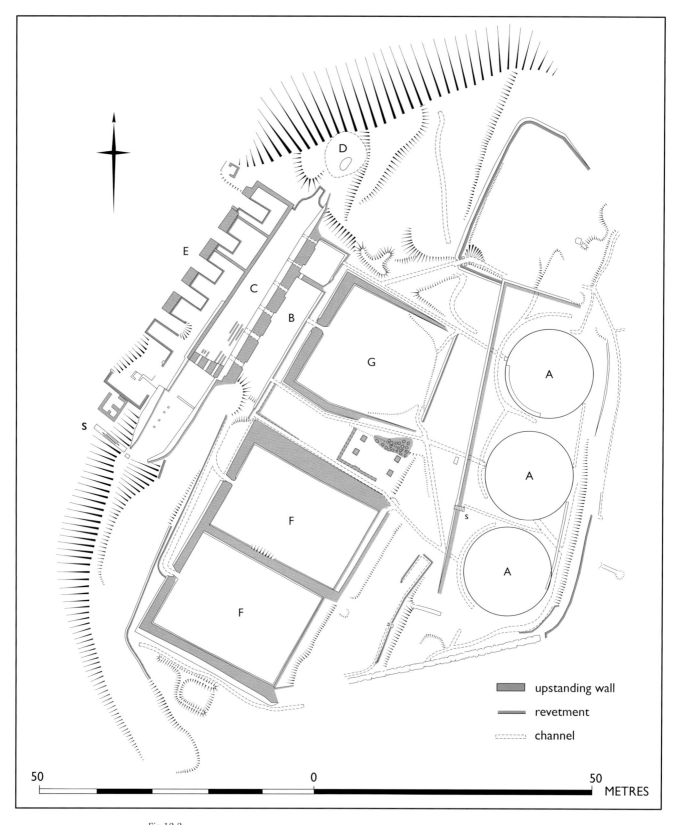

Fig 12.3

Plan of the china clay works built into the bottom of the slope at Shaugh Bridge to process the clay slurry piped down from Shaugh Lake clay works (see Fig 12.1; 12.4):

A circular settling pits; B thickening tank; C kiln; D base of demolished chimney; E cart loading bays; F & G later rectangular settling pits; S steps.

ship it out and providing access to wider transport networks. In the case of Redlake the clay drys were sited at Bittaford, beside the Great Western Railway (GWR) mainline, whereas at Shaugh Bridge there was access to good roads as well as to the nearby railway. At Shipley Bridge, near South Brent, despite being off the moors, there was still the cost of removing the clay from the drys along several miles of narrow lanes with steep gradients, all of which added to the cost and may have contributed to the Brent Moor Clay Company's ultimate failure.

The concrete pipeline from Redlake survives and can be traced across the moor, following a sinuous course that roughly coincides with the tramway and terminates at the clay drys. The manholes that can be seen at regular intervals along the pipeline gave access for clearing blockages. In North Wood, below Cadover Bridge on the River Plym, the ceramic pipes that once transported the liquid clay from Shaugh Lake to the drys at Shaugh Bridge survive *in situ* beside the modern footpath.

Clay drys

Two well-preserved clay drys survive in the National Park at Shaugh Bridge and Shipley Bridge, and a less extensive example exists on Crownhill Down near Smallhanger. The Redlake drys at Bittaford have not survived, although some of the buildings have been adapted for other purposes and a fine granite-built chimney stack remains in place.

The Shipley Bridge clay drys

The Shipley Bridge site, where clays from the Bala Brook beds at Petre's Pits were processed, began in the 1850s and although poorly documented, it is recorded that this site was operated by two chronologically separate companies.

The China Clay Company Ltd was in business by 1858, and although some clay was produced the company was short-lived, due apparently to the poor quality of the product (Robinson 1980, 4). A second attempt at working the Bala Brook deposits took place in 1872 when

Fig 12.4
Aerial view of an area of modern clay works on Shaugh Moor, Lee Moor and Wotter. The clay works, which were established in the 1830s, sit uncomfortably amid prehistoric reaves and hut settlements on Shaugh Moor to the right and the medieval tin streamworks along the Blackabrook to the left. Remnants of the earlier clayworking phases survive in the form of the finger dumps and water-filled clay pit centre left (NMR 24678/024; © English Heritage. NMR).

the Brent Moor Clay Company reopened the works and stayed in business for a further eight years before succumbing to the depressed price of clay in 1880 (Wade 1984, 15). A newspaper article of 1923 stated that the works were to be reopened using the plant remaining from 1872, but it is not thought to have been successful (Robinson 1980, 4). Before any clay working, in 1847 the site was used for the distillation of naphtha (*see* chapter 13) from peat cut on the east side of Brown Heath near Redlake and transported to Shipley by a tramway across Zeal Plain. The majority of the remains at Shipley Bridge are associated with the 1858 and 1870s clay working, and what is remarkable about this place is that evidence of the two periods occupy different zones of the site, which can be easily differentiated by the visitor (Newman 2002c).

Once the unrefined slurry was delivered to the processing works the first priority was the removal of residual mica and quartz sand. In the earlier, 1850s, phase at Shipley Bridge this was achieved using the less-developed method of three, shallow rectangular pits located at descending intervals down the hillside. The liquid clay/sand mix was run into the upper pit, which was allowed to overflow into the second or middle pit carrying the clay with it but leaving the coarse sands behind in the first pit. The finer sands would settle in the middle pit, which overflowed into the lowest pit, where only mica remained to be trapped. Once cleaned in this way the liquid clay was then run from the lowest pit into deep circular settling tanks to be de-watered, whereby the water accumulated above the settling clay and was drained off using a wooden pipe pierced with holes placed vertically in the tank down which the water could escape, leaving only the clay.

The remains of this early phase makes up the southern portion of the site, and is delineated from the later works to the north by an east–west ditch, probably dug as a storm drain to prevent the pits from flooding and becoming contaminated with peaty water. This process used the moderate sloping ground to keep the liquids flowing. All the features survive as earthworks and although all of the pits were once lined with dressed granite, they have been comprehensively robbed as a source of valuable building material. The square pits (1–3) are between 0.2m and 0.7m deep, each with a substantial earthwork bank on the downslope side. The two upper pits cover an area of 180 square metres each, while the lower, shallower pit (3) is approximately 100 square metres.

A little lower down are the settling tanks (4–6): these were probably circular, although one has been badly disturbed and the stone linings have been robbed from all three. They have a diameter of between 12m and 15m and are each 1.3m deep. The location of any further drying processes for this early works is not known.

By the 1870s, when the second phase at Shipley Bridge began, more advanced techniques had been introduced to separate the sand and mica in a device called a drag. The mica drag consisted of a series of narrow, inclined brick or stone-built channels within which the mica would settle as the clay slurry flowed along it. The remains of this feature (7) survive well, apparently not a victim of robbing, and it has three separate 200mm deep channels with rounded ends and a common outfow. The larger sand drag (8) is a flat-bottomed pan with a rounded end, lined with bricks; the floor has a small drop in height approximately half way along. Having passed through these drags the cleaned clay slurry was run down the slope into a series of settling tanks (9–14), within which the water was slowly run off to leave behind the clay. One of these tanks (a) is L-shaped and the other five are circular and of differing diameters, the largest being 18m and the smallest being 8.8m; each is between 2m and 2.5m deep. These features have also been extensively robbed of their stone linings, although that of pit 11 appears to have survived almost intact, as have traces of the lining on the L-shaped pit. The stone robbing was a complicated operation, which involved digging an access route into each pit and a trackway for carts to take the material away. The robbed-out and heavily disturbed pits now comprise approximately circular earthworks with sloping sides, with virtually no masonry left.

Once the bulk of the water had drained away, the clay, became more viscous and was fed through a large-diameter iron pipe into the thickening tank (15), in which de-watering continued. This is the large rectangular stone building adjacent to the modern car park. The structure is set into the slope: the back wall forms a revetment, but the front wall is a thick, robust structure with four buttressed openings. These housed heavy wood or iron hatch doors, which have been removed but which opened outward. Once the moisture level of the clay had reached the correct level, the doors were opened and the clay shovelled into a large open drying pan that once occupied the area covered by the modern car park. At Shipley Bridge this final stage in the process relied on air-drying contained within a corrugated iron shed. This was slow and inefficient, but typical of a small enterprise where costs needed to be kept low and for which the expense of a heated kiln – which became available from the 1850s – would probably have been unaffordable.

South of the car park, on the opposite side of the road, two collecting tanks (16), constructed using upstanding banks with stone facings, cleaned the water from the processes before releasing it into the river Avon.

Shaugh Bridge

The remains of the works at the foot of the slope east of Shaugh Bridge reflect similar processes to those described for the Shipley workings, but on a somewhat larger and more enduring scale. It is believed this plant was installed *c* 1870–80 (Smith and RCHME 1996, 3), or possibly earlier, and served the clay pits at Shaugh Lake around Cadover Bridge until 1952, when more advanced plant was installed at Lee Moor, where operations continue today. Mica was removed from the clay slurry in lagoons close to the clay pits and the slurry was then transported 1.5km across the slopes of North Wood and West Down in a clay pipeline, which survives beside the modern footpath, to the clay drys.

An archaeological survey of this site has revealed at least three phases, reflecting gradual expansion of the facility (Smith 1996 and RCHME, 12--13). Three deep, round settling pits at the east end of the site (A) originally worked alongside a thickening tank (B) farther down the slope, similar to that at Shipley, and a drying kiln (C). The kiln was equipped with a furnace at the south end and a tall chimney stack to the north. This has been demolished since abandonment and survives only as a low rubble mound (D). After passing from the settling pits into the thickening tank, the still-wet product was shovelled into the kiln through the hatch doors, as at Shipley, but dried by the use of heat, which was much quicker than the air-drying method used at Shipley Bridge. Below the kiln is an array of six

stone-built bays (E) where the finished clay, having passed through the kiln, was loaded onto carts. At a later date, probably in the early 1880s, two additional settling tanks were added (F). They are rectangular in plan and of much larger capacity than those already in place. A third tank (G) of irregular outline was added on the north end sometime after 1886, at which date it is omitted from the OS 25-inch map, although it appears on the 1905 map.

The Shaugh Bridge china clay works, in contrast to those at Shipley Bridge, has not been robbed for stone and most of the permanent masonry features survive more or less intact, although, as mentioned, the chimney does not survive. It is, however, visible in a photograph of the site in the early 20th century; this photograph also shows that the clay drys once had a fine, steeply pitched slate roof (Greeves 2004b, 61). Much detail survives *in situ* at the site, including many of the open channels through which the slurry passed between the various processes.

The remains at Shipley and Shaugh Bridges reflect an essentially simple process, much aided by the nature of the material and by the abundance of water available on Dartmoor. The active clay works, although now supplemented by modern technology, rely on similar processes as those reflected in the working landscape of the past (*see* Fig 12.4). There is, however, a substantial difference in scale: the size of the pits and the extent of the settling lagoons now used cover many hectares.

Wotter and Lee Moor

Despite the unquestionably destructive nature of china clay extraction and processing, and its disregard for the pre-existence of natural and cultural landscapes – an unavoidable consequence of opencast pits – the industry has contributed some important elements to the human story on Dartmoor. Beyond the noticeable evidence of clay works, one major contribution of the clay industry to the social landscape is the existence of industrial settlements at Wotter and at Lee Moor, which owe their origins and growth to accommodating the clay workforce; although beyond the archaeological brief of this book, their contribution to the Dartmoor story is considerable.

Conclusion

Currently, because of the conservation issues that surround the ongoing and future activity of this industry, the artefacts from its past are undervalued. At some time in the future, however, clay working will cease around Dartmoor and the value of these places as evidence of past economic and social phases of the Dartmoor historic environment will be better appreciated, in the same way that the granite and tin industries have come to be seen as integral components of Dartmoor's cultural identity. There can be no doubt that the field archaeologists who choose to examine this industry in the future will inherit a spectacular and complicated array of field remains. In the meantime the fragments that survive from early endeavours provide insight into the development of one of Dartmoor's most economically successful extractive industries.

13

Miscellaneous industries: peat, gunpowder mills, ice works and tramways

In addition to exploitation of the major minerals, several smaller-scale industrial endeavours have also left their mark on the Dartmoor landscape. Each represents the 19th-century spirit of enterprise described above through attempts to utilise Dartmoor's plentiful natural assets. These include peat cutting, harvesting a natural resource; the production of ice, which capitalised on the cold wet climate; and gunpowder manufacture, using Dartmoor's remote location for this potentially hazardous operation. The latter two, both single enterprises, have been the subject of detailed investigations (Harris 1988; Pye 1994), and the results of an investigation into the peat cutting industry is due for publication shortly (Newman 2010).

Peat cutting

Peat is a natural substance that forms on the wetter high ground of the moors, and is a result of thousands of years of accumulated, part-decomposed plant material. In the correct wet conditions it can exist to several metres in depth. It is highly water retentive and is responsible for storing the rainfall on the high ground where large, wet peat bogs retain water and provide the sources for several of Devon's major rivers. When extracted from the ground by slicing it into shaped blocks and allowed to dry out, it transforms into a hard material that burns slowly with a distinct aroma or 'tang'. Cut peat was usually referred to as 'turf' by Dartmoor people, whereas the thin, grassy upper layers – also valued as a fuel – were known as 'vaggs'.

The cutting of peat for fuel was once a crucial component in the everyday domestic life of those living on Dartmoor. In an area with few trees to provide firewood and no access to coal, dried peat has been burned on domestic hearths for hundreds of years. Peat cutting for domestic fuel was a key privilege possessed by Dartmoor's tenants and commoners since at least the 13th century (Gill 1970, 98).

Peat can also be transformed into charcoal, for which it was much in demand in the medieval period for tin smelting. Those involved in the peat charcoal trade, were referred to as the *carbonarii*, and were described in 1371 as 'digging turves for charcoal in order to sell it', but it is known that this practice was occurring from at least the time of King John in the early 13th century (H S A Fox 1994, 162).

Although the demand for charcoal by tinners was satisfied commercially by the *carbonarii*, it was not until the 19th century that peat was extracted on an industrial scale, when peat works were established to cut and transport the material from the moors, to be distributed as a domestic or industrial fuel, or to convert the peat to produce naphtha, a product of similar characteristics to paraffin, by a process of distillation. Harris (1968, 105–15) discusses the historical aspects of these peatworks, but essentially there were four major locations where peat was cut commercially, three of which were served by their own railway transport system. These were at Zeal Hill in the Avon Valley, at Rattlebrook on north-west Dartmoor, and at Blackabrook Valley around Greena Ball, Fice's Well and Holming Beam. The Blackabrook Valley and Zeal Hill peat workings both began in the 1840s with the intention of producing naphtha, but both were short lived and closed after only a few years. Attempts to cut peat commercially at Walkham Head in the 1870s were on a small scale and mainly unsuccessful (Newman 2010). However, earlier in the 19th century peat was harvested on a massive scale from this area to supply lead-smelting furnaces at Mary Tavy (Le Messurier 1966, 49).

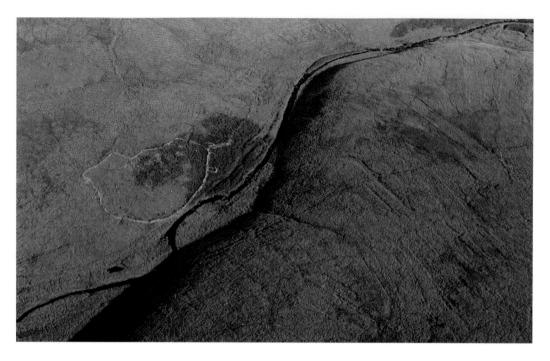

The Rattlebrook peat works commenced work on a more extensive scale in 1868, and in 1878 a company was created, with the intention of producing compressed peat blocks that could be used as an alternative to coal.

Peat cutting continued intermittently through much of the 19th century and into the 20th, with various companies promoting differing schemes for using peat, but usually with little success. And the works at Rattlebrook finally closed in the 1950s, although peat continued to be cut sporadically elsewhere on Dartmoor to within living memory. The works at Rattlebrook once had a range of large stone buildings, but these have been mostly destroyed, surviving only as rubble although they can be seen still standing in contemporary photographs (Hemery 1983, pl 450). Only Dunnagoat Cottage, or 'Bleak House' as it has become known – a residence built for the works caretaker – has any substantive surviving remains.

William Crossing provides a detailed contemporary account of how peat was worked at the start of the 20th century (Le Messurier 1966, 48–55), describing the tools and techniques. Peat was traditionally cut by hand using specialised iron tools. A ditch was first cut in the surface 40yd (36m) long by 3ft (0.9m) wide, called a 'journey'. This was expanded laterally as the peat turves were cut from the sides in rows. By the time each of these pits or 'ties' was exhausted, the result was a large rectangular pit with straight sheer sides, which could be well over 1m deep depending on the depth of the usable peat (Fig 13.1). Once removed from the tie, the peat was dried near by.

Compared with most of Dartmoor's archaeology, field evidence of the peat industry is rarely a cause of excitement to the observer and has, so far, failed to attract researchers. Some areas where peat was extensively cut in the 19th century, such as near Blackabrook on the north moor, have a rather desolate appearance, made all the more uncomfortable for the visitor by the wet nature of the ground; and the evidence itself is rather unimpressive. But in no way should this imply lack of importance as a part of the Dartmoor story. The evidence comprises many hectares of turf ties, the courses of the tramways running from the works (*see below*) and the scant ruins of buildings; and several small shelters in the heart of the moor might be associated with peat cutters rather than with tinners on the basis of their locations. For example, Statts House, a ruined stone-built structure with an internal fireplace, on Marsh Hill is by tradition considered to have origins as a peat cutters' shelter (Harris 1968, 108).

The evidence of peat or 'turf' ties is widespread in the areas where suitable peat was available, particularly in the Blackabrook Valley, Rattlebrook Head, Avon Head, the Skir Gut area and Redlake. Although peat ties could potentially be surviving from as early as at least the 13th century, it is most likely that those for which clear evidence survives are more recent, probably 19th and early 20th century; medieval and post-medieval ties are likely to have been partly smoothed over and disguised by nature long ago.

Tramways and railways

Apart from the peat ties, among the most enduring evidence of the 19th-century peat industry are the railways that served to transport this bulky material from the uplands to the edge of the moor for distribution; these were among several light railways and tramways constructed in association with extractive industries on Dartmoor. In the 18th and 19th centuries the road network to and from the moors was generally reported to be poor; for example Charles Vancouver in 1808 stated that many of Devon's roads had the disadvantage of following direct routes over undulating ground and the surfaces were in poor condition, with deep ruts and numerous potholes (Vancouver 1808, 368–71). Eleven years earlier William Marshall had mentioned that many roads in steep areas of West Devon

were stepped as a result of erosion through overuse (Marshall 1796, 30). If moorland industries were to become economically viable, then the movement of heavy materials on a large scale, such as the products of a quarry or a peat works, necessitated the construction of either improved roads for conventional horse-drawn wheeled vehicles, or a tramway. The latter could, by use of engineering, negotiate the steep gradients encountered when ascending or descending the uplands.

The Haytor tramway, built 1820 and described in chapter 10, was Devon's first such transport system. It was closely followed by the Plymouth and Dartmoor Railway, a conventional horse-drawn tramway with iron rails that extended from Plymouth to King's Tor, opened in 1823, and extended to Princetown by 1825 (Kingdom 1991, 6). This tramway needs to be understood not just as a functional means of overcoming a transportation problem, but also in the context of the industrialisation and capitalisation of central Dartmoor in the early 19th century, as discussed elsewhere. It was a key component in the opening up of Dartmoor for exploitation and its existence was very much in step with the spirit of improvement in the early 19th century. It enabled the free

Fig 13.2
A surviving section of the Plymouth and Dartmoor Railway near Clearbrook. Each of the granite blocks, known as 'chairs', has paired holes on the upper surface to receive iron pegs for fixing the rails to them (photo: Phil Newman).

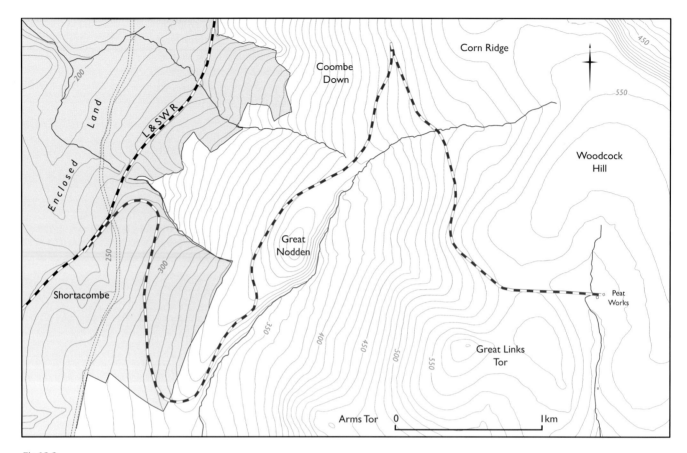

Fig 13.3
Map showing the route of the Rattlebrook Peat Railway built in 1879, based on the 1st edition 1:2500 Ordnance Survey map of 1886. The railway branches from the London and South Western Railway, then climbs 300m to the crest of Great Links Tor, before a short descent to the peat works. A hairpin with changeover points was incorporated into the Corn Ridge section as a means of negotiating the steep ascent (height data licensed to English Heritage for PGA through Next Perspectives™).

movement of goods and people into an area ripe for all kinds of enterprise and development, which at that time was focused around Princetown in the heart of the moor. The moorland section of the tramway was later used as the course of the Princetown branch line, built in 1883 and operated by the Great Western Railway Co. (Kingdom 1991, 6), but sections of the original 1823 railway survive and are particularly clear running across Roborough Down. This iron tramway was constructed using alignments of small, square, flat-topped granite blocks or 'chairs' (Fig 13.2), paired along the course of the track bed, onto which rails were fixed by iron pegs, driven into small holes in the blocks.

Of the Dartmoor industrial railways, the Rattlebrook peat railway (Fig 13.3), built 1878–9, involved the most impressive engineering and has the clearest surviving evidence. Originally horse-drawn but later mechanised (Harris 1968, 111), it follows a sinuous course between a siding of the London and South Western Railway and the works at Rattlebrook Head, rising 250m in altitude across Combe Down before dropping 100m down to the works over a total linear

distance of 7.5km, using numerous cuttings and an embankment en route.

Peat from the Blackabrook Valley works was also transported on a tramway down to Princetown for processing. The scant earthwork remains of the track bed can still be seen cutting across the boggy ground on the eastern side of Mistor Marsh. A clearer section, comprising a raised embankment can be seen south of the B3357 near Rundlestone. The course of the tramway can be traced to the precinct of the prison, where naphtha distillation was done for a short period in the 1840s while the prison was disused (Harris 1968, 106).

The Redlake railway was the last industrial line to be constructed across the high moors, between the Redlake clay pits, on the Erme–Avon watershed, and the clay drying sheds at Cantrell Gate. E A Wade (1982) discusses the history of this line in great detail. It opened in 1910 to ferry men and equipment up to the clay pits and from the very start, loads were pulled by locomotives. Considering the total length of the line – 13.3km – major engineering was minimal apart from a stone bridge across a disused tin streamwork at Left Lake.

Gunpowder mills

The buildings and earthworks of the gunpowder mills near Cherrybrook Bridge, represent a remarkable survival of remains from a non-extractive 19th century Dartmoor industry (Fig 13.4). Eighteen ruined buildings nestle along both sides of the Cherrybrook (Fig 13.5) and once contained all the industrial processes required in the manufacture of gunpowder. Also, a series of dwellings, built to house employees of the powder company, survive and remain occupied. One particularly notable aspect of this manufacturing complex is the use of water power, where leats from the Cherrybrook and the East Dart River have been diverted to the site to activate the seven waterwheels that powered the machinery housed within the buildings.

Known locally simply as 'Powder Mills' or Powdermills, the site was opened in *c* 1846 under a licence issued by the Duchy of Cornwall, who owned the land, and remained in operation until 1897. Although gunpowder had many uses, including for war, it is thought that the Powdermills were started mainly to meet the demands of local mining and quarrying, which was flourishing in the 1840s and 1850s and required large amounts of powder to blast through rock. A slump in copper mining in the 1870s and a growing preference in other sectors of the mining industry towards more advanced explosives such as dynamite, may have eventually sealed the fate of gunpowder manufacturing, hence its demise before the end of the 19th century following 50 years of continuity (Pye 1994, 225).

Gunpowder contains three ingredients: saltpetre (potassium nitrate), charcoal and sulphur. These three needed to be carefully amalgamated to form the finished product, achieved through a series of separate operations developed to avoid the powder combusting mid-process. At Powdermills a detailed archaeological and historical survey in 1990 established the purpose of some of these buildings and the types of machinery they may have contained with as much certainty as the remains will allow (Pye and Robinson 1990; Pye 1994). However, as no contemporary plan of the site survives, there has to be some uncertainty, as several of the processes were housed in similar structures. In the description that follows and in Fig 13.4, the numberings are those used by Pye, although the articles cited should be consulted for further details.

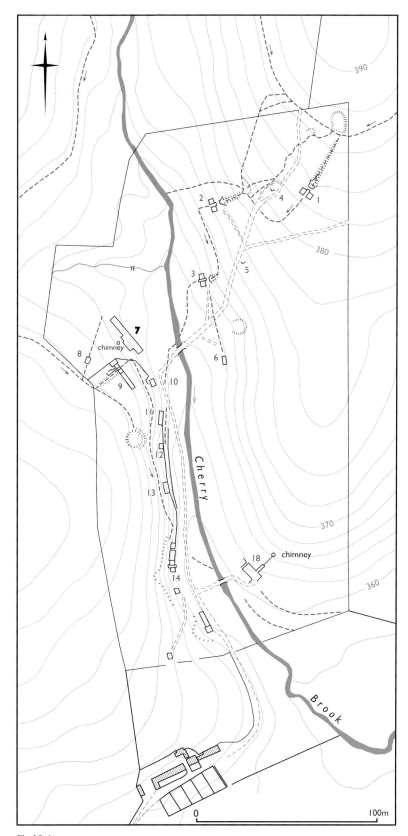

Fig 13.4

Plan showing the layout of the gunpowder mills near Postbridge, based on an RCHME 1:2500 survey (see text for discussion of numbered features).

227

Fig 13.5
Aerial view of the
gunpowder mills looking
east. Building 18, the
charcoal house is in the
right foreground and
building 14, one of the
incorporating mills is at the
centre top (NMR
24954/011; © English
Heritage. NMR).

Essentially the processes that followed the preparation of the raw materials were: grinding and mixing, in which the materials were ground separately in a water-powered mill with rotating grindstones; and blending, also a water-powered process in which the mixed ingredients were rotated in wooden barrels. It is believed that both processes were housed in building 14.

The next phase was incorporating the results of the former processes. The mixture was compressed into a single compound by using a thick, edge-set circular stone known as an 'edge-runner', similar to the apple crushers common at that time, but powered by a waterwheel. The edge-runners were set in pairs on opposite ends of a short shaft, connected by gearing to the main shaft of the waterwheel; they rolled like wheels in a tight circular movement over a flat surface, compressing the ingredients of the gunpowder as they passed over them. The edge-runners were made from limestone to eliminate the risk of sparks.

There are three incorporating mills at Powdermills on the east side of the Cherrybrook Valley (1–3), each sited so that a single leat, bringing waters from the East Dart River and the Cherrybrook could serve all three mills, in a sequence descending the hill. The leat channels and masonry-clad launder embankments all survive *in situ*. Despite minor architectural differences, the buildings have similar layouts, each constructed in a robust fashion from large blocks of granite with walls 2m thick in places. This was a precaution against the real and frequent threat of accidental combustion of the gunpowder mix.

The buildings (Fig 13.6) have a symmetrical footprint comprising a central waterwheel pit and a two-storey rectangular structure attached to either side. Large rectangular openings in the wheelpit walls have polished axle settings across the base and accommodated the drive shafts that powered the mills in the upper storey, where large granite blocks, which supported the mills, survive *in situ*. Building 14 is likely also to have functioned as an incorporating mill at some stage in the life of the factory.

Following incorporation, the charge of half-finished powder was stored in a small building, one for each of the mills (4, 5 and 6), which now survive only just above ground level.

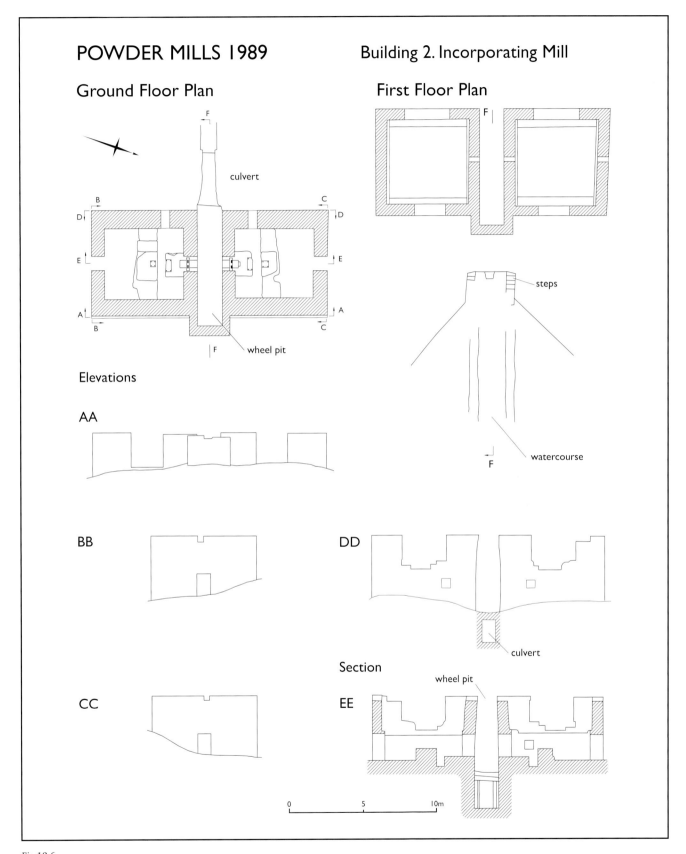

Fig 13.6
Plan and elevations of one of three incorporating mills, from a survey by Exeter Archaeology (© Exeter Archaeology, with permission).

Other major buildings from the 1990 survey whose identity has been suggested by Pye are the press house (13), where the product was compressed hydraulically powered by a waterwheel; and the charcoal house (18), in which willow, alder and other types of wood were converted into charcoal. The charcoal house is a large, although ruined, building with an external flue and an impressive, intact chimney stack. Building 7 also has an intact external chimney, although the building itself is a ruin, and is likely to have contained a steam boiler used for drying the gunpowder. The uses of some of the lesser buildings is uncertain, although Pye has suggested likely processes known to have occurred at gunpowder mills elsewhere.

Unlike so much of Dartmoor's industrial heritage, especially those elements located on the uplands, the structures and earthworks at Powdermills remain remarkably well preserved, having mostly escaped the robbing of materials or demolition in the days before an awareness of conservation issues. Apart from all being roofless and their timber components having decayed long ago, in many cases the structures have no sign of demolition or collapse. The stone structures of the three incorporating mills, all made from large blocks of dimensioned granite, survive as intact shells, with clear central wheelpits. Some of the other buildings have suffered partial loss of fabric through decay, but in most cases enough is standing to provide an understanding of the layout and both the tall chimney stacks survive to their full height; a testimony to the enduring materials and building styles of this region.

The ice works

Perhaps one of most ambitious entrepreneurial projects to ever take place on Dartmoor was the ice works, sited high on the north slopes of Sourton Tor, where between 1875 and 1886, James Henderson, a renowned West Country engineer, built a works for the production of 'natural' ice. The concept was simple: water from a spring was conducted into shallow, artificial ponds to freeze. Using a special press patented by Henderson, the ice was compressed into blocks, which could be stored at the site before being transported to Plymouth for use in preserving fresh foods, especially fish. Success relied heavily on the cold upland climate, for which northern Dartmoor was renowned, to make and allow for the storage of the ice, even during spring and summer, when compressed ice could theoretically remain frozen. This somewhat unpredictable, though crucial, aspect of the enterprise alone made it an unusually speculative venture. Also, artificial ice making, as opposed to the natural process used by Henderson, was already done elsewhere by the 1870s, and these two circumstances conspired towards sealing Henderson's venture as a short-lived financial disaster. The predictable end came when a fall in the price paid for ice coincided with several mild winters.

Helen Harris (1988) has written a detailed article describing these and other aspects of the Sourton ice works. A similar operation on Bodmin Moor, also created by Henderson c 1880, used ice from the surface of Dozmary Pool collected and compressed in a similar way. The Cornish venture was slightly more enduring and operated until 1900 (Hodge 1973, 23).

The earthwork remains of the ice works are located on the northern slope of Sourton Tor, north-west of the outcrops. This exposed position, on the ledge of the outer north-west escarpment of the upland, was probably chosen for its propensity for cold winds, although not so remote to make transport a problem, being just over 1km from the main Plymouth road. Upon abandonment Henderson was required to render the site safe, presumably by backfilling any steep drops, but the earthworks are still remarkably clear. The main element of the site is a series of shallow ponds, now dry, created by digging linear earth banks into the slope, as terraces, behind which a broad concave hollow was excavated. There are five of these long banks and one shorter example, sited one above the other. The interiors of the long earthworks have subdivisions, creating a total of 30 rectangular ponds.

These 'Ice Ponds' were depicted on the first edition OS 25-inch map of the area of 1885 (Fig 13.7), when the operation was still ongoing, apparently showing the ponds filled with water. A small spring emanates from the slope just above the western end of the ponds and may have been the source of water for the works, although it is known that experiments to compress driven snow were also attempted at the site to provide a second source of ice (Harris 1988, 182).

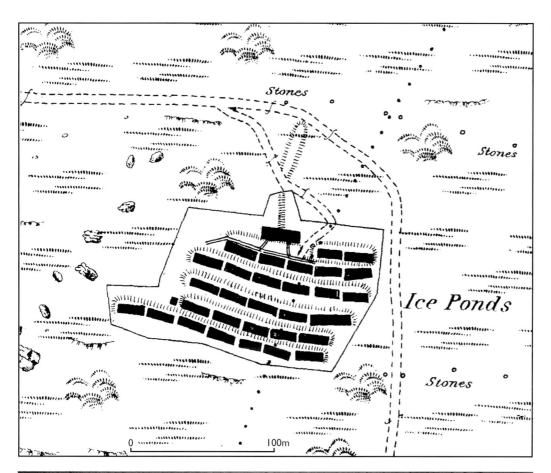

Fig 13.7
Extract from the 1st edition
Ordnance Survey map of
1885, showing the ice works
at Sourton Tors, with ponds
apparently filled with water.

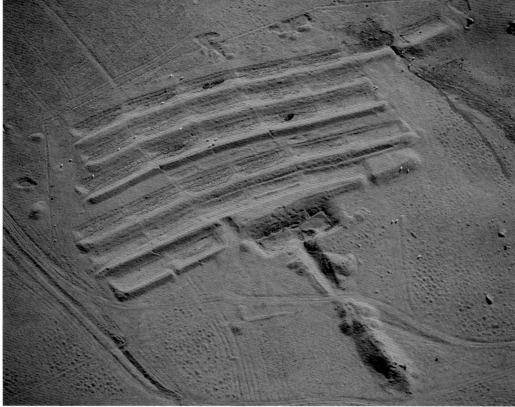

Fig 13.8
Aerial view of the ice works
at Sourton Tors (NMR
24680/033; © English
Heritage. NMR).

231

At the lower end of the works, a 25m × 6m rectangular building is where Harris suggests the ice blocks were stored (Harris 1988, 193). Although this structure appears to have been demolished upon abandonment, the outlines of the walls are visible. It was sunk into a substantial, purpose-built hollow and the material that was removed in the process was dumped on the linear spoil heap farther down the slope. (Fig 13.8) This sunken position, would have provided insulation to help delay thawing when the atmospheric temperature was warmer.

Conclusion

The late 18th- and 19th-century spirit of enterprise that gripped the uplands of Dartmoor is perhaps manifest most clearly in Henderson's ice works, albeit late in this episode and among the last industrial projects to take place on the higher moors. From at least the 12th century Dartmoor had supported human industrial activity; in particular tin, a valuable commodity, had been worked extensively on the moor, although the scale of individual stream-working operations was likely to have been modest. Peat cutting, also practised from an early date on a small-scale and mostly sustainable way, had similarly endured for centuries, providing domestic fuel for moorland dwellers and charcoal for tin smelters. Granite was there for the taking for its early exploiters, who simply needed to search for appropriate pieces then fashion them as required, before carting the results away – a method ideally suited to a localised industry meeting the domestic needs of the inhabitants.

Indeed, the exploitation of the natural resources of Dartmoor were both sustainable and viable as long as they remained localised. With the advent of capitalist venture starting in the 18th century and blossoming in the 19th came a belief that investment in developing these industries could result in profitable enterprises for those bold enough to invest. It is intriguing therefore to consider why so few of these schemes, along with those of the so-called agricultural improvers discussed in chapter 9, were successful or enduring.

For the tin mines, especially those sited on the granite zone, one of the problems was that the tin lodes were much shallower, less extensive and therefore less productive than those elsewhere, such as in Cornwall or in the Tamar Valley. Although the exploitation of tin continued throughout the 19th century into the 20th, the price of the ore fluctuated. For example, the price of £150 per ton in 1872 had plummeted to £68 per ton by1878 (Schmitz 1979, 34). It was at these times when the price was depressed that the Dartmoor tin industry struggled and was therefore never able to support large or enduring tin mines. Most mines had a history of stopping and starting under different companies at frequent intervals, many of which resulted in a loss.

For the peat industry, and attempts to produce liquid fuels, the process proved too inefficient and the central uplands proved too remote. At the Rattlebrook peat works, where numerous attempts were made to produce a range of peat-based products between 1868 and 1931, the cost of installing a railway had at one point contributed to the poor economy of the product (Harris 1968, 111). Later, however, the cost of energy required to dry the peat rendered the enterprise financially unsustainable (Newman 2010).

For the Haytor granite quarries, the elaborate transport system must have increased costs enough to make it difficult to compete. It required the blocks to be transhipped twice to get them to their destination markets – from tramway to barge and from barge to seagoing vessel; hence the early demise of Haytor among the granite quarries on Dartmoor.

For all Dartmoor' industries, competition from the same industries at places with less acute transport costs and with less inhibiting climates was always a crucial factor. These problems always made such schemes on Dartmoor of marginal viability and at the mercy of remote markets. When prices slump marginal businesses are always the first to suffer, and such was the story for tin and copper mining on Dartmoor, whose decline in the 1870s and 80s may also have been responsible for the demise of the gunpowder works.

In essence, although Dartmoor abounds in natural resources, when it came to commercial operations to exploit them those resources were either not plentiful enough or could not be harvested economically enough to fulfil the over-optimistic and often wholly unrealistic expectations of the entrepreneurs who had invested their cash.

14

Security and defence
in the modern period

Context

No issue on Dartmoor has caused more consternation among conservationists than the continuing presence of military training, which many consider an inappropriate activity within a national park. Yet ironically, several of the monuments that are protected and cherished within Dartmoor National Park have their origins in military behaviour and conflict, giving rise to the need for organised military responses to threats. The impact of these activities and the resulting artefacts provide an important dimension to our understanding of Dartmoor's landscape and how past human activity is manifest within it.

Permanent reminders of human response to social disharmony in the past are everywhere in a landscape such as Dartmoor's and its environs. The emergence of small independent communities created a need by some, or at least a perceived need, for defence, and resulted in the building of hillforts in the late prehistoric period. In the 9th-century AD Alfred built the *burh* at Lydford as a defence against Viking raids, and indeed, it saw action serving that purpose in 997. By the Middle Ages timber, stone and earth castles were constructed at several places. Although they were not always necessarily built to be exclusively defensive, for they were also designed to project the strength of the individuals who occupied them, their existence is rooted in discordance and rivalry among human groups. The threat of invasion by sea has always been a key element in Britain's coastal archaeology since Roman times, but Dartmoor is far enough from the coast not to possess permanent evidence of such episodes. However, medieval and Tudor fire-beacon networks took advantage of Dartmoor's high vantage points, and several

sites associated with beacons, especially along the southern escarpment, include Ugborough Beacon and Penn Beacon (Russell 1955, 265–6).

As Britain began to play a greater role in European and then global conflicts, armies needed to be trained in readiness, and during the late 19th century the professionalisation of the army and the reorganisation of local territorial forces, coupled with increased fire power, meant that large training areas were needed. Dartmoor, with its open spaces and low population, provided an ideal location. Manoeuvres commenced on Roborough Down in 1853 and soon afterwards the military established a more permanent presence on Dartmoor, setting up army camps and ranges at Okehampton in the 1890s and at Willsworthy in the early 20th century. In the early days of this military presence, the moors were favoured for their low population, which allowed the firing of small-arms for target practice with relative safety, although it was not long before artillery was being used as well, and for which Okehampton Range was specifically created. Later, the arduous conditions sometimes presented by the uplands were seen as an ideal landscape for character-building and endurance for soldiers, in preparation for the terrains and weather they might encounter in conflict zones.

Twentieth-century conflicts have also left their mark on Dartmoor. During both world wars training on Dartmoor was intensified, particularly in the Second World War (1939–45) when much of the north moor was requisitioned by the War Department and used by the allied forces in preparation for D-Day in 1944. Glider poles and anti-aircraft defences, including decoy aerodromes and searchlights batteries, all played their part in defending the West Country from the threat of Nazi aggression.

Traces of Cold War defences are also to be found on Dartmoor, where several underground monitoring posts were built to detect the effects of nuclear explosions.

Whatever the future holds for military activity within Dartmoor National Park, the material evidence from its past, including more recent periods of training on the moors, are now an important component of Dartmoor's human landscape. Despite past efforts by some conservation groups to see this evidence erased, surviving artefacts are now valued as part of the Dartmoor story and in management terms are treated like any other archaeological site. Military remains on Dartmoor have not previously been considered in any mainstream archaeological work, although recording of the artefacts has been occurring for more than a decade. The following descriptions are the first time the remains of military training have been integrated into a general study of Dartmoor's historic landscape.

Military Training Areas (MTAs)

According to William Crossing the earliest encampment of troops on Dartmoor was on Hemerdon Ball in the early 19th century, at a time when an invasion by Napoleon was feared. Crossing, however, provides no detail of the event (Le Messurier 1966, 97).

An early indication of how valued the open spaces and low population on Dartmoor was considered, especially for artillery, occurred in June and July 1869, when an artillery exercise took place at Hartor, west of Princetown. It was recorded in newspaper articles of the time (*WM* 23 June 1869 to 17 July 1869) that several artillery pieces were set up near the road as it exits the west side of Princetown, and used to bombard a series of temporary trenches and emplacements – complete with wooden cut-outs of soldiers – on Hartor, and the area surrounding it. The aim of the exercise was to compare the effectiveness of various types of artillery shells available at the time.

This exercise was a major operation involving Royal Engineers, who dug the temporary entrenchments, and a tented encampment near the road to accommodate the troops. However, it is surprising how little surface evidence of this event survives, even though the trenches and gun pits were said to be up to 2ft 6in (0.82m) deep and Hartor, itself

was fortified with turf-covered walls containing loopholes. It seems likely that the army was required to clean up the evidence upon completion of the tests and all that can be identified today is a limited number of small shell craters north-east of the tor. If so, then this is an early example of how the fragile evidence of military activity has been so easily erased at many places on Dartmoor.

A little north of Hartor are the remnants of a rifle range, comprising a target butt and a series of inscribed stone distance markers. Their date is unknown. They are not associated with the operation described above and the traditional belief is that they were used by prison guards to improve their marksmanship, although this interpretation has been questioned (Gerrard 1998, 24–5). This range certainly existed in 1884 when depicted on the OS 1st edition 25-inch map.

Large-scale military training exercises took place on at least two known occasions during the later 19th century on south-west Dartmoor: the so-called 'Autumn Manoeuvres' in 1853 and 1873. Tented camps were set up on Yennadon, Wigford Down and Saddlesborough with a headquarters established on Roborough Down, while the action took place on Ringmoor Down. Some excellent photographs and a series of wood engravings of the 1873 event survive and have been published, showing officers and men engaged in various activities (Le Messurier 1966; Greeves 2004b; Gray 2001). These activities cannot be detected archaeologically, so the survival of these images is of particular importance.

Contemporary photographs also survive showing an annual encampment on Haytor Downs on south-east Dartmoor between 1884 and at least 1900 (Le Messurier 1967, 145), where the volunteer battalions of the Devonshire Regiment participated in eight days of instruction. Again, this episode has left little field evidence, although a rectangular earthwork terrace on the north side of the Saddle Tor outcrop is the likely site of a marquee visible on one of the photographs and may have been the venue where, according to William Crossing, the Ashburton hand bell ringers entertained the troops. By 1900 these encampments were said to last for a full month, with 3,500 troops mustered, and to involve complicated logistics, including a hospital, post office and transport office (Le Messurier 1966, 102).

Fig 14.1
Aerial view of Okehampton
Battle Camp (NMR
24681/034; © English
Heritage. NMR).

By the 1870s, the army was in search of a suitable location to train gunners in the use of field artillery. After a visit to Okehampton by two members of the committee appointed to the task in 1875, partly at the suggestion of the town clerk, they agreed to establish a practice camp in Okehampton Park, south of the town. The site was well suited to the purpose, with good flat camping ground and a plentiful water supply, and a location close to Okehampton Railway Station. Most important perhaps, the adjacent high moorland areas were well suited to the purpose of an artillery range, comprising predominantly moorland with apparently little farming activity and no population, with the exception of one farm at East Okement. Thus Okehampton Range became the British Army's first purpose built artillery range.

The first of a series of annual events took place in 1876, when Royal Artillery units pitched a temporary camp. Later, as a result of various Acts of Parliament, the War Department was able to acquire the land it needed and by 1892 a permanent camp (Fig 14.1) was established and the north quarter of Dartmoor Forest was taken as an artillery range under

licence from the Duchy of Cornwall (Wessex 2001, 13). It eventually occupied 6,180ha. From this period Okehampton Range was used for approximately five months every summer, when artillery units from all over Britain would arrive on the train at Okehampton Station equipped with their guns, limbers and teams of horses (*see* Fig 14.6). The camp at Okehampton was never intended to be used as a permanent barracks, and accommodation for the ranks was in tents on flat fields south of the main complex and on a series of terraces within the camp. The permanent buildings contained the infrastructure necessary for the visiting units. The first of the surviving buildings to be erected was the stable for officers' horses, but a number of other essential buildings, built of stone and brick – including officer accommodation, the hospital and several lesser structures – were in existence by 1899. Although the camp has since been continuously added to and refurbished, many 1890s structures survive (Wessex 2001, fig 4).

Between 1908 and 1912 the War Office consolidated their hold on Dartmoor and augmented their training area through the

purchase of 3,200 acres (1,450ha) of land at Willsworthy on the western side of the moor. The purchase included Reddaford Farm, from which the tenants were removed in 1907 (Greeves 2007). The farm now lies in ruins as a consequence of the military's arrival. Because Willsworthy was purchased by the War Department rather than leased or licensed, the perimeter of the estate is marked by a series of boundary stones inscribed with the letters WD and with individual numbers (Fig 14.2). The Willsworthy firing range was never used for artillery, but it contains a number of rifle ranges, some now disused. The original Willsworthy camp has been demolished in favour of a new building at Horndon.

In total there are five training areas still in use within Dartmoor National Park (Fig 14.3): the two original camps at Okehampton (6,180ha) and Willsworthy (1,450ha), plus Merrivale (3,319ha), Cramber Tor (841ha) and Ringmoor Down (610ha), added latter. Of these, only the first three have been, and still are, used for live firing. The others are what is known as 'dry training' areas, where live ammunition cannot be used and where other forms of battlefield training have taken place. Only Willsworthy is owned by the Ministry of Defence (MOD); others are licensed from their landowners, which includes the Duchy of Cornwall. The total area used by the military was substantially reduced after the Second World War, during which period the War Office had acquired through ownership, lease, licence or requisition, more than 31,00ha of Dartmoor moorland. By 1948, largely as a result of a Public Inquiry, land holdings were reduced to 15,160ha. An additional former rifle range with extensive structural remains of shooting butts, now disused, survives on Rushslade Common, within private land on the south-east side of the moor.

Firing ranges: field evidence

Archaeological investigations within Okehampton Training Area (Francis 2002) have revealed a continuous cycle of change. As new weapons were introduced and older systems withdrawn from service, the character of the firing range and its various installations has altered. Thus the range developed from its original purpose of artillery practice, to include rifle ranges and later to accommodate anti-tank weapons as the artillery moved elsewhere in Britain. Finally, in more recent years the use of fixed target ranges has been confined to Willsworthy range; all the permanent installations on Okehampton have effectively become disused as the range was developed for other battlefield training. The evidence for most of these former uses can be divided into four categories: target positions, including target railways for moving targets and mechanisms for 'disappearing' targets; weapons positions, particularly for anti-tank training; observation posts; infrastructure, including field telephone systems and signalling. Also, it is important to note that the entire network of metalled and un-metalled roads within Okehampton Training Area owe their existence to the arrival of the firing ranges, and were well established before the publication of the first edition OS 25-inch map of 1885. Before that time the central areas of north Dartmoor were only accessible on foot or on horseback.

The most noticeable legacy of Okehampton range is the surviving splinter-proof observation posts, or OPs, which were associated with the use of the range for artillery. These structures,

as their name suggests, were used by observers to spot the accuracy of the gunnery and relay the results back to the batteries. They were sited to provide a good field of view over the target area. Their robust construction reflects the fact that they were sited between the guns and the targets. The installation date for each OP is not known but their construction is thought to have begun in the early 20th century. There were once 22 OPs, but after becoming disused many were demolished and only seven remain standing; others are now turf covered rubble or foundations. Each of the surviving OPs has a unique design, although OPs 15 (Fig 14.4) and 17 are very similar. The largest OP is No. 22 (Fig 14.5), sited beside the ring-road near East Okement Farm. Its construction date was recorded as 1924, and it was specifically installed for officers under training, although the structure was later altered.

The construction methods of the surviving OPs varies, but each comprises a rectangular chamber surrounded by reinforcing materials that could resist the impact of a hit from an artillery shell, should the occasion arise. At the front of the structure, facing away from the

Fig 14.2 (opposite, top)
A boundary stone at Willsworthy bearing the inscription WD for War Department, one of a series of stones that define the boundary of Willsworthy Training Area (photo: Simon Probert).

Fig 14.3 (opposite, bottom)
Map of Dartmoor National Park showing the locations of the military training areas currently in use.

Fig 14.4
Observation post (OP15) at Okement Hill within the Okehampton Training Area (NMR AA011985; © English Heritage. NMR).

Fig 14.5
Observation post (OP22) near East Okement Farm within Okehampton Training Area (NMR AA011982; © English Heritage. NMR).

battery, a narrow horizontal opening enabled the observers to view the target area. The smaller OPs had no doors and entry was by climbing over the concrete half-walls that formed the fronts, with iron rungs embedded into the concrete to serve as steps. Some were constructed mostly from stone, but include several other materials, such as concrete and steel. Others are made entirely from concrete reinforced with steel. Surviving OP 3 at Curtery Clitters was constructed around a timber frame and a timber-lined chamber. All the surviving OPs were reinforced with stone facings on the exteriors and were embanked with earth, which today is topped by a turf.

The other major installations for which evidence survives in the firing ranges are the target areas, both for rifle training and for artillery practice (Fig 14.6). Moving and disappearing targets, usually plywood cut outs of soldiers, used mechanisms concealed in long trenches whereby the targets could either move along in a straight line or pop up and disappear. The mechanisms have usually been removed but in one or two cases some ironwork survives. Good examples may be seen on Willsworthy range, where bunker positions for the operator of the mechanism also survive. Many moving targets, particularly those for artillery and anti-tank weapons, ran on small railways, either pulled by static engines at one end or by self-propelled target carriers. Although occasionally the iron tracks survive *in situ* (Fig 14.7), often partly turf-covered, most target railways survive as shallow, flat-bottomed linear cuttings from which the ironwork has

been removed. One of the clearest of these runs in a straight line for 970m, approximately north–south along Black Hill. This range is likely to have been in use for artillery from 1907, but later may have been used by infantry with light anti-tank weapons, probably during the Second World War (Francis 2002).

The shed at the end of the cutting, which accommodated the target carrier, and other associated features have all been demolished. In the East Okement Valley, south of the farm, there is a particularly fine target railway associated with the early use of artillery. This has the remains of a robust concrete shed, used to house the target carrier, earth-banked to protect it from stray rounds. It was later adapted to become an observation post, now known as OP 6. On exiting the shed, the railway takes a U turn then continues north for *c* 900m and comprises a substantial cutting averaging 2.8m wide × 1.8m deep. This is likely to be one of the oldest target railways in Okehampton training area and was, like the example on Black Hill, first recorded on a War Department map of 1907. The motive power is not recorded but it may have moved using gravity alone, then was pulled back uphill using ponies.

One of the clearest surviving static target range layouts is the 'H' range anti-tank area on the northern crest of Row Tor. These are among the later emplacements and date to *c* 1969, to accommodate 94mm medium anti-tank weapons (Francis 2002). At the north end of the range, beside the track, there are two bays comprising timber-lined earthen banks sitting on concrete platforms with earth-banked sides,

Fig 14.6
An early postcard view of artillery practice on Okehampton Range, probably in the period before the First World War. The guns are positioned to the west of Okement Farm. Irishman's Wall can be seen running down the west side of Belstone Tor in the background.

Fig 14.7
A target railway on
Okehampton Training Area
at Black Down, with iron
rails and points in situ
(NMR AA011993;
©English Heritage. NMR).

where the weapons were housed. There is also a smaller officers' observation position of similar construction. Both buildings provided protection when the weapons were fired. Approximately 310m to the south is a high earth embankment where the static targets were set. These were large steel plates propped in front of the bank, one of which survives *in situ*. A pair of weapons emplacements of similar, though smaller, design survive on the north end of Black Down; these were used for training with smaller anti-tank weapons, including rocket-propelled missiles from the tube-launched light anti-tank weapon (LAW).

Of interest within Okehampton Training Area are several earthwork redoubts and trenches, some of which are believed to be experimental types that were being developed possibly during the period between the Boer War (1899–1902) and the First World War (1914–18). A magazine article of May 1908 mentioned that near Okehampton Camp, apart from 'their usual course of practice on the moor

… some important experimental work is being carried out' (*Devonia Magazine* 1908, **8.5**, 115). Most of these are sited on the slopes of East Mill Tor, including several semicircular defensive banks, some of which are described as 'infantry redoubts' on the War Department map of 1907. They have been severely damaged by shellfire and have clearly served as targets at sometime. Also on the 1907 map is a series of four deep, linear trenches with embanked parapets, sited on the northern crest of the tor. These were described as 'experimental parapets' on the map of 1907 and may have been to test the effect of artillery on infantry trenches. A similar set of experiments was carried out on the artillery ranges on Salisbury Plain (McOmish *et al* 2002, 142).

More trench earthworks have been noted near the disused quarry hollow north of Rowtor (Fig 14.8). Although backfilled and in some cases badly damaged, their outlines are clear and can be recognised as being of standard layouts for front-line trenches of the First

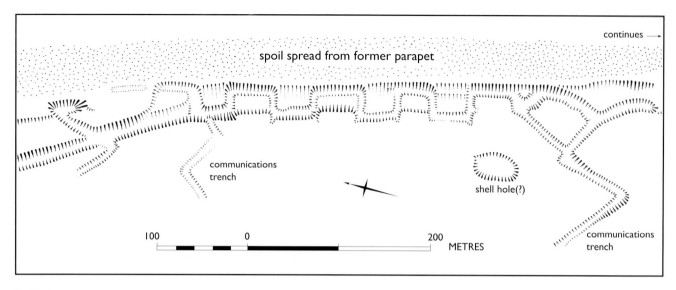

Fig 14.8
Earthwork plan of First World War 'practice' trenches north-west of Hartor Hill within Okehampton training area.

World War, as described in army manuals such as *British Trench Warfare 1917–1918* (War Office). One is a recessed, trench 100m long and has a crenellated plan, preserving the outlines of the main trench and the recessed firing positions, 3.5m to 4m wide at 9m intervals. There are also a number of smaller discrete trenches to the south, which resemble sections of support trenches (ie zigzag-shaped with three trenches emanating from a central junction). On the Western Front these two types would have been used together as part of a trench layout. There is no record of when these features were dug, but it is possible that the remains represent a site where men trained in trench digging before being sent to the front; or possibly these trenches were also experimental, slightly pre-dating the First World War. Training trenches of this type are characteristic of Britain's military training areas: examples are known from Salisbury Plain, Wiltshire, (Brown and Field 2007, 170–80), and the Otterburn Ranges in Northumberland (Nicol and Brown 2006), among others.

The Second World War (1939–45) and the Cold War

During the Second World War Dartmoor played a major part in the training of allied forces from several nations. Given its proximity to the major naval dockyard at Plymouth, it also had a role in the defence against aerial attack and the potential threat of invasion by airborne forces. The most notable feature of the landscape associated with this period is Harrowbeer Airfield on Roborough Down. This has not yet been archaeologically surveyed, but it is known to have many fine surviving features. Airfields of this period fall into in a number of distinctive types, dependent on their function and whether or not they were conceived as permanent or temporary stations. Local topography determined their exact layout, but all were built using a standard set of components, including hangars, control towers, aircraft dispersal areas and anti-aircraft defences (English Heritage 2003).

Although at Harrowbeer the runways have been removed, many of the hard-standing areas where temporary buildings stood are still visible and the control tower survives incorporated into a private dwelling. Particularly notable are the 12 aircraft dispersal bays, capable of housing up to 24 fighter aircraft. They comprise well defined, roughly curved, semi-circular earthen banks with a single straight bank dividing the interior of the arc into two bays. The banks were to protect the aircraft from the blast of any bombs that fell near by. At the T-junction of the banks, a partly sunken, prefabricated structures accommodated the crews during air raids, although these are currently not accessible. These dispersal bays are a common feature of Second World War fighter airfields, but it is less common to find examples of all of them at a single airfield surviving and in such good preservation.

At least three bombing decoys were set up on Dartmoor in about 1941: at Shapley Tor, at Hillson's House and on Roborough Down. The last, of a type known as a 'Q' site, dates from 1941 and displayed a sequence of lights to simulate the night-time appearance from the air of an active aerodrome (Dobinson 1996). The lamps were mounted on raised concrete bases, many of which survive, and their locations have recently been re-discovered by local enthusiasts after vegetation clearance (inf. from RAF Harrowbeer Interest Group). This represents an extremely rare survival for this type of evidence.

On Hameldown, near the head of Grimslake, a number of decayed timber posts represent the remarkable survival of Second World War defences against an airborne invasion using gliders (Fig 14.9). The remaining poles are set out in lines across the fairly flat and featureless upper reaches of Hameldown, which, because of its expanse, was perceived as a suitable place to land gliders laden with troops as part of an airborne invasion. Only the core timber of these once substantial poles survives. Elsewhere on Dartmoor, similar though isolated poles have been recorded on Holne Moor and Thornworthy Down, which may have served the same purpose; if so, these must have been a common sight on the flatter open spaces of the moor.

On Peek Hill, on south-west Dartmoor, there are the earthwork and concrete remains of a range of air defensive activities established from 1942 onward, and which continued to be operated into the post-war and Cold War period. The site is poorly represented on contemporary Ordnance Survey maps, even in the 1950s when they were most active, possibly because the installations were considered confidential. These subtle field remains are the main evidence of their existence. Peek Hill is a high shelf with a small outcrop that provides clear views in most directions, but particularly to the south-west towards Plymouth and its dockyard. A concrete foundation survives on a natural mound, upon which stood a prefabricated structure known as an Orlit, since demolished. From here the Royal Observer Corps (ROC) crew could spot enemy aircraft using basic optical equipment. Although the surviving evidence probably dates from the early 1950s it is likely to have been located near the site of a wartime predecessor. A few metres away is an underground monitoring post or bunker, also used by the ROC, but constructed in 1956 to record nuclear bomb blasts and the drift of fallout, should such a

weapon ever have been used against Britain. It is one of several that once existed around Dartmoor, although most have been demolished. This example remained in use until 1991 (inf *Subterranea Britannia* database). It comprises a flat-topped rectangular earth mound encasing a partly sunken concrete bunker. These structures were often concealed below ground, but here the local geology probably prevented this. Access was down a vertical shaft with a raised hatch. The position of the hatch and the two air vents are still visible, although blocked off since abandonment. The standard three-man ROC bunker had two rooms, the larger monitoring room being 4.6m × 2.3m. This unassuming mound serves as a chilling reminder that even a tranquil place such as Dartmoor would not have been unaffected had the worst happened during the Cold War.

Just north of the observer post are the scant remains of RAF Sharpitor, a transmitting station established early in the Second World

Fig 14.9
Anti-glider poles on Hameldown (NMR AA045893; © English Heritage. NMR).

War as part of the Gee Chain. This was a radio navigation system used to guide British bombers on missions to occupied Europe. Sharpitor served as the master station of the south-west part of the chain. Under planning conditions laid down in 1956, when the transmitter was upgraded, the site, which was always considered temporary, had to be demolished upon abandonment and the moorland reclaimed. This was carried out to great effect in 1970 following closure, although ghostly outlines of many of the buildings survive and the layout is clear. The main feature of the installation was a 64m (210ft) tall wooden tower, which stood just to one side of the outcrop. This was replaced by a steel version as part of the 1956 upgrade, but it has since been removed. The foundations of a number of temporary buildings are located just to the north, including Nissen huts. These sat on low brick foundations, still visible in places although turf covered. North-west of the technical site is an array of similar foundations for temporary huts to accommodate the unit of up to 36 personnel, including housing, guardroom, cookhouse, canteen recreation room and other facilities. Wilkinson (1996) describes the activities and day-to-day life of the personnel sent to operate this remote

outpost. Despite more than 25 years of military activity on Peek Hill, today the visitor needs to look very hard to find the material remains, so thoroughly has the site been erased.

At Hawk's Tor, close to Beatland Corner on the south-west edge of the moors, another Second World War installation has suffered less thorough demolition. This was the site of a transmitter station, which formed part of the Chain Home RDF system, later known as radar (Fig 14.10). It worked on a similar principle to Gee, but was used to detect approaching enemy aircraft. The Hawks Tor transmitter, number CH15M in the chain, comprised two tall timber or steel masts, resembling modern electrical pylons. The masts may have been up to 360ft (120m) tall and at Hawks Tor they were 75m apart. Each mast was mounted on four flat-topped concrete pedestals and both sets of four survive in place at this site (Fig 14.11). In front and just below each mast position is the remains of the transmitter block, a concrete bunker covered with earth for protection from aerial attack. These have been demolished by explosives, though not removed, and survive as disturbed mounds with vestiges of exposed concrete. On the north-west side of the site lie the concrete bases of administration buildings and a guard room. There are also air raid

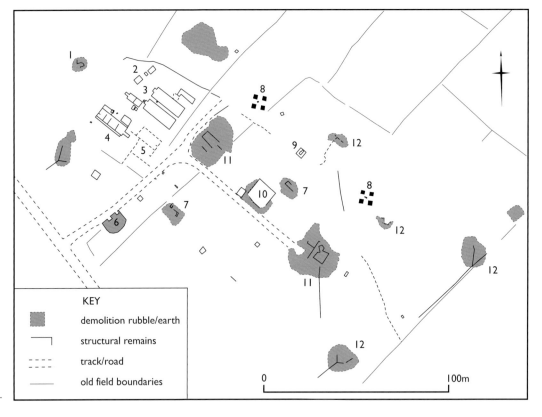

Fig 14.10
Plan of Hawk's Tor Chain Home RTF station.
The ruins include Nissen hut bases and demolished earth-covered bunkers: 1, gun emplacement; 2, toilets; 3, administration building; 4, guard rooms; 5, dog pens; 6, guard hut; 7, air raid shelter; 8, mast base; 9, generator base; 10, duty room; 11, transmitter/receiver block; 12, slit trench.

KEY

demolition rubble/earth

structural remains

track/road

old field boundaries

0   100m

Fig 14.11
One of two sets of concrete
plinths at Hawk's Tor,
which supported one of
the transmitter towers
(photo: Phil Newman).

shelters and a probable gun emplacement. All the main buildings are linked together by a much decayed metalled road.

Smaller reminders of Second World War allied training are also widespread on the open moors. Small circular mortar emplacements, sometimes so perfectly formed as to mislead OS surveyors into recording them as hut circles, survive in several places, but are particularly numerous around Roos Tor and Beckamoor Combe. The earthworks are usually circular (*c* 3–4m in diameter), but sometimes more irregular, each comprising a level hollow surrounded by a bank. On the exterior can be found between one and three small rectangular pits in which ammunition was stored. A particularly clear example survives near Haytor Quarry (*see* Fig 10.7) – a place where American troops are known to have trained – where the circular earthwork was built beside a disused enclosure. A cluster of small craters 150m to the east appear to represent one of the target zones.

Pits at a number of locations can probably be explained as bomb craters from enemy aircraft either missing their target or jettisoning bombs. Straddling the slope of Crownhill Down is an evenly-spaced line of four conical pits of up to 2m deep, whose lack of a spoil heap rules them out as mine shafts. Others have been observed between Legis Tor and Gutter Tor and to the north of Black Tor (Meavy).

Finally, slit trenches, or foxholes, are a common feature over much of Dartmoor where military training has taken place during the past century, but most are likely to date from the Second World War, when large areas of moorland were used for training. These features represent a standard battlefield technique used by infantry to 'dig in', whereby soldiers excavated a small, temporary trench in which they could take cover. The evidence, though sometimes slightly silted up, comprises a rectangular trench *c* 0.5–1m wide × 1.5–2m long with a low bank, formed from the material removed, along one side.

Conclusion

The material evidence of military activity on Dartmoor is seldom spectacular, and has frequently been partly demolished, or in some cases levelled. These 20th-century remains have inspired little emotion or interest among those who have written so exhaustively and enthusiastically about Dartmoor's landscape and heritage in recent years. Nevertheless, a military presence has been part of this landscape since at least the 1850s, and with that comes tradition and heritage. The field archaeology associated with more than 150 years of military activity is now very much a part of the Dartmoor story. An awareness and appreciation of the fact that these artefacts and monuments bear witness to the presence of the many service personnel sent to Dartmoor for peacetime training, or to prepare for the First World War trenches in 1914–18, the Normandy invasions in 1944 and modern conflicts of the 21st century, hopefully means they are less likely to become further erased as a result of the desire for tidiness.

15

Conclusion: Dartmoor's archaeology in the 21st century

In this book the development of Dartmoor's human landscape has been examined, recorded and analysed through the archaeological and historical tools at our disposal. Incomplete though our data are, one major conclusion has to be that, far from being a wilderness, Dartmoor is a landscape whose modern appearance owes a great deal to past human intervention.

There are several upland districts in Britain, including Dartmoor, that are considered in today's terms as on the margins of agricultural viability, owing to their altitude and climate. As a result, episodes of human activity have been less rapid in their succession and less intense in terms of the physical changes they wrought. One outcome of these circumstances is that activities associated with later episodes have been generally less destructive of the field evidence from that of earlier times, compared with more intensively farmed, urbanised or industrialised areas of the country, where change was more rapid and profound.

On Dartmoor these factors have influenced the survival of chronologically distinct categories, or layers, of archaeological evidence and left them to accumulate over considerable periods of time. As we have seen, people have colonised, settled, adapted and exploited the land and the natural resources of Dartmoor for more than five and a half millennia. This means that for the modern resident, visitor or researcher, experiencing Dartmoor involves not only the latest phase of its human story, but also many aspects of its remote past. This broad vista across the past, which close examination or even casual observation of Dartmoor can provide, places it among the most culturally important landscapes in the United Kingdom, rightly protected under National Park designation.

Naturally, for such an important and cherished place, the decisions concerning conservation and protection need to be based on sound

knowledge, and those involved in that process have to be in possession of the information they need to fulfil their roles. Providing accurate information for those who manage the landscape is therefore one the major direct benefits of archaeological investigation.

A more indirect reward comes from the constant renewal of ideas, research themes and interpretations, which, when thoughtfully disseminated, provide a source of great interest to the public, who in turn may be inspired to find out more themselves. In so doing, more people develop a strong affinity for the archaeology and value it enough to support and expect its further protection and the need for greater understanding.

So, whatever we perceive the benefits to be, the study of Dartmoor's archaeology will continue, as new people with modern methods and fresh ideas shine further light on this superlative resource: there is still much to discover. At the time of going to press archaeological work in progress on Dartmoor, or awaiting publication, includes recent excavations within hut circles at Bellever (Hughes 2009) and at Kestor. Both will provide much needed dating evidence for domestic sites of the 2nd millennium BC, from ceramic finds and radiocarbon dates, which have been so lacking. At Kestor, crucial information about the effect of bracken growth on Dartmoor's archaeological deposits is also being explored (Gerrard 2007).

Of particular current interest is the role of peat as an influential environmental component in understanding the past on Dartmoor. The recent recognition of a fallen stone row, sitting on the old land surface of Cut Hill (Fyfe and Greeves 2010), demonstrates the possibilities for discovery of further prehistoric material under the peat of the central uplands. This site was overwhelmed by peat in later prehistoric times, but erosion in the more recent past revealed it. Dartmoor is renowned for its spectacular upstanding archaeology, but this reminds us of the potential for a whole hidden world of archaeological material buried beneath the peat. It has also demonstrated how the intrusion of peat altered both the natural environment of Dartmoor and the human response, as the higher ground, where peat is predominant, has long been devoid of any permanent human presence. The peat is also beginning to release other secrets through new programmes of palynological work looking at pollens and organic material trapped within it, which provides much information about the environment in the past. As to the peat as a resource for fuel in medieval and later times, and a subject of entrepreneurial speculation in the 19th century, work that has just started will also bring light to bear on this neglected topic (Newman 2010).

But as we generate more information, more questions arise and there are many potentially rewarding lines of enquiry that future researches may wish to address on Dartmoor, of which the following would be just a start. Among the earliest enigmas yet to be solved are the enclosures on Dewerstone and Whittor, of which we know practically nothing other than their similarity with sites elsewhere in the region for which Neolithic dates have been established; apart from the uncertainty of Dewerstone's and Whittor's dating, their function also remains within the domain of the theorist.

For the 2nd millennium BC we need to know much more about the relationship of the sepulchral and so called 'ritual' monuments, such as stone circles and rows, with the domestic settlements and reaves; the lack of modern excavations of barrows and the resulting lack of dates needs to be addressed. There is also the problem of what exactly was occurring on Dartmoor in the early to mid-1st millennium BC. Does the absence of evidence really equate to evidence of absence? As archaeologists begin to recognise more material from this period, perhaps more will come to light? Then, for the later 1st millennium BC, the Dartmoor hillforts are practically untapped by modern archaeological techniques, as is the case for much of the rest of Devon, with the exception perhaps of Hembury in east Devon. From a landscape perspective, the relationship of Dartmoor's hillforts to the upland and the context for their peripheral locations is still largely unexplained. Also, the prehistoric

landscape of Dartmoor should not be considered an isolated entity in terms of Devon's regional archaeology – it needs to be integrated into the study of prehistory in Devon as a whole and of the entire south-west peninsula.

For the medieval period, the archaeological data are less sparse and are enhanced by the information from documents. Excavations of domestic sites using modern techniques have also been more numerous than for prehistoric houses. However, although the modern landscape of Dartmoor was fashioned from this period onwards, uncertainty still prevails as to when colonisation and permanent settlement began, and how the process advanced. A full and integrated landscape project, embracing medieval settlement, agricultural land use and industry, has yet to be done on Dartmoor, but would certainly prove hugely rewarding in the same way that Fleming's research into the reaves so enhanced our understanding of Dartmoor in the 2nd millennium BC (Fleming 2008).

Likewise for tinworking. If we are to fully appreciate its importance, further landscape survey will be essential to establish just how extensive the medieval industry was, particularly in the enclosed lands and woodlands that surround the upland, where survey has barely started. Tinworking has in the past been considered separately to the other facets of the medieval and post-medieval landscape on Dartmoor, researchers often focussing only on smelting and dressing; but the fact that tinners and settler-farmers shared this land needs to be integrated into future studies to benefit the study of both, as has been demonstrated on Bodmin Moor (Austin et al 1989).

Within the discipline of industrial archaeology in Britain, in the past decade there have been major changes in approach. The importance of recording machines and processes as the primary purpose of the discipline has made way for studying industrial sites and landscapes as a means of understanding the historic and social context for change (Gwyne and Palmer 2005). Few of Dartmoor's late 18th- to 20th-century industries have been the subject of anything beyond precursory investigations by field archaeologists. Mines, quarries and clay pits all have potential as research topics. Much could be gained if Dartmoor were to be the subject of an industrial landscape study to look both at the extractive industries and at improver farming as an expression of

18th- and 19th-century capitalism in conflict with the customary rights of the traditional inhabitants – a period made all the more interesting by the emergence of the preservation movement of the later 19th century.

Beyond the fascination of these more ambitious research aims, there is still the pressing need to apply basic recording principles to many aspects of Dartmoor's archaeology for the purposes of management and protection, as outlined above. Whereas the uplands have been more thoroughly examined by archaeologists, the woodlands and pastures of the peripheries have been subject to less intense investigation. This needs to be addressed if the relationship between these two areas is to be better understood.

Finally, this book has examined a great deal of archaeological evidence and has encouraged the reader to try to appreciate the modern landscape through consideration of its material past. But in cultural terms, we should not perceive Dartmoor as a place filled only with relics of the past; it is a working landscape and indeed the survival of its past depends on attitudes towards its management in the present and in the future. The survival of hill farming and the continuation of this traditional style of management must be high on our agenda, if we are to continue exploring, experiencing and enjoying the field archaeology of Dartmoor.

REFERENCES

Abbreviations

Bar Comm Report of the Barrow Committee in *Report and Transactions of the Devonshire Association*

DC Daily Courant (newspaper)

DEC Report of the Dartmoor Exploration Committee in *Report and Transactions of the Devonshire Association*

DNPA Dartmoor National Park Authority

DRO – Devon Record Office

OS Ordnance Survey

RCHME Royal Commission on the Historical Monuments of England

WM Western Mail (newspaper)

Addyman, P 1997 *The Saxon Town and Medieval Castles at Lydford, Devon.* Unpubl leaflet from a 'Viking' conference held at Tavistock

Alcock, L 1972 *'By South Cadbury is that Camelot …' Excavations at Cadbury Castle 1966–70.* London: Thames and Hudson

Allan, J 1994 'Medieval pottery and the dating of deserted settlements on Dartmoor'. *Proc Devon Archaeol Soc* **52**, 141–7

Amery Adams, W 1946 'The Old Haytor Granite Tramway'. *Rep Trans Devonshire Assoc* **78**, 153–60

Amesbury, M J, Charman, D J and Fyfe, R 2008 'Bronze Age upland settlement decline in southwest England: testing the climate change hypothesis'. *J Archaeol Science* **35.1**, 87–98

Anon 1671 'An accompt of some mineral observations touching the mines of Cornwall and Devon'. *Philosoph Trans* **69**, 2096–113

Anon 2003 *The Ball Clays of Devon and Dorset.* Newton Abbot: Ball Clay Heritage Soc

Armitage, E 1912 *The Early Norman Castles of the British Isles.* London: J Murray

Austin, D 1978 'Excavations at Okehampton Deer Park, Devon 1976–1978'. *Proc Devon Archaeol Soc* **36**, 191–240

Austin, D 1985 'Dartmoor and the upland villages of the south-west of England', *in* Hooke, D (ed) *Medieval Villages: A Review of Current Work.* Oxford Univ Arch Comm Monogr **5**, 71–9

Austin, D, Gerrard, G A M and Greeves, T A P 1989 'Tin and agriculture in the Middle Ages and beyond: landscape archaeology in St Neot Parish, Cornwall'. *Cornish Archaeol* **28**, 5–251

Bahn, P 1996 *The Cambridge Illustrated History of Archaeology.* Cambridge: Cambridge Univ P

Baring-Gould, S 1900 *A Book of Dartmoor.* London: Methuen

Barnatt, J 1982 *Prehistoric Cornwall: The Ceremonial Monuments.* Northants: Turnstone

Barnatt, J 1989 *Stone Circles of Britain.* Oxford: BAR Brit Ser **215**

Barnatt, J and Smith K 1997 *Peak District.* London: Batsford

Barrett, J C, Freeman P W M and Woodward, A 2000 *Cadbury Castle Somerset: the Late Prehistoric and Early Historic Archaeology.* English Heritage: London

Bate, C S 1871 'On the prehistoric antiquities of Dartmoor'. *Rep Trans Devonshire Assoc* **4**, 491–515

Bate, C Spence 1872 'Researches into some ancient tumuli on Dartmoor'. *Rep Trans Devonshire Assoc* **5**, 549–57

Belcher, M N and Birchell, R G G 2008 *Geophysical Survey Carried Out at Lydford, Devon.* Unpubl report, SiteScan

Beresford, G 1979 'Three deserted settlements on Dartmoor: a report on the late E Marie Minter's Excavations'. *Medieval Archaeol* **23**, 98–158

Blake, W J 1915 'Hooker's synopsis chorographical of Devonshire'. *Rep Trans Devonshire Assoc* **47**, 334–48

Bonney, D 1971 'Former farms and fields at Challacombe, Manaton, Dartmoor', *in* Gregory, K J and Ravenhill, W (eds) *Exeter Essays in Geography. Exeter*: Exeter Univ P, 83–91

Borlase, W 1758 *The Natural History of Cornwall.* Oxford: Jackson

Bowden, M, Mackay, D and Topping, P 1989 *From Cornwall to Caithnes: Some Aspects of British Field Archaeology. Papers presented to N V Quinnell.* Oxford: BAR Brit Ser **209**.

Bowden, M 1991 *Pitt-Rivers: the Life and Archaeological Work of Lieutenant-General Augustus Henry Lane Fox Pitt Rivers, DCL, FRS, FSA.* Cambridge: Cambridge Univ P

Bradley, R 1998 *The Significance of Monuments.* London: Routledge

Bradley, R 2007 *The Prehistory of Britain and Ireland.* Cambridge: Cambridge Univ P

Brailsford, J W 1938a 'Bronze Age stone monuments of Dartmoor'. *Antiquity* **12**, 444–63

Brailsford, J W 1938b 'Excavations at the promontory fort near Okehampton Station'. *Proc Devon Archaeol Soc* **3**, 86–91

Bray, A E 1879 *The Borders of the Tamar and Tavy* (3rd edn). London: Kent

Brooke, J (trans) 2001 *The Kalmeter Journal.* Truro: Twelveheads

Brown, M *Dartmoor 2001: a Dartmoor Diary of Yesteryear.* Newton Abbot: Forest

Brown, G and Field, D 2007 'Training Trenches on Salisbury Plain: archaeological evidence for battle training in the Great War'. *Wiltshire Studies* **100**, 170–80

Buckley, A 1994 *The Bailiff of Blackmoor 1586: Thomas Beare.* Camborne: Penhellick

Burl, A 1976 *The Stone circles of the British Isles.* New Haven: Yale Univ P

Burl, A 1993 *From Carnac to Callanish: the Prehistoric Stone Rows and Avenues of Britain, Ireland and Brittany.* New Haven: Yale Univ P

Burnard, R 1887–90 'On the Track of the "Old Men" Dartmoor' Pt 1 & 2'. *Trans Plymouth Instit* **10**, 95–112, 223–42

Burnard, R 1889 'The Great Central Trackway'. *Rep Trans Devonshire Assoc* **21**, 431–6

Burnard, R 1891 'Antiquity of Mining on Dartmoor'. *Trans Plymouth Instit* **11**, 85–112

Burnard, R 1890–94 *Dartmoor Pictorial Records* (facsimile edition, 1986). Exeter: Devon Books

Burnard, R 1896 *Plundered Dartmoor*. Devon: DPA

Butler, J 1991a *Dartmoor Atlas of Antiquities: Vol 1 The East*. Exeter: Devon Books

Butler, J 1991b *Dartmoor Atlas of Antiquities: Vol 2 The North*. Exeter: Devon Books

Butler, J 1993 *Dartmoor Atlas of Antiquities: Vol 4 The South East*. Tiverton: Devon Books

Butler, J 1994 *Dartmoor Atlas of Antiquities: Vol 3 The South West*. Tiverton: Devon Books

Butler, J 1997 *Dartmoor Atlas of Antiquities: Vol 5 The Second Millennium BC*. Tiverton: Devon Books

Butler, J 2000 *Travels in Victorian Devon 1846–70*. Tiverton: Devon Books

Casseldine, C and Hatton J 1994 'Into the mists? Thoughts on the prehistoric and historic environmental history of Dartmoor'. *Proc Devon Archaeol Soc* **52**, 35–47

Cherry, B and Pevsner N 1989 *The Buildings of England: Devon*. London: Penguin

Collis, J 1972 'Cranbrook Castle, Moretonhampstead, Devon: a new survey'. *Proc Devon Archaeol Soc* **30**, 216–21

Creighton, O H and Freeman, J P 2006 'Castles and the medieval landscape', *in* Turner, S (ed) *Medieval Devon and Cornwall: Shaping an Ancient Countryside*, 104–22. Macclesfield: Windgather

Crossing, W 1912 *Guide to Dartmoor* (1981 repr). Newton Abbot: David and Charles

Crossing, W 1989 *Princetown: Its Rise and Progress* [a series of newspaper articles originally published in 1906]. Brixham: Quay

Cunliffe, B 1986 *Danebury: Anatomy of an Iron Age Hillfort*. London: Batsford

Cunliffe, B 2005 *Iron Age Communities in Britain*. London: Routledge

DEC 1894 'The Exploration of Grimspound: First Report of the Dartmoor Exploration Committee'. *Rep Trans Devonshire Assoc* **26**, 101–21

DEC 1895 'Second Report of the Dartmoor Exploration Committee'. *Rep Trans Devonshire Assoc* **27**, 81–92

DEC 1897 'Forth Report of the Dartmoor Exploration Committee'. *Rep Trans Devonshire Assoc* **29**, 145–65

DEC 1899 'Sixth Report of the Dartmoor Exploration Committee'. *Rep Trans Devonshire Assoc* **31**, 146–55

DEC 1901 'Seventh Report of the Dartmoor Exploration Committee'. *Rep Trans Devonshire Assoc* **33**, 129–38

DEC 1906 'Eleventh Report of the Dartmoor Exploration Committee'. *Rep Trans Devonshire Assoc* **38**, 101–13

DEC 1935 'Twelfth Report of the Dartmoor Exploration Committee'. *Rep Trans Devonshire Assoc* **67**, 115–30

Dell, S and Bright, J 2008 *Dartmoor's Sett Makers' Bankers*. Okehampton: Dartmoor Co

Dines, H G 1994 *The Metalliferous Mining Region of South-West England*. London: HMSO

Dobinson, C S 1996 *Twentieth-century Fortifications in England, volume 3. Bombing decoys of WWI : England's Passive Air Defences, 1939–4*. York: CBA

Donn, B 1765 *A Map of the County of Devonshire* (facsimile edn 1965) DCRS: Exeter

DNPA 2004 Dartmoor Factsheet: General Information

DNPA 2007 *Dartmoor National Park Management Plan 2007–2012*

Durrance, E M and Laming, D J C (eds) 1982 *The Geology of Devon*. Exeter: Exeter Univ P

Emmett, D D 1979 'Stone rows: the traditional view reconsidered'. *Proc Devon Archaeol Soc* **37**, 94–114

Endacott, A 2003 *Okehampton Castle*. London: English Heritage

English Heritage 2003 *Historic Military Aviation Sites: Conservation Management Guidelines*. Swindon: English Heritage

Eogan, G 1964 'The excavation of a stone alignment and circle at Cholwichtown, Lee Moor, Devonshire, England'. *Proc Prehistoric Soc* **30**, 25–38

Ewans, M C 1964 *The Haytor Granite Tramway and Stover Canal*. Newton Abbot: David and Charles

Feachem, R W 1971 'Unfinished hillforts', *in* Hill, D and Jesson, M (eds) *The Iron Age and its Hillforts*. Univ Southampton Monogr Ser **1**

Finberg, H P R 1949 'The Stannary of Tavistock'. *Rep Trans Devonshire Assoc* **81**, 155–84

Finberg, H P R 1969 *Tavistock Abbey*. Newton Abbot: David and Charles

Fleming, A 1978 'The prehistoric landscape of Dartmoor. Part 1: South Dartmoor'. *Proc Prehist Soc* **44**, 97–123

Fleming, A 1983 'The prehistoric landscape of Dartmoor. Part 2: North and East Dartmoor'. *Proc Prehist Soc* **49**, 195–241

Fleming, A 1988 *The Dartmoor Reaves*. London: Batsford

Fleming, A 2008 *The Dartmoor Reaves* (2 edn). Oxford: Oxbow

Fleming, A 1994 'Medieval and Post-medieval cultivation on Dartmoor: a landscape archaeologist's view'. *Proc Devon Archaeol Soc* **52**, 101–18

Fleming, A and Ralph, N 1982 'Medieval settlement and land use on Holne Moor, Dartmoor: the landscape evidence'. *Medieval Archaeol* **26**, 101–37

Fox, A 1952 'Hillslope forts and related earthworks in South-West England'. *Archaeol J* **109**, 1–22

Fox, A 1954 'Excavations at Kestor: an Early Iron Age Settlement near Chagford in Devon'. *Rep Trans Devonshire Assoc* **86**, 21–62

Fox, A 1955 'Huts and enclosures on Gripper's Hill, in the Avon Valley, Dartmoor'. *Rep Trans Devonshire Assoc* **87**, 55–62

Fox, A 1957 'Excavations on Dean Moor, in the Avon Valley, 1954–6. The Late Bronze Age settlement'. *Rep Trans Devonshire Assoc* **88**, 18–77

Fox, A 1958 'A monastic homestead on Dean Moor, S Devon'. *Medieval Archaeol* **2**, 141–57

Fox, A 1996 *Prehistoric Hillforts of Devon*. Tiverton: Devon Books

Fox, H S A 1991a 'Occupation of the land: Devon and Cornwall', *in* Miller, E (ed) 152–74

Fox, H S A 1991b 'Farming practice and techniques: Devon and Cornwall', *in* Miller, E (ed) 303–23

Fox, H S A 1994 'Medieval Dartmoor as seen through the Account Rolls'. *Proc Devon Archaeol Soc* **52**, 149–71

Francis, P 2002 *Okehampton Artillery Range, Devon: Report and Photographic Survey* (Defence Estates)

Fraser, R 1794 *General View of the County of Devon with Observations on the Means of its Improvement*. London

French, H and Linehan, C D 1963 'Abandoned medieval sites in Widecombe-in-the-Moor'. *Rep Trans Devonshire Assoc* **95**, 168–179

Fyfe, R and Head K 2009 *Bellever, Dartmoor Palaeoenvironmental Assessment and Radiocarbon Dating*. Unpubl typescript prepared for DNPA: Univ Plymouth

Fyfe, R M and Greeves, T 2010 'The date and context of a stone row: Cut Hill, Dartmoor, south-west England'. *Antiquity* **84**, 55–70

Gallant, L, Luxton, N and Colman, M 1985 'Ancient fields on the South Devon Limestone Plateau'. *Proc Devon Archaeol Soc* **43**, 23–37

Garmonsway, G N (trans and ed) 1972 *The Anglo-Saxon Chronicle*. London: Dent

Garwood, P 2007 'Before the hills in order stood: chronology, time and history in the interpretation of Early Bronze Age round barrows', in Last, J (ed) 2007 *Beyond the Grave: New Perspectives on Barrows*. Oxford: Oxbow

Gawne, E 1970 'Field patterns in Widecombe Parish and the Forest of Dartmoor'. *Rep Trans Devonshire Assoc* **102**, 49–69

Gawne, E and Somers Cocks, J V 1968 'Parallel reaves on Dartmoor'. *Rep Trans Devonshire Assoc* **100**, 277–91

Gawne, E and Sanders, J 1998 *Early Dartmoor Farmhouses. Longhouses in Widecombe*. Chudleigh: Orchard

Gearey, B R, West, S and Charman, D J 1997 'The landscape contexts of medieval settlement on the south-western moors of England: recent palaeoenvironmental evidence from Bodmin Moor and Dartmoor'. *Medieval Archaeol* **41**, 195–209

Gent, T 2007 'The re-excavation of a deserted medieval longhouse at Hutholes, Widecombe-in-the-Moor, Dartmoor'. *Proc Devon Archaeol Soc* **65**, 47–82

Gerrard, S 1997 *Dartmoor*. London: Batsford

Gerrard, S 1998 *Hart Tor Prehistoric Settlement*. Meavy Valley Archaeology Site Report **8** (published privately)

Gerrard, S 2000 *The Early British Tin Industry*. Gloucester: Tempus

Gerrard, S 2008 *The Dartmoor Archaeology and Bracken Project. Interim Report for 2008*. ACE Archaeol Club Rep

Gibson, A 1992 'The excavation of an Iron Age settlement at Gold Park, Dartmoor'. *Proc Devon Archaeol Soc* **50**, 119–46

Gibson, A 2005 *Stonehenge and Timber Circles*. Gloucester: Tempus

Gill, C (ed) 1970 *Dartmoor: a New Study*. Newton Abbot: David and Charles

Gover, J E B, Mawer, A and Stenton, F M 1969 *The Place Names of Devon*. Cambridge: Cambridge Univ P

Grant, N 1995 'The occupation of hillforts in Devon during the late Roman and post-Roman periods'. *Proc Devon Archaeol Soc* **53**, 97–108

Gray, T 2000 *Travels in Georgian Devon: the Illustrated Journals of the Revd John Swete (1789–1800)*. Tiverton: Devon Books

Gray, T 2001 *Dartmoor Engraved*. Exeter: Mint

Greeves, T 1980 'A history of Whiteworks Tin Mine: part one 1790–1848'. *Plymouth Mineral Mining Club J* **11**, 11–16

Greeves, T 1981a 'The archaeological potential of the Devon tin industry', in Crossley, D W (ed) *Medieval Industry*. CBA Res Rep **40**, 85–95

Greeves, T [A P] 1981b *The Devon Tin Industry 1450–1750: an Archaeological and Historical Survey*. Unpubl PhD thesis, Univ Exeter

Greeves, T 1986 *Tin Mines and Miners of Dartmoor, a Photographic Record*. Exeter: Devon Books

Greeves, T 1991 'Blowing and knocking: the Dartmoor tin mill before 1750'. *Dartmoor Mag* **23**, 18–20

Greeves, T 1992 'Four Devon stannaries: a comparative study of tinworking in the sixteenth century', in Gray, T, Rowe, M and Erskine, A (eds) *Tudor and Stuart Devon: the Common Estate and Government*. Exeter: Exeter Univ P, 39–74

Greeves, T 1996 'Tin smelting in Devon in the 18th and 19th Centuries'. *Mining Hist* **13**, 84–90

Greeves, T 2003a 'Devon's earliest tin coinage roll 1302–3'. *Rep Trans Devonshire Assoc* **135**, 9–29

Greeves, T 2003b 'Was Brentor a Dark Age settlement'. *Dartmoor Mag* **71**, 8–10

Greeves, T 2004a 'The beamworks of Dartmoor – a remarkable heritage of the tinners'. *Dartmoor Mag* **75**, 9–11

Greeves, T 2004b *Images of England: Dartmoor*. Gloucester: Tempus

Greeves, T 2007 *Reddaford Farm, Willsworthy, Peter Tavy: an Archaeological and Historical Survey*. Salisbury: Wessex

Greeves, T 2008 *Yellowmead Farm, Willsworthy, Peter Tavy: an Archaeological and Historical Survey*. Unpubl ts

Greig, O and Rankin, W F 1953, 'A stone-age settlement system near East Week, Dartmoor: Mesolithic and post-Mesolithic industries'. *Proc Devon Archaeol Soc* **5.1**, 8–25

Griffith, F M 1994 'Changing perceptions of the context of prehistoric Dartmoor'. *Proc Devon Archaeol Soc* **52**, 85–99

Grinsell, L V 1953 *The Ancient Burial Mounds of England*. London: Methuen

Grinsell, L V 1974 'Dartmoor barrows'. *Proc Devon Archaeol Soc* **36**, 85–180

Gwyn, D and Palmer, M 2005 'Understanding the workplace: a research framework for industrial archaeology in Britain'. *Industrial Archaeol Rev* **27**, 9–-8

Hamilton Jenkin, A K 1974 *Mines of Devon: the Southern Area*. Newton Abbot: David and Charles

Hamilton Jenkin, A K 1981 *Mines of Devon: North and East of Dartmoor*. Exeter: Devon Library Services

Harris, H 1968 *Industrial Archaeology of Dartmoor*. Newton Abbot: David and Charles

Harris, H 1981 'Nineteenth-century granite working on Pew Tor and Staple Tor, Western Dartmoor'. *Rep Trans Devonshire Assoc* **113**, 29–51

Harris, H 1988 'The Sourton Tor iceworks, north-west Dartmoor, 1874–1886'. *Rep Trans Devonshire Assoc* **120**, 177–200

Harris, H 2002 *The Haytor Granite Tramway and Stover Canal*. Newton Abbot: Peninsula

Haslem, J 1984 *Anglo-Saxon Towns in Southern England*. Chichester: Phillimore

Haynes, R G 1970 'Vermin traps and rabbit warrens on Dartmoor'. *Post-Medieval Archaeology* **4**, 147–64

Heggarty, A 1991 'Machrie Moor, Arran: recent excavations at two stone circles'. *Proc Soc Antiq Scot* **121**, 51–94

Hemery, E 1983 *High Dartmoor: Land and People*. London: Robert Hale

Herring, P 2005 'Medieval fields at Brown Willy, Bodmin Moor', in Turner, S (ed) *Medieval Devon and Cornwall*. Macclesfield: Windgather, 78–103

Herring, P, Sharpe, A, Smith J R and Giles, C 2008 *Bodmin Moor: an Archaeological Survey. Volume 2: the Industrial and Post-medieval Landscapes*. Swindon: EH

Higham, R 1977 'Excavations at Okehampton Castle, Devon. Part 1: the keep'. *Proc Devon Archaeol Soc* **35**, 3–42

Higham, R A, Allan, J P and Blaylock, S R 1982 'Excavations at Okehampton Castle, Devon. Part 2: the bailey'. *Proc Devon Archaeol Soc* **40**, 19–152

Hitchens, F and Drew, S 1824 *The History of Cornwall, from the Earliest Records and Traditions, to the Present Time*. St Austell: Penaluna

Hodge, J 1973 'An iceworks at Dozmary Pool'. *Old Cornwall* **8**, 20–3

Hoskins, W G 1954 *Devon.* London: Collins

Hoover, H C and Hoover, L H (trans) 1950 *Georgius Agricola de Re Metallica.* New York: Dover

Hughes, S, 2009 *A Bronze Age Roundhouse at Bellever Tor, Dartmoor Forest, Devon: Results of an Archaeological Evaluation.* AC Archaeology **ACD08,2/0**

Jamieson, E 2006 *Blackaton Deserted Medieval Settlement, Dartmoor, Devon.* EH Res Dept Rep Ser **24/2006**

Johnston, R 2005 'Pattern without a plan: rethinking the Bronze Age coaxial field systems on Dartmoor, south-west England'. *Oxford J Archaeol* **24**, 1–21

Johnson, N and Rose, P 1994 *Bodmin Moor: an Archaeological Survey Volume 1: the Human Landscape to c 1800.* London: English Heritage

Kain, R and Ravenhill, W (eds) 1999 *Historical Atlas of South-West England.* Exeter: Exeter Univ P

Kelly, J 1866 'Celtic remains on Dartmoor'. *Rep Trans Devonshire Assoc* **4**, 45–8

Kemp, A J 1829 'Account of some monuments conjectured to be British, still existing upon Dartmoor'. *Archaeologia* **22**, 429–35

Kingdom, A R 1991 *The Yelverton to Princetown Railway.* Newton Abbot: Forest

Kytmannow, T 2008 *Portal Tombs in the Landscape. The Chronology, Morphology and Landscape Setting of the Portal Tombs of Ireland, Wales and Cornwall.* Oxford: Archaeopress BAR Brit Ser **455**

Last, J 2007 *Beyond the Grave: New Perspectives on Barrows.* Oxford: Oxbow

Le Messurier, B (ed) 1966 *Crossing's Dartmoor Worker.* Newton Abbot: David and Charles

Le Messurier, B (ed) 1967 *Crossing's Hundred Years on Dartmoor.* Newton Abbot: David and Charles

Le Messurier, B 1979 'The post-prehistoric structures of central north Dartmoor'. *Rep Trans Devonshire Assoc* **111**, 59–73

Linehan, C D 1966 'Deserted sites and rabbit warrens on Dartmoor, Devon'. *Medieval Archaeol* **10**, 113–44

Lewis, G R 1965 *The Stannaries: a Study of Medieval Tin Miners in Cornwall and Devon* (repr 1908 edn). Truro: Bradford Barton

Lockyer, N 1906 *Stone Henge and other British Stone Monuments Astronomically Considered.* London: Macmillan

Lukis, W C 1881 'Report on the monuments of Dartmoor'. *Proc Soc Antiq*, 470–81

Lockyer, N 1906 *Stone Henge and other British Stone Monuments Astronomically Considered.* London: Macmillan

Maddicott, J R 1989 'Trade industry and the wealth of King Alfred'. *Past and Present* **123**, 3–51

Manning, W H 1976 'The conquest of the West Country', *in* Branigan, K and Fowler, P J (eds) *The Roman West Country: Classical Culture and Celtic Society.* Newton Abbot: David and Charles

Marchand, J 1995 'A high rock called Crockerntor'. *Proc Devon Archaeol Soc* **53**, 1–10

Marshall, W E 1796 *The Rural Economy of the West of England Including Devonshire and Parts of Somersetshire, Dorsetshire and Cornwall.* London: Nicol

Masson Phillips, E N 1966 'Excavations at a Romano-British site at Lower Well farm, Stoke Gabriel'. *Proc Devon Archaeol Soc* **23**, 3–29

Maxfield, V 2000 'The Roman Army', *in* Kain, R and Ravenhill, W (eds) 1999 *Historical Atlas of South-West England.* Exeter: Exeter Univ P, 77–9

McOmish, D, Brown, G and Field, D 2002 *The Field Archaeology of the Salisbury Plain Training Area.* Swindon: English Heritage

Mercer, R 1981 'Excavations at Carn Brea, Illogan Cornwall, 1970–73: a Neolithic fortified complex of the 3rd millennium bc'. *Cornish Archaeol* **20**, 1–204

Miller, E (ed) 1991 *The Agrarian History of England and Wales, Vol 3, 1348–1500.* Cambridge: Cambridge Univ P

Milton, P 2006 *The Discovery of Dartmoor: a Wild and Wondrous Region.* Chichester: Phillimore

Newman, P 1993 'Week Ford Tin Mills, Dartmoor'. *Proc Devon Archaeol Soc* **51**, 185–97

Newman, P 1994 'Tinners and tenants on SW Dartmoor: a case study in landscape history'. *Rep Trans Devonshire Assoc* **126**, 199–238

Newman, P 1998 *The Dartmoor Tin Industry: a Field Guide.* Newton Abbot: Chercombe

Newman, P 1999 'Eylesbarrow (Ailsborough) Tin Mine'. *Proc Devon Archaeol Soc* **57**, 105–48

Newman, P 2000 *The Town and Castle Earthworks at Lydford, Devon.* EH AI Rep Ser **AI/25/2000**

Newman, P 2002a 'New observations at Headland Warren'. *Dartmoor Mag* **66**, 22–4

Newman, P 2002b *Headland Warren and the Birch Tor and Vitifer Mines.* EH AI Rep Ser **AI/34/2002**

Newman, P 2002c *Shipley Bridge China Clay Works, South Brent Devon.* EH AI Rep Ser **AI/35/2002**

Newman, P 2003 *Deckler's Cliff Field System, East Portlemouth, Devon.* EH AI Rep Ser **AI/16/2003**

Newman, P 2004 *Brentor: an Earthwork Site on Western Dartmoor, Devon.* EH AI Rep Ser **AI/12/2004**

Newman, P 2010 *Domestic and Industrial Peat Cutting on North-western Dartmoor, Devonshire: an Archaeological and Historical Investigation.* (unpub report for the Dartmoor Mires Project)

Nicol, K and Brown, M 2006 *The Otterburn Ranges: All Quiet on the Western Front.* London: Defence Estates

Oliver, G and Jones, P (eds) 1845 *A View of Devonshire in MDCXXX with a Pedigree of Most of its Gentry. By Thomas Westcote.* Exeter: Roberts

Ormerod, G W 1872 'Notice of pre-historic remains formerly existing near the Drewsteignton Cromlech'. *Rep Trans Devonshire Assoc* **5**, 73–4

Oswald, A, Dyer, C and Barber, M 2001 *The Creation of Monuments: Neolithic Causewayed Enclosures in the British Isles.* Swindon: English Heritage

Page, J Lloyd-Warden 1892 *An Exploration of Dartmoor and its Antiquities.* London: Seeley

Page, W 1906 *The Victoria County History of Devon.* London: J Street

Parsons, H 1956 'The Dartmoor blowing house'. *Rep Trans Devonshire Assoc* **88**, 189–96

Passmore, A 1998 'Finds at Upper Merrivale: the larger stone artefacts'. *DTRG Newsletter* **14**, 10–11

Pattison, P 1999 'Challacombe revisited', *in* Ainsworth, S, Field, D and Pattison, P (eds) *Patterns of the Past: Essays in Landscape Archaeology for Christopher Taylor.* Oxford: Oxbow, 61–70

Pattison, P and Fletcher, M 1994 'Grimspound, one hundred years on'. *Proc Devon Archaeol Soc* **52**, 21–34

Pearce, S 1978 *The Kingdom of Dumnonia.* Padstow: Lodenak

Pearce, S M 1983 *The Bronze Age Metalwork of South Western Britain.* Oxford: BAR Brit Ser **120**

Pengelly, W 1877 'Presidential address to the Geological Section of the British Association'. *Rep Brit Assoc* **47**, 54–66

Penhallurick, R D 1986 *Tin in Antiquity.* London: Institute of Metals

Pennington, R 1973 *Stannary Law. A History of the Mining Law of Cornwall and Devon.* Newton Abbot: David and Charles

Perkins, J W 1984 *Geology Explained: Dartmoor and the Tamar Valley.* Newton Abbot: David and Charles

Pettit, P 1974 *Prehistoric Dartmoor.* Newton Abbot: David and Charles

Piggott, S 1931 'Ladle Hill – an unfinished hillfort'. *Antiquity* **5**, 474–85

Pollard, S 1966 'Neolithic and Dark Age settlements on High Peak, Sidmouth, Devon'. *Proc Devon Archaeol Soc* **23**, 35–59

Polwhele, R 1793–1806 *The History of Devonshire* (1977 repr). Dorking: Kohler and Coombes

Preston-Jones, A 1994 'Decoding Cornish churchyards'. *Cornish Archaeol* **33**, 71–95

Price, D G 1985 'Changing perceptions of prehistoric tinning on Dartmoor'. *Rep Trans Devonshire Assoc* **117**, 129–38

Probert, S 1989 'Beardown Warren, Princetown, Dartmoor', *in* Bowden, M, Mackay, D and Topping, P (eds) *From Cornwall to Caithness: Some Aspects of British Field Archaeology.* Oxford: BAR Brit Ser **209**, 229–33

Probert, S 2004 *Okehampton Castle and Park, West Devon.* EH AI Rep Ser **AI/03/2004**

Pryce, W 1778 *Mineralogia Cornubiensis* (facsimile edn, 1972) Truro: Bradford Barton

Pye, A 1994 'An example of a non-metalliferous Dartmoor industry: the gunpowder factory at Powdermills'. *Proc Devon Arch Soc* **52**, 221–40

Pye, A and Robinson, R 1990 *An Archaeological Survey of The Gunpowder Factory at Powdermills Farm, Postbridge, Devon.* Exeter: Exeter Mus Arch Field Unit

Pye, A and Westcott, K A 1992 *Archaeological Survey of the Pumping Engine-House at Wheal Betsy, Mary Tavy.* Exeter: EMAFU

Quinnell, H 1994a 'New perspectives on upland monuments – Dartmoor in earlier prehistory'. *Proc Devon Archaeol Soc* **52**, 49–62

Quinnell, H 1994b 'Becoming marginal? Dartmoor in later prehistory'. *Proc Devon Archaeol Soc* **52**, 75–83

Quinnell, H 1999 'Excavations of a causewayed enclosure and hillfort on Raddon Hill, Stockleigh Pomeroy'. *Proc Devon Archaeol Soc* **57**, 1–75

Quinnell, H 2003 'Devon beakers: new finds, new thoughts'. *Proc Devon Archaeol Soc* **61**, 1–20

Quinnell, H 2009 'The pottery', *in* Hughes, S, *A Bronze Age Roundhouse at Bellever Tor, Dartmoor Forest, Devon: Results of an Archaeological Evaluation.* AC Archaeology No ACD08,2/0

Radford, C A R 1952 'Prehistoric settlement on Dartmoor and the Cornish moors'. *Proc Prehistoric Soc* **5**, 55–84

Ravenhill, W 1965 *Benjamin Donn: a Map of the County of Devonshire 1765.* Exeter: DCRS and Univ Exeter

RCHME 1998 *Hawns and Dendles, Cornwood, Devon: an Archaeological Survey by the Royal Commission on the Historical Monuments of England.* RCHME Surv Rep

Riley, H 1995 'Holne Chase Castle, Holne, Devon: a new survey by the Royal Commission on the Historical Monuments of England'. *Proc Devon Archaeol Soc* **53**, 91–5

Riley, H 2006 *The Historic Landscape of the Quantock Hills.* Swindon: English Heritage

Riley, H and Wilson-North, R 2001 *The Field Archaeology of Exmoor.* Swindon: English Heritage

Rippon, S 2007 'Emerging regional variation in historic landscape character: the possible significance of the "Long Eighth Century"', *in* Gardiner, M and Rippon, S (eds) 2007 *Medieval Lasndscapes.* Macclesfield: Windgather.

Risdon, T 1810 *The Chorographical Description or Survey of the County of Devon.* London: Rees and Curtis

Roberts, A 1999 'Late Upper Palaeolithic and Mesolithic hunting-gathering communities 13,000–5,500 BP', *in* Kain, R and Ravenhill, W (eds) 1999, 47–50

Robertson, J G 1991 *The Archaeology of the Upper Plym Valley.* Unpubl PhD thesis Univ Edinburgh

Robinson, R 1980 'The early china clay industry on Brent Moor'. *Plym Min and Mining Club J* **2**, 3–5

Rowe, S 1830 'Antiquarian investigations in the Forest of Dartmoor, Devon'. *Trans Plymouth Instit* **1**, 179–212

Rowe, S 1848 *A Perambulation of Dartmoor.* Plymouth: Hamilton

Rowe, S 1896 *A Perambulation of the Antient* [sic] *and Royal Forest of Dartmoor.* (facsimile edition, 1985) Exeter: Devon Books

Russell, P 1955 'Fire beacons in Devon'. *Rep Trans Devonshire Assoc* **87**, 250–302

Saunders, A D 1980 'Lydford Castle, Devon'. *Medieval Archaeol* **24**, 123–64

Schmitz, C J 1979 *World Non-Ferrous Metal Production and Prices, 1700–1976.* Chichester: Frank Cass

Shorter, A H 1938 'Ancient fields in Manaton Parish, Dartmoor'. *Antiquity* **12**, 183–9

Silvester, R J 1979 'The relationship of first millennium settlement to the upland areas of the South West'. *Proc Devon Archaeol Soc* **37**, 176–90

Silvester, R J and Quinnell, N V 1993 'Unfinished hillforts on the Devon moors'. *Proc Devon Archaeol Soc* **51**, 17–31

Simmons, I G 1965 'The Dartmoor oak copses: observations and speculations'. *Field Studies* **2**, 225–35

Smith, R and RCHME 1996 *Shaugh Bridge China-Clay Works: an Archaeological Evaluation.* Truro: CAU

Somers Cocks, J 1970 'Saxon and early medieval times', *in* Gill, C (ed) 1970, 76–99

Somers Cocks, J 1983 *A Dartmoor Century 1883–1983: One Hundred Years of the Dartmoor Preservation Association.* Devon: DPA

Spooner, G M and Russell, F S (eds) 1967 *Worth's Dartmoor* (2 edn). Newton Abbot: David and Charles

Stanbrook, E 1994a *Dartmoor Forest Farms.* Exeter: Devon Books

Stanbrook, E 1994b 'Crane Hill Rabbit Warren: a little known venture'. *Dartmoor Mag* **36**, 16–17

Stanier, P 1999 *South West Granite: a History of the Granite Industry on Cornwall and Devon.* St Austell: Cornish Hillside

Straw, A 1999 'Palaeolithic: the earliest human occupation', *in* Kain, R and Ravenhill, W (eds) 1999, 43–6

Thorn, C and Thorn, F 1985 *Domesday Book (9) Devon.* Chichester: Phillimore

Thorndycraft, V R, Pirrie, D and Brown, A G 2004 'Alluvial records of medieval and prehistoric tin mining on Dartmoor, southwest England'. *Geoarchaeol* **13**, 219–36

Timms, S 1980 *Archaeology of the Devon Landscape.* Exeter: Devon County Council

Timms, S 1985 'The Royal town of Lydford'. *Devon Archaeol* **3**, 19–23

Timms, S 1993 'From ancient monuments to historic landscapes: the quest to conserve Devon's archaeological heritage'. *Proc Devon Archaeol Soc* **51**, 1–16

Todd, M 1987 *South-West to AD 1000.* London: Longman

Todd, M 1998 'A Hillslope Enclosure at Rudge, Morchard Bishop'. *Proc Devon Archaeol Soc* **56**, 133–52

Turner, J 1990 'Ring cairns, stone circles and related monuments on Dartmoor'. *Proc Devon Archaeol Soc* **48**, 27–86

Turner, S (ed) 2006 *Medieval Devon and Cornwall: Shaping an Ancient Countryside.* Macclesfield: Windgather

Turner, S 2007 *Ancient Country: the Historic Character of Rural Devon.* Exeter: DAS Occas Pap **20**

Tyler, F C 1930 'The stone remains in Drewsteignton'. *Rep Trans Devonshire Assoc* **62**, 249–60

Vancouver, C 1808 *General View of the Agriculture of the county of Devon.* Newton Abbot: David and Charles (1969 reprint)

Wade, E A 1982 *The Redlake Tramway and China Clay Works.* Truro: Twelveheads

Wainwright, G J, Fleming, A and Smith, K 1979 'The Shaugh Moor Project first report: The investigation of a cairn group'. *Proc Prehistoric Soc* **45**, 1–33

Wainwright, G J and Smith, K 1980 'The Shaugh Moor Project second report: The Enclosure'. *Proc Prehistoric Soc* **46**, 65–121

Wakeham, C 2003 'Maristow estate farmhouses 1800–1913: a chronological development'. *Rep Trans Devonshire Assoc* **135**, 111–71

Walker, J 2005 *Dartmoor Sun.* Tiverton: Halsgrove

Watson, J Y 1843 *A Compendium of British Mining.* London: privately printed

Webster, C 2008 *The Archaeology of South-West England – SW Archaeological Research Framework.* Taunton: Somerset CC

Weddell, P J and Reid, S J 1997 'Excavations at Sourton Down, Okehampton 1986–1991'. *Proc Devon Archaeol Soc* **55**, 39–147

Wessex 2001 *Okehampton Camp: Archaeological Desk-based Assessment and Earthwork Survey.* Salisbury: Wessex

Wessex 2007 *Doe Tor Farm, Lydford, Devon: Historic Site Appraisal and Survey.* Salisbury: Wessex Archaeology

Wilkinson, J G 1862 'British remains on Dartmoor'. *J Brit Archaeol Soc* **18**, 23–53; 111–33

Wilkinson, B 1996 'RAF Sharpitor'. *Dartmoor Mag* **44**, 6–8

Williams, J 1862 *The Cornwall and Devon Mining Directory.* Hayle: Banfield Bros

Williamson, T 2007 *Rabbits, Warrens and Archaeology.* Gloucester: Tempus

Willock, E H 1936 'A Neolithick site on Haldon'. *Proc Devon Archaeol Soc* **2**, 244–63

Wilson, D M and Hurst, D G 1964–68 'Medieval Britain', *in Medieval Archaeol* **8**, 232; **9**, 170; **10**, 168; **11**, 264; **12**, 155

Worth, R H 1931 'A flint implement of Palaeolithic type from Dartmoor'. *Rep Trans Devonshire Assoc* **63**, 359–60.

Yates, D T 2006 *Land, Power and Prestige: Bronze Age Field Systems in Southern England.* Oxford: Oxbow

GAZETTEER OF ARCHAEOLOGICAL SITES
MENTIONED IN THE TEXT

The following gazetteer is intended as a guide for readers wishing to locate or visit sites described in the foregoing chapters. Eight-figure grid references are provided for use on OS 1:10 000 and 1:25,000 scale maps. For large, grouped, spread or linear features, a single grid reference is provided for the approximate location only.

Only sites and landscapes described in the main text and illustrations are listed. Further information on archaeological remains and historic buildings within Dartmoor National Park is available from the English Heritage National Monuments Record (NMR), Kemble Drive, Swindon SN2 2GZ; telephone 01793 414600, or visit the *Pastscape* website: http://www.pastscape.org.uk/

The majority of sites described are on open moorland with public access; those that are known to be on private land with no access or permitted access are indicated. However, it is the responsibility of individuals to ensure that any location they visit on Dartmoor has public or permitted access, and that they do not enter firing ranges when red flags are flying (for more information and firing schedules visit the MoD Dartmoor website: http://www. dartmoor-ranges.co.uk).

c = centre of large sites, grouped, spread or linear features; npa = no public access; pa = permitted access

2 Mesolithic to Early Bronze Age

Neolithic barrows

	NGRs (SX)
Butterdon	6601 5859
Corringdon Ball	6696 6129
Cuckoo Ball	6595 5820
Spinster's Rock	7009 9078 (*pa*)

Neolithic enclosures

Dewerstone	5390 6402
Whittor	5424 7865

stone circles

Brisworthy	5646 6548
Grey Wethers	6387 8313
Langstone Moor	5563 7819
Mardon Down	7674 8768
Merrivale	5535 7463
Scorhill	6545 8737
Whitemoor	6327 8961

menhirs

Beardown Man	5957 7960
Drizzlecombe	5921 6699
Hanging Stone	5837 6369
Longstone Hill	566- 912-
White Moor Stone	6335 8948

stone rows

Assacombe	6604 8261
Challacombe	6897 8081
Cholwichtown	*destroyed*
Corringdon Ball	6661 6117
Cosden (The Cemetery)	6438 9158
Cut Hill	5992 8279
Drizzlecombe	5917 6697
Hartor	5762 7169
Hingston Hill	5968 6925
Langstone Moor	5501 7878
Merrivale	5543 7479
Sharpitor	5573 7064
Shovel Down	6598 8594
Stall Down	6324 6231
Stall Moor	6352 6473
Trowlesworthy	5763 6391
Wotter	5584 6200

round cairns, barrows and stone settings

Broad Barrow	7057 7989
Corringdon	6699 6128
Cosdon	6432 9158
Crownhill Down (barrow group)	5720 5979
Dendles Waste	6153 6279
Drizzlecombe	5925 6707 (*c*)
Eastern White Barrow	6654 6515
Fernworthy	6554 8407
Giant's Basin	5919 6693
Hartor	5770 7170
Hingstone Hill	6968 6925
Lakehead Hill (a)	6435 7776
Lakehead Hill (b)	6434 7748
Lakehead Hill (c)	6435 7746
Langcombe Hill	6124 6636
Mardon Down	7675 8743
Pinchaford Ball	7626 7651
Shaugh Moor	*destroyed*
Shoveldown	6595 8601
Soussons	6751 7869
Stall Down	6352 6229

Two Barrows	7064 7920
Watern Hill 'King's Oven'	6715 8128
Wigford Down	5469 6495
Yar Tor 'Money Pit'	6807 4040
Yellowmead	5749 6783

cists

Crow Tor	6052 7867
Down Tor	5838 6956
Lakehead Hill (1)	6407 7646
Lakehead Hill (2)	6449 7760
Merrivale	5548 7476
Thornworthy	6674 8433

3 Settlement and land division in the 2nd millennium BC

hut circles and settlements

Bellever Tor	6445 7679
Bellever (excavation)	6486 7675
Broadun	6354 7993
Crapps Ring	6444 7814
Deadlake	5642 7819
Dean Moor	6775 6545
NW of Devil's Bridge	5771 7305
Drizzlecombe	5933 6724
Grimspound	7007 8090
Holne Moor (excavations)	6781 7097
Hammerslake	7732 8136
Kestor (excavation)	7075 8090
Langstone Moor	5558 7797
Legis Tor	5698 6523
Merrivale	5550 7495
Raddick Hill	5745 7095
Round Pound	6639 8685

253

Roundy 5772 7025
Ryder's Rings 6787 6436
Shapley Common
    (excavation) 7012 8175
Shaugh Moor (excavations) *destroyed*
Standon Hill 5502 8251
Throwleigh Common 6575 9073 (c)
Vag Hill 6823 7336
Watern Oke 5645 8350
Wigford Down 5435 6509
Yestor Bottom 5676 7286

reaves and reave settlements
Brent Fore Hill 6735 6122 (c)
Butterdon Down 7505 8837 (c)
Corndon Tor 6860 7452 (c)
Emsworthy Rocks
    settlement 7471 7713
Great Western Reave 5656 7143 (c)
Holne Moor 6742 7120 (c)
Holwell settlement 7537 7777
Hurston Ridge 6721 8247 (c)
Kestor 6640 8655 (c)
Riddon Ridge 6652 7649 (c)
Roos Tor 5392 7695 (c)
Shaugh Moor 5536 6293 (c)
Throwleigh Common 6575 9073 (c)
Venford Reave 6738 7105 (c)
Wigford Down 5438 6472 (c)
Walkhampton Common
    Reave 5604 7132 (c)

4 The Iron Age and Romano-British periods, *c* 750 BC to AD 410

Iron Age settlements and hillforts
Borro Wood 7485 7160 (npa)
Brentor 4707 8040 (pa)
Cranbrook 7385 8900
East Hill 6748 9415
Hembury 7260 6840
Holne Chase 7615 8242 (npa)
Kestor 6638 8684
Metheral 6684 8402
Nattadon 7045 8670
Prestonbury 7466 9000 (npa)
Round Pound 6639 8685
Shapley Common 7012 8175
Wooston 7650 8970 (pa)

5 Early medieval Dartmoor, AD 410–1066

early medieval
Brentor 4706 8043 (pa)
Lydford 5101 8481
Tavistock Abbey 4813 7439

6 Castles and status around medieval Dartmoor

castles
Buckfastleigh (Hembury) 7254 6843

Lydford (Stannary Gaol) 5095 8478
Lydford (ringwork) 5081 8470
Okehampton 5833 9424

7 Medieval farming and settlement on the uplands

medieval settlements
Birch Tor 6849 8076
Blackaton 6975 7824 (npa)
Butworthy (Butterbury) 5498 7938
Challacombe 6935 7955 (pa)
Dean Moor 6773 7538
Dinna Clerks 6921 7509
Down Tor 5814 6971
Hentor 5918 6635
Houndtor 7464 7877
Houndtor Two 7449 7910
Hutholes 7020 7585
Okehampton Park 5804 9293 (c)
Okehampton Park
    (Site 52) 5822 9322
Okehampton Park
    (Site 53) 5853 9332
Sourton *destroyed*

field systems
Challacombe Down 6928 7986 (c)
Hexworthy 6528 7315 (c; npa)
Butworthy (Butterbury) 5466 7928 (c)
Blackaton Down 6976 7823 (c; npa)
Deancombe 5839 6900
Gutter Tor 5788 6676 (c)
Hentor 5898 6613 (c)
Holne Moor 6856 7153 (c)
Higher Godsworthy 5351 7748 (c; npa)
Sherberton Common
    (R & F) 6948 7364 (c)
Dunstone Down (R & F) 7090 7663 (c)
Shapley Common 6923 8261 (c)
Headland Warren 6846 8104 (c)
Headland Warren (R & F) 6930 8163 (c)
Routrundle 5530 7178 (c)
Yar Tor and Corndon
    Down 6817 7365

later desertions
Classiwell 5809 7005
Deancombe 5839 6900
Hawns 6129 6254
Kingsett 5767 6993
Lower Lowery 5563 6924
Middleworth 5717 7917
Newleycombe 5876 6994

8 The medieval tin industry, 1150–1700

Crockerntor Tinners'
    Parliament 6157 7576

tin works
Brim Brook 5906 8774 (c)
Beckamoor Combe 5353 7550 (c)

Birch Tor 6859 8059 (c)
Dick's Pits 5467 8592 (c)
Dry Lake 6605 7041 (c)
Down Tor (channels) 5862 6961
Drivage Bottom 5994 6986
Eylesbarrow 6012 6852
Gibby Beam 6680 6782
Hartor Brook 5863 7203 (c)
Hartor Brook (channels) 5792 7203
Hartor Brook (reservoir) 5820 7078
Henroost (reservoir) 6507 7096
Huntingdon 6603 6697 (c)
Newleycombe 5946 6999 (c)
O Brook 6561 7064
Owlacombe Beam 7659 7339 (npa)
Ringleshuttes 6696 6992 (c)
Skir Gut 6475 7033 (c)
Vitifer 6795 8080 (c)
Walkham Head 5736 8011 (c)
Whiteworks 6094 7093 (c)
Willabeam 5934 7014
West Webburn (leats) 6957 8135

tin mills
Avon Dam (only during
    drought) 6722 6553
Black Tor Falls 5748 7164
Gobbett 6453 7280
Horrabridge 5149 6959 (npa)
Lower Merrivale 5526 7535
Mill Corner (Cole's Mill) 5935 6676
Nosworthy (left bank) 5678 6958
Outcombe 5801 6860
Runnage 6716 7957
Upper Merrivale 5519 7664
Venford 6856 7118
Week Ford 6618 7232 (pa)
Yealm Steps 6171 6385

tinners' huts
Beckamoor Combe 5353 7569
Drivage Bottom 5982 6995
Fishlake 6460 6807
Fur Tor Brook 5852 8222
Hookney Tor 6953 8123
Runnage 6727 8014
Steeperton Brook 6206 8816

9 Warreners and improvers in the post-medieval and early modern periods

larger warrens
Beardown 6000 7545 (c; npa)
Ditsworthy 5827 6628 (c)
Headland 6128 8100 (c)
Hentor 5899 6579 (c)
Huntingdon 6610 6700 (c)
Legistor 5711 6537 (c)
Merrivale 5540 7533 (c)
Trowlesworthy 5737 6468 (c)
Vag Hill 6789 7259 (c)
Willings Walls 5814 6534 (c)
Wistman's Wood 6137 7710 (c)

smaller warrens

Skaigh	6289 9335 (c)
Zeal Burrows	6801 6323
Sheepstor	5623 6826 (c)
Yalland	6896 6317 (npa)
New House	6728 8052 (c)

isolated burries

Drivage Bottom	5971 6993
Dendles Wood	6150 6203
Rook (unverified)	6022 6136
Corringdon Ball	6751 6056

improvers and newtakes 1780–1880 (only deserted farmsteads and newtakes listed)

Doetor Farm	5361 8490
Yellowmead Farm	5303 8248
Swincombe	6392 7257
Fernworthy	6609 8393
Nun's Cross	6060 6982
Merrivale Newtake	5561 7621
Rippon Tor Newtake	74747552
Brown's House	6145 7985
John Bishop's House	6411 7257
Teignhead	6353 8434
Manga	6391 8485
Eastercombe (Vag Hill Warren)	6828 7329

10 Moorstone and granite

Dewerstone Quarry	5370 6407
Emsworthy Rocks Quarry	7486 7700
Fernworthy (gatepost)	6572 8371
Foggintor Quarry	5667 7351
Hare Tor (trough)	5391 8448
Harrow Barrow Quarry	7532 7689
Haytor Quarry	7593 7741
Haytor Granite Tramway	7618 7774
Heckwood Quarry	5444 7374
Holwell Quarry	7515 7772
Holwell Tor (pound stone)	7551 7771
Ingra Tor Quarry	5557 7213
Merrivale (edge runner)	5551 7494
Red Cottages	5660 7475
Rubble Heap Quarry	7557 7728

Set makers bankers (illustrated)	5447 7544 (c)
Swelltor Quarry	5596 7328
Tor (Merrivale) Quarry	5460 7527
Trowlesworthy	5769 6460
Western Beacon	6542 5752

11 Mining for tin, copper and silver-lead

Bagtor Mine (reservoir earthwork)	7581 7583
Belston Consols (wheelpit)	6329 9390
Birch Tor and Vitifer Mines	6818 8097 (c)
Blackabrook Mine	5698 9176
Brookwood Mine	7177 6753 (c; npa)
Cuddlipton Down Mine	5291 7941 (c)
East Birch Tor Mine	6929 8096 (c)
East Hughes Mine	5937 6997
Eylesbarrow (Ailsborough) Mine	5982 6817 (c)
Haytor Consols (tramway)	7489 7600 (c)
Gobbett Mine	6463 7277 (c)
Golden Dagger Mine	6838 8018
Great Wheal Eleanor	7351 8340
Henroost Mine	6602 7108
Hexworthy Mine	6564 7086 (c)
Hooten Wheals	6556 7080
Huntingdon Mine	6678 6700
Huntingdon (wheelpit)	6658 6650
Keaglesborough Mine	5773 7010
New (West) Vitifer Consols	6789 8275
Reddaford Leat	5340 8322 (c)
Ringleshuttes Mine	6713 6994 (c)
Steeperton Mine	6141 8840
Virtuous Lady Mine	4730 6987
Wheal Betsy	5101 8138 (pa)
Wheal Caroline	6680 8079 (c)
Wheal Emma	7150 6748 (npa)
Wheal Frederick	5457 8537
Wheal Freindship	5058 7927 (c; npa but pa in some parts)

Wheal Jewel	5183 8138 (c)
Wheal Katherine	6073 6828 (c)
Whiteworks Mine	6122 7092 (c)
Yarner Mine (engine house)	7837 7837

12 China clay

Left Lake	6471 6344
Petre's Pits	6584 6480
Redlake	6451 6688
Redlake Tramway	6495 6647 (c)
Shaugh Bridge	5338 6357
Shaugh Moor	5611 6394 (c)
Shipley Bridge	6803 6290

13 Miscellaneous Industries: peat, gunpowder mills, ice works and tramways

Zeal Tor Tramway	6598 6493 (c)
Rattlebrook Railway	5456 8870 (c)
Blackabrook Tramway	5784 7500 (c; pa)
Rattlebrook Peat Works	5598 8709
Powder Mills	6278 7734 (c; pa)
Sourton Tor Ice Works	5460 9000
Bleak House (Dunnagoat Cottage)	5596 8647

14 Security and defence in the modern period

Observation Post (OP) 6	6029 8984
Observation Post (OP) 15	6024 8776
Observation Post (OP) 22	6010 9112
East Mill Tor (earthworks)	5976 8973 (c)
Harrowbeer Airfield	5154 6774 (c)
Roborough Down (bomb decoy)	5113 6474 (c)
Rowtor (earthworks)	5955 9226
Peek Hill	5574 6995
Hawk's Tor	5507 6225
Roos Tor (earthworks)	5435 7731
Crownhill Down (craters)	5694 5990

INDEX